# Democratizing Application Development with AppSheet

A citizen developer's guide to building rapid low-code apps with the powerful features of AppSheet

**Koichi Tsuji**

**Suvrutt Gurjar**

**Takuya Miyai**

BIRMINGHAM—MUMBAI

# Democratizing Application Development with AppSheet

**Group Product Manager**: Alok Dhuri

**Publishing Product Manager**: Harshal Gundetty

**Senior Editor**: Nisha Cleetus

**Technical Editor**: Maran Fernandes

**Copy Editor**: Safis Editing

**Language Support Editor**: Safis Editing

**Project Coordinator**: Manisha Singh

**Proofreader**: Safis Editing

**Indexer**: Pratik Shirodkar

**Production Designer**: Alishon Mendonca

**Business Development Executive**: Puneet Kaur

**Marketing Coordinators**: Rayyan Khan and Deepak Kumar

Production reference: 1301122

Published by Packt Publishing Ltd.

Livery Place

35 Livery Street

Birmingham

B3 2PB, UK.

ISBN 978-1-80324-117-3

www.packt.com

*To my whole family and all my friends, who understand and support me all the time. Special thanks to my wife, Yoshiko, for being my loving partner throughout our joint life journey.*

*– Koichi Tsuji*

*To my mother, Sujata, and to the memory of my father, Prabhatkumar. To my wife, Ujwal, and my daughters, Anishka and Anushree. They all have been my strongest support system.*

*– Suvrutt Gurjar*

*To my mother, Michiyo, and father, Kazuhiro, without whom this book would not have been completed.*

*– Takuya Miyai*

# Contributors

## About the authors

**Koichi Tsuji** is the leading author of this book and is a self-proclaimed "world-leading" AppSheet citizen developer. He founded Vendola Solutions LLC, based in Japan, and has provided extensive services dedicated to AppSheet to support his clients. Through his company, he runs the AppSheet online educational platform to train new AppSheet app creators and also builds feature-rich apps on behalf of his clients. He strongly believes that "nothing is impossible with AppSheet." To prove this, he is always considering new ideas, tips, and tricks to take AppSheet as a platform to the next level. He has been active in the AppSheet global community for many years and has introduced a number of new ideas, which are admired by app creators.

*I want to thank the people who have supported me in growing my own business, especially all my friends working in the Google AppSheet team who closely support me daily. Thanks also to the editors and the team at Packt for their help and support throughout the process.*

**Suvrutt Gurjar** has worked in the IT industry since 1998. Up until 2014, he played various roles, starting as project lead. Later, as a delivery manager, he managed software deliveries for Fortune 500 client accounts, managing teams of 300+ software professionals. Prior to his IT career, he worked in the industrial automation field for over 13 years. He has commissioned several prestigious industrial automation projects and has written a great deal of industrial automation software. He has worked on the AppSheet platform since late 2016 as a freelance developer and has developed complex AppSheet apps for global clients. To date, Suvrutt has been among the top five all-time contributors in terms of solutions and likes in the official AppSheet community.

*I would like to thank my wife, Ujwal, for her continuous support and encouragement. I thank my coauthors, Koichi and Takuya, and technical reviewer, Thierry D'hers, for their excellent collaboration and guidance. Finally, I thank the technical editor and the team at Packt for their help and support throughout the process.*

**Takuya Miyai** has worked in the IT industry for years, with expertise in Salesforce. He holds a number of Salesforce certifications. After encountering AppSheet and being fascinated by its future possibilities, his direction in life completely changed. Since joining Vendola Solutions LLC, he has actively worked as an AppSheet professional consultant to help AppSheet communities and clients. He also acts as an active community member for no-code solutions.

*I thank my coauthors, Koichi and Suvrutt, for their excellent collaboration and guidance. Thanks to the Packt team for giving me a great opportunity in joining this book project and for their help throughout the process.*

# About the reviewer

**Thierry D'hers** is a seasoned engineering and product executive in the self-service, business intelligence, and visual analytic software industries, with over two decades of experience. Thierry's career has spanned companies as diverse in size and growth maturity as Hyperion Solutions (now Oracle), Microsoft (for over 15 years), and Tableau Software. Most recently, Thierry served as chief product officer for FocusVision and AppSheet (acquired by Google in 2020). Thierry currently advises start-ups and nonprofit organizations on product strategy and data analytics systems. Thierry has recently joined Vivun, a SaaS start-up, to lead its product and engineering team.

# Table of Contents

Preface                                                                      xv

# Part 1 – Introduction and Getting Started

## 1

## Getting Started with AppSheet                                            3

How AppSheet apps are generally built    4
Prerequisites                            5

Converting your ideas into an
AppSheet app                                                                 5
Summary                                                                      5

# Part 2 – App Editor and Main Features

## 2

## Understanding App Editor and Data Sources                                9

Preparing your data in the right format 10

Creating a new app from your own
data                                     11

Exploring the basics of the AppSheet
editor                                   13

Analyzing the table and column
settings                                 17

Checking table settings                  17

Configuring column types                                                    19
Understanding REF-type columns                                              30
What is dereference and dereference list?                                   35
Creating drop-down lists to assist data entry                               41
Making a slice from a table                                                 44

Summary                                                                     47

# 3

## Presenting App Data with UX/Views    49

Technical requirements    50

Reviewing the basics of the UX pane    50

What is a view in AppSheet?    51

UX – view types    54

Single-sheet-type views    55

List-type views    63

Other view types    76

Displaying views    79

Controlling actions associated with view events    80

Changing behavior in the table, gallery, and deck views    80

Format rules to highlight important data    82

Creating a new format rule    82

Branding with theme colors and icons    83

Theme    83

Primary color    83

App logo    84

Launch image    84

Header and footer    84

Managing the app's internal terminology through the Localize tab    85

Summary    86

# 4

## Manipulating Data with Functions and Expressions    87

Technical requirements    88

Understanding functions, expressions and AppSheet Expression Assistant    88

Type-casting    91

Making decisions with Yes/No functions and expressions    92

Making decisions with conditional functions and expressions    97

Manipulating text with text functions and expressions    101

Manipulating multiple values with list functions and expressions    104

List functions and expressions    106

Performing arithmetic calculations with math functions and expressions    112

Performing date, time, and duration calculations with date and time expressions    116

Extracting components of a datetime value    117

Performing duration calculations    117

Understanding week-based calculation functions    119

Calculating duration in decimal value results    122

Performing record-level operations with table functions and expressions    124

Understanding the difference between column- and row-level functions    127

**Understanding important miscellaneous functions**    **130**

Using functions related to the app user    130

Using the CONTEXT() functions    133

Using the TEXT() function    134

**Using multiple functions in single expressions**    **136**

**Summary**    **138**

# 5

## Manipulating Data with Behaviors and Actions    139

**Technical requirements**    **139**

**Understanding actions and action types**    **140**

What are actions?    140

Action types and their usage    141

Important settings in the Actions settings pane    143

**Using app actions for navigation and working with CSV files**    **147**

Deep link expressions for navigation actions    148

Unconditional navigation    148

Conditional navigation    149

CSV export or import actions    150

**Configuring data change actions**    **152**

Actions for setting the values of some columns in a row    152

Using bulk actions to change data in multiple rows    153

Changing data in summary views with bulk actions    154

Adding a row to another table using values from the current row    156

Reference actions    157

**Using external actions for external communications**    **161**

External actions for starting an email, a message, or a phone call    161

External actions for navigating to a website and opening a file    162

**Sequentially executing multiple actions with grouped actions**    **164**

Event actions    165

**Offline or sync behavior of an app**    **166**

Sync – app to cloud    167

Offline use    167

Sync – cloud to data source    169

**Summary**    **169**

# 6

## Controlling App Users and Data Security    171

**Controlling who can access an app**    **172**

**Adding app users to your apps and defining editing permissions**    **173**

Adding new users as normal users    173

Adding new users as a co-author    175

Defining the app role for each user    175

**Controlling permission levels with expressions**    **178**

Using the userrole() expression to control permissions    178

Using the useremail() expression to control
permissions                                    180
Passing an expression to the table permission
control                                        181

**Controlling what data is sent to a**

user's device and security options             183
Creating a new security filter per table       183
Implementing additional security measures
for safety                                     185

**Summary**                                    187

7

**Managing the App Environment**                                                189

**Analyzing app features and
transferring the app ownership**               190
The Plan requirements tab                       190
Transferring the app ownership                  192
Setting editor settings, copying, and deleting
apps                                            194

**Performing app version management** 197
The version history of an app                   197
Upgrading the app version for all users        200
Creating a stable version of an app            202

**Deploying an app with all features**         203
Checking an app's deployment readiness         204

White labeling an app                           206
Additional options under the Deploy tab         207

**Monitoring app usage and app sync
performance**                                  213
Knowing the user's app usage pattern           214
Using Audit History for the row-level user
activity                                        217
Analyzing an app's sync performance            223

**Sending on-demand messages to app
users**                                        226
**Summary**                                    227

# Part 3 – Advanced Features and External Services

8

**Automating Recurring Data Changes and Scheduling Tasks**                       231

**What is AppSheet Automation?**               232
**Understanding a Bot and its
components**                                   233
**Event – Data change or Schedule**            235
Creating a new Bot                             235
**How is a Process constructed?**              240

Steps for a Task or Data change action          240
Adding a new step to a Process                  240
Setting up a task in a Step                     241
Data change actions                             243

**Learning about Bot setup through a
practical example**                            244

Setting up the column used to trigger the Bot for a data change event   246

Creating a new Bot by adding a new Event   248

Adding a new Step to send an email   250

Running a data change action from a Step   255

Trying and testing Automation   256

**Summary**   **257**

# 9

# Using Intelligence and Advanced Features   259

**Enabling advanced features**   **260**

**Searching data from an app with Smart Assistant**   **261**

**Building your own predictive models**   **263**

Creating a new predictive model   264

**Building an OCR model**   **267**

**What are AppSheet OCR models?**   **267**

What types of images are scannable by OCR?   267

How do you set and train an OCR model?   267

**Summary**   **270**

# 10

# Extending App Capabilities with Third-Party Services   271

**Technical requirements**   **272**

**Displaying images with dynamic text**   **272**

Services to use   274

A quick guide on using the URL service for a basic text label image   275

Dynamically changing the label contents   278

Customizing the styles   278

**Using QuickChart to generate a dynamic chart as an image**   **279**

Building a radial gauge chart   280

Bonus tips – a working sample expression for a progress bar chart   284

Generating a QR code for the image dynamically   286

**Integrating with Google Workspace products**   **287**

Adopting a card-style message rather than plain text   291

**Google Apps Script and use cases**   **294**

Displaying the latest currency exchange rate   295

Google Apps Script sample code   296

Reading data from a spreadsheet   297

**Summary**   **298**

# Part 4 – App Templates and Tricks for App Building

## 11

## Building More Apps with App Templates 303

Creating your apps portfolio for
other app creators 304

Sharing your apps with teams and others 304

Using others' app templates to help
with your app development 311

Using app templates from the
AppSheet website 312

Building templates for your
self-reference 315

Summary 316

## 12

## Tips and Tricks 317

Technical requirements 318

Formulas (expressions) 318

Creating a URL to access images and other files 318

Calculations between time and duration 320

Number division (decimal to be used) 322

Actions 323

Forcing sync upon navigating to the target view 323

Setup guide 323

Reference action to update the parent based
on the child 324

Updating child rows based on a data change
to the parent row 326

Column settings 330

Establishing many-to-many relationships 330

App settings 331

Adding a table with a large number of rows 331

Reading a Google Drive folder as a table 332

Bots and automation 340

Creating sequential numbers by using a bot 340

Creating a dynamic URL to open files created
by a bot 343

Setup guide 343

Views 348

Creating a chart or map view 348

Summary 353

# 13

## Appendix                                                                                          355

Joining the AppSheet community to
be a citizen developer                    355

AppSheet is growing endlessly              356
Summary                                    356

## Index                                                                                             357

## Other Books You May Enjoy                                                                         368

# Preface

This book enables citizen developers to create their own simple or complex hybrid apps for business or personal use. It teaches you how to combine features so that an app is efficient and easy to use for the end user. Many citizen developers regularly use spreadsheets in their business and day-to-day jobs. They can use the AppSheet platform to take their spreadsheet work to the next level with its ease of use. The AppSheet platform allows citizen developers to run their businesses more efficiently and manage them in the field, beyond the office.

As the book progresses, you will learn how the AppSheet editor works and how it is used to configure, test, and deploy an app. You will learn how to effectively use data sources, create app views, and deploy actions, and discover how you can make your app secure through security options and user-friendly through UX options. You will learn how to create, store in the cloud, and send files through emails by using AppSheet Automation bots. You will learn how to integrate third-party services. Also, you will build an app throughout the book so that you get hands-on experience.

By the end of this book, you will be able to build medium-complexity AppSheet apps using the AppSheet features discussed in the book.

## Who this book is for

This book is aimed at beginner- and intermediate-level citizen application developers in small- or medium-sized businesses, and business users who want to develop their own business apps. You are expected to have a basic knowledge of Google Sheets or Excel and an understanding of different spreadsheet formulas. Knowledge of SQL and some basic software development knowledge is beneficial but not necessary.

## What this book covers

*Chapter 1, Getting Started with AppSheet*, introduces the AppSheet platform. Before creating our first app, we first need to understand some basics about the platform so that you know what you are doing and why. We will go through the overall process and what is important to know.

*Chapter 2, Understanding App Editor and Data Sources*, explores the basic skills needed to create a new app and use the app editor. We will also discuss data sources, such as tables, columns, and sliced tables.

*Chapter 3, Presenting App Data with UX/Views*, describes how an app is presented to app users, what kind of views you can use, and how to format your data with colors and icons. This chapter also discusses branding and localizing if your app requires these features. We will also discuss how to control an app with UX options.

*Chapter 4, Manipulating Data with Functions and Expressions*, dives into the major AppSheet functions with which you can create expressions to manipulate data in your apps. You will learn to construct expressions with the help of practical use cases. You will learn different types of functions, such as yes/no, conditional, text, list, math, date, time, and duration functions. If you are already familiar with Google Sheets or Excel formulas, that will be beneficial. You will also learn to combine functions of different types to construct more complex expressions.

*Chapter 5, Manipulating Data with Behaviors and Actions*, examines actions, which enable you to implement app behaviors such as making quick data changes, in-app or out-of-app navigation, and CSV uploads/downloads. With external actions, you can navigate out of an app to a website, compose an email/text message, or make a phone call. You can directly invoke actions by tapping on an action icon or indirectly through events, such as record save or record select. In this chapter, you will learn how you can use different action types to improve app behavior. You will also learn how to best configure an app's offline and sync behavior.

*Chapter 6, Controlling App Users and Data Security*, explains how to control who can use an app and at what permission level. You can also control data itself in different ways, such as filtering data on the server side by applying a security filter.

*Chapter 7, Managing the App Environment*, shows you how to use multiple options in AppSheet's **Manage** tab to monitor and set up an app's environment. Here, you can select team colleagues as app co-authors and transfer app ownership. You can see the app's version history, define a stable version, and upgrade an app version. You can check an app's deployment readiness for any environmental errors. You can monitor an app's usage by various users, automation, and an app's sync time performance, even at table and column levels. You will learn how to deploy an app and also how you can send on-demand messages to app users.

*Chapter 8, Automating Recurring Data Changes and Schedulinge Tasks*, conducts an extensive review of AppSheet Automation. Automation is built to handle more complex challenges such as sending emails, creating files with templates, and manipulating data in the background. It can also run business processes quicker than directly from an app.

*Chapter 9, Using Intelligence and Advanced Features*, explores three AI-driven features and the basics of each feature. AppSheet is generally a data-driven platform for developing feature-rich business applications, but it is also powered by AI to give additional and advanced functionalities, such as data searching, predictions, and data scraping out of image files.

*Chapter 10, Extending App Capabilities with Third-Party Services,* discusses open source services, which are in abundance these days. We will select a few external services that will add some flavor to your app views, such as a dynamic image with text on a colored background and a dynamic image-based static chart, and also look at how to set up integrations with Google Workspace applications such as Google Chat.

*Chapter 11, Building More Apps with App Templates,* shows you how you can share apps as "public" apps on your own portfolio page for any AppSheet user to view or copy them. Portfolio apps demonstrate a feature or business functionality that other app creators can learn from. Additionally, the AppSheet website has a collection of template apps that demonstrate certain business functionalities. We will learn how you can further build your app by copying the template or portfolio apps of other app creators. We will also discuss how you can build your own template apps for future reuse and reference.

*Chapter 12, Tips and Tricks,* offers you the most practicable and useful tips and tricks of AppSheet to help you develop custom functionalities to satisfy the unique needs of business applications. As AppSheet app creators spend more time with AppSheet, they will naturally find out that the learning curve to develop their own functionalities is a step up when they reach a certain skill or knowledge level. This is because app creators are expected to take the advanced step of implementing their own business logic in a single application. The tips in this chapter are not only related to data manipulation but also advanced UX settings to bring customized user experiences, as well as the advanced usage of bots to automate complicated business processes with ease.

*Chapter 13, Appendix,* concludes the book. When you have reached the end of book, you will have a good understanding of how to build an app with most of the AppSheet features. The next step is to join the AppSheet community and discuss with other citizen developers how they solved their challenges. The community is a good source to gain ideas and increase your own skill level. We will also briefly discuss what you can expect in the future from Appsheet.

## To get the most out of this book

Before you start to build your apps, you need to create a Google account, as you need to have access to Google Drive, Google Sheets, and other Google services, such as Google Docs. You can create a new account at `https://accounts.google.com/signup`.

When the Google account is created (skip creation if you already have an account, of course), it's time to create your AppSheet account. Follow these steps to create an AppSheet account:

1.  Go to `www.appsheet.com` and log in with your Google account from the top-right corner.
2.  Click the **Get started** button. Then, select the name of the cloud service to be used for authentication. Select **Google**. After that, follow the guide so that you give permission for AppSheet to have access to your data by using your Google account.

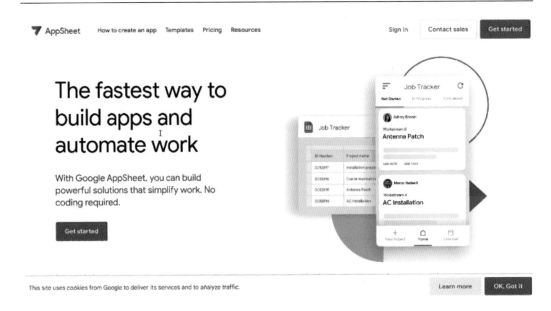

Figure 1.1 – The AppSheet home page

3.   Now, your account is generated and tied to your Google account.

You will also now have your AppSheet account ID, which is a seven-digit number. This account ID is used when a new app is created. Your unique app name will look similar to `Inventory-5689905`. As you created your AppSheet account with your Google account, all your images, files, and templates will be stored in Google Drive by default.

When creating any kind of app, it needs a data source. It could be a spreadsheet, such as a Google sheet or Excel file in OneDrive, or even a real database, such as a cloud SQL database. Whatever the data source is, it always needs to be in the cloud. For example, trying to connect an Excel file from your laptop or phone won't be possible, as that file is not in the cloud. These are the data sources you can use with an AppSheet app:

- Google
- Google Calendar/Drive
- Microsoft Excel Online
- Smartsheet
- Airtable

- Salesforce

- Dropbox

- Box

- Apigee

- OData

- BiqQuery

- A cloud database (SQL, for example)

In this book, we will use Google Sheets as a data source because it's one of the most common ones. *Therefore, please make sure to access AppSheet using a Google account to follow along with this book.*

## AppSheet editor styles used in this book

The style and layout of the app editor we refer to in the book along with the screenshots are all taken from the app editor at the time of writing (October 2022). AppSheet changes the style and layout of its editor quite frequently, so you may see a different layout.                    ar

## Downloading/referring the sample apps

While we are explaining AppSheet's features and functionalities to you throughout the book, you can refer to the sample apps that we prepared for this book. All of the sample apps can be found on the portfolio page at `https://www.appsheet.com/portfolio/5689905`. In each chapter, we will name the relevant sample app, which you can check for reference. These sample apps will help you to see how things are set up. You can even copy the sample apps to your account. We hope these sample apps will help you get familiar with AppSheet quickly.

Check them out!

## Download the color images

We also provide a PDF file that has color images of the screenshots and diagrams used in this book. You can download it here: `https://packt.link/FigT2`

## Conventions used

There are a number of text conventions used throughout this book.

`Code in text`: Indicates code words in text, database table names, folder names, filenames, file extensions, pathnames, dummy URLs, user input, and Twitter handles. Here is an example: "Mount the downloaded `WebStorm-10*.dmg` disk image file as another disk in your system."

A block of code is set as follows:

```
IFS(
        WEEKDAY([DATE)=1, "Weekly Holiday",
        WEEKDAY([DATE])=7, "Half Working Day",
        AND(WEEKDAY([DATE])1,   WEEKDAY([DATE])7),   "Working
        Day"
)
```

When we wish to draw your attention to a particular part of a code block, the relevant lines or items are set in bold:

```
IFS(
        WEEKDAY([DATE)=1, "Weekly Holiday",
        WEEKDAY([DATE])=7, "Half Working Day",
        AND(WEEKDAY([DATE])1,   WEEKDAY([DATE])7),   "Working
        Day"
)
```

Any command-line input or output is written as follows:

```
$ mkdir css
$ cd css
```

**Bold**: Indicates a new term, an important word, or words that you see on screen. For instance, words in menus or dialog boxes appear in **bold**. Here is an example: "Select **System info** from the **Administration** panel."

> **Tips or important notes**
> Appear like this.

# Get in touch

Feedback from our readers is always welcome.

**General feedback**: If you have questions about any aspect of this book, email us at customercare@ packtpub.com and mention the book title in the subject of your message.

**Errata**: Although we have taken every care to ensure the accuracy of our content, mistakes do happen. If you have found a mistake in this book, we would be grateful if you would report this to us. Please visit www.packtpub.com/support/errata and fill in the form.

**Piracy**: If you come across any illegal copies of our works in any form on the internet, we would be grateful if you would provide us with the location address or website name. Please contact us at copyright@packt.com with a link to the material.

**If you are interested in becoming an author**: If there is a topic that you have expertise in and you are interested in either writing or contributing to a book, please visit authors.packtpub.com.

## Share Your Thoughts

Once you've read *Democratizing Application Development with AppSheet*, we'd love to hear your thoughts! Scan the QR code below to go straight to the Amazon review page for this book and share your feedback.

https://packt.link/r/1803241179

Your review is important to us and the tech community and will help us make sure we're delivering excellent quality content.

# Download a free PDF copy of this book

Thanks for purchasing this book!

Do you like to read on the go but are unable to carry your print books everywhere?

Is your eBook purchase not compatible with the device of your choice?

Don't worry, now with every Packt book you get a DRM-free PDF version of that book at no cost.

Read anywhere, any place, on any device. Search, copy, and paste code from your favorite technical books directly into your application.

The perks don't stop there, you can get exclusive access to discounts, newsletters, and great free content in your inbox daily

Follow these simple steps to get the benefits:

1. Scan the QR code or visit the link below

https://packt.link/free-ebook/9781803241173

2. Submit your proof of purchase
3. That's it! We'll send your free PDF and other benefits to your email directly

# Part 1 – Introduction and Getting Started

In this part, we will show you how you can get the most out of this book. We will review the general steps involved in building AppSheet apps and also discuss the prerequisites for becoming an effective AppSheet citizen developer.

This part has the following chapter:

- *Chapter 1, Getting Started with AppSheet*

# 1
# Getting Started with AppSheet

AppSheet is a leading low-code platform for creating business apps. The platform was originally created to develop apps for mobile devices back in 2014 and has been growing ever since. AppSheet became a reputable **Digital Transformation** (**DX**) platform and helps app creators to develop business apps compatible with devices such as mobile phones, tablets, and laptops, most importantly, *without writing a single line of code.*

AppSheet will offer you a path to develop a robust application that could solve a challenge you face in your business without asking for coding skills and knowledge. AppSheet prepares a set of template apps with which you can start to build your own apps, and you can also create a new app from a scratch using data such as Excel and/or Google Sheets. The beauty of AppSheet is that everyone can get on board easily and start for free.

Google constantly keeps adding new features to enhance the functions of AppSheet. This means AppSheet can be used to create business applications with tons of advanced features to facilitate the daily jobs in your offices and solve your own business problems. However, once we start a journey with AppSheet by building our first app, you may notice that it is not easy to handle this platform to customize app behaviors to meet your own requirements. In the context of the comparison between no-code and full-code development, a no-code approach to building an application is far more efficient and productive than full coding in terms of the required number of man-hours to complete a project. However, to validate this comparison, app creators must be proficient as well as confident in no-coding tools such as AppSheet.

This story applies to AppSheet. An understanding of AppSheet is a key to success for efficient business applications. Hence, *Learn AppSheet* is an essential first step for all app creators who want to freely develop their own unique apps.

This book is designed for absolute beginners to AppSheet as well as those who have a small amount of experience to assist them in learning the platform in a structured manner. The process of development with AppSheet is generally consistent regardless of the type of app you build. It is vitally important to understand the AppSheet way of development when building your apps by learning the basics.

Throughout this book, you will learn the overall processes to develop apps from the beginning to the end to increase your level of confidence in handling the AppSheet Editor. Furthermore, we will touch upon some advanced skills and techniques for you to develop feature-rich applications with AppSheet.

By the end of this book, you should be able to grasp the full process of building an AppSheet app with basic features.

Your path as an AppSheet app creator is endless. Each time you learn something new, you will have something else to aim for ahead of you. We hope this book will provide you with a gateway to being a successful AppSheet creator.

In this chapter, we will cover the following topics:

- How AppSheet apps are generally built
- Prerequisites
- Converting your ideas into an AppSheet app

## How AppSheet apps are generally built

Whenever you create a new app, these basic steps are always followed:

1. First, you prepare the data source, usually a spreadsheet on a cloud platform such as Google Drive.
2. Next, you connect the data source to AppSheet. After you connect the data, AppSheet will automatically generate the app for you.
3. Once the data is connected, the app development process moves to the AppSheet Editor. Through the AppSheet Editor, you define how the connected data will be used and configure various app settings, including creating actions for data manipulation and navigation, designing views and layout, and adding automation bots.
4. You can invite test users to try the app for further improvement.
5. When the app is ready, AppSheet provides an easy way to deploy the app to your team and colleagues.

In summary, those five steps are as follows:

1. Connecting the data source
2. Editing your app definition
3. Deploying the app

By reading this book, you will learn the basic sequence of this app development process. All app developments occur in the AppSheet Editor. We will be covering all the important details of these steps to learn how to configure your app through the AppSheet Editor in the upcoming chapters.

# Prerequisites

To work with AppSheet, it is helpful if you are familiar with spreadsheets such as Google Sheets and Microsoft Excel; AppSheet uses its own expressions but most of them are identical to Google Sheet formulas. The syntax can sometimes be slightly different, but the idea is mostly the same. Also, having an understanding of the basic concepts of how spreadsheets work will help you to build your app's foundation. However, don't worry if you are not familiar with Google Sheets – you will get to know it in the following chapters. In fact, there are a number of AppSheet expressions that are unique to AppSheet and not found in other spreadsheet services. We will cover AppSheet expressions throughout this book, especially in *Chapter 4, Manipulate Data with Expressions and Formulas*.

In addition to familiarity with spreadsheets and formulae, it is helpful if you know a thing or two about databases. AppSheet is a database-driven platform; the concept of the relational database is one of the basic foundations of AppSheet. However, this is not absolutely required, as you learn what you need to know while learning AppSheet.

## Converting your ideas into an AppSheet app

We wish to highlight some important concepts before we begin looking at AppSheet.

Whenever you develop apps with AppSheet, your requirements for the application come first. Building apps means that your ideas are converted to AppSheet apps. You should always have an idea of what you want and expect from your app. For example, you may wish to develop an app with a function to help a company's internal approval process for applications for holidays. You also may wish to add a function to send notifications to concerned parties once the applications are approved.

Once you have a clear idea of what you want, think about what you need to do with the AppSheet Editor. AppSheet provides a wide range of options to customize the behavior of your app. To achieve your goals using the AppSheet Editor, you need to know where in the AppSheet Editor to go and how you need to define your own logic. Finding the shortest paths through the AppSheet Editor is key to making your app development process efficient. To gain that skill, you need to understand AppSheet's basic processes.

## Summary

We hope that you now have an AppSheet account prepared and are ready to start the journey with us. As stated in this chapter, the app-development process consists of certain routine steps, regardless of the kind of app you are trying to create. By learning these essential steps in detail, you will be able to master AppSheet.

In the following chapter, we will start with data preparation and creating a new app, which is always the first step in AppSheet app development. Let's start learning now!

# Part 2 – App Editor and Main Features

In this part, we will describe the whole app-building process. We will create an app together with a lot of features so that you will have a good understanding of what capabilities you have when using AppSheet.

This part has the following chapters:

- *Chapter 2, Understanding App Editor and Data Sources*
- *Chapter 3, Presenting App Data with UX/Views*
- *Chapter 4, Manipulating Data with Functions and Expressions*
- *Chapter 5, Manipulating Data with Behaviors and Actions*
- *Chapter 6, Controlling App Users and Data Security*
- *Chapter 7, Managing the App Environment*

# 2
# Understanding App Editor and Data Sources

With a Google account in hand, you are now ready to start building your first app. In this chapter, we will discuss the process of creating a new app from your own data and how to configure table and column settings. An AppSheet app is built from your own data sources, usually a Google Sheets or Excel spreadsheet. Therefore, the first step of building a new app is to prepare your data. Once the data is ready, you are fully ready to create a new app with AppSheet.

Once a new app is created, the whole development process will happen in the AppSheet editor. With this chapter, you will learn how your spreadsheet data should be organized so that it can be used as a data source with AppSheet. We often see cases where the app creator wrongly models data tables, which will cause a number of problems when you develop your apps. To avoid this problem, proper data modeling is important.

You will learn the basics of setting table and column configurations. We will also conduct a quick run-through of the app editor where all of the app development activities are going to happen. By the end of this chapter, you will know how to easily navigate inside the editor.

In this chapter, we will cover the following topics:

- Preparing your data in the right format
- Creating a new app from your own data
- Exploring the basics of the AppSheet editor
- Analyzing the table and column settings

Data modeling and table schema are the foundation of app development; therefore, it is vitally important that you know the basics of the data settings and how to correctly configure them because it will directly affect the app's behavior in various places. By the end of this chapter, you will know the basics of adding new tables from your own sources and defining column settings.

# Preparing your data in the right format

Before building a new app with AppSheet, the data source for your app needs to be in place. Throughout this book, we are using Google Sheets as the data source for our sample app and demonstration. To proceed, please make sure you have a spreadsheet for your own exercise to start to build your application, and ensure the data is stored in a tabular format. A *tabular format* is simply information presented in the form of a table with rows and columns, where the first row at the top always represents the name of columns and each row represents a subset of the data. A quick way to see whether your data is in a tabular format is to check whether a new subset of the data will be appended at the last row as a new record, instead of being added as a new column.

| | A | B | C | D |
|---|---|---|---|---|
| | ID | YYYY-MM | Income | Cost |
| | A001 | 2022-01 | 100 | 80 |
| | A002 | 2022-02 | 120 | 90 |
| | A003 | 2022-03 | 90 | 70 |
| | A004 | 2022-04 | 110 | 85 |

Figure 2.1 – Monthly income and cost table in a tabular format

*Figure 2.1* is an example table, presenting the monthly income and cost for a company in simplified terms. As you can see, each row represents a subset of data for a particular month. If a new record is added to this table – that is, data for **2022-05** – it will be added to this table as a new row. So, this data will grow downward. Therefore, this table is in a tabular format, which is suitable for AppSheet.

Now, let's see another possible format of the table for the same dataset in the following figure.

| | A | B | C | D | E |
|---|---|---|---|---|---|
| 1 | YYYY-MM | 2022-01 | 2022-02 | 2022-03 | 2022-04 |
| 2 | ID | A001 | A002 | A003 | A004 |
| 3 | Income | 100 | 120 | 90 | 110 |
| 4 | Cost | 80 | 90 | 70 | 85 |
| 5 | | | | | |

Figure 2.2 – Data in a non-tabular format

You can now see the difference in the format compared with *Figure 2.1*. When a new subset of data for a new month comes in, it should be added as an additional column entry under **2022-05**. In other words, the table will grow to the right in the form of an additional column. This format does not fit with AppSheet.

The very first step of app building is to prepare your own data. To move to the next step, please check your data is in tabular format. If not, you need to convert your data before adding it to AppSheet.

If your existing data is not in a tabular format, the easiest solution to convert it into a proper tabular format is to use the Google Sheets function to transpose data with copy and paste.

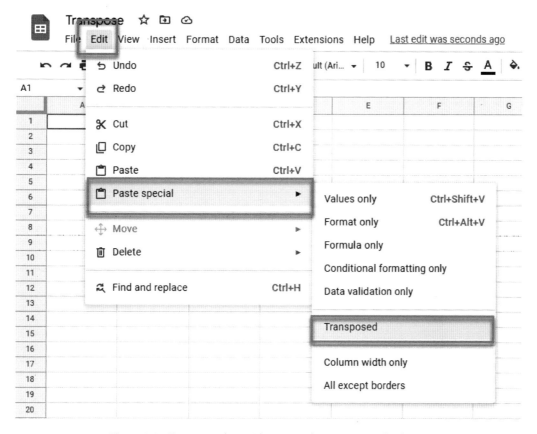

Figure 2.3 – Transpose data with copy and paste in Google Sheets

*Figure 2.3* demonstrates how to transpose the copied data. Using an example of a non-tabular format table in *Figure 2.2*, you copy the whole table by selecting the range of A1 and E4 cells, and then go to **Edit | Paste special | Transposed**. You can transform the non-tabular format into the tabular format table easily. The same function is also available in MS Excel as well.

If you have suitable data, then you are ready to move to the next step.

## Creating a new app from your own data

Considering your data is in the right format as a Google Sheets spreadsheet, let's create your first app using it. Log in to AppSheet, and you will arrive on the **My Apps** page. AppSheet quite frequently changes its UX; the following figure shows what it looks like at the time of writing:

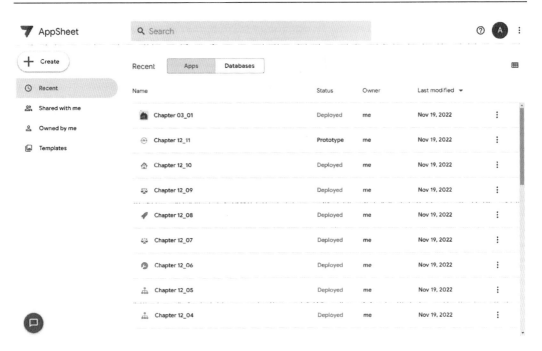

Figure 2.4 – The My Apps page

As the name suggests, this page presents the list of the apps you have created, or apps that you have been added to as a co-author.

Now, let's create a new app by following these steps:

1.  Click the **Create** button in the upper-left corner of this page. When you click on it, you will see two different options, **Start with existing data** and **Start with a template**.

2.  Select the **Start with existing data** option. Then, a dialog box appears where you are asked to name the app you are going to create and to select a category out of the list.

3.  Click the **Choose your data** button at the bottom. Another new dialog box will appear, asking you to select the data source. When you newly start AppSheet with your Google account, you should see a single option for **Google Sheets** with your account's email. Select **Google Sheets** and select the spreadsheet from the file selector.

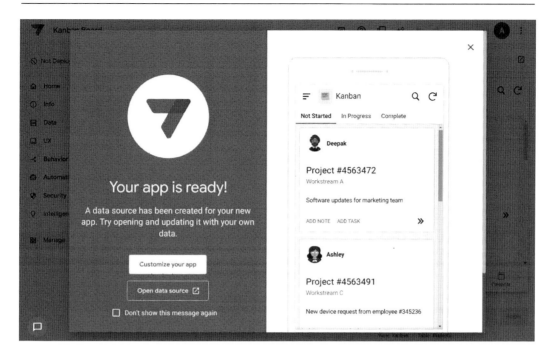

Figure 2.5 – The AppSheet editor is launched after generating a new app

4.  After waiting for a while, AppSheet will create a new app from the spreadsheet you selected, and you will land on a page that looks like *Figure 2.5*.

5.  To proceed, click on the **Start customizing** button.

Now you have successfully created a new app and landed on the AppSheet editor to edit the app in detail.

In the following section, we will walk you through the AppSheet editor to learn its anatomy.

## Exploring the basics of the AppSheet editor

We have successfully created the app by connecting to the data source. To customize the app, we need to change the settings for the data, but before discussing this process in detail, let's briefly walk you through the AppSheet editor you just landed on.

Please have a look at the following figure, where we have outlined the main elements of the AppSheet editor.

> **Note**
>
> The style and layout of the AppSheet editor we quote and the screenshot taken from the editor are all taken from the editor at the time of writing, October 2022. AppSheet makes changes to the style and layout of the AppSheet editor quite frequently, so you may see a different layout.

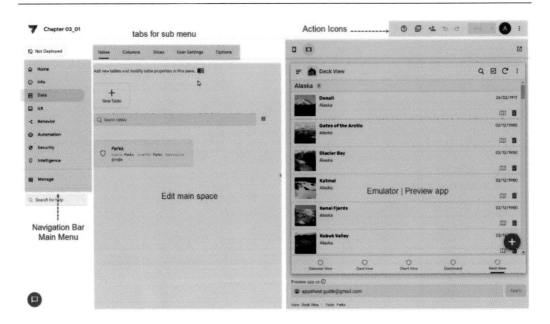

Figure 2.6 – Anatomy of the app editor

Basically, the app editor page has a fixed layout. Let's begin with the main menu, which is located in the upper left of the editor:

- **Navigation bar**: to Whenever you take any action to build your app, you need to select one of the options from this bar. It is located on the left side of the window, and you will see several items. When you select an option from the navigation bar, a sub-menu will appear at the top and the content inside the main space will dynamically change based on your selection from the sub-menu.

- These are the navigation bar options:

  - **Home**: This is the welcome page, where you can find guides to help you build your application, among other things.

  - **Info**: As the name suggests, we can find information about this app, such as various properties and a link to a dashboard that displays the usage and performance of your app.

  - **Data**: This helps with managing table and column configurations. We will dive into this menu in more detail later in this chapter.

- **UX**: This sets up the pages of your app, which are called views in AppSheet, including applying format rules to change the styles, such as font colors and sizes. We will deal with views in detail in *Chapter 3*.

- **Behavior**: This helps with adding and controlling AppSheet actions. Actions are one of the key elements for AppSheet apps to manipulate data and assist navigation. We will learn about actions in detail in *Chapter 5*.

- **Automation**: AppSheet provides a feature to automate processes such as sending emails, creating files, and other useful automation functions. We will deal with AppSheet automation in *Chapter 8*.

- **Security**: This is a menu for controlling the security aspects of your app in terms of defining the required authentications for app users and other security-related permissions. We will cover this topic in detail in *Chapter 6*.

- **Intelligence**: AppSheet provides a few advanced features driven by artificial intelligence, such as advanced data searching inside the app and optical character recognition. We will cover this menu in *Chapter 9*.

- **Manage**: This menu provides miscellaneous options across the app. We will cover the **Manage** menu in *Chapter 7*.

- **Tabs for sub-menu**: This is a list of the available sub-menus for the selected option under the main menu of the navigation bar. Once you select one from the main menu, the sub-menu associated with the selected option will be presented.

- **Edit main space**: This is the main field where your work on the definition of your app will happen. Based on the selection from the main and sub-menus, the content displayed in this space will change.

- **Emulator | Preview pane**: You can access your app based on the definition you have set through this preview pane. You can preview the latest app live as you develop. This is one of the most powerful tools in AppSheet because you can immediately access the latest app after making changes to the app definition to see how your changes will affect the physical apps.

Please refer to the following figure to see what the preview pane looks like.

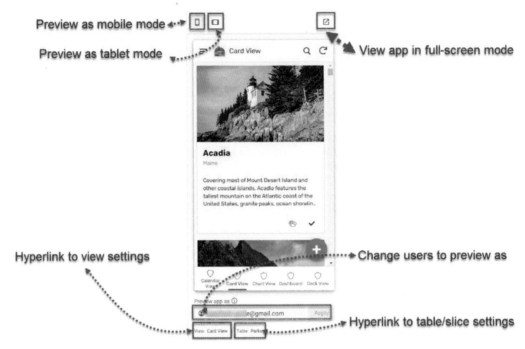

Figure 2.7 – The preview pane

You can preview your latest app in different modes by switching from mobile to tablet and vice versa through the icons at the top. You can open the app in full-screen mode on your browser as well. At the bottom of the pane, there is a hyperlink to view the settings and to customize the view you are currently previewing. Another hyperlink will take you to the table or slice settings of the view that it comes from.

- **Action icons**: Various action icons and links to take you to other pages are in the top-right corner of the editor. Most importantly, the icon for sharing your app is here. Sharing apps will be discussed in *Chapter 6*.

- Now that we have explored the menu options, you can go ahead and build your app.

In the following section, we will talk about the table and column settings after you add your data to the app.

To end this section, we will call your attention to one of the important actions inside the AppSheet editor. Whenever you make any changes to the app definition through the AppSheet editor, your changes are pending. Please make sure to save your changes. Before you save, you can undo and/or redo the change by clicking on the icons beside the **SAVE** button.

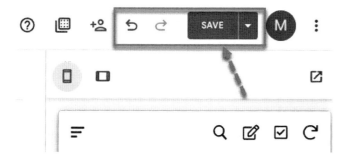

Figure 2.8 – Saving your changes in the AppSheet editor

When you work through the editor and have made any unsaved changes, the button is highlighted. Please ensure you save changes constantly so that you don't lose your work by closing the page without saving.

# Analyzing the table and column settings

When you are working on a spreadsheet, such as Google Sheets or Excel, you may not pay attention to the data types. However, data types in AppSheet are quite important to define because they will affect the other behaviors inside the app, such as actions and expressions you may use inside the app. AppSheet is a database-driven application and platform, so it is important to define how your data is going to be dealt with inside AppSheet.

There are two different places you need to visit to change settings if required:

- Table settings
- Column settings

## Checking table settings

In the navigation bar, go to **Data** and click on the **Tables** tab. We have started to build a new app from a Google Sheet, and you will see one tile in this **Tables** tab. Expand the tile by clicking on it. The expanded tile will look like the following screenshot:

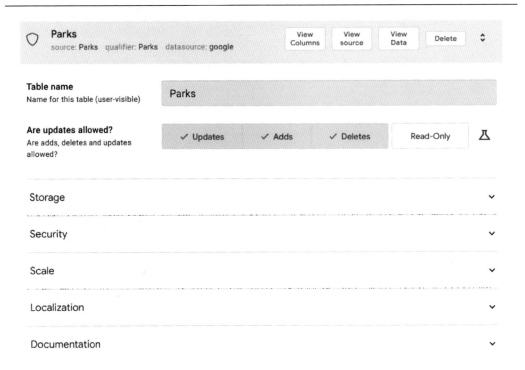

Figure 2.9 – Table settings

In this table settings tile, there are a few optional items, but most importantly, we need to determine the permission level for editing this table.

Figure 2.10 – Permissions to edit data for a table

In this section, we define how the app users will interact with this table. As you can see, there are four different options to select:

- If you select **Read-Only**, then, as the name suggests, the data in this table cannot be edited at all, meaning users can only view the contents.
- If **Updates** is selected, users can edit the data in the app.
- If you want to allow users to add new records, then the **Adds** option should be highlighted.
- Similarly, if you want to allow users to delete records, the **Deletes** option should be selected.

You need to select these options based on the requirements of your app. Since this is the start of your app development journey, just leave them as they are. As we will see in *Chapter 5* of this book, AppSheet provides actions to manipulate data and assist navigation from one view to another. You have to bear in your mind that the selection of the permission level in this section will affect the available actions as well. For instance, if you allow users to add records to this table, then the action to add new records will be automatically generated, and vice versa if you deselect the **Adds** option.

If your spreadsheet has multiple sheets, then you need to add them one by one. At the top of the **Tables** tab, there is a button called **New Table**. To add a new sheet as a table in AppSheet, please click this and select the file and sheet to add new tables.

The next step is to move to the `Columns` table to check and change the column definitions.

## Configuring column types

One of the most important steps when building an app is to configure the data types for all the columns. When we are working on a spreadsheet such as Google Sheets or Excel, we are not really paying attention to the *data type* when we apply formatting to the cells, such as text, date, and number type.

In AppSheet, the app behavior will be automatically aligned with your definition of the columns in the table. Defining the appropriate data types for all the columns in the table is vitally important. Let's review how you define data and learn how it will affect your apps.

### Available data types

To define the data type, go to **Data | Columns**. Then, you can expand the table you are going to work on.

Figure 2.11 – Column settings

This page presents a list view of the columns that are coming from the spreadsheet, which is the data source you added to the app. We can see the following in the preceding figure:

- The first column on the left lists the names of the columns coming from your data.

- The second column contains the data type settings, where we define the data type for each column. When you click the drop-down menu beside the data type for this column, you will see a list of data type options. When you're developing with AppSheet, it is necessary to ensure the right data type is selected for all the columns.

Figure 2.12 – Selecting a data type for each column

The list of the available data types is quite long, so we will not run through them here, but you can visit the AppSheet documentation to find out more: https://support.google. com/appsheet/answer/10106435?hl=en.

For instance, if you are going to capture numbers, then naturally the type for this column should be the **Number** type. If you are going to capture the location data in terms of latitude and longitude, then the **LatLong** type would be the right choice.

If you want to upload and display image files, then your choice for this column should be the **Image** type. For files other than images, such as PDF or XLSX, the **File** type is appropriate. You first need to review your requirements for the type of data you want to capture for each column, and then you select the right type and assign it to each column.

Note that AppSheet app behavior changes with your selection of data type. For instance, if you select the **Image** type, then you will see the action icon to assist the process of uploading the file. If you select the **Phone** type, then actions to call users and send messages will be automatically generated. AppSheet will change the UX for you without explicitly taking action, such as adding rows and changing UX settings. This is an added advantage and makes the app more efficient.

## What are keys and labels?

If you are familiar with databases such as SQL and MS Access, you possibly know about a table's key. AppSheet is a database-driven application, and it is built on the concept of a relational database. So, when you add a new table to AppSheet, you need to decide which column should be assigned the key column for this table by ticking **Key** in the **Update Behavior** section. This is mandatory, and only one column can be the key column. As standard practice, we add a column called ID to all the tables. We will learn about AppSheet expressions later on, but we usually pass the UNIQUEID() expression, which will generate unique and random text mixed with numbers to ensure the uniqueness of the values stored in this key column. You can see the typical settings for the key column for the table in *Figure 2.13*.

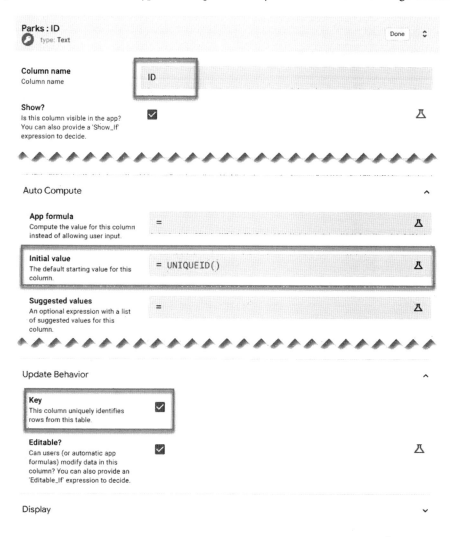

Figure 2.13 – Typical settings for the key column

For each record, the key value must be unique. It should never be duplicated across any two records. Because the key value for a record is unique, it can be used to uniquely identify a record of a table.

There is another column setting you need to be aware of, which is **Label**. What does **Label** mean in AppSheet? In short, the column that is set to **Label** is the most important column in the table. We can select one image column and one non-image column as labels. AppSheet's official documentation (`https://support.google.com/appsheet/answer/10106376?hl=en`) provides clear information.

The **Label** column should have a more user-friendly name than the key column to identify a record. For example, an `Items` table may have a `UNIQUEID()` expression to create a random unique value, which may generate `e6f43da4` as data. It is not user-friendly to read, but the column set to **Label** could be an item name, such as `Blue Pen`, which is more easily readable. Even though it is preferable to have unique label columns for records in a table, just like the key columns, having duplicate label names may not always cause serious issues.

---

**Note – normal columns versus virtual columns**

First of all, the question we need to answer is what is a **virtual column**? When we add a table from a spreadsheet, all the columns in the sheet in the first row will be regarded as columns for this added table. In other words, it can be said that those columns physically exist. Let's call those existing columns *normal columns*. With AppSheet, we can add any type of column to a table by adding *virtual columns*. Unlike normal columns, virtual columns do not really exist in the table, so they are called virtual columns as they exist virtually in the AppSheet app.

There are virtual columns that AppSheet systematically adds automatically, but we can also add them explicitly as we want.

To add a new virtual column, we go to the **Data | Columns** tab, and there is an action button called **Add Virtual Column** on the header in each table. To make a virtual column work, it is mandatory for us to pass the expression into an *app formula* field in the column settings without exceptions. A virtual column can be described as a "calculated column," as it will present the result of the calculation of AppSheet expressions, which is passed to the "app formula" field. The value for the column is always systematically calculated and presented based on the value or expression we enter into the app formula. Please remember that the value for the virtual column is always re-evaluated whenever the app is run or, more precisely, when the app is synced with the backend server. With this virtual column behavior, the values in a virtual column are up to date whenever you visit your app.

---

Now, we have reviewed the basics for data type setting. For data column configuration, there are other items that will assist in data entry, showing or hiding columns, validating data, and controlling other app behaviors. We will now look at some other options for column settings.

## Other settings for each column

There are a few settings groups for each column, as shown here:

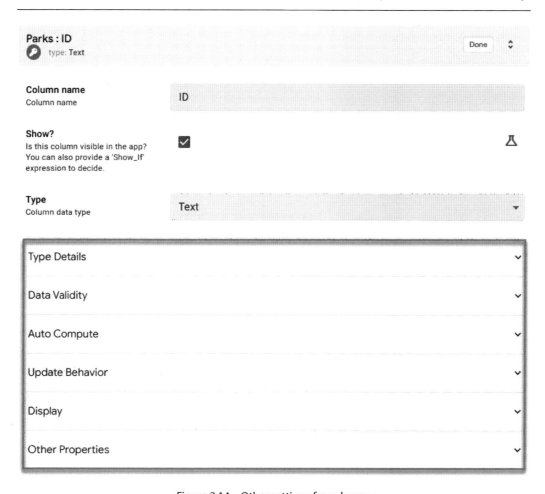

Figure 2.14 – Other settings for columns

Let's review each of them in detail:

- **Show?:** By default, this setting is enabled, as you can see in the preceding figure, but we can disable it as well. In that case, this column will be hidden globally from the app. For instance, the **ID column** will hold unique and random values, as we explained earlier, as a result of passing the UNIQUEID() expression into it. The returned value of the UNIQUEID() expression is not human-readable text, such as cc47ed23, so it will not make sense to present those values on the surface of the app. However, to run the app, we can't remove this column from the data source. We can simply hide the column entirely across the app by unchecking this option.

  As you can see, there is a flask icon beside this setting, which indicates that we are able to pass an AppSheet expression to control the behavior. Using this expression is a common practice, where the app creator shows or hides the column dynamically and conditionally. If the condition is met, meaning the expression you pass returns true, then the column will appear on the views of the app.

For instance, you have a column with the number type called Age, and users are asked to put their ages into this column. Apart from this number type column, there is a column with the date type, which is only required to be filled in when the user enters a value higher than 20 in to the Age column. Then, you can click the flask icon and **Expression Assistant** will appear. We will discuss this expression assistant in *Chapter 4*, but we simply pass the [Age] >= 20 expression in this case. Once you've learned AppSheet expressions, including conditional expressions such as IF(), IFS(), and SWITCH(), you can apply more complex conditions to toggle, show, or hide behavior.

- **Type Details**: The context of this menu will change based on the data type you select. For instance, if you select the **Number** type, then it will give you the option to define the maximum and minimum allowable numbers to constrain data entered by users. This section will give you additional settings associated with the data type you select.

- **Data Validity**: At the top of the list in the **Data Validity** section, as you can see in *Figure 2.15*, there is a field called **Valid If**, which will act as data validation. For instance, if you want to restrict users who can enter data to only those who meet certain conditions and criteria, you need to specify those conditions in this field with an AppSheet expression.

At the bottom, there is a checkbox called **Require?**. As the name suggests, if you want to make it mandatory to enter values into this column, this option is checked. When an app user creates a new record or edits the existing data in this table, they then cannot leave this column blank.

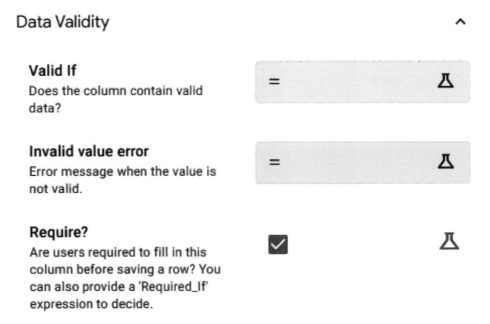

Figure 2.15 – Data validity settings

For example, let's assume you have a column with a date type called `Request date` for an app where your users submit a request to the IT department for support. When users create a new request, this column will contain the date of the request, as its name suggests. Then, you also need to restrict the date value to the date when the request is made. In that case, the condition (expression) should be passed as valid if filed as `[Request Date] =TODAY()`.

With this condition, the user will not be able to enter a date value other than today's date. Note that there is a field called **Invalid value error**. This is the field where you write the text message that will be presented to the app user if invalid data is entered in this field. For example, you can enter text here such as `The request date must be today`. This will guide the user to enter the date without any error in the column.

- **Auto Compute**: First of all, let's see the list of settings in this section. This section is a chunk of settings that will assist data entry into the column, by generating the default value and a list of optional values for data entry. See the following figure:

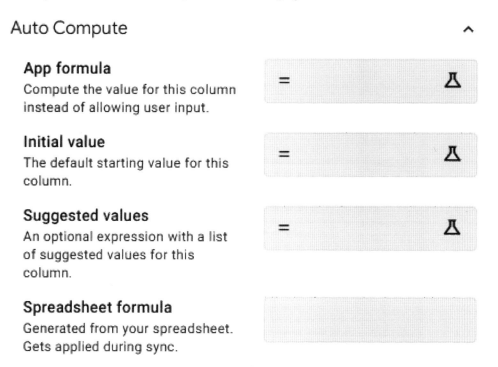

Figure 2.16 – Auto Compute settings

- **App formula** is where you pass a calculation or fixed static text. Whenever a user edits the record, the value saved to this column will be recalculated and the expression will be re-evaluated, and then the result of the expression will be saved as data for this column.

- For instance, say you have two columns in your table, [Income] and [Expense], which have the price type. A new column could be called [Net income], or something like that, where the calculation result of [Income] minus [Expense] is entered. To assist this calculation and make it automated, you simply pass the [Income] - [Expense] expression. Then, once users enter the values in both columns, the app will automatically calculate the value for this [Net income] field. This will help you and your users to effectively collect data by preventing possible miscalculations. This is one of the most frequently used settings.

> **Note**
> When you pass an expression or value to the app formula field, then the same column will become a non-editable column because it will prevent users from editing the value manually, but the expressions passed to this field will always supersede others. In other words, this field will become a calculation field.

- Secondly, there is a field called **Initial value**. As the name suggests, we enter an expression or fixed static value, such as text, in to this field, and then this value or expression will appear as the default value when a user adds a new record to this table.

- Another option is **Suggested values**, but we will cover this option later in the *Creating drop-down lists to assist data entry* section to learn how it works.

- Let's take a look at the last option, **Spreadsheet formula**. The recommendation from AppSheet is not to use spreadsheet formulae in the cells for the sheet you use as the data source for your app. This is because almost all spreadsheet formulae can be converted into AppSheet expressions. Using a spreadsheet formula is going to increase the complexity of your app development process as well as slow down the app's performance. However, you may need to have spreadsheet formulae in your data sheet. When you add a spreadsheet with a spreadsheet formula in cells to AppSheet as a table, you will notice that the formula will be added automatically to this field for the column setting where the spreadsheet function is placed. This is an indication that the value for this field will be determined and evaluated with the spreadsheet formula instead of a user manually entering the value from the app. In turn, please make sure this field is not editable from the app. Once again, please bear in mind that the best practice for AppSheet is to remove the spreadsheet formula and replace it with the equivalent AppSheet expression.

- **Update Behavior:** In the previous *What are keys and labels?* section, we discussed the role of the key in AppSheet tables. If you set this column as the key column for this table, then it will be ticked off. As soon as the column is set to **Key**, the same column is forced to be non-editable.

In this **Update Behavior** section, there are other optional settings to control the behaviors:

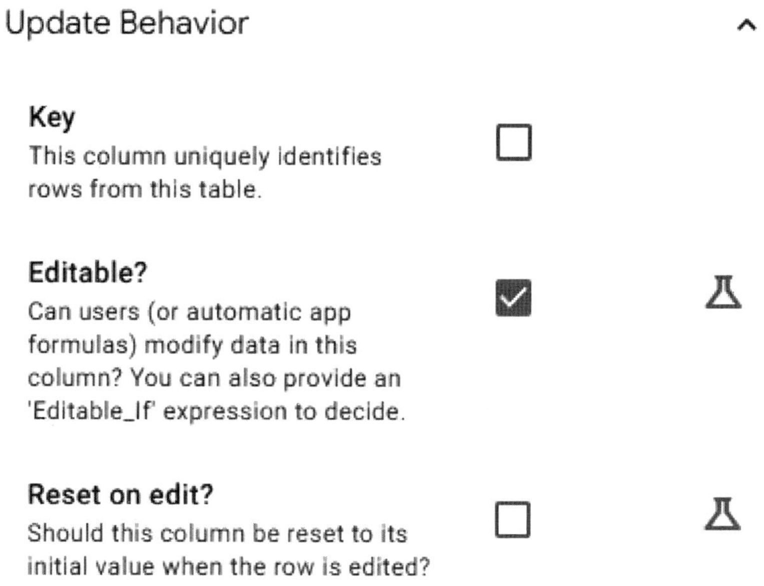

Figure 2.17 – Update Behavior settings

We select **Editable?** when users can edit the value and data for this column. As we also discussed previously, the column would become "not-editable" if there was an app formula or a spreadsheet formula, as these expressions will automatically generate the values.

Then, the **Reset on edit?** option is disabled by default. If we enable this option, it will work in conjunction with the **Initial value** setting. If this option is disabled and a new record is added to this table, then the initial value will be respected when a user adds a new record and will be saved to the column, unless the user explicitly changes the initial value manually. Furthermore, nothing is going to happen to the same column value when the user edits the same record through the form views.

However, by enabling this option, when the user comes to the same record and edits the values in the columns, the value in the column will be cleared and reset to the initial value.

You can customize this **Reset on edit?** behavior further conditionally by passing an expression through the flask icon beside the option field. The expressions, which yield the result in terms of `yes` or `no`, will be accepted in this case. When the expression results in `true`, then the **Reset on edit?** option is activated. For instance, if you want to clear the value in a column and revert back to the initial value only when the value in the particular column of `Col1` is edited, then the following expression should be passed: `[_thisrow_before].[Col1]<>` `[_thisrow_after].[Col1]`.

- **Display**: This label was explained earlier in this chapter, so please refer to the note in the previous section.

In this section, there are two other settings:

- With **Display name**, we can change the column name that will appear within the app. Without passing a value, the app will present the column name that resides in your data source. However, there is an instance in which you need to present the column names differently from their original names. For instance, say you have a [DOB] column in your table; it's better to present the name as Date of birth to make it more meaningful and self-explanatory in order to prevent confusion among users.

- With **Description**, the texts being passed to this field will replace the column name only when a user accesses the column through the *form view*. In *Chapter 3*, we will review AppSheet views. With AppSheet, new data entries or edits to existing data are made through the form-type view. A description is used as a question or instructions to show the user what value should be entered in to this column through the form view. Continuing the example from the previous paragraph, with the [DOB] column, we can pass Please enter your date of birth as a description. With views other than the form view, the DOB will appear as the column name, but when the user goes to the form view to enter the data, the description set in this field will appear to guide them.

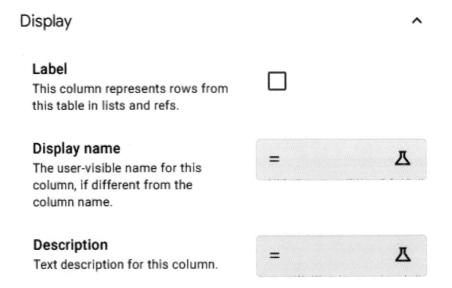

Figure 2.18 – Display settings

- **Other Properties**: In this section, there are four settings available:

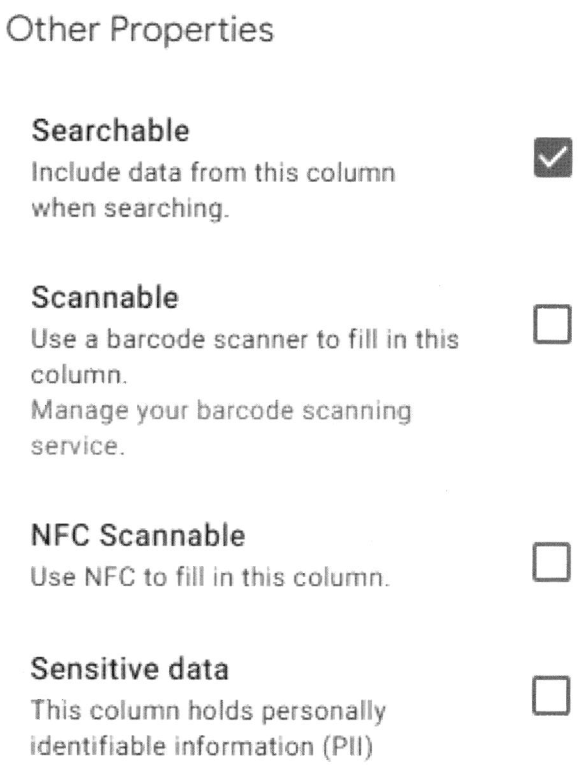

## Other Properties

### Searchable
Include data from this column
when searching.    ✓

### Scannable
Use a barcode scanner to fill in this
column.
Manage your barcode scanning
service.    ☐

### NFC Scannable
Use NFC to fill in this column.    ☐

### Sensitive data
This column holds personally
identifiable information (PII)    ☐

Figure 2.19 – Other Properties settings

Let's review each setting in detail:

- **Searchable**: AppSheet provides a search function to find the data you are looking for. This is done using the search input box, which appears in the header of your app. The data matching the search word will be filtered when you are on the list type of views, such as a table-type view. We will learn what list-type views are in detail in *Chapter 3*. However, only the columns that have this setting enabled will be subject to this search function.

- **Scannable**: To enable this option, you can scan bar codes and QR codes using the AppSheet app to insert a value in to the column field through the form-type view. The AppSheet scanner can cope with the latest standard codes. In the form view, the scanner icon will appear to assist with data entry. Without manually typing anything into the form, you can scan the code. Once AppSheet successfully scans a code, the value extracted from the code will be passed to the target field. This is a powerful AppSheet feature that improves the experience of capturing bulk data.

- **NFC Scannable:** AppSheet provides the ability to scan **Near-Field Communication (NFC).** Most smartphones these days are equipped with an NFC scanner. With such smartphones, AppSheet scans the NFC tags and captures the data inside the tags. Let's assume you have NFC tags in which the product ID value is saved for each product in your warehouse. By creating an inventory management app, the app can scan the tabs by tapping a smartphone over an NFC tag in order to quickly capture the product ID. Compared with manually filling in the product ID value in the app, this scanning experience will increase productivity.

- **Sensitive data:** In general, all data that is edited through AppSheet will be kept in the AppSheet activity logs. When we add a new record or edit existing records, those values will be saved in AppSheet system logs. If you wish to prevent this from being retained in the activity logs as they are confidential or personal information, you can simply enable this option. The data in this column will not be retained in the AppSheet logs any longer.

> **Note – regenerating the tables**
>
> While you are working on the table and column settings, it is possible to go back to your spreadsheet to edit the source data, such as adding a new column or changing column names and/or the order. In such cases, you need to make it a rule to regenerate your table all the time; otherwise, the AppSheet editor will not function, as AppSheet will not know the scheme in your spreadsheet has been changed unless you tell it.
>
> As shown in the following figure, you need to hit the **Regenerate Structure** button as soon as you make changes in your spreadsheet that is the source of the table.
>
>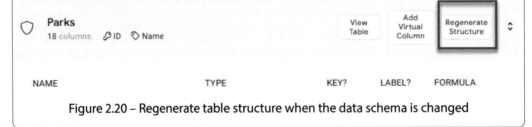
>
> Figure 2.20 – Regenerate table structure when the data schema is changed

We have reviewed the base settings for the column. In the following sections, we will highlight some of the key points regarding the data types that you should know.

We will walk you through the REF type, which is quite an important concept if you want to understand the relationships between the tables.

## Understanding REF-type columns

As mentioned earlier, AppSheet is a database-driven application with the concept of a *relational database* as its foundation. When we add multiple tables to an app, we quite often need to make relationships between tables. For instance, say you are building an invoice management application that makes invoices for your business. One table will be the data source to store the data for a single invoice, such as the date of issue, the counterparty, and other base information for your invoice. Usually, you add a list of product items to an invoice. In this case, another table should be introduced to store the information for these products. Then, the question is, *how do we connect those tables?*

AppSheet provides a simple solution to building a relationship between these two tables – a data type called REF.

We will use the sample app to explain how REF works. Please visit the portfolio site and open the sample app called Chapter 02_01: https://www.appsheet.com/templates/sample?appGuidString=c01096c0-833c-4b88-9ee5-981dbb555b54.

This sample app consists of three tables. See the following screenshots for these tables:

| | A | B | C | D |
|---|---|---|---|---|
| 1 | Invoice_ID | Date | Counter_Party | Descriptions |
| 2 | INV_0001 | 1/1/2022 | ABC Corp. | Monthly Invoice |
| 3 | | | | |

Figure 2.21 – The invoice table

Each row in the invoice table represents one invoice with data such as the date of issue and the name of the counterparty.

| | A | B | C | D | E | F |
|---|---|---|---|---|---|---|
| 1 | ID | Invoice_ID | Product_Name | Price | Quantity | Total |
| 2 | Item-001 | INV_0001 | Pro_001 | 2.5 | 2 | 5 |
| 3 | Item-002 | INV_0001 | Pro_002 | 4 | 3 | 12 |
| 4 | | | | | | |

Figure 2.22 – The items table

Each row in the items table represents one line item that is associated with one invoice.

| | A | B | C |
|---|---|---|---|
| 1 | Product_ID | Product | Unit Price |
| 2 | Pro_001 | Water | 2.5 |
| 3 | Pro_002 | Coffee | 4 |
| 4 | Pro_003 | Soft Drink | 3 |
| 5 | Pro_004 | Beer | 5 |
| 6 | | | |

Figure 2.23 – The product table

This is a master table that stores a list of the products with details such as names and unit prices.

With these three tables, let's see how to connect them. First of all, let's focus on the relationship between the invoice and items tables. One invoice could have multiple related items. In other words, those two tables have a *one-to-many* relationship.

To establish a *one-to-many* relationship in AppSheet between two tables, AppSheet provides a simple solution.

As you can see in the table of items, there is an Invoice_ID column, which should be set to the REF type. In the world of databases, the column set to the REF type is called the *foreign key*. A foreign key is a field in one table (in this case, it is the Invoice table) that refers to a key value in another table. The table with the foreign key is called the **child table** (in this case, the Items table), and the table with the key value is called the **parent table** or **referenced table**.

Please refer to the following figure, where you will see that the **Invoice_ID** column in the Items table is set to the REF type and the **Source table** field is set to the Invoice table. With this setting, one of the keys in the parent table of **Invoice** will be saved to this column.

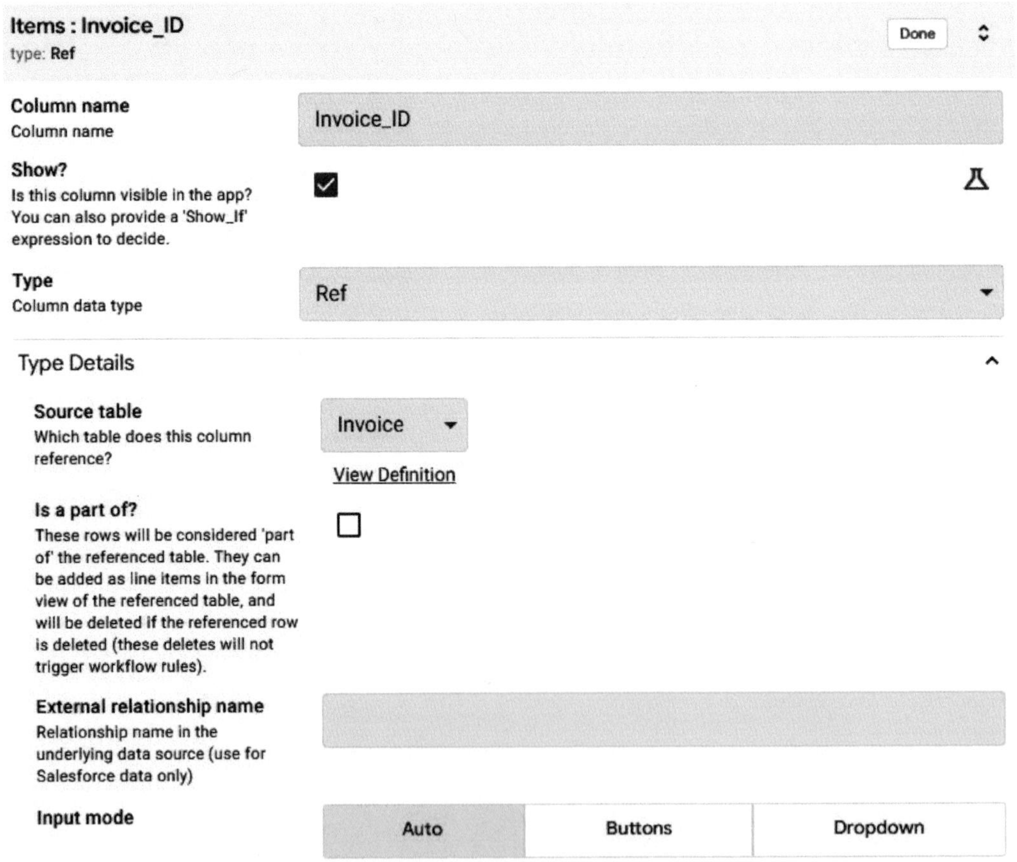

Figure 2.24 – The Invoice_ID column with the REF data type

Whenever a new row is added to the `Items` table, then the users will select one record in the parent table, `Invoice`. Once the value in the `REF` column is saved, the *parent-child* relationship will be established.

As soon as we save the column settings, note that the new column is added to the parent table, which is named something like `Related xxxxx`. This is a system-generated virtual column with the list type by default. This column does not exist in your source data table and only exists in AppSheet virtually. In AppSheet, this virtual column is called a **reverse reference**.

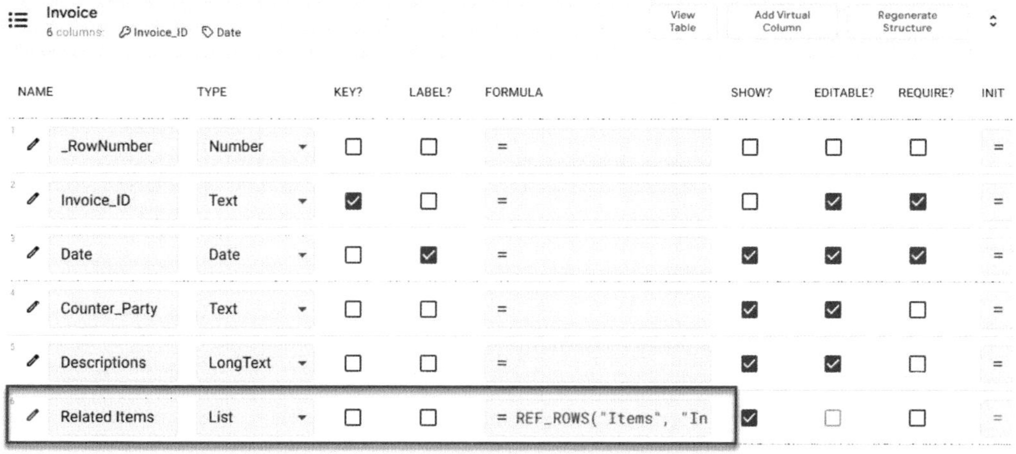

| | NAME | TYPE | | KEY? | LABEL? | FORMULA | | SHOW? | EDITABLE? | REQUIRE? | INIT |
|---|---|---|---|---|---|---|---|---|---|---|---|
| ✏ | _RowNumber | Number | ▾ | ☐ | ☐ | = | | ☐ | ☐ | ☐ | = |
| ✏ | Invoice_ID | Text | ▾ | ☑ | ☐ | = | | ☐ | ☑ | ☑ | = |
| ✏ | Date | Date | ▾ | ☐ | ☑ | = | | ☑ | ☑ | ☑ | = |
| ✏ | Counter_Party | Text | ▾ | ☐ | ☐ | = | | ☑ | ☑ | ☐ | = |
| ✏ | Descriptions | LongText | ▾ | ☐ | ☐ | = | | ☑ | ☑ | ☐ | = |
| ✏ | Related Items | List | ▾ | ☐ | ☐ | = REF_ROWS("Items", "In | | ☑ | ☐ | ☐ | = |

Figure 2.25 – A system-generated virtual column – reverse reference

This column stores a list of key values in the related rows in the child table of the `Items` table. "Related rows" means all the records in the `Items` table, where the `INVOICE_ID` column holds the same key values as the key value of the record in the `Invoice` table.

The `Items` table will construct the inline view on the detail view (we will learn about AppSheet views in detail in *Chapter 3*). A list of the child records will appear as an inline view, as shown in the following figure:

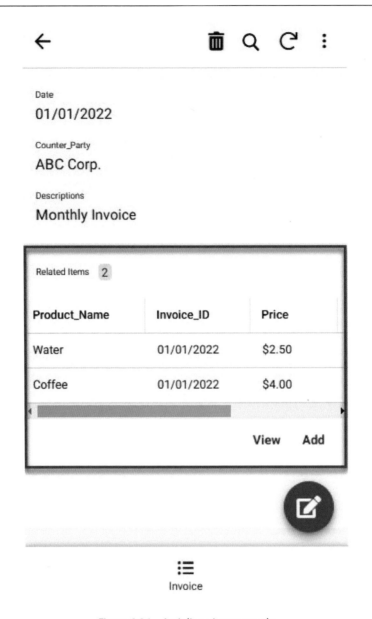

Figure 2.26 – An inline view example

When we visit the detail view for one of the parent records of the Invoice table, the data for the related child records will be automatically displayed, thanks to this system column. The user can add new records by clicking the **Add** action button at the bottom of the inline view. Records added from here will be automatically associated with the same parent record. This is because the parent record's key will automatically populate the REF column when you add a new record from the inline view.

> **Note – Is a part of?**
>
> For REF columns, there is a setting called **Is a part of?** in the type details section. When this option is enabled, the child records related to a parent record will be considered *part of* the referenced table. The child records can be added from the form view of the parent record. Another effect of enabling this option is that all the child records will be deleted if the parent record is deleted.

We have now learned about the basics of the REF column. In the following section, we will introduce the useful functions that the REF column provides.

## What is dereference and dereference list?

Let's go back to the Items table, which we set as the child table to the parent Invoice table. These two tables are now linked by the Invoice_ID column, which is the foreign key.

In the Items table, the users will select a product and assign values to create invoices. It is unproductive for users to manually type the name of the product every time they enter new data, since we have a table storing a list of the products. In this case, the REF column will be put to use. Just simply set this Product column as REF and reference it to the Product table.

Once you save the changes and try to add a new record to test through the preview pane in the AppSheet editor, you will notice a drop-down list from which you can select one of the items from the Product table. This is another advantage of the REF column. It will generate a list of the referenced table, the parent Product table in this case, and let users select one of the items for data entry.

Setting the column to REF is going to change the behavior of the app. Presenting a list from the referenced table is one of these new behaviors. When you refer to a parent table, please make sure a column other than the key column is the label. Quite often, the key column is set to LABEL and a list of keys will be presented in the drop-down list. Please ensure the most important and readable column is set to be the label.

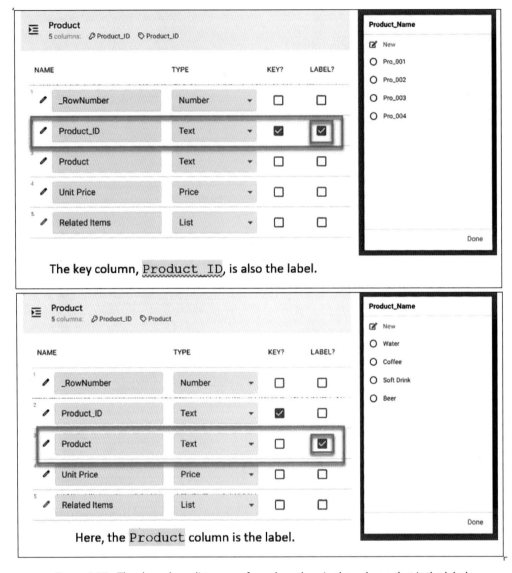

Figure 2.27 – The drop-down list comes from the values in the column that is the label

Now, we will introduce the concept of dereference and a dereference list that is important to know.

### Understanding the dereference concept

Continuing with the Items table, we have the Unit Price column, which represents the unit price for the selected product. Now, we have set the Product_Name column to REF, referenced as the Product table. As you can see in the Product table, we already have the unit price for each product.

AppSheet provides an easy way to pull data from another table using the REF  column as a gateway to the referenced table. As previously discussed, the table with the REF  type is the child table, while the referenced table is called the parent. Looking back at these tables, we have a Unit price column in the parent table. With the existence of a REF  column in the child table, we can use a special expression called a **dereference expression**, which is sometimes called **de-ref**.

First of all, let's have a look at the syntax for this special expression: [ref-column].[target-column in referenced table].

We will learn about the basics of AppSheet expressions in *Chapter 4*, but we hope this expression is simple enough to understand. When this expression is used in the child table of Items, it will extract the unit price data in the parent table of Product.

The syntax for this expression is simple. The column set to the REF  type is connected by a dot to the column name in the parent table that you want to access.

Have a look at this working example of the invoice management app to learn how we construct this expression:

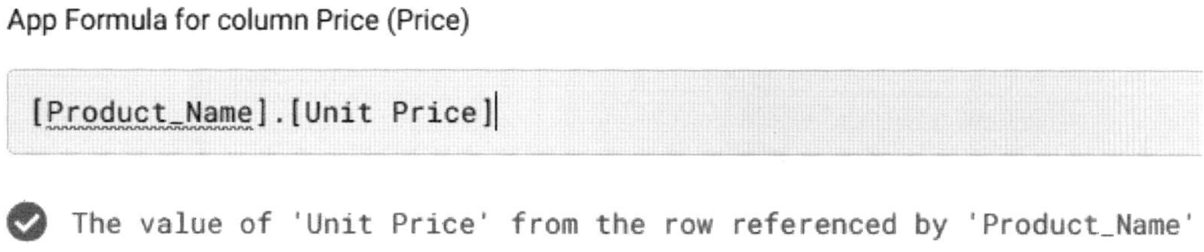

App Formula for column Price (Price)

```
[Product_Name].[Unit Price]
```

✅  The value of 'Unit Price' from the row referenced by 'Product_Name'

Figure 2.28 – Dereference expression example

We set the [Product_ID] column as the REF  column earlier. In this practical example, we are now pulling the unit price for the selected product. By passing this expression into the app formula, the unit price is extracted from the referenced table when the user selects the product from the REF  column.

The dereference expression is the most commonly and frequently used expression when we have established table relationships using REF  columns, as this gives us an instant way to pull the data from the referenced table automatically.

This is nothing to do with the subject we are dealing with in this section, but in the Items table, we have other columns, Quantity and Total. As the names indicate, we enter the number of items sold per product as well as the total prices for each sold product. To automate this calculation, we can simply pass the expression into an app formula, and now the settings for the Items table look as follows:

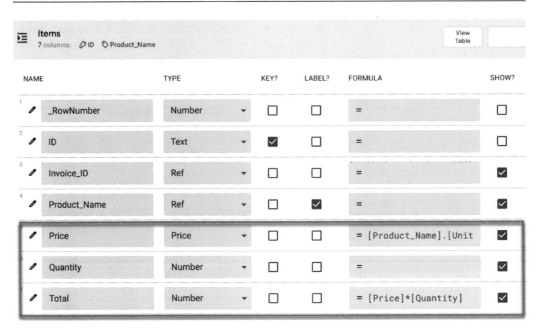

Figure 2.29 – Items table settings with expressions

In addition to the dereference expression, there is another useful function called a dereference list. Let's see how we can use this in our sample app.

### Understanding a dereference list

We keep adding product items to construct an invoice. Then, it is possible to get the total prices for an invoice before we present it to a client, by summing up the values in the Total column we just created in the child table. To solve this challenge, we can use the *reverse referencing* column for this type of calculation. Let's what it means.

As previously mentioned, we have a Related Items reverse reference column in the Invoice table, where the key values for the associated records in the Items table are listed. To calculate the total prices for an invoice (the sum of the Total column), AppSheet provided us with an instant solution. To get this calculation done, add a virtual column for the parent table of Invoice and pass the expression to the app formula, which is called a **dereference list** expression.

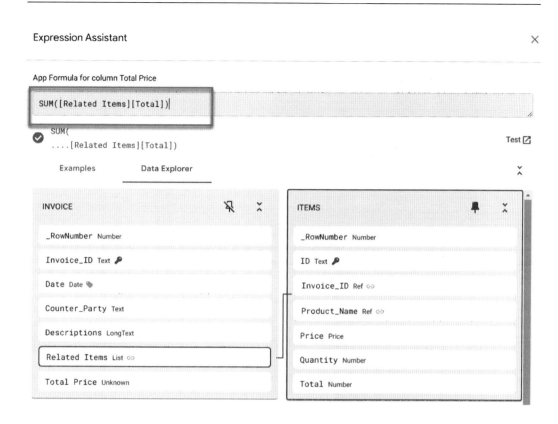

Figure 2.30 – A dereference list expression example

The `Total` column we created is in the child table of `Items`. What we are trying to do now is sum up this column to get the total amount for this invoice. In the `Invoice` table, we have a `Related Items` column from where we can access the items that are related to an invoice. The dereference list expression allows us to access the target column values in the related `Items` records from the `Invoice` table.

Let us review the basic syntax for the dereference list expression: `[Reverse reference column] [target column in child table]`.

We reviewed the dereference expression to get the value in the column of the parent table into the child table, by using the special syntax. The syntax was to connect the two column names with the dot notation. The dereference list expression looks similar, but there is no dot between the two column names.

We place a reverse reference column name, followed by the column name we wish to access in the child table (`Items`), and we can get those values. Let's replace the basic syntax based on the sample use case and see what it looks like: `[Related Items] [Total]`.

As you see, the reverse reference column of `Related Items` is connected to the target column of `Total` in this expression. This expression will return the list of the values, which are saved in the `Total` column in the `Items` table.

To confirm the result through the AppSheet view, please have a look at the following figure:

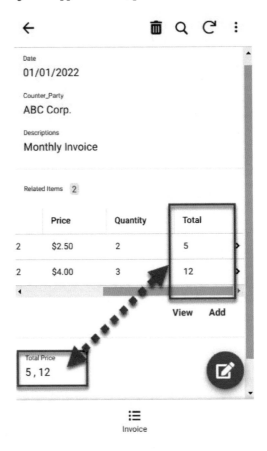

Figure 2.31 – Sample invoice data

This sample invoice data has two items. Their total prices are 5 and 12 respectively. At the bottom of the view, the result can be confirmed as **5, 12**.

We hope you can see that we successfully pulled column values from related child records. But the return value is in the list type and it appears as comma-separated values, not total prices. What we want to achieve here is summing up those values.

In order to sum them up, we need to alter the expression further by wrapping a dereference expression with the `SUM()` expression.

To get the total prices for a single invoice, the required expression is as follows at the end: `SUM([Related Items][Total])`.

Before you alter the expression by adding the SUM() expression to the dereference expression, it is possible that your virtual column type was set to the List or Enumlist type, but you need to change it over to either number or the price type to get the expression validated.

In this section, we quickly reviewed the unique expressions of dereference and the dereference list, which are quite frequently used with AppSheet. Understanding both expressions is quite important to improve your skills to deal with data inside your AppSheet apps regardless of what kind of app you will be working on. In the following section, we will introduce a few ways to construct drop-down lists. Drop-down lists help users to enter data in a field, and they are also quite commonly used with AppSheet apps as well as dereference and dereference list expressions.

## Creating drop-down lists to assist data entry

Enum is one of the data types in AppSheet. It displays a drop-down selection and allows users to select one of them. There is another data type called EnumList, with which users can select multiple items of their choice from the drop-down list. In either case, we will get a useful drop-down list to choose from.

### Learning about ways to construct the choices

There are a few other ways to present selection choices to the users. These are common settings across data types, which are REF, Enum, and Enum ref, and others, such as text-type columns.

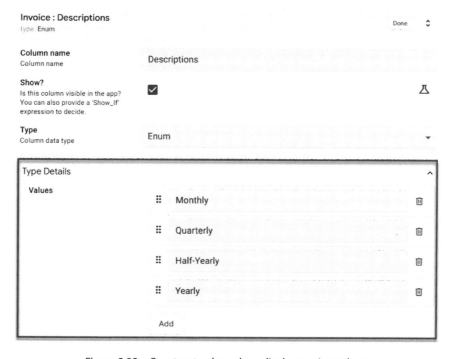

Figure 2.32 – Construct a drop-down list by passing values

The preceding figure demonstrates the most basic ways to construct the choices for a drop-down list. To add a new choice, select the **Add** button. There are other optional settings as well:

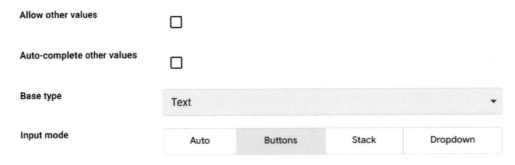

Figure 2.33 – Other settings for Enum/EnumList columns

When **Enum** or **EnumList** is selected as the data type, there are a few ways to create a drop-down list to present the data entry choices. Let's have a look at them one by one. For training purposes, we will demonstrate the three ways to generate a drop-down list for the `Descriptions` column of the `Invoice` table of the example app:

- **Enter the choices in the Values section**: Once Enum is selected for the data type of the column, a section called **Values** is presented in the **Type Details** section. As illustrated in the following figure, just type your choices there.

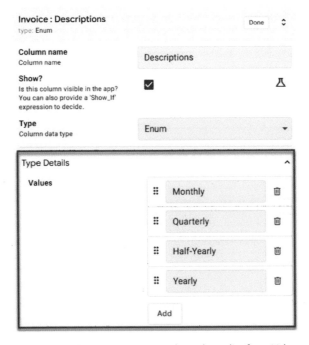

Figure 2.34 – One way to create a drop-down list from Values

This applies to `EnumList` and other types of columns, such as text.

- **Passing expressions to the Valid If field**: The drop-down list can be constructed by passing an AppSheet expression into the **Valid If** field. See the following screenshot:

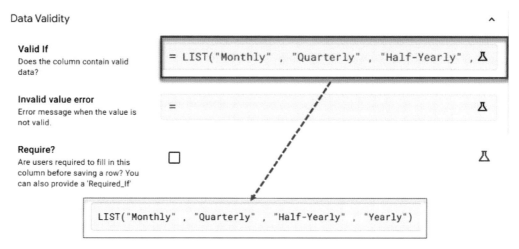

Figure 2.35 – Using the Valid If field for the construction of our drop-down list

A `LIST()` expression is often used to construct a list manually, as demonstrated here.

In general, the **Valid If** field is there for the purposes of data validation. In other words, values stated in this column need to follow the condition defined in the **Valid If** field. By passing the list of the values with the expression, the users will be forced to select one of the items from the list – in the case of `Enum`, as a part of the validation rules.

- **Passing expressions to Suggested values**: Using the **Suggested values** field, we can implement a similar effect to create a drop-down list. As illustrated in the following screenshot, you can pass an expression that returns a list of multiple values.

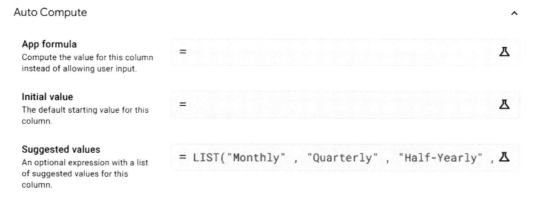

Figure 2.36 – Using the Suggested values field to construct the dropdown

Unlike using the **Valid If** field, users will see the list of the choices, but they can type the value arbitrarily rather than being forced to select one of the values in the list.

As we have seen so far, AppSheet provides multiple ways to construct drop-down lists. As soon as we set the column to the REF type and select the referenced table, then AppSheet automatically generates the list to assist with data entry. However, other ways, such as using Enum/EnumList, require you to state the list of values explicitly.

To end this chapter, we will briefly review the concept of the slice. The **slice** is one of the basic concepts every AppSheet creator must know about to add basic and advanced features to their apps. When we build an app, there are occasions when we do not want to show every row and every column from a table, but just present a subset of the rows from the table. We can apply filters to the table using the slice function.

## Making a slice from a table

So far in this chapter, we have seen how to add tables to the app and have configured them with data type definitions, among other things.

Once a table is added, you may wish to display only certain rows or columns of your table. For instance, you might want to present a subset of the data in terms of the current year, while the table has data for the past 10 years for example.

To create a new slice, go to **Data | Slices** and click the **New Slice** action button. Then, you will see the page shown in the following figure.

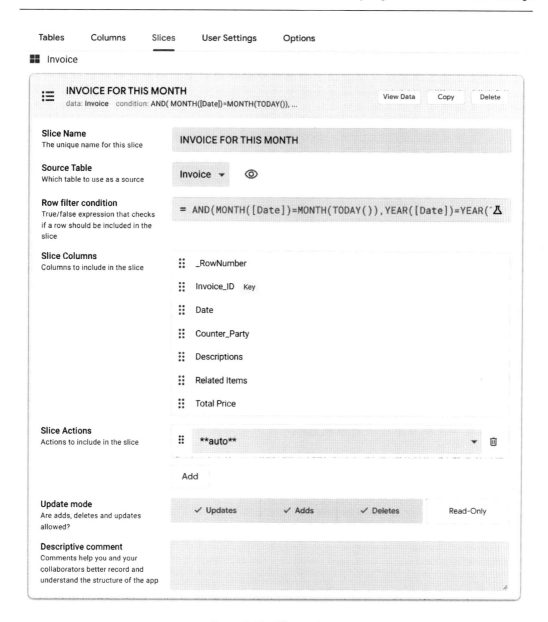

Figure 2.37 – Slice settings

A slice is a subset of a table. We can apply filters to rows as well as columns. Slices have broadly the same functionality as filters in Excel spreadsheets. Unlike the Excel filter function, however, we can apply the filter to a set of columns.

A slice extracts only the required records and columns, but there is more. We will learn about AppSheet actions later in this book, but you can control which actions will be taken from a table to a slice. For instance, if you have certain actions in a table, you can define which action will be used in a slice or not. If you added an action to a table to change the value in a target column but do not want to include this action for some reason, then you can rule out this action to construct a slice.

Furthermore, you can change the edit permission level and make it different from the source table's permission level. Let's say you set a table's edit permission to add, update, and delete, meaning a user will have full edit permission to manipulate data in this table. By creating a slice, you can make this sliced table read-only, for example.

This will virtually exist inside the AppSheet app, so it is appropriate to say the slice can be called a *virtual table*, in which the subset of the records matching the filter condition will appear in the slice.

The **Row filter condition** option is a key setting for slices. Using the example app for invoice management, let's make a slice where the set of records matches the current month. In the Invoice table, we have the Date column where we capture the date of issuance of the invoice. To apply the filter for rows, we pass an expression that will return yes or no:

Row filter for slice INVOICE FOR THIS MONTH (Yes/No)

```
AND(
MONTH([Date])=MONTH(TODAY()),
YEAR([Date])=YEAR(TODAY())
)
```

Figure 2.38 – Row filter condition example expression

After we pass this condition, each row in the source table will be evaluated one by one. In this case, the expression will check whether the value in the **Date** column matches the current month and year. Once this condition check returns yes, then these rows are gathered into a slice.

The rest of the settings are there to control which columns are added to a slice or not, and which actions in a source table are added to a slice and decide the permission levels.

Once you create a new slice, the next step is to create a new view from a slice. We will discuss this in *Chapter 3* regarding AppSheet views and how to create a new view from a slice.

# Summary

In this chapter, we learned about the basics of the AppSheet editor, data controls, and the settings that you need to get familiar with for development with AppSheet. We suggest that you gain some practical experience and apply the different settings that you just learned in a sample app or sandbox app. Playing with the AppSheet editor without worrying that the app is going to break should help you learn how the changes you made affect the behavior of the app.

We also covered AppSheet expressions. To configure table and column settings, we can use and pass expressions that will help us dynamically change the behavior of our AppSheet app. We will review expressions in detail in the later chapters of the book. Once you have learned about expressions, come back to this chapter again, as you can use expressions across all the table and column settings to dynamically and conditionally change an app's behavior. AppSheet can build a powerful and flexible application that will dynamically change behavior based on the conditions.

We will start to discuss AppSheet expressions in *Chapter 4*. In the next chapter, we will cover one of the most important visible elements of an AppSheet app, which is UX and views.

# 3
# Presenting App Data with UX/Views

**User Experience** (**UX**) plays a significantly important role in app development. This is because it is the **view** that is presenting your data to the eyes of the users whenever they visit your apps. From the user's perspective, the app's appearance is everything.

As an app developer, you always need to pay the utmost attention to how to organize and design your app so that it is user-friendly. If the app is not managed well in terms of UX – including a data entry interface, and not simply limited to navigation from one view to another view – your app users may feel uncomfortable using your app. **AppSheet** natively provides you with a number of options to change those views. Choosing the right options and also building the appropriate view for your data are both important.

In this chapter, we will describe how an app is presented to app users and what types of view you can use. We will also explore how you can format your data with colors and icons to highlight important data. We will also discuss how to change the main theme of your app through *branding* and how to change the default system language through *localization* settings.

In summary, we will cover the following topics in this chapter:

- Reviewing the basics of the UX pane
- UX – view types
- Controlling actions associated with view events
- Format rules to highlight important data
- Branding with theme colors and icons
- Managing the app's internal terminology through the **Localize** tab

By the end of this chapter, we hope you will be confident in controlling the views of your apps.

# Technical requirements

To assist you in learning about view types, we have prepared a sample app that you can access from the portfolio site for this book. You can find the `Chapter 03_01` sample app at `https://www.appsheet.com/templates/sample?appGuidString=e158a182-2b72-4fcc-818d-78c5cb7ecf6c` to follow along. This sample app contains all the available view types produced using the same dataset on national parks in the US.

While you go through this chapter, we suggest you try out the hands-on exercises using our sample app from the aforementioned portfolio page. This is the most efficient way you can learn about each option for the different types of views. We also recommend that you revisit this chapter while you are developing apps, as we have organized this chapter to work as a guidebook and/or documentation for you.

# Reviewing the basics of the UX pane

Let's focus on the **UX** pane in AppSheet. It is a collection of various settings to control the visible parts of your app.

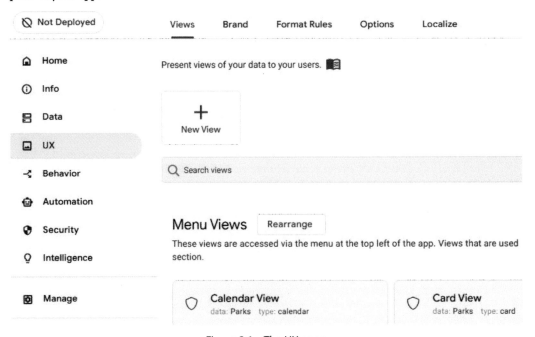

Figure 3.1 – The UX pane

Once you select the **UX** pane, you will see various options as tabs on the top of the screen. The **view** tab is significantly important as you will be setting up all of the views through this particular tab. This is the place you will visit the most while creating the app.

Apart from the **view** tab, there are other tabs that will be reviewed later in this chapter. To start the discussion for this chapter, let's focus on the **view** tab first.

The **view** tab is the place you will work on all of the views you have within your app. The **view** tab gives you full control to customize the app's views in detail. During the app development process, you may need to create a new view, customize it, hide unnecessary views, or relocate the position of a view inside the app. All these tasks are done through the **view** tab. To understand views in AppSheet and their controls, let's review what a view is and how it generally works.

## What is a view in AppSheet?

As mentioned earlier, views are important elements in the app development process with AppSheet. Views are everything your app user will see and touch on your app. To understand views, you could consider them as a parallel to a *page* on a website. Views in AppSheet comprise all the visible elements of your app, including the actual app data, action icon, and navigation menu.

In-app views are always generated from either a data table or a slice. It is important to select the most suitable view type for the user out of the multiple view types offered. Using different types of views with the same data may create different user experiences, so you always need to consider how to style such an in-app view for every occasion.

Once you connect your data – which normally means connecting your spreadsheet to your AppSheet – you will be able to see views automatically created by AppSheet on the preview screen on the right-hand side. Those automatically created views are called **system-generated views**. These make the app development process with AppSheet easier as a built-in AI inside AppSheet assists you in creating a ready-to-use app on launch.

However, normally it is required that you customize the views further as your app development journey progresses. The question is, which type of view will you pick to present data to your users? Well, it always depends on the context of your data and app – there is no fixed answer to this question.

Let's assume you have just added a data table on the app editor. You will see the **views** in the preview window in the app editor, but they are generally system-generated ones. However, now that your data is successfully connected, you are ready to add a **new view**. Let's see how we go about doing so.

### Adding new views

It is easy to add a new view. Once you go to **views** tab on the **UX** pane, you will see the button to add a new view.

Press this button to add a new view. You will then see the following new window.

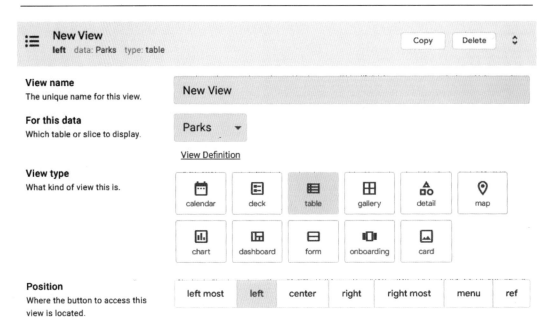

Figure 3.2 – Settings for a new view

In this window, we have a few basic options we need to select according to our app's requirements. Let's have a look at all these options in more detail.

## View name

We need to assign a unique **view name** to all new views. The name can be whatever you want. But you need to be careful – you cannot create multiple views with the same name, as the view name always needs to be unique.

The view name you assign here is going to be used elsewhere inside the app editor. For instance, when you build an action to navigate from view to view, we need to pass the view name as an argument for the expression. In order to identify the target view for such an expression, we need to give a unique name to each new view we create.

Our recommendation is that you make the view name readable and intuitive – you should be able to tell what the view is by reading its name.

## For this data

From the **For this data** dropdown, you can select the name of the table (or slice) the view is created from. Please select the source tables the view is going to be based on. After you create a slice (filtered table), you can select any one to create a view. At all times, any view you create resides on either the table or slice you selected.

> **Note**
>
> Views on AppSheet are always generated from a data table or slice. It is possible you may encounter a problem where changes you applied to your data slice (such as column orders or filtering by column) are not applied to your view. This is because the view is created from other data, such as a source table instead of a slice. Please make sure to check which data source, be it a table or slice, is selected in the **For this data** field to troubleshoot this problem.

## View type

As we briefly mentioned at the beginning of this chapter, AppSheet provides various view types. Through the **view type** option, you can decide which type of view you will create.

Once you select the **view type**, you will be able to see additional options for configuration. These additional options vary based on your selected view types. We will discuss the different types of views available in AppSheet in later sections.

## Position

This is used to specify the location where the view is going to appear in your app. Please refer to the following screenshot to see the multiple options for **Position**. In total, we can choose from seven options for where the view will appear inside your app. Please select the most appropriate location for the view to be presented.

If **ref** is selected as the position, it is not going to be placed anywhere visible on the app but will instead be presented when you make an action to navigate to that view.

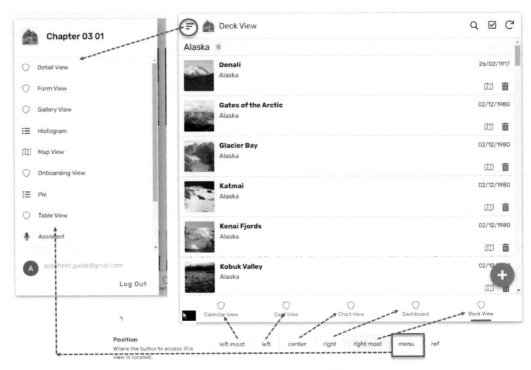

Figure 3.3 – Setting the position of a view

Before you start building your app, it is important to understand the various types of views available. Based on this knowledge, you can then consider which one is going to best fit your needs.

Once you select another view type, you may notice that **view options** in the View settings window are different. This is because each view type has a different set of optional controls to customize the view. Before we look in detail at each view type, let's see an overview of view types available in AppSheet.

## UX – view types

At the time of writing, 11 different types of views are available. Roughly speaking, view types are categorized into the following:

- Single-sheet-type views
- List-type views
- Other types

The single-sheet-type views are represented by views such as the **detail** and **form** view. The data in those views comes from a single record from the table. Next, the list-type views are represented by **table**, **deck**, and **card**, among others, where the view is used to present a set of records as a list. There are a few view types available that are categorized as *other*, such as **dashboard** and **chart** views.

As mentioned earlier, each view type has its own set of options that vary based on the view type you select. Let's now dive into the details for each view type. While we are going through the next section, we will try to mention as many of the options as possible so that you are fully aware of what sort of options you will have with each view type.

## Single-sheet-type views

Let's have a look at the single-sheet-type views, namely the detail view and form view. These are standard views used to present data in your app, as well as to allow users to enter and edit data in the app.

### Detail view

The detail view is a typically used view type in AppSheet to present data on one record as a single sheet. In other words, every detail view represents a single data record with column values residing on that record.

This view is automatically generated upon adding a new data table to the app (called a system-generated view). You can leave it as is or add your own detail view to replace the system-generated detail view.

Detail views provide quite a few options with which you can customize styles. Let's have a look at these options now:

- **Use card layout**: By turning this option on, a card view-styled header will appear, and you can customize the style of the card view and specify it as the header of the detail view. To learn how to apply your own card view style, please refer to the *card view* subsection under the *list-type views* section later in this chapter. A single card view is placed on the top as a header. Images, texts, and data actions are wrapped inside a card. This makes the view look more appealing.

**Acadia**
Maine

VIEW MAP
(LATLONG)

ID
0.954418110453728

Coordinates
44.35°N 68.21°W

LatLong
★

Date established
26/02/1919

Area
49,075.26 acres (198.6 km2)

Recreation visitors
3,537,575

Description
Covering most of Mount Desert Island and other coastal islands, Acadia
features the tallest mountain on the Atlantic coast of the United States,
granite peaks, ocean shoreline, woodlands, and lakes. There are freshwater,

Figure 3.4 – The header in the card view layout and the style at the top

- **Main image:** If you want to place the image in the header at the top of the detail view, specify the image/thumbnail type column in the record. The size of the displayed image can be changed through the **Image style** option field, where we have options of **Fill**, **Fit**, and **Background**.

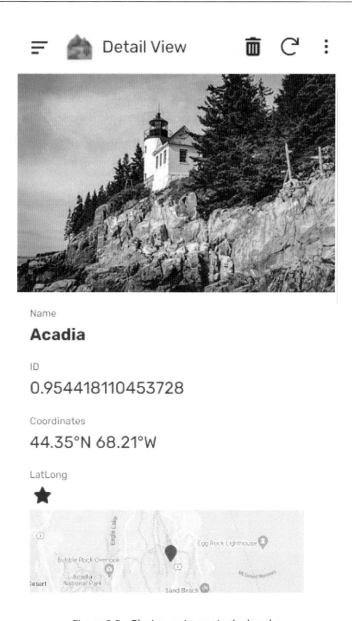

Figure 3.5 – Placing an image in the header

If you have an image or thumbnail type column in the source table for your view, then this option is set to auto by default to use the image as the header. If you do not want to use an image as the header, leave this option as **None**.

- **Header column:** If you want to display some text in the header part at the top of the view, specify the column. If nothing is specified, no text will be displayed.

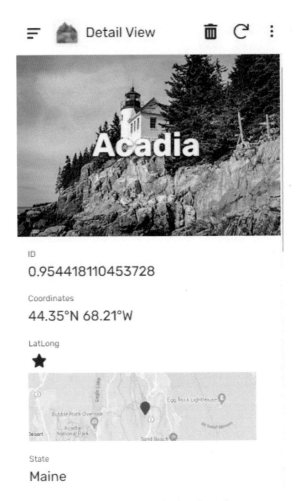

Figure 3.6 – Applying the header column

The header is useful to appeal to the users of the app, giving them more information about the view they are currently seeing. To improve user experience and make your app more intuitive, we suggest you apply the header for all the detail views you have within the app as much as possible. If you apply both Main Image and Header columns at the same time, the header value is overlaid on top of the image.

- **Quick edit columns**: With this option enabled, you can make the column editable through the detail view, without having to change to the form view. Originally, to edit the data of the record, the edit action was executed from the detail view, and app users were prompted to visit the form view to edit the existing data. This is AppSheet's default behavior. However, once the quick edit column option is enabled, the values in the column (which are editable by the app user) can be directly updated on the detail view without moving to form view.

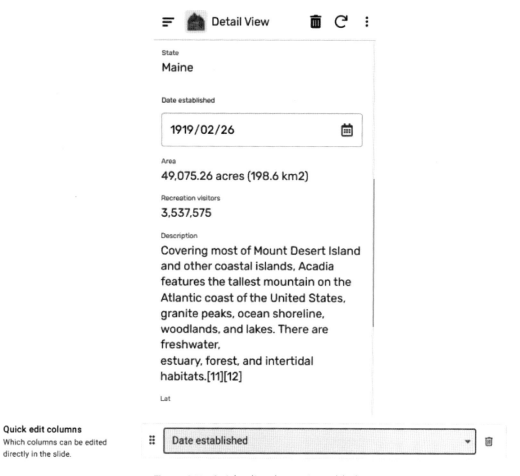

Figure 3.7 – Quick edit columns is enabled

In the preceding example, we made the Date established column quick to edit. This column is shown as a clickable input field at the top of the view.

> **Note**
> Any column in the **Quick edit columns** option must itself be set to **Editable** in the column setting; otherwise, the quick-edit mode will not be applied.

- **Sort by**: When the **Slideshow mode** option is enabled in the subsequent option settings, arrow icons are displayed on the left and right of the detail view, and you can move to the detail view of the previous and following records in the order sorted by the column you specify in this option.

- **Column order**: This option specifies the order of the columns to be displayed in the detail view from top to bottom. If **all other columns** is specified, the columns will be displayed in the order specified in the table/slice that is the source of the view. If you wish to change the column order, please select the column from top to the bottom on this stacked input field. The selected column will be shown on the detail view in the exact same order you specify in this option. The only columns that are selected one by one here will be shown in the detail view.

- **Display mode**: With this option, we can select the style that the data will be presented in from the available options for the layout.

See the following example in *Figure 3.8* to see how each option changes the layout for the views:

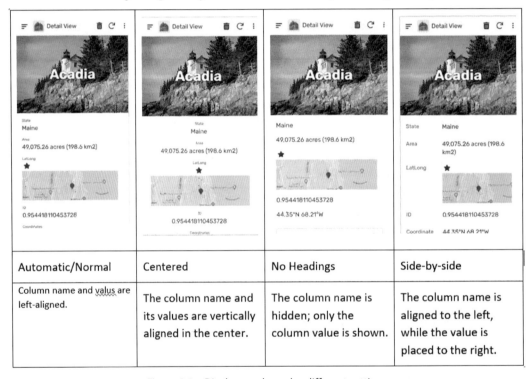

| Automatic/Normal | Centered | No Headings | Side-by-side |
|---|---|---|---|
| Column name and valus are left-aligned. | The column name and its values are vertically aligned in the center. | The column name is hidden; only the column value is shown. | The column name is aligned to the left, while the value is placed to the right. |

Figure 3.8 – Display mode under different settings

- **Image style**: As we learned earlier in this section, we can select a main image to be displayed as the header for the view. With this option, we can control the size of the image.

With the **Fill** setting, the main image will dominate the whole header. **Fit** will retain the aspect ratio of the original image and display it by fitting to the available header space. **Background** will set the image as the background image for the detail view.

- **Max nested rows**: This is to control the number of records in the inline view to display the related child records. The default is five records and you can change this to any number.

- **Slideshow mode**: When this setting is enabled, arrow icons are displayed on the left and right of the detail view, and you can move to the detail view of the previous and following records. On mobile devices, users can swipe left or right on the screen to do this.

As we discussed, there are many options you can use with the detail view to style the view however you like. Try and test all these options out to learn how they work.

### Form view

The form view is used to register new data (that is, add new records) and also edit existing data. Whenever users update data through the app, the form view acts as a gateway to push data into the data table.

Once the form view is opened, app users can edit the values for each column. They always need to save the form afterward.

The form view options are as follows:

- **Page Style**: This specifies the style of the form view. All the columns in the record are distributed vertically on one screen:

  - **Simple**: The default form view style where the data entry input fields are displayed vertically.

  - **Page count and tabs**: If you have a column whose data type is set as the **Show** type with **Type details** set to **Page_Header** for the category, the columns located below this **Show** type column will be grouped and fit onto a single page. If you have another **Show** type column, then the column located below that will instead be placed onto a separate page. This helps us to make form views with multiple pages using tab separation. If **Page Count** is selected, a multiple-page form view is applied, where each page is split using the multiple-dot icon at the top. For the **Tabs** option, then pages will be split using tabs at the top of the form view.

  - In terms of the **Show** type column, please refer to the AppSheet official documentation from https://support.google.com/appsheet/answer/12463320.

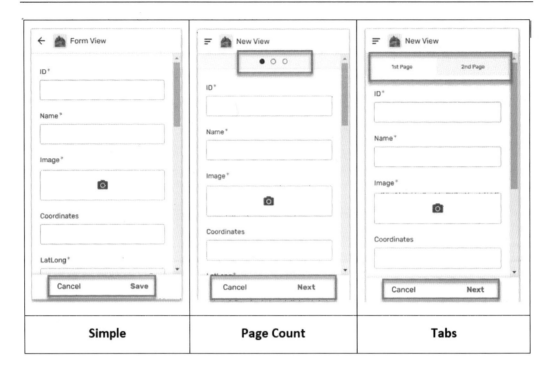

Figure 3.9 – Form view with different page styles

*Figure 3.9* provides a quick sample of form views after applying the different page styles. As you can see, once we apply either a page count or tabs style, you will see the headers move around the pages, and the footer also changes, moving from one page to the next.

- **Form style**: Set the display position of the column name. **Side-by-side** will display the column name on the left with its value on the right-hand side.

- **Column order**: You can explicitly change the column order from top to bottom as you please.

- **Save/cancel position**: Data entered into form views must be saved by the user. This option controls the position of the cancel/save button, either at the top or bottom of the view.

- **Max. nested rows**: This has the same setting option as the detail view to control the number of related child records in the inline view.

- **Auto save**: By enabling this option, the form view will automatically be saved without pressing the **Save** button when the value is entered in the last column.

- **Auto re-open**: On saving a form view, a new form will be automatically opened to allow the entry of new data. This setting is effective when you want to register new records continuously.

- **Finish view**: This option specifies the view to be displayed after saving the form view. Select the name of the view from the list shown immediately after the form view is saved.

- **Display name**: Set the label name of the view to be displayed on the app, while the actual view name is preserved under the hood.

### Onboarding view

As the name implies, the **onboarding view** is a view type introduced for the purpose of presenting guidance to users accessing an app for the first time. One record constitutes one page, and by clicking the screen transition button at the bottom, you can go to the next page, the last page, and then navigate to another view. It is an effective way to present information by briefly summarizing the purpose and usage of the application to users visiting the app for the first time.

To construct this type of view, there are five options you need to set up:

- **Image**: Select the image that will be the main component of the page.

- **Title**: Select the column to be the title of the page to display at the bottom of the image.

- **Short blurb**: This is the part that displays the body and summary of the page. Select the column that contains the text you want to display.

- **Second short blurb**: Select the text you want to display in a paragraph separate from the first short blurb.

- **Finish view**: With this option, you specify the next view to navigate to after reaching the last page in the onboarding view.

## List-type views

Let's have a look at the list-type views. The majority of AppSheet view types belong to this category. List-type views present a list of data in a single view. For instance, the table view, a popular view type, is used to present your data as a table with multiple rows of data. In other words, list-type views are useful when you wish to present a set of data (rows). In this section, we will run through all the available list-type views.

## Calendar view

The **calendar view** displays data in a calendar format based on the values in the Date, Time, and DateTime columns. As you can see in *Figure 3.10*, the calendar looks very similar to Google Calendar.

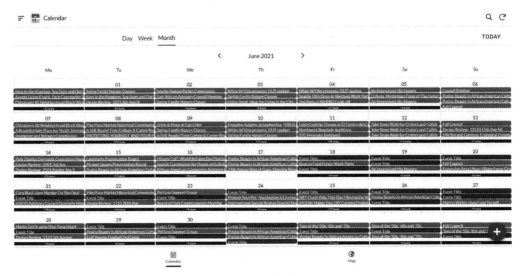

Figure 3.10 – A calendar view example

The following table illustrates the list of options for the calendar view:

| | |
|---|---|
| Start date | Specify the column that points to the start date of the period using the Date/DateTime/Time type columns in the table. |
| Start time | Specify the column that indicates the start time of the period using the day/hour/date/time type columns in the table. If the Date and Time values are shown as DateTime in one column, specify this DateTime column. |
| End date | Specify the column that points to the end date of the period using the Date/DateTime/Time type columns in the table. |
| End time | Specify the column that indicates the end time of the period using the day/hour/date/time type columns in the table. If the Date and Time values are shown as DateTime in one column, specify this DateTime column. |
| Description | Specify the label name to be displayed on the marker for the record displayed on the calendar. |
| Category | Specify the column used to color-code the marker generated from one record displayed on the calendar. |
| Default view | Sets the default value for the display format (monthly, weekly, or daily) that is displayed when the user opens the calendar view. |

Table 3.1 – List of options for the calendar view

A calendar view is typically used to display events with DateTime ranges.

## Deck view

The **deck view** presents the records in the source data table as a list where the information of one record is displayed vertically, stacked as an elongated card. It is one of the most frequently used views to present a list of data from a data table.

Each card in the deck view offers three places where you can display text values in addition to showing an image, which can optionally be placed on the left. Furthermore, you can show a set of icons for the user to invoke actions, such as changing data or navigating to another view. See the example view in *Figure 3.11.*

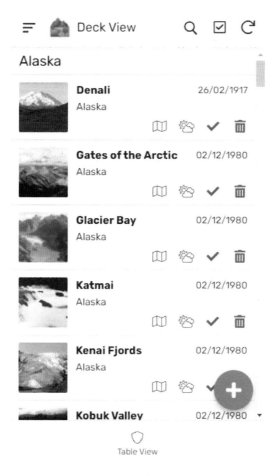

Figure 3.11 – A deck view example

The deck view presents your data in a perfectly aligned manner for users of mobile devices. To fully customize the deck view, let's study the list of options available for this type of view.

## View options for the deck view

Through this set of options, you can freely control the layout as well as actions that will be invoked when users select one item from the deck view. In this section, we will review all the options to control the visible part of the view:

- **Sort by**: In the deck view, the records are listed one above the other, and you can set the specific order. If multiple columns are specified, they will be sorted from top to bottom.

- **Group by**: Records with the same value in the specified column are grouped and displayed. The column selected for a group is displayed as a header and the set of rows under each group will be under each header. You can determine the order for these group header values to be either ascending or descending.

- **Group aggregate**: For grouped columns, the result of a simple calculation is displayed next to the group name. A typical calculation is **COUNT**, which displays the number of records belonging to that group.

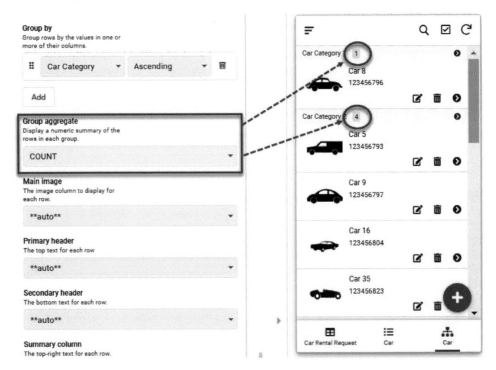

Figure 3.12 – The Group aggregate option

As you can see in *Figure 3.12*, the count for the associated records under each group is indicated as a number. As well as **COUNT**, the other options available for aggregate calculations are **SUM**, **AVERAGE**, **MIN**, and **MAX**.

- **Data locations**: There are a few places where we can present app data inside the view, namely **Main image**, **Primary header**, **Secondary header**, and **Summary column**. To apply these, simply specify the columns and positions for the text displayed on the given card. A diagram is shown in *Figure 3.13*, which explains the relationship between those four options and their locations inside the deck view.

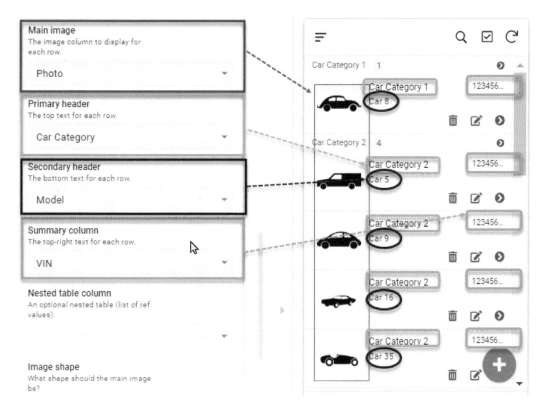

Figure 3.13 – The relationship between an option and its location

It is up to you as an app creator to determine whether you want to show or hide the column value for each available position. If you select **None** instead of a column name, then nothing will be displayed for that position.

- **Nested table column**: If the table has a **List type** virtual column with the base type set to the REF type, then you can specify the REF column for the **Nested table column** option. The **List type** column will be displayed inline, specified as the default view in the list type of the table specified in the reference destination. In the following example, the default view of the **List type** REF destination table is set to the chart type. Based on this condition, let's examine the example view in *Figure 3.14*.

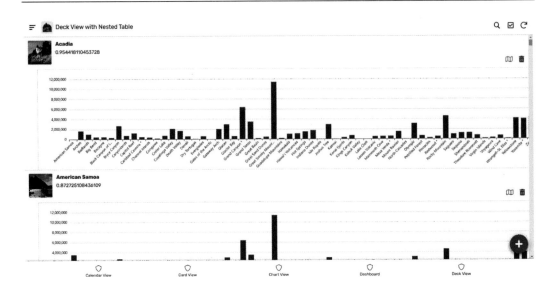

Figure 3.14 – An example view with the nested table column option

In the latter part of this chapter, we will cover a detail view where the **List type** column with the REF base type is displayed as an inline view. In the deck view, you can show exactly the same inline view with the `Nested table` column option.

- **Image shape**: If you choose to use an image, you can specify its display style. The full image option allows you to show the entire image without cropping.

- **Show action and Actions**: You can choose to display or hide the action bar at the bottom right of the deck view. When displaying it, you can specify which actions will be shown or hidden. If you turn off **Show action bar**, then none of the actions will be displayed.

## Table view

The **table view** is AppSheet's most versatile list-type view that displays records on a table. It gives users an experience similar to working with a spreadsheet. One row of data consists of one record of the source table, and the detail view opens by default. With the table view, we have the option to enable quick edit mode as well. By enabling this mode, you can edit data directly without going through the form view. This will improve the efficiency of the editing process.

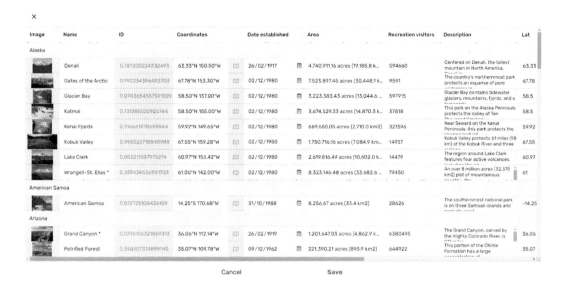

Figure 3.15 – A table view example

We recognize that the table view is the most frequently used AppSheet view, so it is important to know how to customize it with the available options. The **Sort by**, **Group by**, and **Group aggregate** options work with the table view essentially in the same way as with the deck view.

Let's learn in detail about the various options available for the table view:

- **Column order**: This allows you to specify the display order of the columns from the left. In the default state, the columns will be displayed in the same order as it appears on the table/slice from which the view is generated, but you can change this to any order. The columns not selected in this option will not appear in the view, giving you the ability to select specifically which columns will be shown or hidden in the table view.

- **Column width**: This is a setting for the column width. You can explicitly select the default column width to either **narrow** or **wide**.

- **Enable quick edit**: Turning this setting on will show an edit icon above the view, which you can click to make all records editable while preserving the appearance of the table view. By selecting this option, you can edit the data across multiple records simultaneously. All columns where you set **Editable?** as true can be edited once you invoke this action. See *Figure 3.16*.

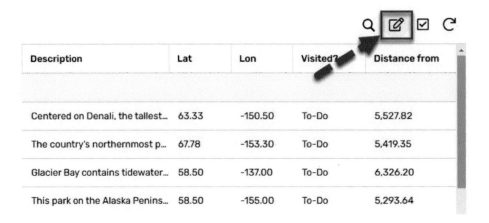

Figure 3.16 – The icon to enable quick edit mode

Once you enable quick edit mode, the table view looks as shown in *Figure 3.17*, where the column values are editable through the table-style interface.

| Image | Name | ID | Coordinates | | Date established | | Area | Recreat |
|---|---|---|---|---|---|---|---|---|
| | Alaska | | | | | | | |
| | Denali | 0.787200224332493 | 63.33°N 150.50°W | | 26/02/1917 | | 4,740,911.16 acres (19,185.8 k... | 594660 |
| | Gates of the Arctic | 0.992234396483703 | 67.78°N 153.30°W | | 02/12/1980 | | 7,523,897.45 acres (30,448.1 k... | 9591 |
| | Glacier Bay | 0.0983654557591029 | 58.50°N 137.00°W | | 02/12/1980 | | 3,223,383.43 acres (13,044.6 ... | 597915 |
| | Katmai | 0.731385522925744 | 58.50°N 155.00°W | | 02/12/1980 | | 3,674,529.33 acres (14,870.3 k... | 37818 |
| | Kenai Fjords | 0.316661978698944 | 59.92°N 149.65°W | | 02/12/1980 | | 669,650.05 acres (2,710.0 km2) | 321596 |
| | Kobuk Valley | 0.498523718840988 | 67.55°N 159.28°W | | 02/12/1980 | | 1,750,716.16 acres (7,084.9 km... | 14937 |
| | Lake Clark | 0.852211387975274 | 60.97°N 153.42°W | | 02/12/1980 | | 2,619,816.49 acres (10,602.0 k... | 14479 |

Figure 3.17 – The table view with quick edit mode

This view works like an AppSheet form view. After users make changes to data, they must then save their work by clicking the **Save** action icon at the bottom. Selecting **Cancel** will leave the data unchanged, and any data change will be aborted.

## Gallery view

As the name suggests, the **gallery view** generates an image gallery from a table with columns of either the image or thumbnail type.

Figure 3.18 – A gallery view example

The available options for customization are minimal. You can select the **Sort by** option to change the order of the images, as well as change the size of each tile through the **Image size** option.

## Card view

The **card view** displays the information of records on cards and displays them in a list. A card is a container for some short pieces of information coming from a single data record. It resembles a playing card in size and shape, and you can provide calls to action to the user by placing a set of action icons on the card as well.

In the **Layout** options,  you can select the style you like from multiple layout presets. What you have to do is map the data to be placed on the card. As an option common to all styles, you can set the action to be executed when each card is clicked. Using a card view as a gateway, you can guide the user to proceed through the app's workflow, such as editing data and navigating to another view.

Let's have a look at the available card styles.

## List layout

The **list** style is similar to the deck view. We can place an image on the left of the card, along with two lines of text from two columns. If you click the three dots icon on the right, multiple action icons can be added as calls for action.

In the **Layout** section, you can select the layout type with the radio button, as shown in the following screenshot. Once the layout is selected, the list of settings fields appears, based on your selection. To apply your change, select the element you wish to change by clicking on the layout.

Figure 3.19 – List layout settings

The **list** layout is the simplest layout in the card view, as described previously, and looks like a banner. By selecting one of the other layout styles, you can add more content in addition to what the list layout offers. Let's have a look at these now and learn about these additional elements that help you construct your card view layout.

## Photo layout

The **photo** layout is used to add a main image to the bottom of the **list** layout. The **photo** layout, unlike the **list** layout, does not have an ellipsis icon with which we can choose multiple actions. Instead, you can specify the action to be invoked when users click or tap the card. This is done by selecting one of the available actions from the drop-down list to the right of the card. See the following screenshot:

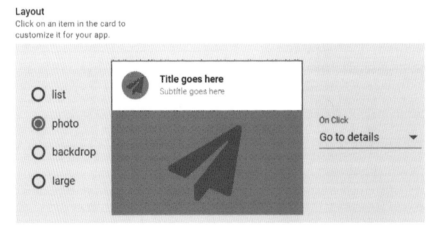

Figure 3.20 – Photo layout settings

## Backdrop layout

With the **backdrop** layout, the whole card is constituted from the main image with one text value overlaid on top of the image.

Figure 3.21 – Backdrop layout settings

This style is similar to the gallery view.

### Large layout

The **large** layout is a further extension of the **photo** layout. A subtitle, a text body, and a total of four action icons can be presented on a single card.

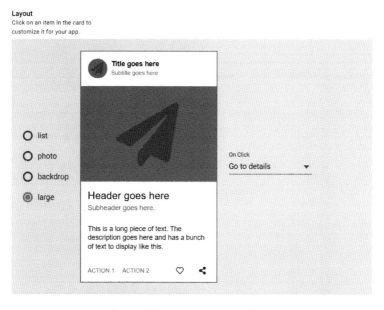

Figure 3.22 – Large layout settings

In the layout settings window, you can select each of the available elements one by one, and pick up the name of the column and/or actions to place them into the layout. You also have the option to select None for each element so that it will be hidden on the final card view at the end.

## Map view

As the name suggests, the **map view** presents location data, including latitude and longitude and addresses, as pins over a Google Maps tile in the background.

Figure 3.23 – A map view example

## Map column

A **map column** specifies the column from which the data is taken for the pins displayed on the map. The columns that can be specified are either Lat long type or Address type columns. Select one of those columns from the source table.

### Secondary data table

In addition to the column we select in the map column, we can add one more source to display as pins over the map. To add this, you specify the table or slice to which the target column belongs. You can select the same table as the one specified for the map column previously. This is useful when you have two columns in the same table and wish to display pins for them.

### Secondary data column

With this option, you can select the Latgong/Address type column in the table/slice specified above and display additional pins. There are a total of two columns that can be displayed in one map view on which the pins are generated.

## Map type

This option allows you to specify the style of the map. If you specify **Aerial**, Google Maps satellite imagery will be the default style. Regardless of which style you specify as the default, users can still switch styles on the map view.

## Minimum cluster size

When displaying a large number of pins on a map, it can slow down the display speed of the application and even affect performance in general. Additionally, innumerable pins being displayed on the map all at once makes it less aesthetically pleasing. The map view offers a cluster function that groups adjacent pins and displays them as a group, allowing you to hide a large number of pins on the map.

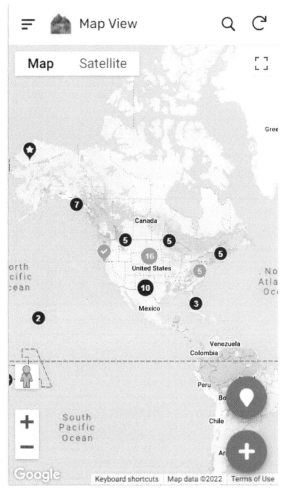

Figure 3.24 – Map view with clusters

As you can see in *Figure 3.24*, adjacent pins are grouped into single clusters. Each cluster indicates the number of pins inside, and you can dissolve a cluster and show the individual pins by clicking it.

## Other view types

We reviewed single-sheet-type and list-type views so far, but the AppSheet provides us with some views which do not belongs to either of those two types. On this book, we defined them as "other types".

### Dashboard view

In the **dashboard view**, multiple views are displayed on the screen as one view. It is an effective view type that enhances the visibility of data and improves the user experience by displaying various types of views together.

Simply speaking, the dashboard view wraps several other views into a single view. Let's see what sort of options we have with this view:

- **View entries:** Select the views to be used in the dashboard. On the right side of each view, you can specify the size at which it will be displayed on the dashboard from four options: **Large**, **Wide**, **Tall**, or **Small**.

- **Use tabs in mobile view:** Since the screen space is limited on mobile devices, multiple views are displayed with tabs. When accessing a dashboard view on a mobile phone with this setting turned off, the user has to scroll up and down to move to a different view on the dashboard. This option makes using the dashboard view on mobile devices more efficient.

- **Interactive mode:** As a simple example, shown in the following screenshot are two views inside the dashboard, where the left-hand table view is set to **Tall** and the right-hand detail view is set to **Large**. Both views are generated from the same table but use different view types.

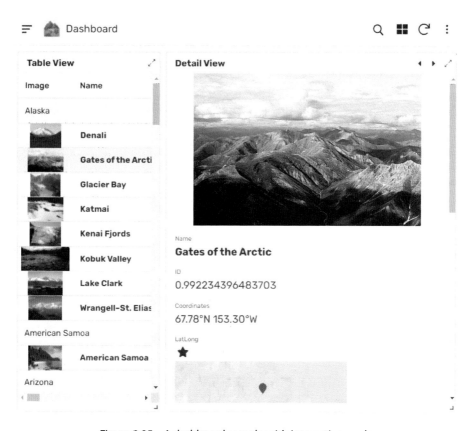

Figure 3.25 – A dashboard sample with interactive mode

When the interactive mode is turned on, selecting (clicking) a record displayed as a list in a table view switches the display of the remaining view – in this example, the detail view, according to the record selection. Once interactive mode is turned on, each view placed on the dashboard will work interactively. When the app users select one record from the list type view, the rest of the view(s) will be sorted based on the user selection.

It is possible that you have views in a dashboard coming from two tables that have a parent-child relationship with a REF column connection. Let us assume we have an invoice table as the parent table with a related child table, named `invoice-details`. One invoice will have multiple records in invoice-details table, which is a typical parent-child relationship. Then, we place two table views in our dashboard view. One uses the invoice table, while the other uses `invoice-details` with interactive mode turned on. This means that once the user selects an invoice in the table view, then the rest of the other table view will filter out the records, showing only the records associated with the selected invoice.

Interactive dashboards are a powerful feature available with AppSheet, giving users the ability to find the data they need.

**Tips**

A form view cannot be selected or installed in a dashboard. As an alternative, the general approach is to set up a detail view with the column you want to edit set to quick edit mode, allowing you to edit it from the dashboard.

## Chart view

AppSheet provides a chart library. With the **chart view**, you can convert numeric data into charts. These charts provide opportunities for analysis as well as quick insight into your data. Once you select the chart view, you will see the list of available chart types, as shown in the following screenshot:

**Chart type**
The type of chart to show.

**Group aggregate**
How to aggregate data for aggregate charts.

**Chart columns**
Which columns to include.

**Chart colors**
Use custom colors for this chart.

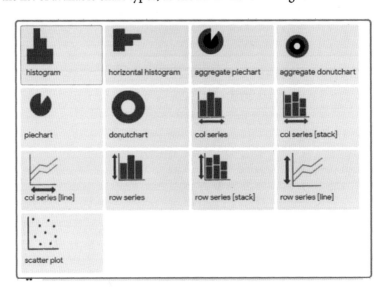

Figure 3.26 – A list of chart types

**Note**

The AppSheet documentation (https://help.appsheet.com/en/articles/961557-charts-the-essentials) explains these chart-style options in detail.

In this section, we quickly reviewed all the available view types along with the specific features of each view type. We hope you learned the basic skills to build the custom views required as you continue on your journey with AppSheet.

In the next section, we will learn about the **Display** pane, which is a common setting across all views. Let's move on.

# Displaying views

When you scroll down inside the **views** setting window, you will see a **Display** section. It allows you to change the visual appearance of a view, such as the view icon and display name. Furthermore, you can conditionally control whether to show or hide a view by selecting the **Show if** option.

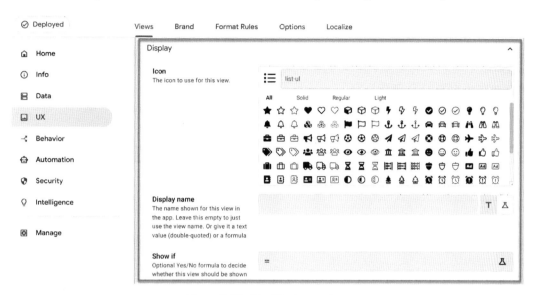

Figure 3.27 – The Display settings

The three settings are explained here:

- **Icon**: This is where you select an icon for your views.

- **Display name**: The display name is like a label name for the view. The name you specify here will appear on the app with the icon you selected in the previous option.

- **Show if**: This is a very useful feature in AppSheet. We pass an expression in this field to set a condition for when this particular view will be shown or hidden. For instance, if the user login ID (email) does not match xxx@sample.com, then you can hide the view. If you have multiple app users grouped by admins and regular users, you can specify a certain view to become available to admin users, while the regular user group will not be able to access that view. In short, in this scenario, you can create an *admin-only* view using a **Show if** expression.

There are other settings common across the view types. In the next section, we will examine the connection between views and actions. You can set views to trigger actions when events occur on the view, such as an item being clicked by a user or a form being saved. Such events are called view events.

# Controlling actions associated with view events

For some view types such as table and deck views, you can specify the action (moving to a detail view, invoking a data change action, and so on) that will be invoked when a row is selected on a table view. It's a great way to implement your own logic by associating actions with **view events**.

There are a few different view events available with AppSheet, such as the row select event, or swiping one list item to either right or left on the deck view. The available view events vary from one view type to another, so let's see the types of events available for each view type and how to associate actions with those events. Firstly, let's have a look at the table, gallery, and deck views, as these are the most commonly used.

## Changing behavior in the table, gallery, and deck views

Inside the **views** setting window, you will find the **Behavior** section.

There are three view types that we cover in this section – table, gallery, and deck views. Once you create those views, you may not notice the actions attached by default to the view you just generated.

For instance, on the table view, when you click a line item, you will see the detail view. This is AppSheet's default *behavior*. When the user selects one of the rows from a table view by clicking it, the action is triggered behind the scenes. By default, a **navigating to the detail view** action is invoked. So, selecting a row by clicking on the table, gallery, and deck view is called as an **event** in AppSheet. In the **Behavior** section, you can set actions to be invoked when this event happens. Firstly, let's have a look at the table and gallery views.

### Behavior settings in the table and gallery views

Once you scroll down to the **Behavior** section in the table/gallery view settings, you will see the settings shown in *Figure 3.28*:

Figure 3.28 – Behavior options under the table/gallery view settings

With the **Event Actions** field, you can direct the action to be invoked upon a row being selected by the user. As we discussed earlier, views are made out of data tables or slices, for which you may have a number of actions. Rather than **\*\*auto\*\***, you can select another action from the drop-down list.

For the deck view, we have additional view events.

## Behavior settings for deck views

In the deck view setting window and **Behavior** section, you will see the three options shown in the **Event Actions** setting:

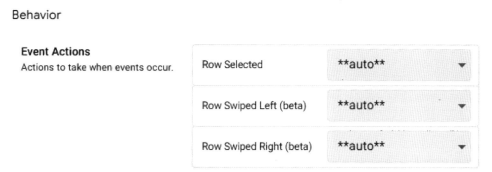

Figure 3.29 – Behavior settings for deck views

The **Row selected** event is the same as the one in the table/gallery view. In addition to that, we have **Row Swiped Left** and **Row Swiped Right** events. In the deck view, users can swipe items right or left, events upon which you can invoke actions.

## Action settings for form views

In form views, you can invoke the chosen action when a form view is saved after the user edits the data.

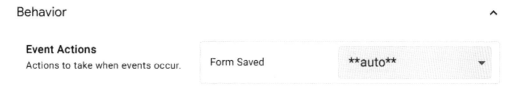

Figure 3.30 – A Form Saved event action

This **Form Saved** event action is used for various purposes in AppSheet. By invoking the data change action, you can automate the process of changing data inside the app. Furthermore, you can invoke a deep link action to guide users to the next view you wish them to land on after the form has been submitted (saved).

So far, we have broadly discussed views. As suggested earlier, you can revisit this section when you develop your own app and views to deepen your knowledge and skills.

In the next section, we will discuss format rules. You will find format rules useful while highlighting data to change the visual appearance of your view and data.

# Format rules to highlight important data

Like the format rules of Excel and Google Sheets, AppSheet allows you to apply your own format rules, such as changing text colors and placing icons beside data in a specified column. You can apply the conditional format rule by using the AppSheet expression to change the app behavior dynamically, whether the format rule is applied or not, based on the contexts.

## Creating a new format rule

The process to set up format rules is rather simple. Let's create a new one.

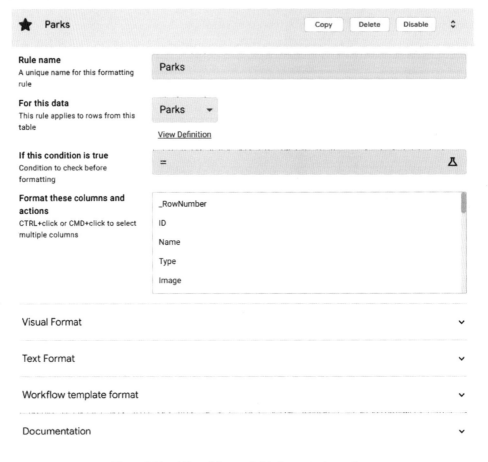

Figure 3.31 – A list of the available format rule settings

Firstly, you need to name the rule. The name should be self-explanatory, as you may need to refer back to these rules later on. The name should give you a quick indication of the rule's purpose. All format rules you make will reside on one table.

The other options are as follows:

- **For this data:** Select the name of the table where you intend to place the format rule.

- **If this condition is true:** We can pass an AppSheet expression into this field. By doing so, you can change the condition to apply the format rule or not dynamically, based on the context.

- **Format these columns and actions:** Select one or multiple columns where you wish to apply the format rule. When multiple columns are selected, then the same rules will be applied across selected column values.

- **Visual Format:** You can manage the appearance of format rules, such as icons, highlight color, and text color.

- **Text Format:** You can apply format rules to change the text styles, such as text size, underline, bold, italic, uppercase, and strikethrough styles.

Generally, the format rule settings are simple enough, and you won't find much difference from the format rules in Excel, Word, and other similar applications.

In the following section, we will talk about the **Brand** tab, which offers settings specific to AppSheet and allows you to control the app theme globally.

# Branding with theme colors and icons

Through the **Brand** tab on the **UX** pane, we are able to customize the appearance of our apps, such as the background image, logo, and main color theme applied across your apps, including the icon and header/footer colors as well as images used in various places inside your app. Let's see what kind of options we have for customization. To follow along with this section, you need to go to **UX | Brand**.

## Theme

Here, we can choose from two options, light and dark. Light is a theme with a white background, while the dark theme changes the overall background of the app to black.

## Primary color

With this setting, we can specify the main color theme of the app using hex or RGBA color codes to apply your brand colors. The selected color will be broadly applied to various elements of your app, such as action buttons and the header and footer across the app.

## App logo

We can change the logo used as the app icon with this option. The app icon will be displayed in various places. You can select a logo from the default list of icons, or add your own logo image by clicking the **Custom** button. The easiest way to use your own image as the logo is to save the file to Google Drive. Then, you will be able to select the file through the Google Drive file picker to apply it as the app logo.

## Launch image

Select the background image when starting/synchronizing the app. You can use images saved in the `.jpg`, `.png`, and `.gif` formats that are hosted externally and can be accessed by a URL. As with the app logo, you can save the image to Google Drive and set the file to be used as the launch image as well.

### Background image

Select the background image for your app. Compatible image formats include `.jpg`, `.png`, and `.gif`, and they can be hosted externally and accessed by a URL. As with the app logo, you can save the image file to Google Drive and select the file to apply it as your launch image.

## Header and footer

We can explicitly control the styles for both the header and footer. We have the following options to control the styles:

- **Show view name in header**: Set whether to display the view name in the header at the top of the app

- **Show logo in header**: Set whether to display the logo of the application to the left of the header at the top

- **Hide menu and search buttons**: A function to turn on/off the hamburger menu and header search function on the upper left

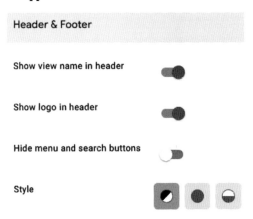

Figure 3.32 – Header & Footer options

Like the format rule settings, branding should be a simple process, as you now know what each option will do for you.

Finally, we will briefly talk about the **Localize** tab, where you can tweak the default system terminology that appears inside the app by default.

## Managing the app's internal terminology through the Localize tab

You can change the names of options such as **Share**, **Sync**, **About**, and **Log out**, and any other terms that appear across the app by default. You can change them to your preferred language or even change them to other English terms in specific contexts.

To achieve this, navigate to **UX** | the **Localize** tab.

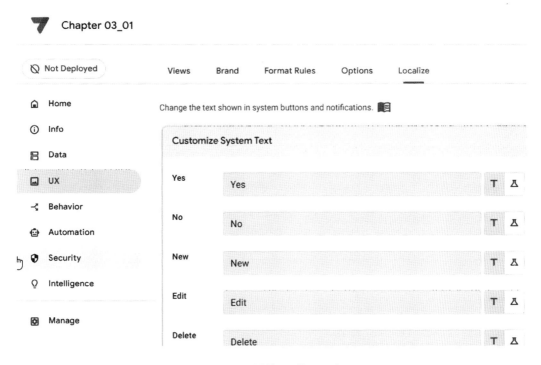

Figure 3.33 – UX | Localize settings

The available system text is shown on the left in the list. Navigate this list and find the system wording you want to change. In the input field to the right of the system text, type any text in your own language to replace the system wording.

For instance, on the same app, you can display **Save** for a certain form view, but you may wish to present **Submit request** for the save form action. You can achieve dynamic conditions like this by passing an expression.

## Summary

This chapter has covered the **UX** pane of AppSheet in its entirety, and we spent most of our time discussing *views*. AppSheet provides a number of different options to control view style and appearance, which gives us the flexibility to change the UX of our app.

Some argue that AppSheet does not have great flexibility to control a view style, but we have the opposite opinion. We have found a high level of flexibility in AppSheet that lets us change the view styles. However, we hope that the AppSheet team will add more functionality in the future.

Once again, it will be difficult to remember all the options we discussed here simply by reading through this chapter once. When you start your journey with AppSheet, please open this chapter once again to refresh your skills to improve the UX of your apps.

During the course of this chapter, we looked at the use of *AppSheet expressions*, which are functions used everywhere in the AppSheet editor. We also covered *branding* and *localization* as well, which allow you to customize the appearance of your app, such as the logo and system language, to meet your business requirements. With the knowledge gained from this chapter, we hope you will be able to build a user-friendly app to attract new users.

In the next chapter, we will go through *expressions* to learn how they work, why they are important, and how to construct expressions effectively.

# 4

# Manipulating Data with Functions and Expressions

In the previous chapter, we learned how to create various types of views so that users can input and view app data using various types of app views. However, any data, be it textual, numerical, or date and time data, needs to be manipulated to match the app's business functionality. Data manipulation means your app can process the data keyed in by users and convert it into other formats or perform calculations on it as per the required business logic. Finally, the app will present the processed data to the user in the most user-friendly format. This processed data, in turn, will provide the app users with just the right information to make decisions or understand the status of the business functionality for which the app was created. In this chapter, we will learn how we can manipulate the data in our apps with the help of AppSheet **functions** and **expressions**.

This chapter covers the following topics:

- Understanding functions, expressions and AppSheet Expression Assistant
- Making decisions with Yes/No functions and expressions
- Making decisions with conditional functions and expressions
- Manipulating text with text functions and expressions
- Manipulating multiple values with list functions and expressions
- Performing arithmetic calculations with math functions and expressions
- Performing date, time, and duration calculations with date and time expressions
- Performing record-level operations with table functions and expressions
- Understanding important miscellaneous functions and associated expressions
- Using multiple functions in single expressions

AppSheet has a substantially large list of **functions**. We will learn how you can effectively use the most often used functions in this chapter. You can use the learning from this chapter to extend the use of other functions in your apps.

## Technical requirements

To assist your learning through this chapter, we have prepared a sample app that you can access from the portfolio site of this book. You can find the set of sample apps that are created for this chapter by visiting `https://www.appsheet.com/portfolio/5689905`.

You can refer to the sample app, `Chapter 04_01`, on the portfolio site to understand the various functions and expressions described in this chapter. You can access Chapter 04_01 app at `https://www.appsheet.com/templates/sample?appGuidString=d4a2289a-fbb2-4e06-b0c8-b0bbeb3646f1`

## Understanding functions, expressions and AppSheet Expression Assistant

In this section, you will learn about what functions and expressions are and where in the app editor you can configure them.

The app users enter data via columns. They may add or update data directly through the form views in the columns or fields of the tables used in apps. They may also add or update data through actions or quick edits in the detail and summary views. Some of the real columns and all virtual columns will have computed data based on the data entered into the other columns. As an app creator, you can manipulate textual data and numerical data, as well as time and date data, by using various AppSheet functions that you will learn about in this chapter.

In spreadsheets, as in computer language programming, there are several functions. Each function has certain inputs; the function processes those inputs, and then those functions produce results as per the definition of the function. AppSheet similarly has a list of multiple functions for manipulating data as well as for app navigation. We will mainly concentrate on the data manipulation functions in this chapter. We will discuss the app navigation functions in *Chapter 5*.

When you construct a string of one or more functions that manipulate the input data to a suitable format, this string of multiple functions is referred to as an **expression**.

In AppSheet, you can configure expressions in multiple places in an app as required for the desired functioning of those respective app elements. You can construct expressions in the column settings of the **App formula**, **Initial value**, **Valid if**, **Editable_if**, **Show_if**, and **Required_if** constraints, the **Display name** settings, **Row filter condition** for the slices, action conditions, the **Localize** pane, the **Automation** panes, and so on.

The following screenshot shows what an expression entry window looks like for the **App formula** setting of a column:

Figure 4.1 – App formula pane for entering expressions

The app editor has an important feature known as the **Expression Assistant**. Whenever you construct any expression in your app, you always enter it through the **Expression Assistant**. As its name suggests, the **Expression Assistant** makes the process of constructing expressions easier. When you click on the **flask** icon in any of the previously described settings such as **App formula**, **valid_if** , **Display name** , or anywhere else where you can enter expressions, the **Expression Assistant** pane opens, as the following figure shows.

Figure 4.2 – Expression Assistant in the app editor

You can start constructing the expression on your own in the grey color settings field that shows the TEXT(..) expression example in *Figure 4.2*.

**Expression Assistant** provides several sample expressions that help you to construct the expressions. To access the example expressions, select the **Examples** tab. The expression examples are listed under different categories of expression types, such as Yes/No, Math, Text, Time, and more. You can refer to the example expressions under the category that you are constructing an expression for. Note that the suggestions by the app editor under the **Examples** option are not necessarily the final expressions that you want to construct. That being said, you can get a good overview and help in constructing your final expressions.

In the **Expression Assistant**, there is another key feature called **Data Explorer**, where you can access the columns from all tables of your app. This feature ensures that you avoid possible errors in typing column names when you manually construct your expressions, and it will also help you to have a bird's eye view of all the available columns in all the tables of your app.

If the expression you have entered is syntactically correct, the **Expression Assistant** displays a green **tick** icon just below the expression settings field, as shown in the preceding figure. The **Expression Assistant** also expands the expression you have entered in a descriptive manner to help you understand the expression in your native language.

If the expression you have entered has any syntactical errors, the **Expression Assistant** flags them with a **red cross** icon. The **Expression Assistant** also displays an error message that explains why the expression's validation has failed, as shown in the following figure:

Figure 4.3 – Error in expression detected by the Expression Assistant

Once your expression is syntactically correct as indicated by the **green tick** icon, you can click the **Test** action icon, which is just below the expression setting field where you entered the expression. The **Test page** will display the results of your expression, as the following figure shows:

Figure 4.4 – Test results pane of the Expression Assistant

The test results displayed are for each row if the expression is a row level expression. You can expand the test results by tapping on the **sitemap** icon. The test results pane then shows how the expression is evaluated at each step of the expression. Based on the test results, you can make any required changes to the expression until you get the desired results as per your app logic requirement.

Once you are satisfied with testing, then you click the **Save** button at the bottom of the **Expression Assistant** to save your expression.

After having the overview of AppSheet functions, expressions, and the **Expression Assistant** in the preceding section, we will now understand the concept of type-casting before we dive into understanding each of the functions and expressions.

## Type-casting

As you are aware, there are several types of columns in AppSheet. **Type-casting** involves converting values from a column of one type into values of another type. Type-casting is often necessary in expressions that need a certain type of value.

Using type-casting, you can convert a number-type column into a decimal-type column by simply writing DECIMAL([Number Column]). You can convert a datetime-type column value into just time or date values by wrapping the column with TIME() or DATE() functions. As an example, you can convert a datetime column named [Record Saved] into just a time-type column value by wrapping the column as follows: TIME([Record Saved]). Alternatively, you can convert a datetime column into a date-type column value by wrapping the column as follows: DATE([Record Saved]).

The following table illustrates a few examples of type-casting:

| Column Type | Column Name | Value | Type-Casting into | Type-Cast Expression | Value After Type-Casting |
|---|---|---|---|---|---|
| Datetime | `[RECORD_SAVED]` | 08/15/2022 10:11:12 | `TIME()` | `TIME([RECORD_SAVED])` | 10:11:12 AM |
| Datetime | `[RECORD_SAVED]` | 08/15/2022 10:11:12 | `DATE()` | `DATE([RECORD_SAVED])` | 08/15/2022 |
| Decimal | `[WEIGHT]` | 1234.56 | `NUMBER()` | `NUMBER([WEIGHT])` | 1235 |

Table 4.1 – Type-casting of column types

Having understood type-casting, we will now start learning about various AppSheet functions. Let us learn about the most often used functions in AppSheet. We will discuss the functions with the help of a sample app. We will also emphasize the peculiarities of the functions and the salient points about when and how those functions should be used.

> **Important note**
>
> You will understand each function in this chapter with the help of use case examples. We will also use some sample data either from the sample app of this chapter or some sample data just as a part of the use case discussion.

We will start with Yes/No expressions.

## Making decisions with Yes/No functions and expressions

Many times, in your app configuration, there will be logic that has just two possible results, Yes or No or TRUE or FALSE. In this section, we will learn about AppSheet functions that lead to these results. Before understanding these Yes/No functions, let us first discuss a few examples of scenarios where a yes or no answer will need to be configured in your apps:

Does a list of flowers, LIST( "Jasmine", "Rose" , "Aster", "Daffodil, "Dahlia"), include "Hibiscus"? The answer, in this case, is No or FALSE.

Does the word *ice cream* contain the word *ice*? The answer is Yes or TRUE.

There is a value of skateboard in the [DESCRIPTION] column in record 1 of a table. Now, the question is – is the [DESCRIPTION] column in record 1 blank? The answer, in this case, is No or FALSE.

You can use AppSheet functions that result in a Yes/No or TRUE/FALSE value when applied to input data, as discussed in the preceding paragraph. The input data can be a list of elements or simply elements of any column type, such as text, date, time, phone, or name, depending on the function used.

It is also appropriate to mention here that the IF(), IFS(), and SWITCH() functions are similar to Yes/No functions. The difference is that these three functions do not stop at evaluating a condition or more than one condition as just TRUE or FALSE, but, depending on the result of these conditions, also allow you to configure some additional options.

Let us now learn about the six AppSheet functions that allow us to provide a yes or no response to questions. We will start by understanding the AND() and OR() functions:

| Use case | Find out whether the marks received in **all three subjects**, math, geography, and science, are greater than 80. |
|---|---|
| | Find out whether the marks in **any one of or all three subjects**, math, geography, and science, are greater than 80. |
| Column types | [MATH], [GEOGRAPHY], and [SCIENCE] are all number-type columns with different values in four records, as follows: |

| Record | MATHS | GEOGRAPHY | SCIENCE |
|---|---|---|---|
| 1 | 88 | 87 | 91 |
| 2 | 85 | 78 | 67 |
| 3 | 71 | 81 | 88 |
| 4 | 65 | 74 | 68 |

[AND_RESULT] is a Yes/No-type column.

[OR_RESULT] is a Yes/No-type column.

| Expression | The AND([MATH] > 80, [GEOGRAPHY]>80, [SCIENCE]>80) expression will result in TRUE if all three arguments or subexpressions within it are true. The expression will result in FALSE if any of the three subexpressions within it is false. |
|---|---|

The OR([MATH] > 80, [GEOGRAPHY]>80, [SCIENCE]>80) expression will result in TRUE if one or more of the three arguments or subexpressions within it is true. The expression will result in FALSE if all three subexpressions within it are false.

With this understanding of the AND() and OR() functions, let us understand the results of applying AND() and OR() functions to the three columns of those records:

| Record | MATHS | GEOGRAPHY | SCIENCE | [AND_RESULT] | [OR_RESULT] |
|---|---|---|---|---|---|
| 1 | 88 | 87 | 91 | TRUE | TRUE |
| 2 | 85 | 78 | 67 | FALSE | TRUE |
| 3 | 71 | 81 | 88 | FALSE | TRUE |
| 4 | 65 | 74 | 68 | FALSE | FALSE |

| Points to note | You can apply the AND() and OR() functions to any number of sub-arguments or subexpressions. |
|---|---|

Each subexpression or sub-argument should evaluate as TRUE or FALSE.

Table 4.2 – Understanding the AND() and OR() functions

Let us next understand the NOT() function, which reverses the result of any expression that evaluates to TRUE or FALSE.

| Use case | Find out whether the marks in **both subjects**, math and geography, are greater than 80 and reverse the result. |
|---|---|
| | Find out whether the marks in **any of the two subjects**, math and geography, are greater than 80 and reverse the result. |
| Column types | [MATH] and [GEOGRAPHY] are number-type columns with different values in four records, as follows: |

| Record | MATH | GEOGRAPHY |
|---|---|---|
| 1 | 88 | 87 |
| 2 | 85 | 78 |
| 3 | 71 | 81 |
| 4 | 65 | 74 |

[AND_RESULT] is a Yes/No-type column.

[OR_RESULT] is a Yes/No-type column.

[NOT_RESULT] is a Yes/No-type column.

| Expression | The NOT (AND ( [MATH] > 80, [GEOGRAPHY] >80) ) expression will result in FALSE if all the arguments or subexpressions within it are true. The expression will result in TRUE if any of the three subexpressions within it is false. |
|---|---|

The NOT (OR ( [MATH] > 80, [GEOGRAPHY] >80) ) expression will result in FALSE if any of the three arguments or subexpressions within it is true. The expression will result in TRUE if all three subexpressions within it are false.

With this understanding of the NOT () function, let us understand the results of applying the NOT () function above the AND () and OR () functions on those records:

| Record | MATHS | GEOGRAPHY | [AND_RESULT] | [NOT_RESULT] |
|---|---|---|---|---|
| 1 | 88 | 87 | TRUE | FALSE |
| 2 | 85 | 78 | FALSE | TRUE |
| 3 | 71 | 81 | FALSE | TRUE |
| 4 | 65 | 74 | FALSE | TRUE |

| Record | MATHS | GEOGRAPHY | [OR_RESULT] | [NOT_RESULT] |
|---|---|---|---|---|
| 1 | 88 | 87 | TRUE | FALSE |
| 2 | 85 | 78 | TRUE | FALSE |
| 3 | 71 | 81 | TRUE | FALSE |
| 4 | 65 | 74 | FALSE | TRUE |

| Points to note | You can apply the NOT () function to a column of the Yes/No type or an expression that evaluates to TRUE or FALSE. The NOT () function basically reverses the result of the inner TRUE or FALSE expression. |
|---|---|

Table 4.3 – Understanding the NOT() function

We will discuss the IN() function in the following table. The IN() function finds out whether a value exists in a list of values of the same type and supplies a yes (TRUE) or no (FALSE) result:

| Use case | Find out whether an item is included in a list of items. |
| --- | --- |
| Column types | Input: A list-type [PLANETS] column with the base type as text and values in a record of LIST("Mercury" , "Venus" , "Earth" , "Mars" , "Jupiter" , "Saturn" , "Uranus" , "Neptune")<br><br>Output: A column called [LIST_TEST] of the Yes/No type |
| Expression | The IN( "Sun", [PLANETS] ) expression will result in No or FALSE because Sun does not exist in the list of planets.<br><br>IN( "Earth", [PLANETS] ) will result in Yes or TRUE because Earth is in the list of planets. |
| Points to note | The IN() function always results in a value of TRUE or FALSE or Yes or No.<br><br>You need to configure the value to search followed by the list to be searched in the IN() function.<br><br>You can use the IN() function to search for a value in lists of prices, text, numbers, decimals, email addresses, and phone numbers. You will, of course, search for a price value in a list of prices, a number in a list of numbers, and so on. |

Table 4.4 – The IN() function – a Yes/No-type function

We will next learn about the CONTAINS() function, which searches whether a larger string contains another string or not:

| Use case | Find out whether a text string is part of another text string. |
|---|---|
| Column types | Input: The [PLANET_NAME] column contains Earth in one record and Neptune in the second record. |
| | Output: A column called [STRING_TEST] of the Yes/No type. |
| Expression | The CONTAINS("Earth" , "ear") expression will return a result of TRUE or Yes. |
| | The CONTAINS("Neptune" , "tunes") expression will return a result of FALSE or No because Neptune does not contain tunes – it contains tune without an "s." |
| Points to note | You need to configure the larger text string to be searched first in the function followed by the text string to search with. You can use the CONTAINS() function to find any part of a string in a larger string. So, both the CONTAINS("Earth" , "arth") and CONTAINS("Earth" , "art") expressions will return TRUE because the arth and art text strings are contained in the word, Earth. |
| | You can use the CONTAINS() function with a list as well. So, the CONTAINS(LIST("Mercury" , "Venus" , "Earth" , "Mars" , "Jupiter", "Saturn" , "Uranus" , "Neptune") , "jUPITER") expression will return TRUE because jUPITER is contained in the list. Note that the "jUPITER" search text does not match Jupiter in terms of letter casing but the CONTAINS() function is not case-sensitive. |

Table 4.5 – The CONTAINS() function – a Yes/No-type function

We will understand the ISBLANK() and ISNOTBLANK() functions next, which check whether a column is blank or not:

| Use case | Find out whether the value of a column in a record is blank or not. |
|---|---|
| Column types | Input: [DESCRIPTION] is a text-type column with no data in it, [ITEM_QUANTITY] is a number-type column, and [PLANETS] is a list-type column. [ITEM_PRICE] is a price-type column. |
| | Output: A column called [BLANK_TEST] of the Yes/No type. |
| Expression | The ISBLANK([DESCRIPTION]) expression will return TRUE and the ISNOTBLANK([DE-SCRIPTION]) expression will return FALSE. |
| | The ISBLANK([PLANETS]) expression will return FALSE and the ISNOTBLANK([PLANETS]) expression will return TRUE. |
| | The ISBLANK([ITEM_PRICE]) expression will return FALSE and the ISNOTBLANK([ITEM_PRICE]) expression will return TRUE. |
| Points to note | ISBLANK() checks whether a column's record value is blank and returns TRUE if so |
| | ISNOTBLANK() checks that a column's record value is not blank and returns TRUE if so |
| | You can use ISBLANK() and ISNOTBLANK() to check whether the column value contents are blank for a list, text, number, decimal, email address, phone number, or name column type |

Table 4.6 – ISBLANK() and ISNOTBLANK() – Yes/No-type functions

You have learned how you can use Yes/No functions in your app for certain decision-making scenarios. We will next learn about conditional functions, which are similar to Yes/No expressions in that they also result in one value depending on several input conditions.

# Making decisions with conditional functions and expressions

Conditional functions and expressions help you to determine any one of multiple alternative result values depending on certain input conditions. Let us discuss a scenario where you can use conditional expressions.

In an examination, the grade is A for aggregate marks above 85%, B for marks between 71% and 85%, C for marks between 61% and 70%, D for marks between 45% and 60%, and E for the rest. In these scenarios, AppSheet conditional functions will allow you to compute any one resulting grade in a results column titled, say, [GRADES], depending on the range of marks as input conditions in the other column, titled, say, [PERCENT_MARKS]. The range of marks is the condition on which to decide the grades. Also note that there are several possible results of grades based on the range of marks, but for any one particular value of marks, only one result is correct. You can enter the conditional expressions in the column where you are expecting the result, the [GRADES] column in this example.

You will often need to configure results based on this type of conditional decision-making in your apps. You can use the three conditional functions mentioned in the following table:

| Function | Recommended use cases. |
| --- | --- |
| IF() | When you have two alternative expressions or results based on a condition that evaluates to TRUE or FALSE, you can conveniently use the IF() function. You can use a nested IF() function for more than two conditions, but instead of a nested IF() function, you can use IFS() or SWITCH() for multiple conditions with more ease. |
| IFS() | When you have one or multiple conditions or results pairs, the IFS() function selects the result of whichever condition first evaluates to true. The IFS() function sequentially evaluates the condition/results pairs in the order they have been configured in the expression. Note that the IFS() function does not have a default result value or expression if none of the conditions mentioned in it is true. |
| SWITCH() | When you have one or multiple conditions or results pairs along with a default result value, you can use the SWITCH() function. The SWITCH() function expression results in a default value if none of the conditions mentioned in it is true. |

Table 4.7 – Conditional functions

Let us understand a few situations where the three conditional functions described in the preceding table would be used.

We will first understand the IF () function, which you can conveniently use to select one of two results based on whether a condition is true or false:

| Use case | If the date falls on Sunday, then it is a weekly holiday; otherwise, it is a working day. |
|---|---|
| Column types | [DATE] is of the date type. |
| Expression | IF( WEEKDAY([DATE])=1, "weekly Holiday", "Working Day") |
| | In this expression, WEEKDAY([DATE])=1 is the conditional part that evaluates to either TRUE or FALSE. If the conditional expression evaluates to TRUE, the IF() function selects the first of the two results or expressions. If the conditional expression evaluates to FALSE, the IF() function selects the second result or expression. In this case, if the WEEKDAY([Date]) returns a value of 1, which means the condition is TRUE and it is a Sunday, then the IF() function selects the first result of Weekly Holiday. Or, if the WEEKDAY([Date]) returns a value other than 1, which means the condition is FALSE and the date falls on a day other than Sunday, that is, any other day number is provided, then the IF() function selects the second result of "Working Day" mentioned in the expression. |
| Points to note | Even though you can use the IF() function for multiple conditions with nested IF(), the IFS() and SWITCH() functions are more convenient for multiple conditions or result pairs. |
| | The two results of the IF() function need to be of the same data type. For example, you cannot configure one result to be of the date type and another one of the number type in the same expression. |

Table 4.8 – Conditional IF() function

Let us next learn about the IFS () function, which allows you to easily configure multiple conditions and multiple results in one function. The function selects a result depending on the first TRUE condition.

| Use case | If the date falls on Sunday, then it is a holiday; if the date falls on a Saturday, then it is a half working day; and for all other dates, it is a working day. |
|---|---|
| Column types | [DATE] is of the date type. |
| Expression | ```<br>IFS (<br><br>        WEEKDAY ([DATE])=1, "Weekly Holiday",<br><br>        WEEKDAY ([DATE])=7, "Half Working Day",<br><br>        AND(WEEKDAY([DATE])>1,  WEEKDAY([DATE])<7),<br>"Working Day"<br><br>        )<br>```<br><br>The parts of the expression can be broken down as follows:<br><br>• The WEEKDAY ([DATE])=1 condition checks whether [DATE] falls on a Sunday and if so, assigns a value of Weekly holiday as the result<br><br>• The WEEKDAY ([DATE])=7 condition checks whether [DATE] falls on a Saturday and if so, assigns a value of Half working day as the result<br><br>• The AND (WEEKDAY([DATE])>1,  WEEKDAY([DATE])<7) condition checks whether [DATE] falls on a day from Monday to Friday and if so, assigns a value of Working day as the result |
| Points to note | As you can see, the expression in the preceding cell has three conditions with one possible result for each condition. Thus, with the IFS () function, you can conveniently include more than two condition/ result pairs.<br><br>However, there is no default result value or default expression included in the IFS () function. Due to this fact, if the conditions in IFS () do not match any of the configured conditions, the result is blank. So, you need to be careful when configuring an IFS () expression that you have configured all the possible conditions in the expression. |

Table 4.9 – Conditional IFS() function

Let us next learn about the SWITCH () function, which allows you to configure multiple conditions or result pairs and also a default condition in case all the preceding conditions are FALSE:

| Use case | If the date falls on Sunday, then it is a holiday; if the date falls on a Saturday, then it is half a working day; and for all other days of the week, it is a working day. |
|---|---|
| Column types | [DATE] is of the date type. |
| Expression | ```SWITCH(WEEKDAY([Date]),```<br><br>```        1, "Weekly Holiday",```<br><br>```        7, "Half Working Day",```<br><br>```        "Working Day")```<br><br>The parts of the expression can be broken down as follows:<br><br>• If the WEEKDAY([Date]) condition evaluates to 1, the result of Weekly Holiday is assigned<br><br>• If the WEEKDAY([Date]) condition evaluates to 7, the result of Half working day is assigned<br><br>• For all other dates, a result of Working Day is assigned |
| Points to note | You will notice that in the case of the SWITCH() function, for the last result, you need not include a condition. All the conditions that do not satisfy the explicitly configured conditions are automatically assigned the last or the default result in the case of the SWITCH() function.<br><br>Also, unlike the IFS() function-based expression, where the first part of the condition, in our current example, WEEKDAY([Date]), needs to be included in all conditions, you will notice that in the case of SWITCH(), the WEEKDAY([Date]) condition is mentioned only once.<br><br>Thus, the SWITCH() expression can be configured more efficiently compared to IFS().<br><br>However, SWITCH() evaluates the second part of the condition only for the "equal to" operator. You cannot configure other operators, such as > (greater than) or < (less than), in the SWITCH() function. The IFS() function can also evaluate conditions with the > or < comparison operators. |

Table 4.10 – Conditional SWITCH() function

You have now learned how you can use conditional expressions in your apps for decision-making based on various conditional inputs. You will next learn about the text functions that help you manipulate textual data in the most user-friendly way for the app user and as required by your app logic.

# Manipulating text with text functions and expressions

In any app, as in the real world, we deal with a lot of text data. We then obviously need to manipulate the text to get just the right format for the app user to easily understand it. At times, you may need to only use part of the text, or at times, you might want to combine the data from multiple columns into a text string to create a meaningful message or information for the app user. You can use the AppSheet text functions to manipulate the text in an app just the way you want. In this section, let us understand the most common text functions that allow us to perform this text manipulation.

Let us start by understanding the CONCATENATE() function, which returns a longer text string by combining column values or other text strings:

| Use case | Combine the item name and quantity in a message to be sent to users. |
|---|---|
| Column types | [ITEM_NAME] and [ITEM_QUANTITY]<br><br>[MESSAGE] is a text-type column. |
| Expression | We use the CONCATENATE() function to combine the column values with other text to construct a combined meaningful text string message.<br><br>The CONCATENATE("The item ", [ITEM_NAME], " has a quantity of ",[ITEM_QUANTITY], " left in the stock.") expression will result in a text string of The item  Lounge Chair has a quantity of  97 left in the stock. for a record containing an [ITEM_NAME] value of Lounge Chair and an [ITEM_QUANTITY] value of 97. |
| Points to note | You can use values from almost all column types in the CONCATENATE() function to create a useful text string.<br><br>You need to separate the subparts made up of free-text strings and the column names used in a CONCATENATE() function with a comma.<br><br>You need to surround the text strings used in the CONCATENATE() function in double quotes. |

Table 4.11 – The CONCATENATE() text function

Let us next learn about a few text functions that help you find out the length of a text string and extract a certain portion of a text string:

| Use case | Get the length of a text string. |
| --- | --- |
| | Get the initial part of a text string. |
| | Get the middle part of a text string. |
| | Get the ending part of a text string. |
| Column types | The [MOVIE_NAME] column is of the text type. |
| Functions used | The LEN() function returns the length of a text string in terms of the number of characters. |
| | The LEFT() function returns the character string starting from the first character of another text string with the specified number of characters in the function. |
| | The RIGHT() function returns the character string starting from the last character of another text string with the specified number of characters in the function. |
| | The MID() function returns the character string starting from a certain position of another text string with the specified number of characters in the function. The starting position, as well as the number of characters to return, is mentioned in the MID() expression. |
| Data | [MOVIE_NAME] has The Jungle Book in the first record and The Lion King in the second record. |
| Expression | The LEN([MOVIE_NAME]) expression will return the length of the string in the [MOVIE_NAME] column. It will return an integer of 15 for the first record and an integer of 13 for the second record. |
| | The LEFT([MOVIE_NAME] , 3) expression will result in a text string of The. |
| | The RIGHT(([MOVIE_NAME] , 4) expression will result in a text string of Book for the first record and King for the second record. |
| | The MID([MOVIE_NAME], 5 , 6) expression will result in a text string of Jungle for the first record and the MID([MOVIE_NAME], 5 , 4) expression will result in a text string of Lion for the second record. |

Table 4.12 – Miscellaneous text functions

Let us next learn how we can use the SUBSTITUTE() function, which helps substitute one part of a text string with another one:

| Use case | To replace a part of a text string with another text string. |
|---|---|
| Column types | The [MOVIE_NAME] column is of the text type.<br><br>[MOVIE_NAME] has The Jungle Book in the first record and The Lion King in the second record. |
| Expression | The SUBSTITUTE[MOVIE_NAME], "The", "A") expression will give a result of A Jungle Book for the first record and A Lion King for the second record. |
| Points to note | The SUBSTITUTE() function has three arguments. The first argument is the text string in which you want to make a substitution. The second argument contains the part of the text string in the first argument that you wish to substitute, and the third argument contains the string that you want to substitute for the string in the second argument.<br><br>You can also use the SUBSTITUTE() function for a single word to partially substitute the part of the word. So, the SUBSTITUTE("Anytime", "time" , "way") expression will result in Anyway. |

Table 4.13 – SUBSTITUTE() text functions

Let us next learn about the FIND() function, which finds the character position, as an integer number, at which a character or another text string occurs for the first time in a string:

| Use case | Find the character number at which a text string starts in another text string. |
|---|---|
| Column types | [DESCRIPTION] is of the text type.<br><br>The [DESCRIPTION] column contains Sunflower in the first record and Railroad in the second record.. |
| Expression | The FIND("flower" , [Description]) expression returns a value of 4 for the first record because the flower text string starts at character number 4 .<br><br>The FIND("Rail" , [Description]) expression returns a value of 1 for the second record because the Rail text string starts at character number 1 . |
| Points to note | The FIND() function returns a value of the position of the first character of the search text string in another text string. So, the result of a FIND() function is always an integer number.<br><br>One peculiar point about the FIND() function is that it is case-sensitive. So, if you configure the FIND("Flower", "Sunflower") expression, it will return a value of 0. This is so because the search string has Flower with the first letter as a capital. The string to be searched, Sunflower, has f in lowercase. So, the FIND() function returns a value of 0.<br><br>You can use the FIND() function in a text string that is composed of multiple words. So, FIND("butter", "peanut butter") will result in a value of 8 because the word butter starts at position 8. Note that the FIND() function also considers space as a character. So, the result of 8 includes the 6 letters in peanut and the space before butter, which starts at position 8 in the text string to be searched.<br><br>You can use FIND() to search text strings that have a combination of special characters, numbers, and currency symbols. So, you can also use the FIND() function as follows: FIND("5", "post office in lane 5 is nearby") or FIND("$4", "The pencil with a price of $4.99 is the best one"). |

Table 4.14 – FIND() text functions

You have now learned how you can use various text functions to manipulate text in a user-friendly manner. Let us next learn about the list functions that are essential in any app. With the list functions, you can perform certain operations or manipulate multiple values combined as a list of a column's values from several records of a table.

# Manipulating multiple values with list functions and expressions

In this section, we will learn what list column types are and also how you can create lists. Thereafter, we will learn about various list functions and expressions with examples.

As you will be aware, in AppSheet, in columns of date, datetime, time, URL, text, phone number, name, number, price, image, or other types, the user can enter a single value per record – so users can enter a single date value in a date-type column, a single time value in a time-type column, a single phone number value in a phone-number-type column, and so on.

However, at times, you may need multiple values of a single data type in a single record. Consider a case where you would like to refer to multiple phone numbers of a customer in their record in a customer table. Those phone numbers may have been entered in another table, such as one called `Customer Contact Details`, in multiple rows, but you want to display them together in a single column in a single record in the customer table.

When you need to display multiple (more than one, up to any number) values of a column type in another single column, you can do so using the list column type. There are two types of list columns in AppSheet:

- **Enumlist**-type list columns are **real columns**. Users mostly use them to enter multiple values in a single record in a single column of the enumlist type.

- There are also list-type **virtual columns**, where the app stores multiple values of any column type. In virtual columns, you as an app creator can enter `SELECT()` expressions that create a list. At times, the app editor might create specific list-type virtual columns, such as reverse reference lists. We call virtual list columns that are automatically created by the app editor system-generated columns.

List columns most commonly have commas separating the element values. The most common notation or syntax to create a list in AppSheet is `LIST(value 1, value 2, value 3..........., value n)`, or simply `{value 1, value 2, value 3..........., value n}`.

So a list column of several dates will look like following in the test results pane of the Expression Assistant:

```
1/1/2016 , 2/1/2016 , 3/1/2016 , 4/1/2016 , 2/1/2016 , 3/1/2016 ,
4/1/2016 , 3/1/2016 , 4/1/2016 , 6/20/2017
```

You can manually construct a list of prices with the following expression in a list type column with element type as Price:

```
LIST( 12.55 , 55.33 , 67.89 , 32.11)
```

In an enumlist-type real column, mostly, users enter several values at a time. An example of an enumlist column is a question in a form asking the user to fill in their favorite sports, as shown in the following screenshot:

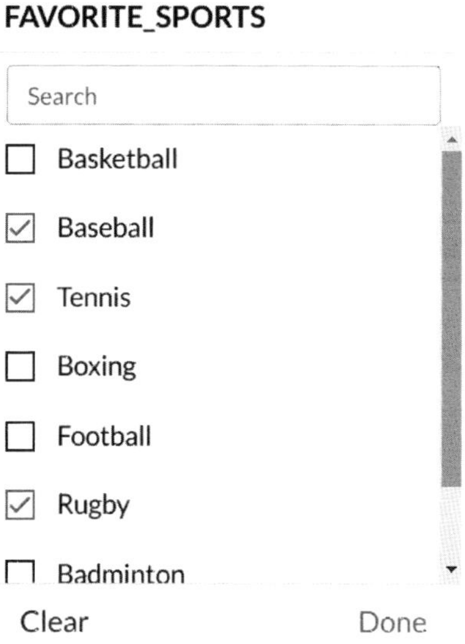

Figure 4.5 – Enumlist column type in a form view

In the preceding screenshot, the user has chosen three sports as their favorite. When the user saves the record, the data source saves the values, as shown in the following screenshot:

Figure 4.6 – Enumlist column type saved in a data source

Using expressions, you can refer to these values as `LIST("Baseball" , "Tennis" , "Rugby")` or simply `{"Baseball" , "Tennis" , "Rugby"}`.

We have now understood how list-type columns are created and how we can refer to them in expressions. We have also seen some examples of how users can enter multiple values in a single record using enumlist columns. Let us learn about various functions and expressions that we can use to construct lists from the data in our apps next. We will also learn how we can manipulate lists.

## List functions and expressions

We will first learn how we can create a list from a column's values in multiple rows of a data source of an app using the SELECT() function. We will also learn how we can create a list by simply combining a data source table name and column name.

You can use the `Table Name[Column Name]` expression to get a list of the values of the `[Column Name]` column in **all the rows in that table**. So, if there are 500 rows in the table, the expression will return a list of 500 elements.

`SELECT(Table Name[Column Name], row level conditional sub-expression that evaluates to true)` will create **a partial list** of elements from the `[Column Name]` column of the table. This partial list created from the SELECT() function includes column values of `[Column Name]` from only those rows wherever `row level conditional sub-expression` for the row evaluates to TRUE. So if the row-level conditional sub-expression evaluates to TRUE for 235 rows in a table of 500 rows, the expression will return a list of 235 elements.

Let us learn how we can create a list of a column's values from all the rows of a table:

| | |
|---|---|
| Use case | Get a list of prices in all rows of the `Items` table. |
| Column types | `[PRICE]` is of the price type. |
| Expression | `Items[PRICE]`<br><br>This expression will list the values of the column mentioned in the expression for all the rows in the table. So, if the table has 1,000 rows, the expression will produce a list of 1,000 values. If the column values in some rows are blank, the list will contain blanks for those rows. However, the count of elements in the list will be 1,000 for 1,000 rows, including blank and non-blank values. |
| Points to note | You can create a list of any column type, such as date, datetime, time, phone number, name, number, decimal, text, or URL, in the table using this expression. |

Table 4.15 – Creating a list of a column's values from all the table rows

Let us next learn how we can use the SELECT() function to select certain values of a column from a table's rows based on certain conditions. We can configure those conditions in the SELECT() function expression:

| Use case | Get a list of prices in the Items table where the price is more than $100. |
|---|---|
| Column types | [PRICE] is of the price type. |
| Expression | SELECT(Items[ITEM_PRICE], [ITEM_PRICE]>100)<br><br>This expression will list the values of the column mentioned in the expression for those rows in the table where the price of the item is greater than $100. So, if the Items table has 1,000 rows and 350 rows have [PRICE] greater than $100, then the SELECT() function-based expression will produce a list of 350 price elements from the [ITEM_PRICE] column. |
| Points to note | You can create a list of any column type, such as date, datetime, time, phone number, name, number, decimal, text, or URL, in the table using this expression.<br><br>You can use more complex subexpressions in the conditional argument in the SELECT() statement. |

Table 4.16 – Creating a list with the SELECT() function

Now that we have understood the concept of lists and how to create them, let us look at a few useful functions related to lists to manipulate list data.

Let us first understand the SORT() function, which sorts a numerical list in ascending (e.g. 0, 1, …98, 99, 100) or descending order (e.g. 100, 99, 98,…,3,2,1) and a textual list in ascending (A to Z) or descending order (Z to A) based on the settings in the function:

| | |
|---|---|
| Use case | Sort a list of prices in ascending order and sort a list of dates in descending order. |
| Column types | [ITEM_PRICES_LIST] is a list-type column with the price base type and has the following values:<br><br>LIST(201.00 , 225.00 , 325.00 , 175.00 , 55.00 , 760.00 , 550.00 , 182.00 , 375.00 , 240.00 , 155. 00 , 135.00 , 300.00 , 178.00)<br><br>[DATE_LIST] is a list-type column with the date base type and has the following values:<br><br>LIST("09/15/2022" , "04/21/2022" , "07/14/2022" , "11/05/2022" , "08/11/2022" , "04/07/2022" , "03/28/2022" , "06/16/2022" , "06/08/2022" , "05/26/2022" , "02/10/2022" , "11/04/2022" , "08/08/2022")<br><br>[PRICE_LIST_SORTED] is a list-type column with the price base type and [DATE_LIST_SORTED] is a list-type column with the date base type. |
| Expression | The SORT( [ITEM_PRICES_LIST], FALSE) expression in the [PRICE_LIST_SORTED] column sorts the elements of [ITEM_PRICES_LIST] in ascending order, resulting in a list of prices in ascending order, as follows:<br><br>LIST(55.00 , 135.00 , 155.00 , 175.00 , 178.00 , 182.00 , 201.00 , 225.00 , 240.00 , 300.00 , 325.00 , 375.00 , 550.00 , 760.00)<br><br>The SORT( [DATE_LIST], TRUE) expression in the [DATE_LIST_SORTED] column sorts the elements of [DATE_LIST] in descending order, resulting in a list of dates in descending order, as follows:<br><br>LIST("11/05/2022" , "11/04/2022" , "09/15/2022" , "08/11/2022" , "08/08/2022" , "07/14/2022" , "06/16/2022" , "06/08/2022" , "05/26/2022" , "04/21/2022" , "04/07/2022" , "03/28/2022" , "02/10/2022") |
| Points to note | You can sort lists of any column type, such as text, name, date, time, datetime, number, or decimal.<br><br>You can configure a sub-expression that evaluates to a TRUE or FALSE result as an argument in the SORT() function for lists with numerical elements, such as numbers, decimals, prices, dates, and times. When the sub-expression evaluates to a TRUE result, the list is sorted in descending order, from the highest to the lowest value. When the sub-expression evaluates to a FALSE result, the list is sorted in ascending order from the lowest to the highest list element values.<br><br>In the case of a list of textual elements with column types such as names or text, the list is alphabetically sorted in ascending (A to Z) order when the sub-expression evaluates to FALSE. When the sub-expression evaluates to TRUE, the textual list is sorted in descending order (Z to A). |

Table 4.17 – Sorting a list with the SORT() function

At times, you would want to know the largest and smallest values in a list. Let us next learn how we can achieve this using the MAX() and MIN() functions. The MAX() function will give the largest value in a numerical list and the MIN() function will give the lowest value in a numerical list:

| Use case | Find the highest- and lowest-priced items in a list of prices |
|---|---|
| Column types | The [ITEM_PRICE] column of the price type in the Items table.<br><br>[MAX_PRICE_ITEM] and [MIN_PRICE_ITEM] are of the price type.<br><br>As we learned, the Items[PRICE] expression will give a list of all prices of all the items in the Items table. |
| Expression | The MAX(Items[PRICE]) expression, configured with the [MAX_PRICE_ITEM] column, will give the highest price in the list.<br><br>The MIN(Items[PRICE]) expression, configured with the [MIN_PRICE_ITEM] column, will give the lowest price. |
| Points to note | You can use the MIN() and MAX() functions on lists of numerical elements, such as numbers, decimals, prices, dates, and datetime and time elements.<br><br>You cannot use the MIN() and MAX() expressions on lists of textual elements, such as text, names, and URLs. |

Table 4.18 – Using the MIN() and MAX() functions to find the smallest and largest values in a list

Let us learn about the INDEX() function next, which will give an element at a certain position (rank) in a list based on the position (rank) mentioned in the function.

We will also learn about the TOP() function, which will make a sublist from another list based on the number of elements mentioned in the function:

| Use cases | Find the value of the first, fifth, or eighth highest-selling item by quantity in the Items table. |
|---|---|
| | Find the value of the top five costliest items in a list of items. |
| | Find the three least-selling items in a list of items. |
| Column types | The [ITEM_PRICE] column is of the price type in the Items table. |
| | The [ITEM_QUANTITY] column is of the number type in the Items table. |
| Data | As we have learned, the Items[ITEM_PRICE] expression will give a list of all prices of all items in the Items table and the Items[ITEM_QUANTITY] expression will give a list of the quantities of all items in the Items table. |
| Expression | INDEX(SORT(Items[ITEM_QUANTITY], TRUE), 1) will return the highest quantity among the quantities of all items. |
| | INDEX(SORT(Items[ITEM_QUANTITY], TRUE), 5) will return the fifth highest quantity among the quantities of all items. |
| | INDEX(SORT(Items[ITEM_QUANTITY], TRUE), 8) will return the eighth highest quantity among the quantities of all items. |
| | TOP(SORT(Items[ITEM_PRICE], TRUE), 5) will return the top five costliest items in the Items table. |
| | TOP(SORT(Items[ITEM_PRICE], FALSE), 3) will return the three cheapest items in the Items table. |
| Points to note | You can use the INDEX() function to get the value of a single element in a list at any position or rank you specify in the expression. Columns that have an expression containing the INDEX() function need to have the same type as the base type of the list because the INDEX() function returns a single value. |
| | You can use the TOP() function to get the values of elements in a list from the starting positions of the list. So, if you configure a value of 5 in the TOP() function, it will give the value of the first five elements in the list. |
| | You can use the TOP() function together with the SORT() function to find the largest or smallest multiple values in a list. Since the TOP() function returns a list of values, the base column type of the TOP() function needs to be the same as that of the original list from which it finds the number of desired elements. |

Table 4.19 – Using the INDEX() and TOP() functions on a list

Let us next learn about the COUNT() function, which will count the number of elements in a list.

| Use case | Count the number of values or elements in a list. |
|---|---|
| Column types | [ITEM_PRICES_LIST] is a list-type column with the price base type and [COUNT_PRICE] is a number-type column. <br><br> The [ITEM_PRICES_LIST] column has the following 14 values: <br><br> LIST(201.00 , 225.00 , 325.00 , 175.00 , 55.00 , 760.00 , 550.00 , 182.00 , 375.00 , 240.00 , 155. 00 , 135.00 , 300.00 , 178.00) |
| Expression | The count of all values in the [ORDER_DETAIL_PRICES] column is computed by the COUNT() function with the following expression: <br><br> COUNT ([ITEM_PRICES_LIST]) <br><br> In current example, COUNT() expression will return a value of 14 because there are 14 elements in the column [ITEM_PRICES_LIST] <br><br> You enter this expression in the [COUNT_PRICE] column. |
| Points to note | You can use the COUNT() function on a list of any type of column, such as number, decimal, price, text, URL, name, or phone number. This is because the COUNT() function counts the number of elements in a list, so the type of the element does not matter. <br><br> A COUNT() function always gives results in terms of integer numbers. So, a column where you have configured a COUNT() function should be of the number type. |

Table 4.20 – Using the COUNT() function on a list

Let us learn about the UNIQUE() function next, which you can use to remove duplicate values in a list:

| Use case | Remove the duplicate values in a list. |
|---|---|
| Column types | [ITEM_PRICES_LIST] and [ITEM_PRICES_UNIQUE] are both list-type columns with the price base type. <br><br> The [ITEM_PRICES_LIST] column has the following values: <br><br> LIST(201.00 , 225.00 , 325.00 , 175.00 , 55.00 , 760.00 , 550.00 , 182.00 , 375.00 , 240.00 , 155. 00 , 135.00 , 300.00 , 178.00 , 550.00) <br><br> You can see that in this price list, there are two values of $550.00. |
| Expression | The UNIQUE([ITEM_PRICES_LIST]) expression will return unique values or non-duplicate values from the [ITEM_PRICES_LIST] list by removing the duplicate value of $550.00 from the list. |
| Points to note | You can use the UNIQUE() function to remove duplicate values from a list of numerical as well as non-numerical elements, such as text, URLs, phone numbers, names, numbers, decimals, or prices. |

Table 4.21 – Using the UNIQUE() function to remove duplicates from a list

Let us next learn about the INTERSECT() function, which will find the common elements between two lists of the same base or element types.

| Use case | Find the common elements in two lists. |
|---|---|
| Column types | [LIST_OF_PRICES] and [LIST_OF_PRICES2] are both of the list type, with the price base type.<br><br>The [LIST_OF_PRICES] column has the following values:<br><br>LIST(115.83 , 44.90 , 28.76 , 47.63 , 43.68 , 36.15 , 57.02 , 63.28 , 73.59 , 16.89)<br><br>The [LIST_OF_PRICES2] column has the following values:<br><br>LIST(17.73 , 30.76 , 44.90 , 59.53 , 43.68 , 67.15 , 57.02 , 83.49 , 93.39 , 16.89)<br><br>You can see that the 44.90 , 43.68 , 57.02, and 16.89 elements are common to both lists. |
| Expression | INTERSECT([LIST_OF_PRICES] , [LIST_OF_PRICES2] ) will give a resulting list of LIST(44.90 , 43.68 , 57.02 , 16.89).<br><br>The elements in the result exist in both the input lists. |
| Points to note | You can use the INTERSECT() function to find the common elements between two different lists of any element type – text, price, number, decimal, and so on. In the majority of the cases, the two lists should have the same element types.<br><br>The result of INTERSECT() is always a list even if the resulting list has no elements or just a single element. |

Table 4.22 – Using the INTERSECT() function to get the common elements from two lists

We have now learned about the most used list functions that you will need in your app configuration. Let us now understand math functions, which allow us to perform various math operations in our apps.

# Performing arithmetic calculations with math functions and expressions

We will learn about the most used math functions in this section. Math functions are mostly useful in numerical calculations and data presentations. You may want to show the user a rounded-off distance value, in kilometers, as an integer, rather than the calculated distance with decimals. You can achieve this using math functions and expressions:

| Use case | Convert a decimal number to the nearest integer number. |
|---|---|
| | Case 1: Convert to the nearest lower integer. |
| | Case 2: Convert to the nearest higher integer. |
| | Case 3: Convert to the nearest higher or lower integer based on whether the value of the decimal number's fraction component is greater than 0.49 or less than or equal to 0.49. |
| Column types | Input: [INPUT_DECIMAL] is of the decimal type. |
| | Output: [OUTPUT_INTEGER] is of the number type. |
| | We will discuss [INPUT_DECIMAL] with two different values of 45.67 and 45.36. |
| Functions used | FLOOR() will round off the decimal number to the nearest lower integer. |
| | CEILING() will round off the decimal number to the nearest higher integer. |
| | ROUND() will round off the decimal number to the nearest lower or higher integer depending on the decimal number's fraction value. |
| Expression | When the value of [INPUT_DECIMAL] is 45.67: |
| | The FLOOR() function will compute the nearest lower integer. |
| | The FLOOR([INPUT_DECIMAL]) expression results in an integer value of 45. |
| | The CEILING() function will compute the nearest higher integer. The CEILING([INPUT_DECIMAL]) expression results in an integer value of 46. |
| | The ROUND() function will compute the nearest lower or higher integer value depending on whether the fraction value of the input decimal number is greater than 0.49 or lower than 0.50. |
| | The ROUND([INPUT_DECIMAL]) expression results in an integer value of 46. This is because, in the input decimal number, 45.67, the fraction part of 0.67 is greater than 0.49. |
| | When the value of [INPUT_DECIMAL] is 45.36: |
| | The FLOOR([INPUT_DECIMAL]) expression results in an integer value of 45. |
| | The CEILING([INPUT_DECIMAL]) expression results in an integer value of 46. |
| | The ROUND([INPUT_DECIMAL]) expression results in an integer value of 45. This is because, in the input decimal number, 45.36, the fraction part of 0.36 is less than 0.50. |
| Points to note | You can use FLOOR() to always find the nearest lower integer and CEILING() to always find the nearest higher integer irrespective of the fraction value in the input decimal number. |
| | You can use the ROUND() function when you want the input decimal number to find either the nearest lower or higher integer value depending on the fraction part of the input decimal number. If the fraction part in the input decimal number is less than or equal to 0.49, the ROUND() function returns the nearest lower integer. For a fraction part greater than 0.49, the ROUND() function returns the nearest higher integer. |
| | You can use the FLOOR(), CEILING(), and ROUND() functions with an integer number itself as input. However, it will lead to the same integer number as a result, so if an integer of 5 is input to either of these three functions, the result will still be 5 because 5 is already an integer. |

Table 4.23 – Math functions – FLOOR(), CEILING(), and ROUND()

Let us next learn how to use the MOD() function to find the arithmetic remainder when we divide one integer by another:

| Use case | Find the arithmetic remainder after dividing one integer by the other. |
| --- | --- |
| Column types | The [YARDS] column of the number type consists of distance values in terms of yards.<br><br>We will discuss the [YARDS] column with three different values: 3520, 1900, and 5200. |
| Function used | We use the MOD() function to find out how many excess yards (that is, the remainder) there are after dividing the values in the [YARDS] column by 1,760. As we know, 1,760 yards make up 1 mile. |
| Expression | When the value of [YARDS] is 3540, the MOD([YARDS], 1760) expression will give a result of 0. This is because 3,520/1,760 = 2, without any remainder.<br><br>When the value of [YARDS] is 1900, the MOD([YARDS], 1760) expression will result in 140. This is because 1,900/1,760 = 1, with a remainder of 140.<br><br>When the value of [YARDS] is 5200, the MOD([YARDS], 1760) expression will result in 1680. This is because 5,200/1,760 = 2, with 1680 as the remainder. |
| Points to note | You need to use integer values in the expression based on the MOD() function.<br><br>The result of a MOD() function is always an integer number. |

Table 4.24 – Math function of MOD()

Let us next learn about the SUM() function, which adds all the values in a numerical-type list:

| Use case | Add the prices in a list to get the total price. |
| --- | --- |
| Column types | [ORDER_DETAIL_PRICES] is a list-type column with the price base type and [TOTAL_PRICE] is a price-type column.<br><br>The [ORDER_DETAIL_PRICES] column has the following values:<br><br>LIST($59.79 , $24.90 , $27.78 , $39.21 , $24.08 , $86.78 , $63.22 , $65.28 , $68.49 , $18.72) |
| Expression | The sum of all values in the [ORDER_DETAIL_PRICES] column is computed by the SUM() function with an expression:<br><br>SUM([ORDER_DETAIL_PRICES])<br><br>In the current example case, the total sum value is $478.25<br><br>You enter this expression into the [TOTAL_PRICE] column. |
| Points to note | You can use the SUM() function on the list of any numerical type of columns, such as number, decimal, or price.<br><br>Since a SUM() function adds the elements of a list, you can configure the column where you have used the SUM() expression to the same type of column as the base type of the list whose elements you are adding. So, if you are adding a list of prices, the results column with a SUM()-based expression should also be of the price type. If you are adding lists of numbers, the results column should also be of the number type.<br><br>As it is obvious, you cannot use the SUM() function on a list of non-numerical column values, such as text, names, URLs, dates, and datetime and time elements. You will get an error in the expression assistant if you try to make a sum of non-numerical columns. |

Table 4.25 – SUM() function

At times, you want to compute a random number within a number range. You can use the RANDBETWEEN() function to compute a random integer number in a range between two integer numbers. Let us learn about the RANDBETWEEN() function.

| Use Case | Find a random value between two integer numbers. |
|---|---|
| Column Types | [RANDOM_NUMBER] of integer type. |
| Function Used | The RANDBETWEEN() function results in a random integer number generated between two integer numbers mentioned in the function when you configure it. |
| Expression | RANDBETWEEN(100, 10000) results in any randomly generated integer number between 100 and 10000.<br><br>RANDBETWEEN(99, 999999) will result in any randomly generated integer number between 99 and 999999. |
| Points to note | The higher the range defined in the RANDBETWEEN() expression, the lower the probability of the generated random number being repeated. |

Table 4.26 – The RANDBETWEEN() function

Let us learn about the AVERAGE() function next, which computes the average when used on a list of numerical elements:

| Use case | Find the average value of the elements in a numerical list. |
|---|---|
| Column types | [ITEM_PRICE] is of the price type in the Items table.<br><br>Items[ITEM_PRICE] will give a list of prices of all items in the Items table. |
| Function used | The AVERAGE() function, when used on a list of numerical elements, will compute the average value of the elements in that list. |
| Expression | AVERAGE(Items[ITEM_PRICE]) will result in an arithmetic average value of a list of prices of all items in the Items table. |
| Points to note | You can use AVERAGE() function with numerical columns such as price, number, decimals etc. |

Table 4.27 – The AVERAGE() function

AppSheet has more math functions, such as ABS(), for finding arithmetic absolute values, and the LOG(), LOG2(), and LOG10() functions, for finding logarithms of numeric values with different base values. We have discussed the most often used math functions, which should give you a good understanding of how you can use other math functions. Let us cover the all-important date and time functions next, which allow us to perform date, time, and duration math.

# Performing date, time, and duration calculations with date and time expressions

Almost every app needs the date and time functions in some form or the other. Scheduling apps, project management apps, time-keeping apps, and attendance apps need date and time functions. In this section, you will learn how you can use date and time functions in AppSheet to compute dates, times, and durations in your apps.

Date and time math is more complex than metric or decimal system math because the relationship between various date and time parameters is very uneven. On the other hand, as we are aware, a metric system is even – that is, the units of measurement are always in multiples of 10. The following table shows how each date and time unit of measurement has a different multiplier to calculate the next unit of measurement:

| Unit of Measurement | 1 Minute | 1 Hour | 1 Day | 1 Week | 1 Month | 1 Year |
|---|---|---|---|---|---|---|
| Equals | 60 seconds | 60 minutes | 24 hours | 7 days | 28, 29, 30, or 31 days | 12 months  365 or 366 days |

Table 4.28 – Date and time parameters

As a result of this uneven relationship between various time and date units of measurement, performing date and time math in an app can be somewhat challenging. Let us start by understanding some basic date and time functions:

| Function | Expression | Typical Value | Result |
|---|---|---|---|
| NOW() | NOW() | 08/09/2022 12:34:37 | Captures the current date and timestamp when the column is saved |
| TIMENOW() | TIMENOW() | 12:34:37 | Captures the current timestamp when the column is saved |
| TODAY() | TODAY() | 08/18/2022 | Captures the date when the column was saved |

Table 4.29 – Functions to capture the datetime, time, or date

If you want to capture any of the three functions in the preceding table in your app, it is a good practice to use NOW() because by using this function, you can get both the TODAY() and TIMENOW() components.

If you want to capture when the app users updated or added a record, you can insert any of the three functions depending on your need. To capture the timestamp when the record was added, insert any of TODAY(), NOW(), or TIMENOW() in the initial value of a column. To capture the timestamp when the record was updated, insert any of TODAY(), NOW(), or TIMENOW() in the app formula setting of a column.

## Extracting components of a datetime value

We will now learn how we can extract individual components, such as day, month, year, hours, minutes, and seconds, from a datetime-, date-, or time-type column. We will take a sample datetime value of `08/17/2022 12:34:37` and see how we can extract individual date and time components from it. Let us assume the datetime-type column name is `[DATETIME_IN]`. The following table shows how you can extract the year, month, or day from a date or datetime column:

| Function | Expression | Result |
|---|---|---|
| `YEAR()` | `YEAR([DATETIME_IN])` | 2022 |
| `MONTH()` | `MONTH([DATETIME_IN])` | 8 |
| `DAY()` | `DAY([DATETIME_IN])` | 17 |

Table 4.30 – Functions to extract the year, month, or day from a date or datetime value

When extracting time components from a datetime- or time-type column, you need to ensure a few points. If the column type is datetime, you need to type-cast it into a time-type column by wrapping the column with the `TIME()` function. Secondly, the functions for time components actually return a duration value, so, first, you need to convert any time value into a duration by subtracting a time of `00:00:00` from the time value. We will consider a datetime value of `08/17/2022 12:34:37` from which to extract the time components by using the relevant functions, as the following table shows:

| Function | Expression | Result |
|---|---|---|
| `HOUR()` | `HOUR(TIME([DATETIME_IN]) - "00:00:00")` | 12 |
| `MINUTE()` | `MINUTE(TIME([DATETIME_IN]) - "00:00:00")` | 34 |
| `SECOND()` | `SECOND(TIME([DATETIME_IN]) - "00:00:00")` | 37 |

Table 4.31 – Functions to extract hours, minutes, or seconds from the date or datetime

Having understood how to extract various date and time components from a date, time, or datetime value, we will learn how we can compute various date and time durations next.

## Performing duration calculations

An important requirement in apps using date and time functions is to calculate the duration of an event. The duration is the day or time difference between two different datetime values. Let us understand duration calculations with the help of some examples.

Some day-to-day life examples of duration include the number of hours worked in a day based on the end time and start time, the number of days to carry out a task based on the end date and the start date, and the number of days until a milestone event based on the current date.

Let us learn how to compute the number of days between an end date and a start date:

| Use case | Number of days between an end date and a start date. |
|---|---|
| Column types | [END_DATE] and [START_DATE] are date-type columns.<br><br>[END_DATE] has a value of 07/15/2022 and [START_DATE] has a value of 03/19/2022. |
| Expression | The HOUR([END_DATE] - [START_DATE])/24 expression will give a result of 118 days.<br><br>In AppSheet, the [END_DATE] - [START_DATE] expression gives the duration in the number of hours between the two dates at the instance of midnight (12:00 AM or 00:00 hours) of both dates. The hours are given in the hh:00:00 format. Thus, [END_DATE] - [START_DATE] results in a value of 2832:00:00 hours.<br><br>Thus, to compute the number of days, the expression needs to first extract only the hours from the hh:00:00 format. We get the hours by wrapping the date subtraction with the HOUR() function as HOUR([END_DATE] - [START_DATE]). This results in an hour value of 2832.<br><br>The previous step has obtained the duration in hours. To get the number of days, the expression divides the number of hours by 24: HOUR([END_DATE] - [START_DATE])/24. We then get a result of 118 days between the two dates. |
| Points to note | Both the [START_DATE] and [END_DATE] columns need to have an identical date format, such as either dd/mm/yyyy or mm/dd/yyyy. |

Table 4.32 – Duration between two dates using the HOUR() function

Let us now understand duration calculations involving time:

| Use case | Number of hours between [TIME_OUT] and [TIME_IN]. |
|---|---|
| Column types | [TIME_OUT] and [TIME_IN] are either both time-type columns or both datetime-type columns.<br><br>[TIME_OUT] has a value of 17:35:00 and [TIME_IN] has a value of 09:30:00. |
| Expression | [TIME_OUT] - [TIME_IN] will result in a duration value of 08:05:00.<br><br>Alternatively, [TIME_OUT] - "08:00:00" will result in a duration value of 09:35:00.<br><br>In this expression, 08:00:00 is a fixed time of 8 hours. |
| Points to note | The result of subtraction between any two time or two date or two datetime column type values is always a duration value.<br><br>You can use the duration expressions based on time-type columns only if both the time values are on the same calendar day.<br><br>If the two time values in the expression are on different calendar days, use datetime-type columns for time calculations. |

Table 4.33 – Duration between two time values

Let us learn how we can subtract durations of time or days from a time or date value next to get the resulting time and date values:

| Use case | Subtract a duration of 4 hours from the time value. |
|---|---|
| Column types | [TIME_OUT] is a time-type column with a value of 17:35:00. |
| Expression | The [TIME_OUT] - "004:00:00" expression will result in a time value of 1:35:00 P.M. or 13:35:00. |
| Points to note | In AppSheet, a time duration value is always denoted with an extra 0 at the beginning. So, if you need to subtract a duration of 10 hours and 30 minutes, you need to write 010:30:00, unlike the time value. For a time value of 10:30 A.M., you need to write 10:30:00.<br><br>When you subtract or add a duration from/to a time value, you always get the result of another time value. |
| Use case | Subtract a duration of 35 days from a [DATE] column. |
| Column types | The [DATE] column is of the date or datetime type. The [DATE] column has a value of 09/21/2020. |
| Expression | The [DATE] - 35 expression results in a date of 8/17/2020. |
| Points to note | When you subtract an integer number from a date or datetime value, as in the preceding example, you are basically subtracting a duration, 35 days in this case, so the result is always another date. |

Table 4.34 – Finding the time or date by adding or subtracting the duration to time or date values

We have now learned how to perform date and time duration calculations. Let us next understand the week-based functions in AppSheet.

## Understanding week-based calculation functions

We often need to make week-based calculations in real life, such as calculating weekly wages or working out the duration of a task starting on a certain week number and ending on a certain week number of the year. AppSheet has a rich repository of weekly calculation functions. The following table lists some week-based functions in AppSheet:

| Function | Return Value | Examples |
|---|---|---|
| WEEKDAY() | A number from 1 to 7 (1 for Sunday and 7 for Saturday) | WEEKDAY("11/20/2022") will result in 1 because 20th November 2022 is a Sunday. |
| WEEKNUM() ISOWEEKNUM() | The week number of the year the date falls in<br><br>The ISO week number (https://en.wikipedia.org/wiki/ISO_8601) of the year the date falls in. | WEEKNUM("11/20/2022") will result in 48, which is the week number for the date 20th November 2022 in the year 2022.<br><br>ISOWEEKNUM("11/20/2022") will result in 46, which is the ISO week number for the date 20th November 2022 in the year 2022. |
| EOWEEK() | The date of the Saturday of the week in which [Date] falls | EOWEEK(("11/20/2022") will result in "11/26/2022", which is the date of Saturday in the week of "11/20/2022". |

Table 4.35 – Week-based functions in AppSheet

Let us see a few expressions that perform week calculations using the functions mentioned in the preceding table:

| Use case | Find the number of weeks between two dates. |
|---|---|
| Column Types | [START_DATE] and [END_DATE] are date-type columns.<br><br>[START_DATE] has a value of 04/22/2022 and [END_DATE] has a value of 08/15/2022. |
| Expression | The WEEKNUM([END_DATE]) – WEEKNUM([START_DATE]) expression results in an integer value of 17. WEEKNUM([END_DATE]) gives a result of 34 and WEEKNUM([END_DATE]) gives a result of 17. The subtraction of these two numbers results in 17.<br><br>Alternatively, ISOWEEKNUM([END_DATE]) – ISOWEEKNUM([START_DATE]) results in an integer value of 17. ISOWEEKNUM([END_DATE]) gives a result of 33 and ISOWEEKNUM([END_DATE]) gives a result of 16. The subtraction of these two numbers results in 17. |
| Points to note | The result of WEEKNUM() is an integer. So, while performing addition or subtraction using WEEKNUM(), the week numbers are rounded to the nearest integer value.<br><br>Also, WEEKNUM() calculations should be performed on two dates in the same calendar year. This is because every new calendar year, WEEKNUM() restarts from 1, so performing WEEKNUM() calculations across multiple calendar years could be erroneous. |

Table 4.36 – Using the WEEKNUM() function

Let us learn how to use the WEEKDAY() function next:

| Use case | Find the number of orders delivered on a Thursday during the entire year of 2021 from the Orders table. |
|---|---|
| Column types | [ORDER_DATE] is a date-type column. |
| Expression | Slice filter expression in the Orders table:<br><br>AND(WEEKDAY([ORDER_DATE])=5, [ORDER_STATUS]="Delivered", YEAR([Order Date])=2021)<br><br>This slice filter expression in the Orders table with return all the orders delivered in 2021 on Thursdays as explained herein:<br><br>WEEKDAY([ORDER_DATE])=5 checks whether the order date falls on a Thursday<br><br>• YEAR[ORDER_DATE] =2021 checks whether the order date falls in the year 2021<br><br>• [ORDER_STATUS]="Delivered" checks that the order has the Delivered status |
| Points to note | The WEEKDAY() function returns an integer for each day of the week. If the date falls on a Sunday, it returns 1, it returns 7 for a date falling on Saturday, and numbers in between for dates falling on other weekdays. |

Table 4.37 – Using the WEEKDAY() function

Let us now understand how we can use the EOWEEK() function, which gives the date of the weekend (Saturday) of the week in which the date supplied as an argument to the function falls:

| Use case | From the list of yearly holidays in the `Holidays` table, get the rows of holidays that fall on weekend days (Saturday and Sunday). |
|---|---|
| Column types | `[HOLIDAY_DATE]` is of the date type. |
| Expression | Slice the filter expression in the `Holidays` table:<br><br>`OR ( EOWEEK([HOLIDAY_DATE])=[HOLIDAY_DATE],`<br><br>`WEEKDAY([HOLIDAY_DATE])=1 )`<br><br>The slice filter expression in the `Holidays` table will result in all the dates when the holiday falls on weekend days, that is, Saturday and Sunday.<br><br>The expression parts evaluate as follows:<br><br>`EOWEEK([Holiday_Date])` results in a Saturday. So, the `EOWEEK([Holiday_Date])=[Holiday_Date]` part checks whether `[Holiday_Date]` falls on the Saturday of the `[Holiday_Date]` week.<br><br>`WEEKDAY([HOLIDAY_DATE])=1` checks if the `[HOLIDAY_DATE]` falls on a Sunday.. |
| Points to note | `EOWEEK()` always gives the date of the Saturday in that week, so when you input any date falling in the same week from Sunday to Saturday, it will return the date of the Saturday in that week. As an example, in the week of 09/18/2022, the dates of the week are 09/18/2022 (Sunday) to 09/24/2022 (Saturday). If you give these dates as input to the `EOWEEK()` function, it will always return the date of `09/24/2022` because that is the end-of-week date for the week that begins on 09/18/2022. |

Table 4.38 – Using the EOWEEK() function

Now that we understand the week-based functions, let us learn how we can use certain AppSheet duration functions that return results in decimal values.

## Calculating duration in decimal value results

There are three duration functions, as listed in the following table, that give results in decimal values when you use them to find the duration between two time values:

| Function | What it does |
|---|---|
| `TOTALHOURS()` | Calculates the duration in terms of hours in decimal values between two time values |
| `TOTALMINUTES()` | Calculates the duration in terms of minutes in decimal values between two time values |
| `TOTALSECONDS()` | Calculates the duration in terms of seconds between two time values |

Table 4.39 – Using duration functions for decimal durations

Let us understand a few expressions that use the three functions described in the preceding table. We will start with the TOTALHOURS() function:

| Use case | Find the number of hours between two time values. |
|---|---|
| Column types | [START_TIME] and [END_TIME] are datetime-type columns. |
| Expression | TOTALHOURS([END_TIME] - [START_TIME]) |
| Test case | TOTALHOURS( "08/12/2022 10:30:00" - "06/21/2021 14:45:00") |
| Result | 10003.75<br><br>As you can see, the preceding result is in decimal form, in hours. The duration is 10003:45, or 10,003 hours and 45 minutes. |
| Points to note | The TOTALHOURS() function always gives results of durations in decimal form, so you can do addition or subtraction on two durations in decimal form to get the resulting duration.<br><br>The fractional part of the duration derived from TOTALHOURS() is basically the duration component in minutes. You can get this duration part in minutes by multiplying the fractional part by 60. |

Table 4.40 – Using the TOTALHOURS() function for decimal durations

Let us understand the TOTALMINUTES() function next, which calculates the duration between two values in terms of minutes in decimal form:

| Use case | Find the number of minutes between two time values. |
|---|---|
| Column types | [START_TIME] and [END_TIME] are datetime-type columns. |
| Expression | TOTALMINUTES([END_TIME] - [START_TIME]) |
| Test case | TOTALMINUTES( "08/12/2022 10:30:45" - "06/21/2021 14:45:15") |
| Result | 600225.5<br><br>As you can see, the preceding result is in decimal form, in minutes. The duration is 600225:30, or 60,022 minutes and 30 seconds. |
| Points to note | The TOTALMINUTES() function always gives results of durations in decimal form, so you can do addition or subtraction on two durations in decimal form to get the resulting duration.<br><br>The fractional part of the duration derived from TOTALMINUTES() is basically the duration component in seconds. You can get the value of this duration in seconds by multiplying the fractional part by 60. |

Table 4.41 – Using the TOTALMINUTES() function for decimal durations

Let us understand the `TOTALSECONDS()` function next, which calculates the duration between two time values in seconds:

| Use case | Find the number of seconds between two different time values. |
|---|---|
| Column types | [START_TIME] and [END_TIME] are datetime-type columns. |
| Expression | TOTALSECONDS([END_TIME] - [START_TIME]) |
| Test case | TOTALSECONDS( "08/12/2022 10:30:45" - "06/21/2021 14:45:15") |
| Result | 36,013,530 |
| Points to note | Since AppSheet does not have provisions for calculating fractions of seconds, the result of the TOTALSECONDS() function is always in terms of an integer number. |

Table 4.42 – Using the TOTALSECONDS() function for durations

You have now learned about all the major date, time, and duration functions in AppSheet. Let us now learn about the table functions that help you to perform operations at the record level in an app.

## Performing record-level operations with table functions and expressions

Many table functions and associated expressions lead to row-level results instead of column-level results. When we say row level, it means these functions return key values of the rows. You can then access a record of a table with that record's key value when the column type is referenced. Let us look at the most used table functions that work at the record level. We will also learn about a few table functions that work at the column level:

| Use case | Find the record with the highest item price in the Items table. |
|---|---|
| | Find the record with the lowest price in the Items table. |
| Column types | [ITEM_PRICE] in the Items table. |
| Function used | MAXROW() will get the key value or the reference of the row with the highest item price in the table. |
| | MINROW() will get the key value or the reference of the row with the lowest item price in the table. |
| Expression | The MAXROW("Items" , "ITEM_PRICE") expression will return the key of the record with the highest price in the Items table. |
| | The MINROW("Items" , "ITEM_PRICE") expression will return the key of the record with the lowest price in the Items table. |
| | You can use more conditions in the MAXROW() and MINROW() functions. The MAXROW("Items", "ITEM_PRICE", [ITEM_CATEGORY]=[_THISROW]. [ITEM_CATEGORY]) expression will return the keys of the records for the items with the highest prices in each of the item categories, so if there are seven different item categories, and item records are available for all seven categories in the Items table, then the expression will return seven records with the highest price, one each in each of those seven categories. |
| Points to note | You can conveniently use the MAXROW() and MINROW() functions in the slice filter expressions when you wish to filter the records with the highest or lowest value of certain columns. As we demonstrated with the item categories example, you can apply more conditions to the MAXROW() or MINROW() functions so that these functions return the maximum or minimum values based on those additional conditions. |
| | You need to use numerical columns, such as number, price, decimal, date, datetime, or time, to find the keys of the records with the maximum or minimum values using these functions. |

Table 4.43 – Using the MAXROW() and MINROW() functions

Let us learn about the ORDERBY() function next, which sorts the records of a table in ascending or descending order:

| Use case | Sort the records of the Items table by name of the items in ascending order (A to Z). |
| --- | --- |
| | Sort the records of the Items table by the item price starting from the highest item price to the lowest item price. |
| Column types | [ITEM_PRICE] is of the price type and [ITEM_NAME] is of the text type in the Items table. [ITEM_ID] is a text-type column and is the key of the Items table generated with the UNIQUEID() function. |
| Expression | We use the ORDERBY() function to sort the keys of the Items table by the item name. The ORDERBY(Items[ITEM_ID], [ITEM_NAME], FALSE) expression will sort the Items table's records in ascending order, starting with the item names beginning with A and ending with item names beginning with Z. The ORDERBY(Items[ITEM_ID], [ITEM_NAME], TRUE) expression will sort the Items table's records in descending order starting with item names beginning with Z and ending with item names beginning with A. |
| | The ORDERBY(Items[ITEM_ID], [ITEM_PRICE], TRUE) expression will sort the Items table's records in descending order, starting with items with the highest price and ending with items with the lowest price. |
| Points to note | The ORDERBY() function sorts the records of the table in ascending or descending order based on any column in the table you mention in the function. |
| | You can use text columns such as name or text type to sort the records. In the case of text-type columns, ORDERBY() sorts the records alphabetically in ascending order (A to Z) when you use the FALSE option or descending order (Z to A) when you use the TRUE option. |
| | You can use numerical columns of the number, decimal, date, datetime, or time type to sort the records. In the case of numerical columns, ORDERBY() sorts the records in ascending order (from the lowest value to the highest) when you use the FALSE option or descending order (from the highest value to the lowest) when you use the TRUE function. |

Table 4.44 – Using the ORDERBY() function to sort a table or slice records

Having understood the main row-level functions, let us next understand the important differences between column-level and row-level functions of a similar nature with the help of some examples.

## Understanding the difference between column- and row-level functions

We will evaluate some column-level as well as row-level functions to learn how we can appropriately use these functions in our apps depending on our requirements:

| Column-level functions | Result |
| --- | --- |
| MIN() | Finds the minimum value in the list of values of a numerical column in a slice or table |
| MAX() | Finds the maximum value in the list of values of a numerical column in a slice or table |
| SORT() | Sorts of values of a text or numerical column's list in a slice or table in ascending or descending order |
| SELECT() | Selects a list of certain values as per the conditions in the expression from the entire list of values of a text or numerical column in a slice or table |

Table 4.45 – Using column-level functions

Next, we will evaluate corresponding row-level functions:

| Row-level functions | Result |
| --- | --- |
| MINROW() | Finds the record from a slice or table with the minimum value of a numerical column mentioned in the function |
| MAXROW() | Finds the record from a slice or table with the maximum value of a numerical column mentioned in the function |
| ORDERBY() | Sorts records from a slice or table in ascending or descending order for a text or numerical column |
| FILTER() | Selects or filters a list of certain records of a slice or table as per certain criteria |

Table 4.46 – Using row-level functions

Let us now learn how these column-level and row-level functions work with the help of a few practical examples from the sample app.

The following screenshot shows an Items table. Note the [ITEM_ID] (the key column in the table), [ITEM_PRICE], and [ITEM_QUANTITY] columns:

**Items**

| ITEM_NAME ↑ | ITEM_ID | ITEM_PRICE | ITEM_QUANTITY | MAX_PRICE_ITEM | MIN_PRICE_ITEM |
| --- | --- | --- | --- | --- | --- |
| Chair - Wooden | 0BB1E451 | $201.00 | 50 | $760.00 | $55.00 |
| Computer Desk | DBA69A6A | $240.00 | 60 | $760.00 | $55.00 |
| Desk - Wooden | D5729520 | $325.00 | 45 | $760.00 | $55.00 |
| Dining Chairs | 395AD3F7 | $375.00 | 55 | $760.00 | $55.00 |
| Dining Table | F5172952 | $550.00 | 80 | $760.00 | $55.00 |
| File Cabinet | 1ADC5DCG | $175.00 | 45 | $760.00 | $55.00 |
| Lamp Shade | DBF97CA4 | $55.00 | 38 | $760.00 | $55.00 |
| Lounge Chair | E69D94D4 | $155.00 | 97 | $760.00 | $55.00 |
| Shoe Rack | 4EC688E5 | $135.00 | 55 | $760.00 | $55.00 |
| Sofa Set | E5729520 | $760.00 | 70 | $760.00 | $55.00 |
| Stand - Wooden | E5172952F | $175.00 | 35 | $760.00 | $55.00 |
| Storage Cabinet | DEB58EA3 | $178.00 | 65 | $760.00 | $55.00 |
| Table - Wooden | DBF97CA4 | $225.00 | 75 | $760.00 | $55.00 |
| TV Stand | E01D7763 | $300.00 | 38 | $760.00 | $55.00 |

Figure 4.7 – Understanding the difference between column- and row-level functions

When you configure column-level expressions based on column-level functions such as MAX (),
MIN (), SELEC (), and SORT (), the functions work on the list values from the column mentioned
in the function. These functions then return a single value or multiple values from that list of a single
column's values.

The following screenshot shows the maximum and minimum prices in the Items table computed by
the MAX () and MIN () functions applied to the [ITEM_PRICE] column's list of values. As you can
see, each row's detail view shows the maximum and minimum prices. The table view in the following
figure also shows the maximum and minimum price columns.

## Details

ITEM_NAME

Chair - Wooden

ITEM_ID

0BB1E451

ITEM_PRICE

$201.00

ITEM_QUANTITY

50

MAX_PRICE_ITEM

$760.00

MIN_PRICE_ITEM

$55.00

Figure 4.8 – Values computed by column-level functions

The expressions we used for the minimum price and maximum price are MIN (Items[ITEM_ PRICE]) and MAX(Items[ITEM_PRICE]), respectively. Here, as we have learned before, the Items[ITEM_PRICE] expression creates a list of all the values of the [ITEM_PRICE] column, and then the MIN() and MAX() functions find the minimum and maximum item prices in that list. As we can see, the MIN() and MAX() columns return the value from the single column.

Similarly, SELECT() and SORT() create lists from the single column.

Now, let us understand row-level expressions. The main point to understand about row-level expressions is that they create a list of key values of the table. Whenever you have a list of key values with the column's element type as a reference, you get a reference to entire rows from those key values – so row-level expressions return an entire row or multiple rows depending on the function and the condition used in that function compared to only a single value or a list of values of a single column in the case of column-level functions and expressions.

The following figure shows that the MAXROW() and MINROW() expressions, when used as slice expressions, have returned an entire row as a result. We have used those expressions to get the rows with the maximum and maximum [ITEM_QUANTITY] values:

**Min Quantity Record**

| ITEM_NAME | ITEM_ID | ITEM_PRICE | ITEM_QUANTITY | MAX_PRICE_ITEM | MIN_PRICE_ITEM |
|---|---|---|---|---|---|
| Stand - Wooden | E5172952F | $175.00 | 35 | $760.00 | $55.00 |

**Max Quantity Record**

| ITEM_NAME | ITEM_ID | ITEM_PRICE | ITEM_QUANTITY | MAX_PRICE_ITEM | MIN_PRICE_ITEM |
|---|---|---|---|---|---|
| Lounge Chair | E69D94D4 | $155.00 | 97 | $760.00 | $55.00 |

Figure 4.9 – Values computed by row-level functions

The slice expression we have used for the row with the maximum `[ITEM_QUANTITY]` value is `[ID]=MAXROW("Items", "ITEM_QUANTITY")` and we get the row with the minimum quantity with the `[ID]=MINROW("Items", "ITEM_QUANTITY")` expression. As we can see, these expressions return a reference to an entire row.

Similarly, `FILTER()` and `ORDERBY()` create lists of key columns with the element type as the reference, thereby returning a reference to entire rows.

# Understanding important miscellaneous functions

Let us now understand a few miscellaneous functions that are very useful in our app configuration. We will learn about three functions, `USERSETTINGS()`, `CONTEXT()`, and `TEXT()`, in this section.

## Using functions related to the app user

As you will learn in *Chapter 6*, AppSheet per-user apps or secure apps need you to add the email IDs of the users to the app from the app editor to enable them to access the app. You will learn in detail how to add a user with the user's email address in *Chapter 6*. *Chapter 6* also explains the `USEREMAIL()` and `USERROLE()` functions and their use in apps, so we will just learn about the `USERSETTINGS()` function in this chapter.

When you distribute an app to your users, there are situations where each user would want the app to show them only certain data, at least for a certain time period. Let us look at some possible scenarios.

In an inventory management app, the manager has assigned the inventory management of large category items to supervisor *A* and small category items inventory management to supervisor *B* for the entire upcoming week. In this situation, supervisor *A* would only like to see large category items in their app for the next week and supervisor *B* would only like to see small category items in their app. They can do so using the USERSETTINGS() option, wherein they can select the respective item category to filter the Items table views as per their respective needs.

In another sales management app, the senior manager asks one of their sales managers to concentrate on closing the deals that were started in the previous or second quarter, *Q2*, so the sales manager now only wants to browse the sales deals created in the previous quarter. They can do so using the USERSETTINGS() option in the app, wherein they have the *Q1*, *Q2*, *Q3*, and *Q4* options for each of the quarters in a year and can select *Q2* to only see the deals created in the previous quarter.

Thus, the USERSETTINGS() option allows you to configure the app in such a way that users can select certain choices that allow them to filter views, records, or similar options in the app for a certain time period until they want to reset or change those settings. The user settings remain persistent on mobile devices until the user changes them. In the app editor, though, the user settings change with each sync of the app.

You can configure the user settings with the **Data | User Settings** option in the app editor, as shown in the following screenshot:

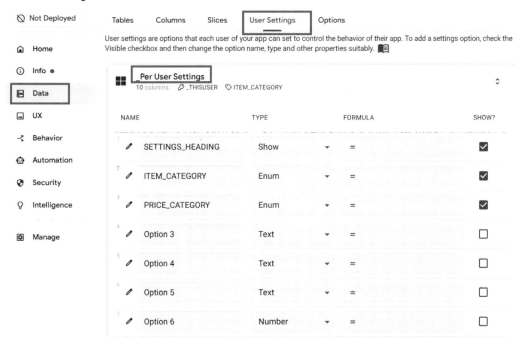

Figure 4.10 – User Settings option in the app editor

As shown in the preceding screenshot, there are 10 user settings columns available for configuration in an app, so you can configure a maximum of 10 user settings for an app user to set in an app. The columns here are like normal columns in tables. You can set almost all types of columns in the user settings, such as text, enum, enumlist, email, number, and decimal. However, as the user settings give options to users to set their preferences, you are most likely to use enum or enumlist column types.

When you configure the user settings, they appear in the menu views for the user, as in *Figure A* on the left-hand side of the following figure. As *Figure B* shows, the actual user settings pane looks like any other form in the app. When the user saves these user settings by clicking on the **Save** button, a full sync of the app takes place.

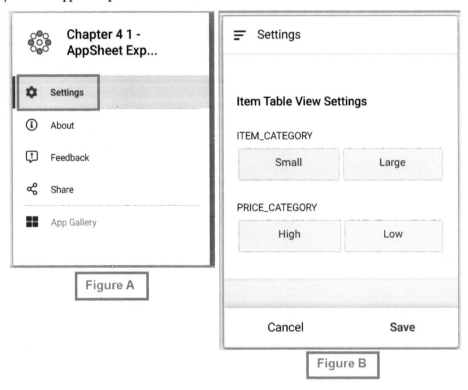

Figure 4.11 – User settings option in menu and user settings form

Next, let us learn how we can configure user settings in various app expressions with the help of the sample app for this chapter.

The columns from a normal table in an app are referred to as `Table Name[Column Name]` for the entire list of that column. If you wish to refer to any specific row's value, then you can use `ANY(Table Name[Column Name])`. You can consider the user settings as a single-row table for each user, with each user having a different single row of the user settings.

A column from **User Settings** is referred to in expressions as USERSETTINGS(COLUMN_NAME). Note that the user settings column names are written as (COLUMN_NAME), using round brackets, compared to [COLUMN_NAME] with square brackets in the case of normal tables. Unlike ANY(Table Name[COLUMN_NAME]), which denotes a single value from a list by using the ANY() function in the case of normal table columns, since there is only one row in a user settings "table," the user settings-based expression does not require the ANY() function. Note that the user settings values are also stored internally in the app definition and are not stored in a data source the way values from other tables used in an app are stored.

As the preceding screenshot shows, the **User Settings** form has two columns for the user to fill in: [ITEM_CATEGORY] and [PRICE_CATEGOTY]. Both columns are of the enum type. The [ITEM_CATEGORY] column has **Small** and **Large** as two enum options. [PRICE_CATEGORY] has **High** and **Low** as two enum options.

There are two slices in the sample app:

- The Item Category slice has a filter expression of USERSETTINGS(ITEM_CATEGORY)=[ITEM_CATEGORY]

- The Price Category slice has a filter expression of USERSETTINGS(PRICE_CATEGORY)=[PRICE_CATEGORY]

When you select any of these user settings, the views, **Items Category** and **Price Category**, accordingly, show the filtered records from the respective slices.

Let us learn about the CONTEXT() functions next, which tell us the context of certain app elements the app user is currently using.

## Using the CONTEXT() functions

As the name suggests, the CONTEXT() functions return the context of certain app elements that the app user is currently using. The app elements returned by CONTEXT() functions are view names, view types, device types, the app name, the table name, and the UUID of the user's device. Let us discuss various CONTEXT() functions with examples.

CONTEXT("View") = "Items" returns TRUE if the app user is currently viewing the "Items" view. When the app user is browsing any other view than the view name in the expression (Items, in this case), it returns FALSE.

CONTEXT("ViewType") = "Detail" returns TRUE if the app user is currently browsing a detail view. You can configure other view types, such as Table, Deck, Gallery, or Dashboard, in the CONTEXT("ViewType") function. If the user is browsing any other view type than the view type mentioned in the expression (Detail, in this case), the expression returns FALSE.

You can also use the CONTEXT () function to get the context of the app name, the table name of the view that the user is browsing, and the UUID of the device that the user is using. However, you will mostly use CONTEXT ("View") and CONTEXT ("ViewType"), so we will only discuss those two options with examples.

Let us now learn how we can use the CONTEXT ("View") and CONTEXT ("ViewType") functions:

| Use case | There is a column called [ITEM_PRICE]. You would want to give a more meaningful heading to the column in the form view when the user is entering the price details and a short name in the detail and table view because the user only browses the data in detail and table views in this case. |
| --- | --- |
| Column types | [ITEM_PRICE] is of the price type. |
| Expression | In the display name property of the column settings, the IF(CONTEXT("ViewType")="Form", "Enter the price in dollars and cents" , "ITEM_PRICE") expression will display a long column heading when the user is browsing the form view and a short column heading when the user is browsing the record in other views.

Assuming the form name is Items_Form, you could alternatively write the preceding expression as IF(CONTEXT("View")="Items_Form", "Enter the price in dollars and cents" , "ITEM_PRICE"). |
| Points to note | In the case of CONTEXT ("View"), the expression is only applicable to the view named in the expression. On the other hand, in the case of CONTEXT ("ViewType") expressions, the expression evaluates all the views in the app that are of the type mentioned in the expression. |

Table 4.47 – Using the CONTEXT("View") and CONTEXT("ViewType") functions

We will learn about the TEXT () function next, which allows us to change the format of date and time values.

## Using the TEXT() function

There are various display formats for dates and times. In an app, you would want to display dates and times in different formats depending on your needs. The TEXT () function allows you to transform the dates and times very conveniently from one format into another. Let us understand the TEXT () function with a few examples:

| Use case | Convert a date field that captures and displays dates in a 12/25/2022 format to display dates in a 25 December 2022 format. |
|---|---|
| | Convert a date field from a 12/25/2022 format to just display the month and two-digit year in the Dec 22 format. |
| | Convert a date field from a 12/25/2022 format to just display the month as well as the year in a two-digit format, such as 12/22. |
| Column types | [DATE] is of the date type. |
| | [DATE_CONVERTED] is a text-type column. |
| | The [Date] column contains the 12/25/2022 date in one record. |
| Expression | The TEXT([DATE], "DD MMMM YYYY") expression will return a value of 25 December 2022. |
| | The TEXT([DATE], "MMM YY") expression will return a value of Dec 22. |
| | The TEXT([DATE], "MM/YY") expression will return a value of 12/22. |
| Points to note | The TEXT() function returns values in the form of a text-type column, so even though you convert a date or time into another format, the output type of a TEXT() function is a text-type column and not a date, time, or datetime column. |
| | A TEXT() expression is a very powerful expression to convert dates and times from one format into another: |
| | You can convert a time format from A.M./P.M. into the 24-hour format and vice versa. A date formatted as dd/mm/yyyy being converted to yyyy/mm/dd or mm/dd/yyyy format is another example. |
| | You can have multiple combinations of date and time formats using the TEXT() function. |

Table 4.48 – Using the TEXT() function

Having understood the main AppSheet functions, next, let us learn how we can combine multiple functions in a single expression to perform more complex calculations and text or data manipulations in our apps.

# Using multiple functions in single expressions

So far, we have mostly concentrated on understanding various AppSheet functions. Most of the expressions we have used have mainly been based on single functions. You can combine various functions in a single expression to come up with more complex logic requirements in your apps.

We will learn about complex expressions based on some use cases and associated expressions to see how we can combine multiple functions in a single expression:

| Use case | In a list of items, find out whether an item's price is above or below the average of all items. |
|---|---|
| Column types | `[ITEM_PRICE]` is a price-type column in the `Items` table.<br><br>`[PRICE_CATEGORY]` a column of the text type. |
| Expression and explanation | The `IF( AVERAGE(Items[ITEM_PRICE])<[ITEM_PRICE], "Above Average Price", "Below Average Price")` expression in the `[PRICE_CATEGORY]` column will categorize items as above or below the average price.<br><br>The expression evaluates as follows:<br><br>The expression uses two functions, namely `AVERAGE()` and `IF()`.<br><br>The inner function is solved first and then the outer function. The `Items[ITEM_PRICE]` expression creates a list of the prices of all the items in the `Items` table.<br><br>The `AVERAGE(Items[ITEM_PRICE])` expression finds the average price from the list of all the item prices.<br><br>Finally, the `IF( AVERAGE(Items[ITEM_PRICE])<[ITEM_PRICE], "Above Average Price", "Below Average Price")` expression uses the `IF()` function to categorize an item as `Below Average Price` or `Above Average Price`. |

Table 4.49 – Using multiple functions in complex expressions – 1

Let us learn another expression that combines three functions of `IN()`, `TOP()`, and `ORDERBY()` in a slice filter expression to filter rows based on certain criteria:

| Use case | From an `Items` table, create a table view of the five items with the least quantities by creating a slice and basing the view on that slice. |
|---|---|
| Column types | `[ITEM_QUANTITY]` is a number-type column in the `Items` table. `[ITEM_ID]` is a text-type key column, initialized with `UNIQUEID()`. |
| Expression | `IN([ITEM_ID], TOP(ORDERBY(Items[ITEM_ID], [ITEM_QUANTITY], FALSE),5) )` |
| Points to note | The expression uses three functions, namely `ORDERBY()`, `TOP()`, and `IN()`. |
| | The inner function is evaluated first and then the outer functions are. The `Items[ITEM_ID]` expression creates a list of the keys of all the items in the `Items` table. |
| | The `ORDERBY(Items[ITEM_ID], [ITEM_QUANTITY], FALSE)` expression sorts the list of the `Items` table records in ascending order by `[ITEM_QUANTITY]`. Note that the `ORDERBY()` function sorts the table record keys by another column in that record. `SORT()` merely sorts any column of the table. |
| | `TOP(ORDERBY(Items[ITEM_ID], [ITEM_QUANTITY], FALSE),5)` gets a list of the first five `Items` table records in the sorted list. Since the sorted records list is in ascending order, the first five `Items` records of the list are the items with the lowest quantities. |
| | Finally, the slice filter expression that uses the `IN()` function, as `IN([ITEM_ID], TOP(ORDERBY(Items[ITEM_ID], [ITEM_QUANTITY], FALSE),5))`, checks whether a table record key is in the list of the five lowest-quantity records. |
| | Note that we could have also used a slice filter expression of `IN( [ITEM_QUANTITY], TOP(SORT(Items[ITEM_QUANITY], FALSE),5) )` to get the five least-stocked items. Often, you can use more than one function and expression to achieve the same result. As a rule of thumb, you should prefer to use an expression with the least number of functions. |

Table 4.50 – Using multiple functions in complex expressions – 2

You can configure much more complex expressions involving multiple functions in your app. However, it is always a better approach to configure your expressions to be as simple as possible, without compromising the business function logic of your apps. We have now fully supplemented our knowledge of AppSheet functions in this chapter, so let us summarize what we have learned in this chapter.

# Summary

In this chapter, you were introduced to AppSheet functions. You learned about what functions are and how you can build expressions using various AppSheet functions. We discussed around 51 functions with associated examples.

You were introduced to the different types of functions, including `Yes/No` functions, conditional functions, list functions, math functions, and time and date functions. With each of these function types, you learned how to construct expressions using these functions with the help of practical use cases.

While learning about these functions and expressions, you were also given important points to note about those functions.

You learned the difference between column-level functions, such as `SELECT()`, `SORT()`, `MIN()`, and `MAX()`, and associated row-level functions, such as `FILTER()`, `ORDERBY()`, `MINROW()`, and `MAXROW()`.

You learned about miscellaneous functions, such as `USERSETTINGS()` and `CONTEXT()`. We discussed in detail what user settings are, how to configure them, and how app users can use them in their apps, with practical examples.

Finally, you also learned about creating more complex expressions using multiple functions in the same expression.

In the next chapter, we will learn how we can manipulate app data with actions and app behaviors.

# 5

# Manipulating Data with Behaviors and Actions

In this chapter, you will learn how to configure various actions to enhance the user experience. **Actions** are powerful behaviors that enable users to make quick data changes in an app and navigate effortlessly to various views in the app. Actions also allow users to navigate outside an app to another AppSheet app or a website.

After learning how to configure various views in an AppSheet app in the previous chapter, we'll cover the following topics in this chapter:

- Understanding actions and action types
- Using app actions for navigation and working with CSV files
- Configuring data change actions
- Using external actions for external communications
- Sequentially executing multiple actions with grouped actions
- Offline and sync behavior of an app

By the end of this chapter, you'll have learned how to use and configure different actions for data changes within an app and navigating within and outside the app. You will know how to configure an app's sync and offline behavior settings so that the app syncs with the data source and works as intended when the app is connected to the internet (online mode) or disconnected from the internet (offline mode). You will also learn about the limitations of your app when used offline.

## Technical requirements

To assist your learning activities through this chapter, we have prepared sample apps that you can access from the portfolio site of this book. You can find the set of sample apps that are created for this chapter by visiting `https://www.appsheet.com/portfolio/5689905`.

You can refer to the sample apps, `Chapter 05_01` and `Chapter 05_02` on the portfolio site to understand the various actions described in this chapter and their settings. We have explained most actions in this chapter with the help of the `Chapter 05_01` sample app.

You can access *Chapter 05_01* at `https://www.appsheet.com/templates/sample?appGuidString=8d319bed-4f58-411a-a7ac-6642a9226f5f`

You can access *Chapter 05_02* at `https://www.appsheet.com/templates/sample?appGuidString=18881e6e-deb3-423d-b76d-ce4b9d08ec0c`

# Understanding actions and action types

In this section, you will learn what actions are and the various types of actions you can configure in an app. You will learn the various configuration settings for actions. You will also learn how the app editor automatically creates certain actions called **system actions**.

## What are actions?

**Actions** are powerful components that help you perform quick behaviors such as data changes and app navigation with the tap of a button in an app. The following screenshot shows an example of what actions look like and how they are placed in the detail view of an app. Actions show up in views as buttons with suitable icons and names or appear as icons with the name showing in the tooltip. Actions can also be indirectly invoked when the user carries out certain events in the app. We will learn about all these options in this chapter.

Figure 5.1 – Actions in the detail view

The preceding screenshot shows icons of four actions, namely **ALL TASKS**, **COMPLETED TASKS**, **ADD TASKS**, and **ARCHIVED** in the detail view of the sample app, `Chapter 05_01 Actions - Projects`. As shown in the preceding figure, users can simply tap on these action icons to invoke them. Apart from the detail views, you can also configure actions in the summary or list views and **dashboard** views. You cannot, however, configure actions in the **form** views.

Additionally, you can also configure the actions to be invoked in the background when the users perform certain app events. Examples of these events are **Row saved**, **Row selected**, and **Row swiped** within an app. Actions can also be invoked through AppSheet automation. We will discuss the invocation of actions through automation in detail in *Chapter 8*.

You can configure actions in your apps from the **Actions** tab found inside the **Behavior** section.

In the following section, we will get an overview of the most used action types.

## Action types and their usage

Here are the main action types and how they behave when invoked:

- **App actions**: These actions allow the user to perform behaviors such as the following:

  - Navigating between various views of the same app or in another AppSheet app

  - Opening forms to insert new records or open forms to edit existing records

  - Performing an import (upload) or export (download) of app data in CSV format

- **Data actions**: Data change actions allow the user to change data within an app. The users can tap on action buttons to edit, add, and delete records in the same table where they invoke the actions, or in the other tables of the app.

- **External actions**: These actions allow the user to perform external behaviors such as the following:

  - Navigating outside an app to a website

  - Starting an SMS, phone call, or email communication

  - Opening a file in the cloud

- **Grouped actions**: These actions group two or more actions of the preceding types to invoke them in sequence.

Now that you have got an overview of the types of actions and how users invoke them in an app, let's learn how you, as an app creator, can create certain actions. The AppSheet app editor also creates certain default actions, called system-generated actions or simply **system actions**. We will cover the system actions created by the app editor first.

### *System-generated actions*

As you configure an app, the app editor automatically adds certain actions called system-generated actions, or simply system actions. Let's learn about when the app editor adds these system actions.

When you configure table update permissions such as adds, updates, or deletes for a table source via the **Table | Data | Are updates allowed** option, the app editor automatically creates the system actions listed in the following table:

| Table Permissions | Updates | Adds | Deletes |
|---|---|---|---|
| System Actions | Edit | Add | Delete |

Table 5.1 – System actions for table permissions

When you configure certain column types in a table using the **Data | Columns** option, the app editor automatically creates and names system actions for those column types, as described in the following table:

| Column Type | Email | Phone |
|---|---|---|
| System Action | Compose Email(ColumnName) | Call Phone(ColumnName) and Send SMS(Column Name) |

Table 5.2 – System actions for Email and Phone column types

The default names of the system actions for the **Email** and **Phone** column types follow the pattern of *Compose Email/Call Phone/Send SMS(ColumnName)*. If there is an *Email* column type called [EmployeeEmails], then the app editor automatically creates a system action called Compose Email(EmployeeEmails).

You also need to switch the **Callable** and **Textable** settings to the **On** position in the **Phone** column type's settings. The app editor will assign the system actions of *Compose Email* and *Call Phone* to the **Phone** column type only if the **Callable** and **Textable** settings are **On**.

When you add the URL, File, and Address column types to an app, the app editor automatically adds system actions, as the following table shows:

| Column Type | URL | File | Address |
|---|---|---|---|
| System Action | Open URL(ColumnName) | Open File(ColumnName) | View Map(ColumnName) |

Table 5.3 – System actions for URL, File, and Address column types

These system actions help the user in opening the file or URL or viewing the address by navigating to a map view when the user taps on those action icons.

The default names of the system actions for the URL and File column types follow the pattern of *Open Column Type(ColumnName).* With a few examples, let's look at how the app editor will automatically name system actions based on column names:

- If there is an URL column type called [DOCUMENT_LINKS], then the app editor automatically creates a system action called Open URL(DOCUMENT_LINKS).

- If there is a File column type called [INVOICE_FILES], then the app editor automatically creates a system action called Open File(INVOICE_FILES).

- For the Address column type, the name of the system action follows the pattern of View Map(Column Name). If there is an Address column type called [Customer Address], then the system action will be called View Map(Customer Address).

You need to be aware of the following specific points about system actions.

> **Tip**
>
> You cannot delete system actions. However, you can hide them from users if you do not want to display certain system actions. We will learn how to set the visibility of actions later in this chapter, as well as the position (called prominence) of the actions in an app.
>
> Even though the app editor automatically creates system-generated actions for the Email, Phone, Message, URL, and File column types, you can also configure these actions as the app creator. However, **View Map** is only a system-generated action associated with the Address column type. You cannot create a View Map action.

In the next section, we will learn about the important settings that you need to configure for creating actions in your app.

## Important settings in the Actions settings pane

You can configure actions via **Behavior | Actions** in the app editor. Here are some of the most important settings in the **Actions** settings pane:

- **Do this**: Here, you select the action type you want to configure. There are as many as 17 different actions of the app, data, external, and grouped types that you can configure, as the following figure shows:

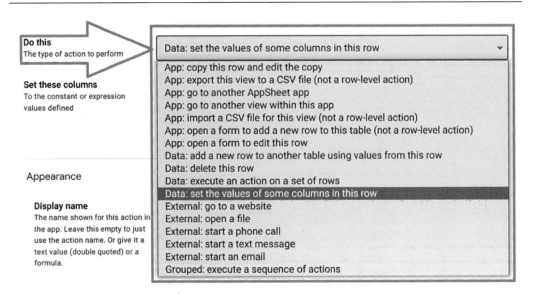

Figure 5.2 – Different types of actions

We will learn the important actions in detail from each of these categories later in this chapter.

- **Appearance**: In this part of the **Actions** settings, you can configure the physical appearance of the actions with the following settings:

  - **Display name**: You can assign a user-friendly display name to an action that gets displayed in the app views. If you have an action called **Project Status-Completed** and you set **Display name** to Completed, the app displays the name **Completed** in the views. However, if you leave the **Display name** setting blank, the action name will show alongside the action icon in the app views.

  - **Action icon**: Currently, you can only configure the icons displayed in the app editor in the action icon settings. You cannot use any custom icons you want to use.

  - **Action prominence**: You can position the action buttons in three places in an app:

    - **Overlay**: The lower-right-hand side of the summary, detail, and dashboard views

    - **Prominent**: At the top of the view in the detail views

    - **Inline**: Next to the columns in the detail views and along with the record values in summary views

  - **Do not display**: This setting will hide the action button from user views. However, the action can be executed based on how it is configured. We will learn how to use this setting later in this chapter.

The following screenshots show the prominence of actions positions in the summary and detail views:

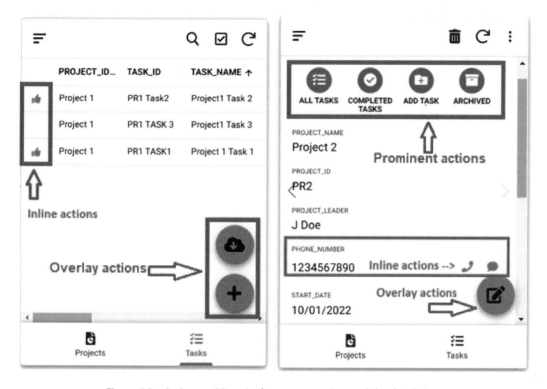

Figure 5.3 – Action positions in the summary view and the detail view

The left-hand side of the screenshot show screenshot actions in the overlay and inline prominence positions in the *summary view*. The right-hand side of the screenshot shows the actions in overlay, inline, and prominent positions in the *detail view*. You can also configure actions in the overlay position in the *dashboard views*.

> **Tip**
>
> When you configure an action in an inline position, you need to attach it to a column. In the detail view, the inline action is displayed next to the column to which you have attached the action. However, when you attach an inline action to a column in the summary table view, the app only displays the action button. The inline action in summary table views hides the column name in column headers and column values to which the action is attached. In such cases, you can create a virtual column with the app formula as text that describes the action. You can then attach the inline action to that virtual column in the summary views.

Let us continue with understanding the settings under the **Behavior** section in the **Actions** settings pane:

- **Behavior**: In this part of the **Actions** settings, you can configure row-level *Y/N* result expressions so that actions display only for those records where the expression results are Y. You can also configure a confirmation message for the user before they invoke the action.

  - **Only if this condition is true**: You can write row-level expressions that evaluate a TRUE or FALSE (Y or N) result in this setting. The actions are visible or available for the rows where these expressions evaluate to TRUE. For non-row level actions such as CSV export or CSV import, you can use conditional expressions based on CONTEXT(), USERROLE(), or USEREMAIL() functions.

The following table lists a few examples of these condition expressions from the example app, *Chapter 05_01 Actions- Projects*:

| Scenario | Only if this condition is true **setting's expression(s)** |
|---|---|
| The **Approve n Call** action in the **Projects** table should be available only if the project status is completed. | `[STATUS]="Completed"` |
| The task **Approved** action should only be visible for those rows where the task status is Completed. | `[TASK_STATUS]="Completed"` |
| The CSV Export action should only be visible in the summary table view named Completed Tasks. | `CONTEXT("View")="Completed Tasks"` |

Table 5.4 – Examples of expressions in the settings of the Only if this condition is true action

Let us now understand the remaining settings under the **Behavior** section of the **Actions** settings pane:

- **Needs confirmation**: In cases where invoking an action can have a large impact on the app, such as changing the data in several columns or rows, you can add a pop-up confirmation message for the user before they invoke the action. You can set the **Needs confirmation** setting to **On** through a toggle setting in the **Actions** settings pane.

- **Confirmation message**: Once you turn the **Needs confirmation** setting on, you can construct a customized confirmation message using expressions. If you are invoking an action that changes the task status in the Tasks table, you can have an expression such as this:

```
CONCATENATE ("Approve all the selected task with task ID ",
[TASK_ID], "?")
```

Note that this confirmation message expression will only work for actions invoked one row at a time and not on rows selected in bulk actions because [Task_ID] will be different for each row.

Now that we got an overview of action types and the settings for configuring them, let's look at the configuration of and use cases for various action types in detail now, starting with app-type actions. App-type actions help the user to navigate between various views of an app or to another AppSheet app. We will also learn how to import (upload) or export (download) CSV files to an AppSheet app.

# Using app actions for navigation and working with CSV files

We will start with app-type navigation actions and explain how to configure conditional and unconditional navigation actions. In the latter part of this section, you will learn about configuring CSV export and import actions.

Users can navigate within an app by using the view names in the bottom bar and menu options. However, users often want to navigate to another view within the app or outside the app from the view they are in. Navigation actions allow you to configure this view-to-view navigation.

Users may also want to navigate to some specific results in the navigated views depending on the current record they are viewing. For example, in this chapter's sample app, *Chapter 05_01 Actions – Projects*, when the user is in the project record detail view, they may want to view task records that are open or completed for that specific project.

In another instance, the user may want to create a new project record by copying an existing project's record with minor changes, such as the start and end date. In this case, they may want to open a new form view with certain fields prefilled from the existing project record. You can configure navigation actions to achieve these specific in-app navigations.

There are two main actions for navigation within an app and from one app to another:

- *App: go to another AppSheet app*
- *App: go to another view within the app*

While configuring these two navigation action types, you will also need to configure expressions called **deep link expressions** in the **Target** setting of the **Actions** settings panes, as the following figure shows. The **deep link expressions** in the **Target** setting navigate the user to another app or another view in the same app when the corresponding action is invoked. The following figure is an example of a navigation action that takes the user to the filtered view of the same app:

Figure 5.4 – Navigation actions

We will now explore the different deep link expressions you can configure depending on the navigation type: to a different summary view, to filtered records of a summary view, to another app, or opening a form.

## Deep link expressions for navigation actions

We will look at commonly used navigation actions and the associated deep link expressions by discussing scenarios from the sample app, Chapter 05_01 *Actions – Projects*. Let's start with the simpler unconditional navigation actions.

## Unconditional navigation

Unconditional deep link expressions almost behave like the primary and menu views buttons. These simple deep link expressions allow the user to navigate from one view to another view without any additional processing, such as filtering the target view at the action level. Let's look at some scenarios and the associated deep link expressions you can use.

- This is an example of unconditionally linking to a view within the app:

  **Scenario 1**: The user wishes to navigate to a view called *Tasks* that lists all the tasks of all the projects from a project record detail view.

  **Action** : App: go to another view within the app.

  **Deep link expression format** : LINKTOVIEW("View Name").

  **Example action** : *Tasks* configured on the Projects table.

  **Example action deep link expression** : LINKTOVIEW("Tasks").

- This is an example of unconditionally linking to the starting view of another app:

  **Scenario 2** : The user wishes to navigate to another app.

  **Action** : App: go to another AppSheet app named Chapter 05_02.

  **Deep link expression format** : LINKTOAPP("App Name").

  **Example action** : Chapter 05_02 *App* configured on the Projects table.

  **Example action deep link expression:** LINKTOAPP("Chapter 05_02-5689905").

- This is an example of unconditionally linking to a specific view in another app:

  **Scenario 3** : The user wishes to navigate to a specific view in another app

  **Action** : App: go to a **Today's Messages** view in another AppSheet app named Chapter 05_02

  **Deep link expression format** : LINKTOVIEW("View name", "App Name")

  **Example action** : *Today's Messages*

  **Example action deep link expression** : LINKTOVIEW("Today's Messages", "Chapter 05_02-5689905")

The careful inclusion of unconditional navigation actions will allow the user to maintain intuitive app navigation without having to go back and forth to the menu or navigation bar at the bottom to navigate. We will learn about conditional navigation actions next, which use more complex deep link expressions.

## Conditional navigation

You can create **deep link expressions** with more complex arguments with *App: go to another view* action types to navigate within the app or to another app. These expressions allow the user to navigate to filtered records in other views or prefilled form views. Let's understand some commonly used examples from the sample app, Chapter 05_01 *Actions – Projects*:

- This is an example of navigating a view that shows certain filtered records from a table:

  **Scenario 1** : In a project record's detail view, the user wants to navigate to a view of all the *Completed* tasks of that particular project.

  **Deep link expression** : LINKTOFILTEREDVIEW().

  **Deep link expression format** : LINKTOFILTEREDVIEW("View Name", "condition expression").

  **Deep link expression description** : The action will navigate from the Projects detail record to the filtered task view. The task will only display **Completed** status tasks belonging to the current project record.

  **Example action**: *Completed Tasks* configured on the Projects table.

  **Example action deep link expression** : LINKTOFILTEREDVIEW("Tasks", AND([TASK_STATUS]="Completed",[PROJECT_ID]=[_THISROW].[PROJECT_ID])).

- This is an example of navigating to a form view with certain fields being prefilled in the navigated form:

  **Scenario 2** : The user wishes to open a new task form from an existing task record by automatically prefilling certain columns, such as project id, project name, and project leader name, from an existing task. This will save the project leader some of the effort of entering repetitive data in the record.

  **Deep link expression** : LINKTOFORM().

  **Deep link expression format** : LINKTOFORM("View Name","Column Name 1 in Form" ,"Value to be populated for column 1",......,"Column Name n in Form" ,"Value to be populated for column n" ).

  **Deep link expression description** : The action will open a new task form on the Tasks table by copying the [PROJECT_ID] and [PROJECT_STATUS] fields from the existing project record from where the user invokes the action. The action will also initialize TASK_STATUS to the **Planned** status.

**Example action**: *Add Task* configured on the `Projects` table.

**Example action deep link expression**: `LINKTOFORM("Tasks_Form","PROJECTS_ TABLE_ID",[ID],"PROJECT_ID",[PROJECT_ID],"TASK_STATUS","Planned", "PROJECT_STATUS",[STATUS])`

- This is an example of navigating to a parent view of the current view from where the action is invoked:

  **Scenario 3**: The user wishes to go back to the parent view of the current view they are in. The user wishes to go back to the `Tasks` summary view from any of the `Tasks` detail views.

  **Deep link expression**: `LINKTOPARENTVIEW()`.

  **Example action deep link expression**: `LINKTOPARENTVIEW()`.

  **Deep link expression description**: The action will take the user to the parent view. So, in the detail view, the action will take the user back to the summary view.

  **Example action**: The **Tasks view** is configured on the `Tasks` table.

  **Example action deep link expression**: `LINKTOPARENTVIEW()`.

As the examples in the previous table show, conditional navigation actions are very useful for enhancing user experience. We will explore some more app action types next, such as CSV file import or export, which helps you in certain app usage scenarios.

## CSV export or import actions

With CSV export or import actions, the user can import (upload) data to an app's data source table from a CSV file. The user can also export (download) data from the summary view of an app into CSV format on their desktop device. Let's note a few important points about these actions:

- CSV export and import are not row-level actions. This means you cannot only configure a CSV action on a specific row in a table.

- These actions are only available for the summary views such as table, gallery, or deck views, and you can only configure these actions in the **Display Overlay** prominence.

- CSV actions are only available on desktop devices used in browser mode. You cannot invoke a CSV action on a mobile or tablet device running on Android or iOS.

- If you want the CSV action to only be displayed for a specific view of a table, you can use `CONTEXT(View)` or `CONTEXT(View Type)` expressions in the action condition to limit the display of the action.

- In the CSV import and export action pane settings, the **CSV Locale** setting is important. The locale of the app data and the **CSV Locale** setting need to match or the CSV import or export may fail or may not be legible. **CSV Locale** is important for certain column types that are locale-dependent, such as date, time, datetime, price, percent, and decimal.

Let's discuss the export CSV action first, which downloads a summary view's rows to your computer in CSV format.

### Exporting a view's records to a CSV file

The action for exporting a summary view's records to your computer is called *App: export this view to a CSV file (not a row level action)*. You and the app user need to be aware of the following important points about the CSV export action:

- The exported CSV contains all the rows that exist in the view. This means that if a summary view has 30 rows, then the CSV export for that view will include all 30 rows in the exported CSV file. The user can apply a slice-based filter to a view. The export CSV action will essentially export the rows that are available in the summary view after filtering. If the user does not apply any filtering, whatever rows are available in the summary view will export.

- The exported CSV file will have all the columns from the table or slice on which the summary view is based. If you do not want to export certain columns to the CSV file, you can create a slice of the required columns and base your view on that slice. The slice should also have the proper row filter expression that selects the desired number of rows the user wants to export.

- When you export a CSV file with a CSV export action, the file downloads to your computer's default downloads folder.

Take a look at the action titled **CSV Export** configured on the Tasks table and visible as overlay action in the Completed Tasks view. Now that we have understood how you can export a view's records to a CSV file, let us understand how a user can import a CSV file to add or update records of a view in an app.

### Importing a CSV file to add or update records of a view

You can import a CSV file stored on your computer into an app. You can upload data from a CSV file into your app's source tables. With the import CSV file action, you can add new rows or update values in the existing rows of the app's data source tables.

You and the app user need to be aware of the following important points about the import CSV file action:

- The app user can select the CSV file from their desktop computer to upload the data to their app.

- The user needs to ensure that the first row in the CSV file is a column header row and the column names are identical to the column names in the app data source, even down to the case. If there is a column called [PROJECTS_NAME] in the app data source, then the uploaded CSV file should also have a column with the same name. Even a minor difference, such as [Projects_Name] or [pROJECTS_NAME], will cause the import CSV file action to fail.

- The order of the columns in the CSV import file does not need to be the same as the order of the columns in the app data source.

- While doing a CSV import that updates columns in the app data source, all columns used in the app data source should be present in the CSV file. However, the user needs to exclude any Show column types from the upload CSV file, or else the upload will fail.

- The CSV upload file should contain values for all existing rows in the data source. If there are 75 rows in the data source, the CSV upload file should also have 75 or more rows. The action will add excess rows (rows in excess of 75) as new records in the app data source.

- The CSV import action will not update virtual columns or change column type.

We will learn about data change actions next, which allow the user to swiftly make data changes in an app.

## Configuring data change actions

With data change actions, a user can edit or delete existing rows or add new rows to an app. We will look at four different types of data change actions.

### Actions for setting the values of some columns in a row

A data change action of the *Data: set the values of some columns in this row* type can change one or more columns in a row. You can configure this action with the settings shown in the following figure:

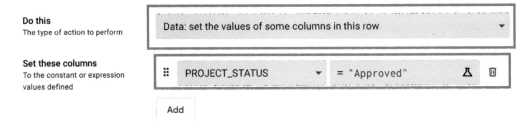

Figure 5.5 – Row-level data change action settings

You can only change the data in columns that have no app formula or no spreadsheet formula through data change actions. You also cannot set virtual columns in data change actions.

### *Using the INPUT() function with data change actions*

In the preceding section, we learned that the data change value is always set to a fixed value of **Approved** whenever the user invokes the action. However, at times, the app's business logic may need to allow the user to select from a choice of enum values, or sometimes, any other user-defined value matching the column type. You can set the row-level data change action's columns with the INPUT() function in such cases, which allows the user to select an action's data change value from several enum choices or even a user-defined value.

The format of the `INPUT()` function is `INPUT("Name of Input", "Default Value")`. You can configure multiple columns of different types that the user can set in a single data change action. You can, for example, configure a date change and an enum column with respective `INPUT()` functions that the user can set in a single data change action.

The `Chapter 05_01` *Actions – Projects* app has a data change action called `Task Quality Comment` that has a text column called `[TASK_QUALITY]` set with the `INPUT()` function. In this case, the user can input any text when they invoke the action.

The `[TASK_QUALITY]` column is set to `INPUT("TASK_QUALITY", "")` in the action. When the user invokes this action, the input pane for the user input looks like the form shown in the following figure:

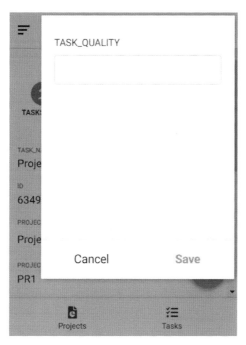

Figure 5.6 – The input function pane

The form in the preceding screenshot shows a blank default value. The user can enter the text regarding the task quality and tap on the Save button to complete the action. Note that as of date, the INPUT() function feature is in BETA stage, so use it with caution or avoid using it on production apps.

## Using bulk actions to change data in multiple rows

**Bulk actions** are basically row-level data change actions, which we learned about in the preceding section. However, they provide a selection mechanism for the user to simultaneously apply a row-level data change action to several rows.

> **Note**
>
> Whenever you configure a row-level data change action in an app, the app automatically displays this bulk action selection setup in summary views such as table, deck, and gallery views.

The following table lists a few common scenarios when an app user will want to change certain column values in *several rows* at a time. In the example app, *Chapter 05_01 Actions – Projects*, the project leader may want to update several records at the end of the day, as the following examples show:

- Set the task status to started, completed, reviewed, or approved for multiple rows

- Set today's date as the task completion date for multiple rows

- Set today's date as the task approval date for certain tasks

As we can see, there are several scenarios in which bulk actions help the user to simultaneously change values in several rows, thereby saving a user from repeatedly changing each row. Now, let's learn how bulk actions work.

## Changing data in summary views with bulk actions

Once you configure one or more data change actions, the app editor automatically inserts a checkbox button in the right-hand corner of the header in the summary views, as **Image A** in *Figure 5.7* shows:

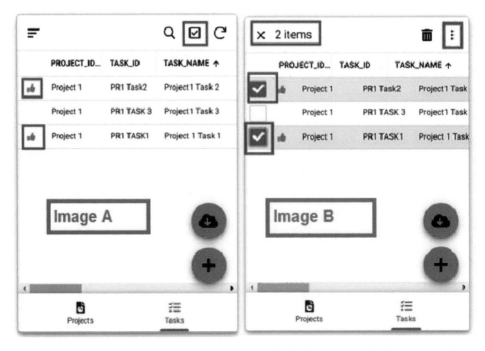

Figure 5.7 – Bulk actions (step 1 and 2: tapping the checkbox icon and selecting rows)

Here is the sequence in which the user can invoke bulk actions in a summary view:

1. As **Image A** of the preceding screenshot pair shows, the app user can tap on the checkbox icon in the view's header when they wish to invoke bulk actions simultaneously on several rows. Thereafter, as **Image B** shows, the user can select the rows on which to invoke the action. Solid checkbox icons start appearing next to each row that the user selects. The view header shows the number of records selected by the user.

2. In **Image B**, the user has selected the first and third rows. Once the user selects the rows for invoking the action, they can tap on the three dots (or action icon) that appear on the view header, as **Image B** shows. Then, a list of available row-level data change actions appears, as the following screenshot shows. The **Delete** and **Approve** data change actions are available to the user to apply in bulk to the selected rows. The user can tap on either of these actions to invoke that action on the selected rows:

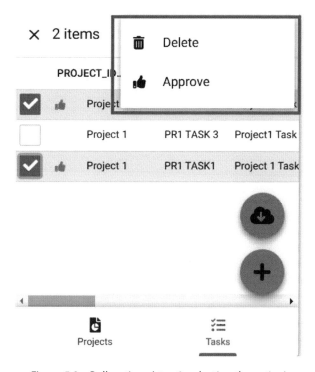

Figure 5.8 – Bulk actions (step 3: selecting the action)

With bulk actions, the actions on each of the selected rows are invoked sequentially. So, if the user has invoked a bulk action on ten rows, ten individual row-level actions will be invoked in sequence.

Bulk actions are only available for row-level data change actions. Bulk actions are not available for navigation and non-row-level actions such as CSV import and export.

> **Tip**
> When you need to invoke a bulk action on several rows, the action needs to be available for all the rows that you select. For example, if you wish to apply the **Completed** status to several rows of an enum column in a summary view, all those selected rows should have a status other than **Completed**. If even one of the selected rows already has the **Completed** status, the **Completed** action will not show in the bulk actions popup window.

Now that we have explored bulk actions in detail, let's explore another data change action type of adding a row to another table.

## Adding a row to another table using values from the current row

The *Data: Add a row to another table using the values from this row* data change action adds a new row to another table using column values from the table from which it is invoked. You can also configure it to add a new row to the same table on which the action is invoked.

We will learn about this action with the help of an action in the `Chapter 05_01 Actions - Projects` sample app. Whenever the user creates a new project with a **Planned** status, the app allows the user to add a standard reporting task for each project. This reporting task will have a start and end date identical to that of the project.

The sample app shows the *Add Reporting Task* action configured on the Projects table. This action becomes visible to the user when the user adds a new project record with a **Planned** status. When the user invokes this action, it adds a new reporting task to the `Tasks` table using a value of `Project_ID` from the newly added project record.

Let's discuss the main settings of this data change action of adding a row to a table. As the following figure shows, in the action settings pane, under **Set these columns** setting, you can configure the columns in the **Table to add to** setting (the table where the new row is added) to populate with the values of the columns in **For a record of this table** setting (the table where the action is invoked and whose column values are used to populate the new row being added).

The following figure shows how the action adds a new reporting task to the `Tasks` table by using values from the newly added row of the `Projects` table:

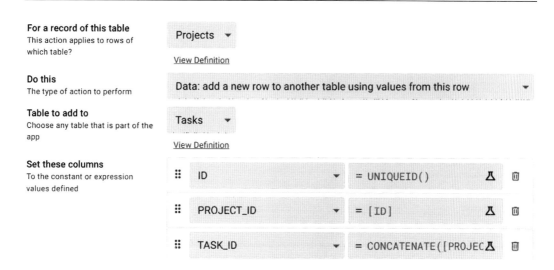

Figure 5.9 – Adding a row to another table using the values from this row

As the screenshot shows, the add new row action populates the [PROJECT_ID] and [TASK_ID] columns (among others) of the Tasks table with the corresponding values from the Projects table. Let us now learn another data change action type of reference actions.

## Reference actions

**Reference actions** are paired data change actions. The user invokes the first of the paired actions from one row, which invokes a second action. The second action is generally a row-level data change action such as updating rows or deleting a set of related records. The record on which the initiating action is invoked and the related records where the data changes can be in the same table or different tables. However, more commonly, the second action on the related rows where data changes is in a different table.

The important thing to note about the reference actions is that they always work in pairs of two actions:

- The main initiating action is of the *Data: Execute an action on a set of rows* type. The initiating action refers to a list of rows, more commonly called referenced rows, from the same or a different table. The second data change action acts on this list of referenced rows.

- The second action, the reference action, generally a data change action, either edits or deletes those related or referenced records. Technically, you can even configure navigation actions as reference actions. However, you can use reference actions more effectively and more commonly for changing data in multiple related or referenced records.

Let's learn how to implement reference actions with the help of an example. The following two figures show a reference action implemented on two tables in the sample app *Chapter 05_01 Actions – Projects* – the Projects table and the associated Tasks table.

When the project status changes to **Archived** in the `Projects` table, the project leader wants to simultaneously change the status of all related tasks of that project to **Archived** in the `Tasks` table. To achieve this, you can create reference actions.

The following figure shows the settings of the initiating action, called **Archive All Tasks**, created on the `Projects` table:

**Action name**
A unique name for this action

Archived

**For a record of this table**
This action applies to rows of which table?

Projects ▾

View Definition

**Do this**
The type of action to perform

Data: execute an action on a set of rows ▾

**Referenced Table**
The table whose action will be executed

Tasks ▾

View Definition

**Referenced Rows**
From the referenced table, these are the rows to act on

= [Related Tasks]

**Referenced Action**
The action to apply to the referenced rows

Tasks Archive ▾

Figure 5.10 – Reference actions (initiating action settings)

This main action, named *Archive All Tasks*, set on the **Projects** table, is of the **Data: Execute an action on a set of rows** type. This action sets the framework for the execution of the second action, named *Tasks Archive*, on the **Tasks** table. The second action is called the reference action. It is a row-level data change action in this example. The main initiating action, *Archive All Tasks*, has five main settings as shown in the preceding screenshot:

- **For a record of this table:** This defines the initiating table from which the reference pair action is invoked. It is `Projects` table in our example.

- **Do this:** The action type needs to be **Data: execute an action on a set of rows.**

- **Referenced Table:** This defines the table on whose rows the second action is applied. It is the `Tasks` table in this example.

- **Referenced Rows:** You need to enter an expression that creates a list of rows in the referenced table to which the second action of the action pair will be applied. You need to ensure that this expression creates a list of key values of the referenced table. Key values identify a row. In this example, the **Referenced Rows** box lists all the child rows from the `Tasks` table related to the initiating action's parent `project` record.

Reference actions can work on two different tables even if the two tables are referenced or not referenced to each other. They can also work on the same table.

Let's look at some common examples of **Referenced Rows** expressions before we look at the configuration of the second action in the reference actions pair:

| "For a record of this table" Setting | "Referenced table" Setting | Common Referenced Rows Expression |
|---|---|---|
| Parent Table | Child Table | `[Related Children]`<br><br>`[Related Children]` is the system-generated reverse reference column in the parent table. Thus, the expression references all the child table rows of the parent table row on which the reference action is invoked. |
| Child Table | Parent Table | `LIST([Reference Column])`<br><br>The expression references the parent table row through the reference column. Child table records always reference the parent table record through the reference column that contains the corresponding parent record's key. |
| Parent Table | Parent Table | `SELECT(Parent Table[Parent Table Key], [Date]>=TODAY()-15)`<br><br>Here, the expression references rows of the same table because referenced action is on the same table. The expression references rows where the date is in the past 15 days. |

Table 5.5 – Examples of referenced rows expressions in reference actions

- **Referenced Action:** Here, you configure the referenced action from the referenced table.

With the help of our example app, we will now look at how to configure the referenced action in the reference actions pair. In the example app, the second action, *Tasks Archive*, is the data change action configured on the `Tasks` table, as shown in the following figure. It changes the `[TASK_STATUS]` column value of all the related or referenced `Tasks` table records to **Archived**:

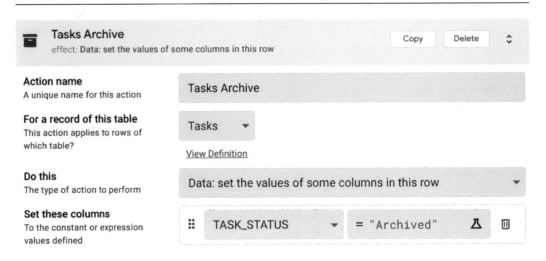

Figure 5.11 – Referenced action settings

Let's summarize this example of reference actions in the example app:

- When the user sets a project status to **Archived**, the *Archive All Tasks* action becomes visible in the detail view.

- The first action, or the initiating action, *Archive All Tasks*, set on the Projects table record, lists all referenced rows or the related child records of the Tasks table.

- The second action, or the *Tasks Archive* referenced action, set on the Tasks table, changes the [TASK_STATUS] column values of all the related children records in the Tasks table to **Archived**.

- When the project leader invokes the *Archive All Tasks* initiating action, it in turn, invokes the *Tasks Archive* referenced action, which changes the status of all the referenced or related child records of the Tasks table to **Archived**.

You can set the prominence of the second data change referenced action to **Do not display** in most cases. This is because when you invoke the initiating action, the referenced action is automatically invoked. You can hide the main initiating action as well if you have configured it as an event action. We will discuss event actions in more detail later in this chapter in the *Event actions* section

We have now learned all the data change actions that change column values of one or several rows in the same or different tables in this section.

Next, we will understand the external actions that allow you to start certain external, out-of-app behaviors from the app, such as starting an email communication.

# Using external actions for external communications

With **external actions**, you can start communications outside the app such as starting a phone call, starting an SMS message, or starting an email communication. Additionally, external actions also allow you to open a file stored in cloud storage that is accessible with a URL. You can also use external actions to go to an external website.

## External actions for starting an email, a message, or a phone call

The following figure shows the standard settings of a **Compose Email** action. The action has expressions used in the **To**, **Subject**, and **Body** settings:

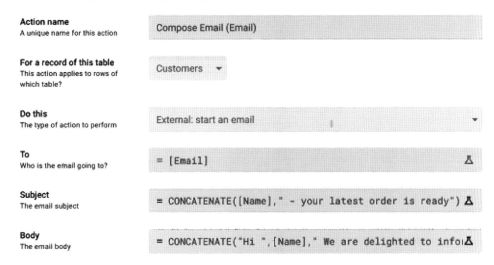

Figure 5.12 – External actions settings (starting an email)

Similarly, you can configure the relevant settings with expressions for the other external actions, as shown in the following table:

| External Action Type | Expression-based Settings |
|---|---|
| Start an email | To, Subject, Body |
| Start a message | To, Message |
| Start a phone call | To |
| Go to a website | Website URL |
| Open a file | File URL |

Table 5.6 – Settings for external actions

These external actions of starting an email, starting a message, or starting a phone call are in a way two- or even three-step actions. As an example, the steps the user needs to take in a *Start an email* action are as follows:

1.  Tap on the action icon.

2.  Select the icon of the desired email provider (such as Gmail or Yahoo Mail) from those available on the user's device.

3.  The email pane opens, and the action automatically fills in `To`, `Subject`, and the email **body** as per the expressions used in the action configuration.

4.  The user then can tap on the `send email` icon of the email provider.

The user needs to perform similar multiple steps for the *Start a message* and *Start a phone call* actions.

## External actions for navigating to a website and opening a file

The following figures show two examples of the *Go to a website* action type through a URL:

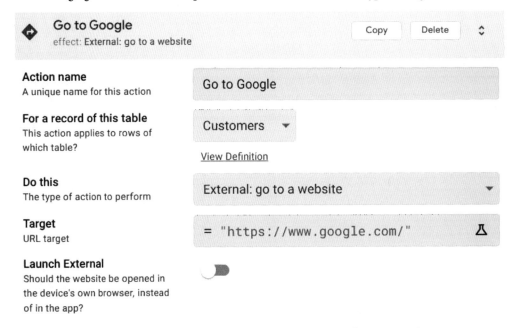

Figure 5.13 – External actions settings (going to a website – step 1)

In this figure, the website URL is directly pasted in the **Target** field of the action. With this setting, the action will always open the Google site when invoked from any row in the table because the Google site URL is hardcoded in the **Target** field.

In the following figure, the **Target** field has an expression:

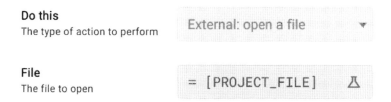

| | Open Url (WebsiteURL) | Copy |
|---|---|---|
| | system generated | |

| **Action name** | Open Url (WebsiteURL) |
|---|---|
| A unique name for this action | |

| **For a record of this table** | Customers ▼ |
|---|---|
| This action applies to rows of which table? | |
| | View Definition |

| **Do this** | External: go to a website ▼ |
|---|---|
| The type of action to perform | |

| **Target** | = [WebsiteURL] |
|---|---|
| URL target | |

| **Launch External** | |
|---|---|
| Should the website be opened in the device's own browser, instead of in the app? | |

Figure 5.14 – External actions settings (going to a website – step 2)

Here, for each row, the action will go to a website URL that is included in the [WEBSITE_URL] column for that row. It can be a different URL for each row.

Let's now see how the *External: Open a file* action works with the help of an example from the sample app, *Chapter 05_01 Actions – Projects*. The following figure shows the Open File(PROJECT_FILE) action's relevant settings.

| **Do this** | External: open a file ▼ |
|---|---|
| The type of action to perform | |

| **File** | = [PROJECT_FILE] |
|---|---|
| The file to open | |

Figure 5.15 – Example of external actions settings – open a file

Whenever you configure a file column type in an app, the app editor creates a system-generated action with the Open File(PROJECT_FILE) name pattern. Here, (PROJECT_FILE) is the name of the file column type. The system action automatically includes the **File** column name in the action name as well as in the **File** setting of the action. The file column type contains the path to the saved file. Once saved, this action allows the user to open the file from the detail view. In the detail view, the file column with its system-generated action looks as shown in the following figure. When the user taps on the action icon (a file icon in the following figure), the file opens:

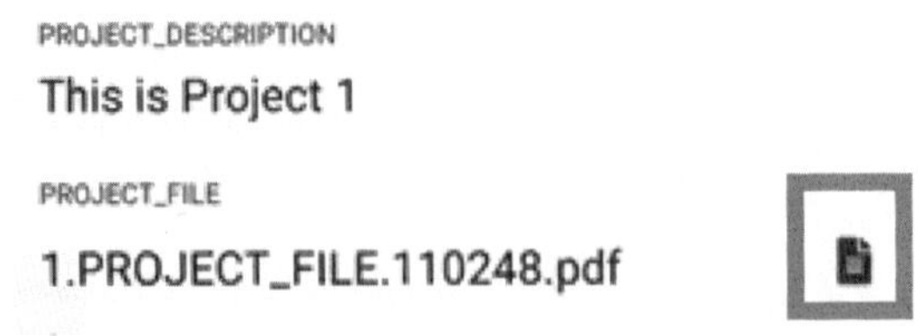

PROJECT_DESCRIPTION

This is Project 1

PROJECT_FILE

1.PROJECT_FILE.110248.pdf

Figure 5.16 – A file column type in the detail view

We have now learned about all the external actions that are system generated and that you can create as an app creator. Next, we will briefly discuss the *View Map* external action, which is exclusively system-generated and cannot be created by you as an app creator.

The app editor automatically creates *View Map* action when you add **Address** or **Lat, Long** column types.

We will learn about grouped actions next. A grouped action includes two or more individual actions that are invoked sequentially through the grouped action.

# Sequentially executing multiple actions with grouped actions

At times, the app may need two or more actions to be invoked one after the other. In such a scenario, you can group several actions in the *Grouped: Execute a sequence of actions* action type.

You can group several actions as a group action. However, there are certain precautions you need to take while configuring the group actions:

- The actions included in the grouped actions need to be from the same table on which you configure the group action. You can, of course, have a reference action from that table included in the group action. This reference action can, in turn, invoke a data change in another table. However, you cannot directly include other types of actions from other tables in the group actions.

- The first action of the sequence of group actions cannot be a delete action. A delete action essentially halts any further processing of the group actions.

- You cannot configure non-row level actions such as export or import CSV actions as one of the group actions. These actions will be executed but will export an empty CSV file.

- You can configure the first action as a row-level data change action and the subsequent action as a navigation action. However, you cannot reverse the order of execution, meaning you cannot configure the first action as a navigation action and the second action as a row-level data change action. If you configure the first action as a navigation action followed by a row-level data change action, then the first navigation action will be invoked and will be completed. However, the second-row level data change action will not be invoked. This is the case because after navigation, the app loses the references to the rows where it needs to make data changes.

In the sample app, `Chapter 05_01 Actions - Projects`, the project leader requires that whenever they approve a project, a call to the project manager starts to update them on the approval of the project. The sample app has a group action called **Approve n Call**. This grouped action is basically a group of two actions, as shown in the following figure:

Figure 5.17 – Grouped actions

The grouped action shown in the figure is composed of two individual actions:

- A row-level data change action called **Approve** that changes a project's status to **Approved**.

- After the **Approve** action, the **Call Project Manager** action is invoked and starts a phone call with the project manager.

- Note that this group action is available for only those projects where the [STATUS]="Completed"

You have now learned how you can use grouped actions to execute multiple actions in sequence. We will next learn about **event actions** that an app user does not directly invoke. You can configure event actions to be invoked by in-app view events. Examples of view events are **row selected** in cases of deck, table and gallery views, or **row saved** in case of a form view.

## Event actions

Event actions get their name from the way they are invoked. These actions are silent to users because users do not directly invoke them by tapping an action button. You configure event actions to be invoked in the background when the user performs an app event. The app events are **row saved** in a form view, **row selected** in a table, a deck or a gallery view, or **row swiped** in a deck view.

The types of event action you can configure are the same as we learned earlier, meaning that technically, you can configure any action as an event action. The summary and form view settings panes allow you to configure event actions associated with the respective events.

The following figure shows an event action called **Add Reporting Task** being configured as an event action on the **Form Saved** event in the `Projects` table form view in the sample app, `Chapter 05_01 Actions - Projects`:

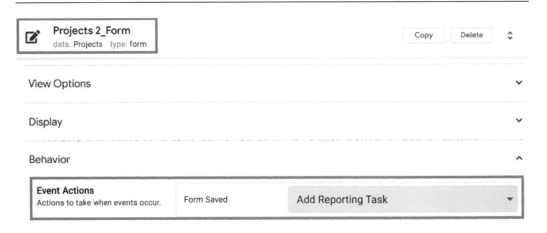

Figure 5.18 – The Form Saved event in the summary view

The **Add Reporting Task** action will be invoked when `Projects_Form`'s **Form saved** event takes place. This action is available for only those rows where the [Status]="Planned".

We have now explored all the major, commonly used types of actions. In the next section, you will learn how an AppSheet app syncs with a data source to get data into an app and save data to an app. We will explore the relevant settings that you need to make to ensure proper sync behavior in the app.

## Offline or sync behavior of an app

An AppSheet app is required to sync with a data source to get updates made by other users. It also needs to sync to save the changes made in the app to the data source. The **Offline/Sync** settings on the **Behaviors** tab allow you to set the sync behavior of the app in line with how the app users will use an app.

When an app is connected to the internet, it is referred to as being used in **online** mode. On the other hand, when the app users use an app when it is not connected to the internet, the app is referred to as being used in **offline** mode. It is sometimes necessary for an app to work offline, especially for apps used in remote worksites or locations where internet connectivity may not be available.

You will need to configure the sync settings to ensure the proper behavior of the app in online or offline usage without loss of data or impacted user experience.

Let us now examine the various sync behavior settings of an app.

## Sync – app to cloud

This option, found under **Behavior** | **Offline/Sync**, has three settings, as listed in the following table. These settings mainly decide how the data changes made in the app are synced to the app's data source in the cloud:

| Setting | | The resulting sync behavior |
| --- | --- | --- |
| **Delayed Sync** | **Automatic Updates** | |
| Enabled | Enabled | As the user makes changes in the app, those changes are synced to the app data source in the background. Changes made by other users that have been stored in the data source are auto-synced to the app approximately every 30 minutes. |
| Disabled | Enabled | As soon as a user makes a change in the app, they are immediately synced back to the data source when the data is saved. The app displays the sync screen with the saving changes, syncing the app message until the sync operation is complete. |
| Enabled | Disabled | The user needs to tap on the sync button to initiate the sync update(s) to the data source. |
| Disabled | Disabled | As soon as a user makes changes in the app, they are immediately synced back to the data source. The app displays the sync screen with the saving changes, syncing the app message until the sync operation is complete. |
| **Sync on start** | | |
| Enabled | | Whenever a user starts the app, the latest data from the data source syncs to the app. |

Table 5.7 – Sync settings (app to cloud)

You need to choose the appropriate combination of settings described in the preceding table based on how your app will be used by the users.

## Offline use

This option has two settings, as listed in the following table:

| The app can start when offline | The resulting sync behavior |
|---|---|
| Enabled | The app can work even when it is offline, meaning there is no internet connection. The changes made by the user are synced to the data source when the app is online again. However, note that the user needs to ensure that the app is online the very first time it is started on a particular device. This is necessary because the device needs to load the app definition and the latest data the app has before it can be used offline. |
| **Store content for offline use** | |
| Enabled | If you want the images and files in the app to be accessible to the user when they are accessing the app offline, you can enable this setting. An app captures images and files and stores them in the cloud if it is designed for capturing images and files. These images are stored in the cloud provider selected for the app.<br><br>The size of these images and other files accessed by an app can be very large. So, AppSheet does not copy images and files associated with an app to the user's mobile device by default. It only copies the table data from the data source to the user's device. When this Store content for offline use setting is enabled, the images and files are downloaded to the device. For this setting to work, the user will need to be online initially to download all these images and files to the device. Depending on the overall size of the image and file data, it can take a substantial amount of time to download this data to the device. |

Table 5.8 – Sync settings (offline use)

The preceding table explains how you can use the offline settings of an app to match your app usage requirements. However, your users need to be careful if using the apps in offline mode for an extended period.

> **Tip**
> The user should not use an app in offline mode for a very long period in a multi-user environment. This is because if other users make changes to the app, the offline user will not know about these changes until the app is online and syncs with the data source. Additionally, when the offline user syncs the app after going online, their changes are likely to override the changes made by other users.

Now that we have learned about the app-to-cloud sync behavior settings, let's now take a look at the reverse direction sync setting, that is, cloud to data source.

## Sync – cloud to data source

This option has two settings, as listed in the following table:

| Server caching | The resulting sync behavior |
| --- | --- |
| Enabled | The AppSheet server caches copies of read-only tables in the app. There may be certain tables in an app that do not change very often. For example, there may be a Products list table in an app. If this table does not undergo changes often, you can mark it as a read-only table. The AppSheet server caches these read-only table copies for up to 5 minutes at a time. |
| **Delta sync** | |
| Enabled | You can enable **Delta sync** to speed up the app's sync cycle. **Delta sync** only reads tables from the data source if they have changed after the last sync cycle. However, the **Delta sync** feature has certain limitations that you should be aware of: <br><br>• There are no spreadsheet formulas in your app and there are no virtual columns that need fresh calculations during each sync cycle. <br><br>• You can use it with data sources such as spreadsheets and not with SQL cloud databases. <br><br>• **Delta sync** depends on the cloud provider's file update timestamp. These cloud provider's file timestamps are not very accurate and hence, the resulting **Delta sync** behavior may not be accurate. |

Table 5.9 – Sync settings (cloud to data source)

In this section, you learned about the various offline or sync behavior settings that you need to configure in each app. You should configure these important settings carefully, taking into consideration how users will use the app to ensure proper offline or online usage and that the behavior of the app is synced.

# Summary

In this chapter, you were introduced to the actions and the app's sync behavior. You learned about system actions and different action types: app actions, data change actions, external actions, and grouped actions. You also learned about the important settings required for configuring actions.

Among the data change actions, you were introduced to the four different data change actions. In navigation actions, we saw how deep link expressions allow you to create more specific navigation behaviors, such as filtered views, opening prefilled forms, or navigating to a different AppSheet app. You also learned how you can export data in CSV format to an app and import data in CSV format from the app.

Finally, you were introduced to the sync settings of an app that will enable an app to get data from and store data to the app's data sources properly. You also learned how you can manage an app's offline behavior.

In the next chapter, we will explore how to make an app more secure and manage the app users.

# 6
# Controlling App Users and Data Security

We have been discussing how to connect data sources to our app and the other basic steps to building an app, such as adding views and actions, as well as learning about the basics of AppSheet expressions. You may find you are ready to test your app with possible app users even though app development is still underway. In this chapter, we will discuss how to add our colleagues and teammates as users of our apps, as well as how to invite someone else to collaboratively build your app as a co-author.

Furthermore, we will explain a basic approach to data protection and the accessibility of data for each app user. AppSheet provides various options to control user permission levels, such as who can view what sort of data and who will have editable permission to manipulate data while other users can only view data.

When the app usage and the number of users interacting with the app concurrently grow, it is common for app creators to control those permission levels based on named users. Learning about this technique is important to ensure the data inside the app is secured and accessible only by users with the correct permissions. For instance, if you create an HR-related application, this will contain confidential and sensitive information. If access to this app is granted to all employees, you must control who can view and access what data, as well as who will be given editable permission to manipulate data inside the apps. This is a typical use case where user permission levels are a concern, but we assume all apps to have different permission levels to some extent.

This chapter will cover the following topics:

- Controlling who can access an app
- Adding app users to your apps and defining editing permissions
- Controlling permission levels with expressions
- Controlling what data is sent to a user's device and security options

By the end of this chapter, you should be able to invite your app users to interact with your app for testing, as well as gaining the basic skills to control user permission levels.

# Controlling who can access an app

On creating a new app, you would be the app owner and have full control to add users who can access and interact with your app. You can share your app with someone else to edit the app with you or simply test the app as an app user.

Before sharing your app, the first step is to check whether it is securely protected. You may use AppSheet to create business applications that contain confidential data and information – in which case, you have to ensure that only permitted users can access your app and the information inside it. As a responsible app owner, you have to control who is permitted to access your app and interact with the content to ensure its security. To manage this, please go to the **Security | Require Sign-In** tab, as shown in the following screenshot:

Figure 6.1 – Settings for requiring authentication

This is the place where you define whether or not the app users who are given access to the app are required to authenticate themselves. We strongly recommend that you always set your app to require sign-in, which means the user needs to be verified to access the app without exception. If not, anyone who has the link to your app can access it. This means the data in the app will be exposed to the public, which you probably do not want.

Now, you may have a new question: what does authentication mean? AppSheet accepts a number of cloud services, such as Google, Microsoft, Apple, and Dropbox, which will be used as authentication services to verify that users attempting to access the app are allowed to use it. You can define what to use as the authentication service to verify user access to your apps. As you can see in *Figure 6.1*, there is an **Authentication provider** option. This is an option where you control which authentication services you will employ to verify the users to let them access your apps.

# Adding app users to your apps and defining editing permissions

The next step is to share the app by adding a list of users who are allowed to interact with it. When adding new users, we can configure the permission levels and their roles inside the app to control what those users can do inside our app. They can either edit data or only view the contents. Let's review the whole process to set this up.

## Adding new users as normal users

The process to add new users to your app is simple. All you have to do is follow these steps:

1. To add new users, just click the icon in the upper-right corner of the app editor, as shown:

Figure 6.2 – Icon to add new users

2. Then, the following new dialog window will be seen:

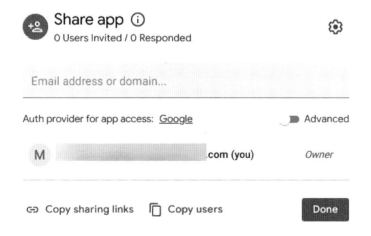

Figure 6.3 – Dialog box to control app users

Here, you can add the email addresses of the users with whom you wish to share the app in the input field.

3.  Once you hit the *Enter* key after typing one email address, the dialog box will look as follows:

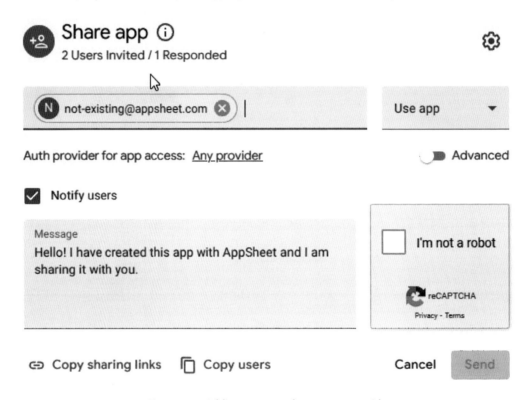

Figure 6.4 – Adding a user to share your app with

If you want this user to simply use the app without editing permissions, then simply check the **I'm not a robot** checkbox and then the **Send** button at the bottom right. This user is added as an app user, and the invitation email will automatically be sent to them. You can customize the body of this message, and have a choice not to send an automated message. If you don't wish to send a notification to the user that they have been given access, please uncheck the **Notify users** option.

If you need to add multiple users at once, then add other email addresses before pressing the **Send** button.

## Adding new users as a co-author

When you wish to share your app with a particular user and give them permission to collaboratively edit it, you need to change the sharing settings. Please have a look at the following figure to see how to set it up:

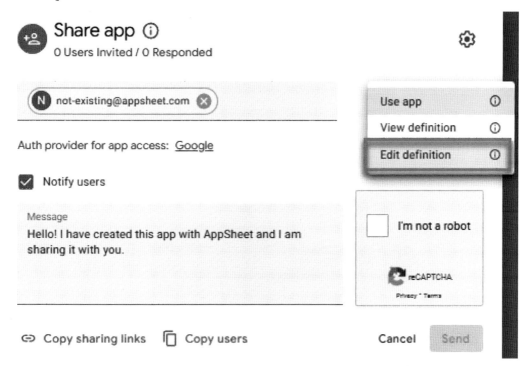

Figure 6.5 – Adding a user as a co-author

As highlighted in *Figure 6.5*, the settings are very simple. Select **Edit definition** when you wish to promote this user to a co-author, who will be given the full authority to develop the app along with you.

This user will see your app on the **My Apps** page on their AppSheet account and can change the app definition, as well as access the app as a normal user.

## Defining the app role for each user

There are other advanced settings available when we add new users. To access the advanced settings, just turn on the **Advanced** toggle button. Once you enable it, you will see the following:

Figure 6.6 – Accessing the advanced settings

There are three options: **Permission, App role**, and **App version**. The **Permission** option is the same as what we discussed in the previous section. **App role** is a useful option to control the app behaviors at the individual user level. Let us explain this option in detail.

AppSheet currently provides two different roles, **User** and **Admin**, which can be assigned as seen in the following screenshot:

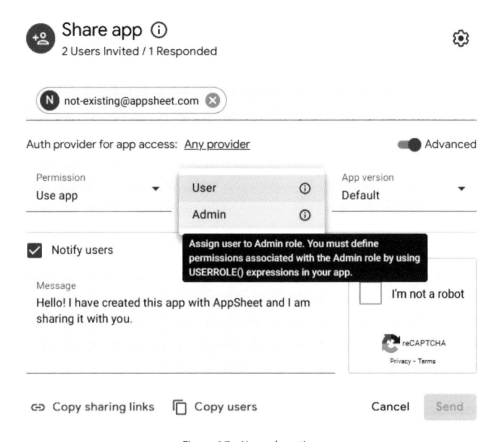

Figure 6.7 – User role options

By default, the app role is set to **User**, but you have the option to change this over to **Admin**. We can get the value of the app role through an AppSheet expression, but we will discuss this later in this chapter in the *Using the userrole() expression to control permissions* section.

You may need to stop sharing your app with users after adding them. If this is the case, you must select the email address of the user you wish to delete and select **Remove** from the list of options. See *Figure 6.7*. Now, this user will completely lose access to the app.

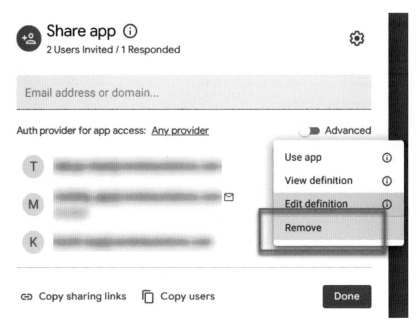

Figure 6.8 – Stop sharing (to delete a user)

At this stage, the app is under development, and it remains a prototype unless you explicitly deploy the app to users for production. Users you share the app with can access your app for review and trial, and users that are co-authors can work with you on developing the app.

In the following sections, we will learn how to manage the permission levels for users that have been added to create a user experience that differs from user to user.

## Controlling permission levels with expressions

Regardless of the purpose of your business app, it is quite a common requirement to allocate different permission levels to every user one by one. For instance, say you are developing an app that all employees of the company will use, but you wish to control the editing permissions, in terms of *who can edit what data*. You might wish to let each user only edit the data associated with them, or grant full permission to admins to edit data. It purely depends on how you would like to control those permission levels.

AppSheet provides different approaches to achieving this goal, but let's review the basic approach, using what we have learned in this book so far.

### Using the userrole() expression to control permissions

Let's assume the possible use case we discussed earlier. As we learned, an app role is assigned to each added user. AppSheet provides the `userrole()` expression to capture the value of this setting when the user accesses the app. For example, we are going to add the `acb@dummy.com` email address as an app user. To achieve that, we just simply add this email address as the app user, but leave the **App role** option as the default, **User**. When this user logs into the app, we are able to capture this app role value with the userrole() expression. In this case, this expression will return User. Alternatively, if you add xyz@dummy.com and explicitly change the **App role** option to **Admin**, then the same expression will return Admin, when this user, xyz@dummy.com, accesses the app.

In previous chapters, we learned how to add a data table, as well as the basics of AppSheet actions. When we add a table where the user can add, update, and delete rows, AppSheet will automatically generate system actions in order to assist them in making those data changes. In this case, AppSheet will automatically add actions to add records, edit the data, and delete rows in line with your table permission levels or settings.

Now, let's assume you configure the settings for a table so that everyone can add, update, and delete rows in this table. After that, you may wish to change the permission for a specific user from what you originally defined for them when adding them to the app. For instance, if you wish to only allow users with the **Admin** role to edit this table across the app, and stop anyone with the **User** role from editing, then the simplest implementation is to pass the expression in the **Edit** action settings. When you set the table permission level to be editable for all users, then AppSheet will generate the **Edit** action automatically. You simply visit this action configuration page and change the **Only if this condition is true** field by passing the userrole() expression. See the following screenshot:

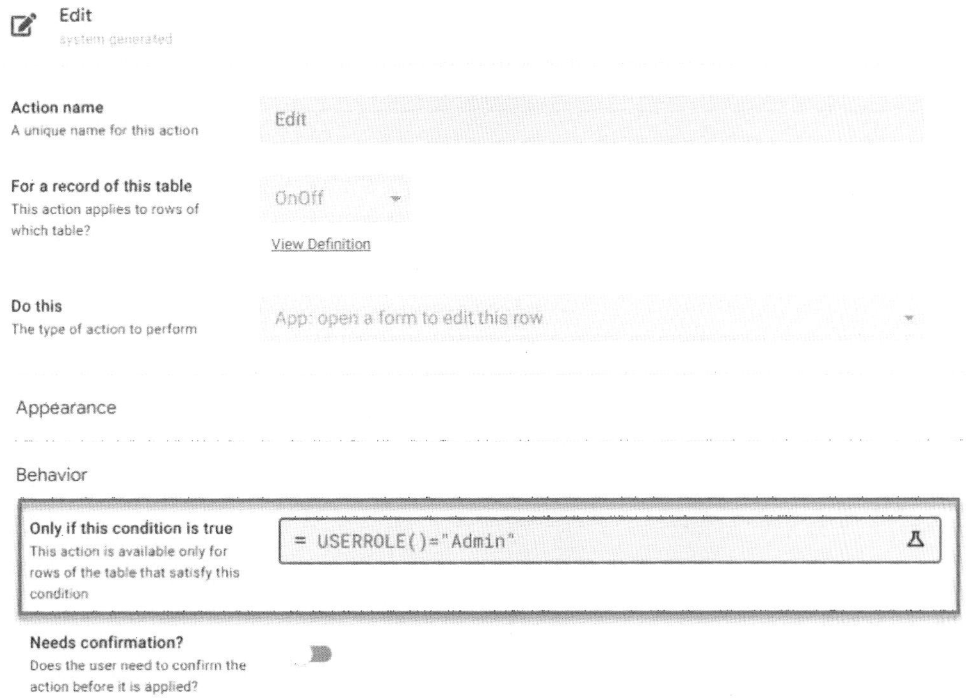

Figure 6.9 – Settings using the userrole() expression for the system-generated Edit action

When this condition is met, a user who accesses the app with the **Admin** role you defined will see the **Edit** action, while users who are added to the app with the **User** role will not see this **Edit** action.

What we are doing is conditionally showing or hiding the **Edit** action icon using an expression, which is the simplest implementation to control the permission level using the **App role** values. You can do the same for other actions, such as adding or deleting records, and even a custom action to control who will be given access to the action icons.

Controlling when to show or hide the icons for actions will in turn help us to control update, add, and delete record permissions.

The userrole() expression can be used anywhere across AppSheet wherever we can define an expression to control app behaviors. For instance, you can control which views you wish to present or hide based on the app role. In that case, you would go to **UX** > **Views** > **Display** > **Show if**, and pass the expression using userrole().

We just learned how to control user-based permissions using the **App role** value, but there is another common approach to controlling the permission level. In the following section, let's review the alternative approach, using the useremail() expression.

## Using the useremail() expression to control permissions

useremail() is one of the most commonly and frequently used expressions in AppSheet to control what users can do with apps. This expression will return the email address as a value when the respective app users access your apps. To explain this approach, let's assume that you have three team members from the admin group: abc@dummy.com, def@dummy.com, and ghi@dummy.com. Furthermore, let's assume you have one table where you wish to ensure that only those three admin group members can add the new record to this table, while app users with other email addresses will not have permission to add new records to this table.

As we reviewed in the previous section, the simplest approach is to change the settings in the action for adding a record. Once you add a table with an add permission where the users can add new records to a table, you will see that the **Add** action has automatically been added. For this **Add** action configuration, we pass the condition by passing the relevant expression. See the working example in the following figure for the system-generated **Add** action:

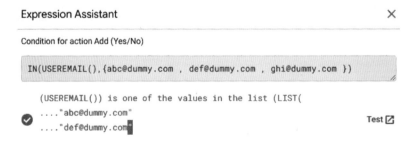

Figure 6.10 – Action settings using the useremail() expression

The basic approach to this is the same as when we demonstrated controlling the user's permission level by using the `userrole()` expression – that is, passing the expression to the **Only if this condition is true** field, but using the `useremail()` expression.

In this sample case, the working expression is as follows:

```
IN(useremail(),{abc@dummy.com , def@dummy.com , ghi@dummy.com })
```

This expression will return `TRUE` or `FALSE` if the email address of the user who is currently accessing the app is one of the three email addresses listed.

We are using the `IN()` expression for the sake of simplicity, but this expression is equivalent to the following:

```
OR(useremail()=abc@dummy.com, useremail()=def@dummy.com,
useremail()=ghi@dummy.com)
```

When any of these admin members access the app, this expression will return `TRUE`, and in turn, the action icon will become available and visible; otherwise, the action icon will be hidden from other app users.

As we have seen so far, by controlling the "visibility" of action icons, based on the values returned by `userrole()` and/or `useremail()`, you can control whether these actions are hidden or visible; then, in turn, you can control the permission level against each added data table.

So far, we have reviewed the approach to controlling the permission levels by showing or hiding the action icon through changes made to the action settings. There are a number of ways to do this in AppSheet, but we wish to share another typical approach to controlling the permission level of each table, which is passing expressions into the table's **Are updates allowed?** setting.

## Passing an expression to the table permission control

In the table settings, there is a field to control the editing permissions, which is the **Are updates allowed?** option. See the following figure:

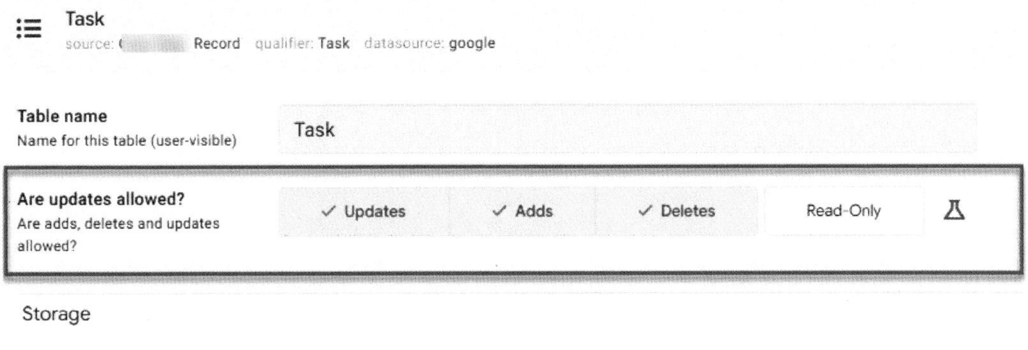

Figure 6.11 – Table settings for update, add, delete, and read-only controls

This **Are updates allowed?** setting is used to specify whether app users can add new records, update records, delete records, or just read the data. This behavior will change based on which options are selected by the app creator(s). However, we can pass an expression to control these behaviors for more complex scenarios.

Upon clicking the flask icon to the far right of this option, the **expression assistant** window will show up, looking as follows:

An expression to dynamically change the update mode of the table on a per-user basis. The allowed values are "READ_ONLY", "UPDATES_ONLY", "ADDS_ONLY", "ADDS_AND_UPDATES", "DELETES_ONLY", "UPDATES_AND_DELETES", "ADDS_AND_DELETES", and "ALL_CHANGES" (Enum)

```
SWITCH(USEREMAIL(),
  "user1@mydomain.com", "UPDATES_ONLY",
  "user2@mydomain.com", "ALL_CHANGES",
  "READ_ONLY")
```

Figure 6.12 – Expression assistant for table permission controls

By default, the SWITCH() expression is inserted as a sample. In the previous sections, we talked about permission control using the userrole() and useremail() expressions in the **Only if the condition is true** settings. We can insert an expression, using those two expressions, userrole() and useremail(), into this field, rather than passing the expressions into the action configuration by modifying the default expression.

To demonstrate and explain what we mean here, let's assume the following.

*Assumption*: This table can be read-only if User is selected as the app role, but Admin users (the email addresses for Admin users are the same as those used in the sample case in the previous section) will be given full control to add, update, and delete records.

So, the expression we would pass would be as follows:

```
IFS(IN(useremail(),{abc@dummy.com , def@dummy.com , ghi@dummy.com
}),"ALL_CHANGES", userrole()="User","READ_ONLY")
```

As you can see, using the IFS expression, we are able to change the permissions conditionally and dynamically to meet the requirement. Inside this expression, there are reserved words that are used to control the permission level:

```
"READ_ONLY", "UPDATES_ONLY", "ADDS_ONLY", "ADDS_AND_UPDATES", "DELETES_
ONLY", "UPDATES_AND_DELETES", "ADDS_AND_DELETES", "ALL_CHANGES"
```

These reserved words should be self-explanatory. Each word represents the permission level that the word suggests. These special reserved terms are only used for the expression in the **Are updates allowed?** field. Based on your business requirements, please select the right permission level out of the list of reserved words.

We have covered the process to share the app and control the permission levels on a single-user basis. In the following section, we'll learn about some other basics of AppSheet control and how to limit the data records to be sent from a data source to user devices. This control will help us secure the data effectively.

# Controlling what data is sent to a user's device and security options

As we discussed in *Chapter 2*, the data in the data source (typically a spreadsheet) will be sent to user devices, such as PCs and mobile phones, when users access the app. When the app users log into the app, the app will first read all the data the app is using from the data source and get that data on the devices the app users are using to access the app. In this case, all the rows in the data sources are sent to user devices without exception. This is pretty much the default behavior of AppSheet. If we imagine tables that have thousands or millions of rows, it will naturally take some time to get the data from the source to the user devices, which will slow down the app's performance due to the high volume of data the app needs to deal with.

We have a solution to improve your app performance, which is by applying conditions specifying which rows will be sent to user devices through the **Security filter** table setting. **Security filter** helps improve the performance of your app by reducing the number of rows to be sent to user devices.

Another popular use case of this setting is to control which rows should be presented to each logged-in user for security purposes. Let's assume you are creating an app for the HR division of the company and the app deals with sensitive data. It could be a list of employees, containing their date of birth and private phone number, which are private information that should not be shared publicly. The app is going to be shared with all employees. If you present your app without implementing any security measures, anyone can access and view the data of other employees. In this case, it is possible for you as the app creator to restrict the access that normal users have so that they can only access their own data, while members of HR can access all employees' data. **Security filter** will help with this.

Let's have a look at how we set this up, using this HR app scenario.

## Creating a new security filter per table

**Security filter** is an optional setting that can be set per table:

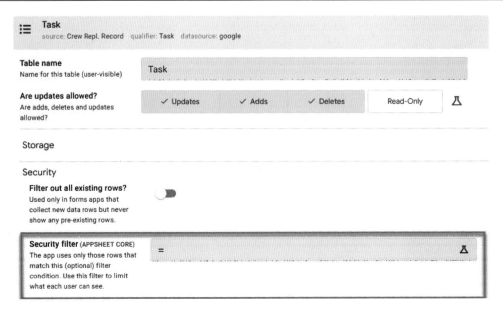

Figure 6.13 – Security filter table setting option

We can also access the **Security filter** setting through the **Security** pane | the **Security filters** tab. Let's imagine there is an `Employee` table in this HR app, and we wish to restrict the app so users can only access their own data while members of HR can access all the data in this table. This employee table has a list of columns, as shown in the following figure:

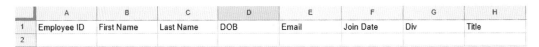

Figure 6.14 – Sample HR data table

As you see, this table contains an `Email` column, where the value of the email address is saved for each employee. Every single row in this table represents the unique data of one employee and the `Email` column holds their private email address. This email address is used by app users when they access your app. You can apply a filter to this `Email` column when you set up **Security filter**. Simply pass the following expression so that the app is only reading the data from this table associated with the user who is currently accessing the app:

```
[Email]=useremail()
```

However, this expression is not sufficient to control what we want to achieve. This expression will hide all the rows for other employees whenever anyone accesses the app. This means members of HR cannot access data for all other employees. The goal is to show all the rows when a member of HR accesses the app.

In the previous section, we learned about the usage of the `userrole()` expression. We can use the same expression on this occasion. Before we alter the expression, we share the app with users who are in the HR division and assign an app role of `Admin`, while other app users have their app role set to `User`.

We can extend the expression by adding `userrole()` expression along with the conditional expression of `IF()`. Then, the revised expression looks as follows:

```
IF(userrole()="Admin", true, [Email]=useremail())
```

This expression is passed to **Security filter** and looks like the following figure.

**Security filter** (APPSHEET CORE)
The app uses only those rows that
match this (optional) filter
condition. Use this filter to limit
what each user can see.

`= IF(USERROLE()="Admin", true, [Email]=USEREMAIL())`    ⚗

Figure 6.15 – Sample expression for the Security filter condition

As you can see, the expression is conditional, as we are using `IF()` as an outer expression. The expression evaluates whether or not `userrole()` is set to `Admin` for users accessing the app. When members of HR access the app, it should return `TRUE`. Then, the second argument in the `IF()` expression is set to `TRUE`, which means **Security filter** will not set a filter, and all the rows will be returned and sent to the user's device. If the `userrole()` expression does not return `Admin`, the condition of the third argument of `[Email]=useremail()` is going to be applied as a security filter.

When the user opens the app, the sync operation will be initiated. The rows that match the conditions in the security filter will be sent from the backend data source to the user devices.

As we saw, **Security filter** gives us additional assurance in terms of safety, as you can freely control what data (records) in the source table will be submitted to user devices.

Before we end this chapter, let's also look into the additional security-related options that reside in the **Security | Options** tab.

## Implementing additional security measures for safety

On the **Security** pane, there is another tab, called **Options**, where additional security-related options can be configured. The following screenshot shows the different options:

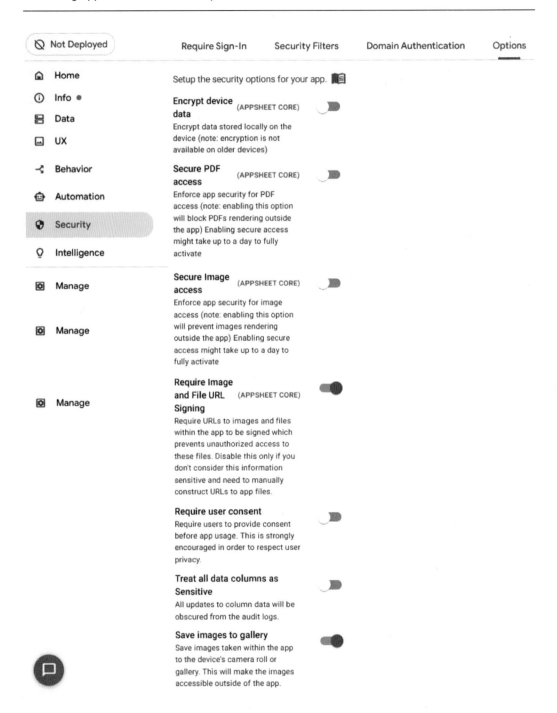

Figure 6.16 – Security tab to configure additional security options

Let's take a quick look at these security options:

- **Encrypt device data**: When you run your AppSheet app, the data is retrieved from the backend data source and stored in the user's device. By enabling this option, data stored locally on user devices is encrypted.

- **Secure PDF access**: On opening a file from an AppSheet app, it will be opened with a unique URL to display the contents. In the case of a PDF, with this option enabled, access to those PDF files is restricted. Only users who have access to the same app can view the files.

- **Secure Image access**: This provides the same protection as **Secure PDF access** but for image files. Only users who are authorized to access the app can open the image file outside the app, using the unique URL.

- **Require Image and File URL Signing**: By enabling this option, URLs to access images and files within the app need to be signed. This prevents unauthorized access to these files and increases the security level.

- **Require user consent**: When users first access the app, the app will ask them for consent. This complies with the various regulatory requirements for privacy, such as the GDPR requirements in Europe and the CCCA laws in California in the US.

- **Treat all data columns as Sensitive**: On updating data inside the app, AppSheet logs will record the contents of those changes, including the column values. By enabling this option, logs will no longer hold column values across the board.

- **Save images to gallery**: This option is to control the app behavior when the user accesses the app from mobile devices. For the image type column, the app user can take a photo and upload it to the image column, using the device camera. When this option is turned on, the image file taken from the device will be saved to the user's devices locally so that the user can directly access those photos from the image gallery on their device.

As app creators, you need to pay attention to the privacy and/or regulatory requirements in terms of data protection and privacy. We recommend you examine each option before you share your app with users to ensure compliance with the requirements.

## Summary

In this chapter, we reviewed how to share your app with users as well as how to control the permission levels in a few different ways. Both sharing apps with users and controlling the permission levels are processes that need to be considered regardless of the type and purpose of the app you are creating in AppSheet. They are always essential in app development processes. We hope you have learned how to share your apps with users once they are ready to test and deploy, as well as control the permission levels assigned to each app user. AppSheet is a tool for generating business applications, which means it will usually contain sensitive data that must be carefully handled. With the knowledge you learned in this chapter, you should be able to control and alter each app user's experience with your app.

Now, you have learned how to share your app for testing and your app might be ready to deploy. In the following chapter, we will discuss the required processes before you fully deploy the app to production. We will also deal with other subjects that you need to pay attention to as a responsible app creator to make sure your apps provide a good experience for the app user by ensuring fast and stress-free performance.

# 7

# Managing the App Environment

In the previous chapter, we had a look at how you can manage app security, the users that can access and use an app, and which users can modify the app definition.

An app, as with any other human-made system, may need frequent changes throughout its life cycle when the underlying business or functionality requirements change. At the same time, you need to ensure that for your users, the app's user experience is as smooth as possible throughout these changes without a major disturbance. In this chapter, we will understand how you can monitor, manage, and define an app environment by monitoring and managing certain administrative and performance parameters of an app. These options are available in the app editor under the **Manage** tab.

After reading this chapter, you will understand the following:

- Analyzing app features and transferring app ownership
- Performing app version management
- Deploying an app with all features
- Monitoring app usage and app sync performance
- Sending on-demand messages to app users

By understanding these topics, you'll have learned about managing the app's environment, which is so important for ensuring that your app works as intended throughout its life cycle.

Even though the options under the **Integrations** tab are part of the **Manage** tab, we will not cover the option Manage | Integrations in this book because it is an advanced topic.

Let's start by understanding the options under the **Manage | Author** tab that help you to analyze your subscription plan requirements.

# Analyzing app features and transferring the app ownership

The **Manage | Author** tab has three major sub-options and three more miscellaneous options. In this chapter, you will learn how you can use the **Author** tab's two sub-options:

- **Plan requirements**: You can use this option for analyzing app features.

- **Transfer**: You can use this option for transferring your app's ownership to someone else.

The **Author** tab also has a third sub-option titled **Author | Team Work** that allows you to share your apps with your team (as defined in the AppSheet account) or share your apps as public sample apps that anyone can browse or copy if the user has an AppSheet account ID. You will learn about those **Team Work** options in *Chapter 11*.

The **Author** tab has yet three more sub-options: **Editor Settings**, **Copy App**, and **Delete App**, used for enabling/disabling certain app editor settings and for copying or deleting apps. You will understand those options by the end of this chapter as well.

Let's start by understanding the **Plan requirements** option under the **Manage | Author** tab.

## The Plan requirements tab

When you create an app, you use some of the features out of an entire list of features available in the AppSheet editor. However, certain advanced features are only available with certain subscription plans. A detailed list of the subscription plans and the features associated with each subscription plan is available at https://about.appsheet.com/pricing/.

The **Plan requirements** option under the **Manage | Author** option analyzes the features you have used in the app and shows any features that do not match your current subscription plan. The option also lets you know what subscription plan you will need to utilize those features.

If you are using features available with a higher-value subscription plan, then you can either upgrade your subscription plan or you can remove certain features from your app that are not available in your current subscription plan.

If you click **Plan requirements**, you will see the first pane that the following screenshot shows:

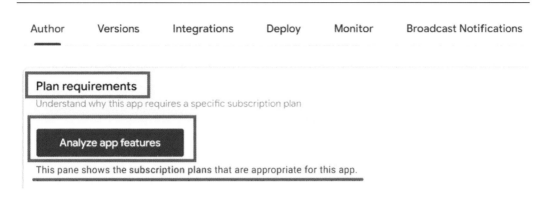

Figure 7.1 – Plan requirements

If you click on the **Analyze app features** button, you get the expanded results pane. This results pane shows what features you have and what plans do not allow those features, as the next screenshot shows:

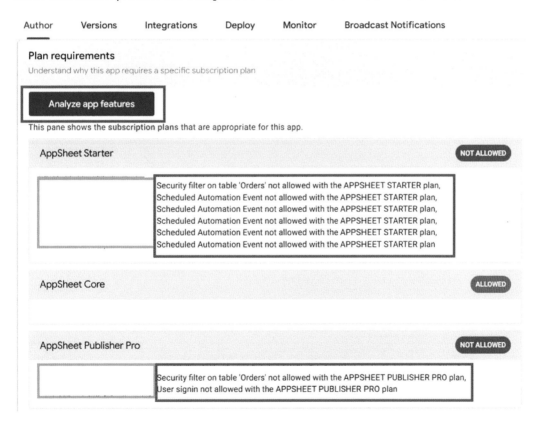

Figure 7.2 – The Analyze app features function

The screenshot shows that the app is using security filters and scheduled automation events. The results show that these features are not allowed with the **AppSheet Starter** and the **AppSheet Publisher Pro** subscription plans. At the same time, the results pane shows the **ALLOWED** message for the **AppSheet Core** subscription plan.

In summary, the **Analyze app features** results pane conveys that the app creator will need an **AppSheet Core** subscription plan in order to use the features they have included in the app.

With this **Plan requirements** option, you can decide on the subscription plan you will need before you deploy the app.

Now, let's understand how you can transfer the ownership of your app to someone else with an AppSheet account ID.

## Transferring the app ownership

The app creator to whom you want to transfer the ownership of an app should be a coauthor of that app. You will learn about the process of adding users or coauthors to your app in *Chapter 6*:

1.  The process of app ownership transfer requires that the coauthor should make a request to transfer an app's ownership to them first. The user requesting the transfer of ownership needs to go to the **Manage | Author** option, where they will see the **Transfer** option, as shown in the following screenshot:

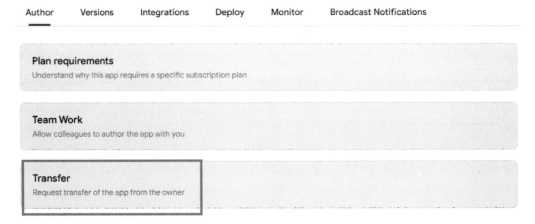

Figure 7.3 – The Transfer option

2.  When the user requesting the app ownership transfer clicks on the **Transfer** option, the **Request transfer** button shows up as shown in the following screenshot:

Figure 7.4 – The Request transfer button

3.  The user requesting the app ownership transfer can then click on the **Request transfer** button to request the transfer. This will send the tranfer request to the current app owner:

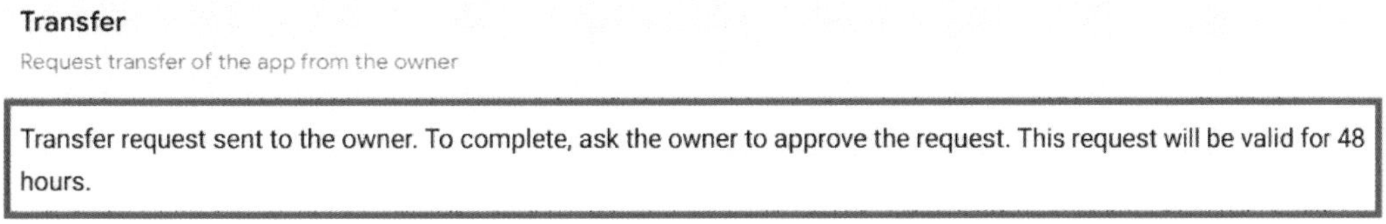

**Transfer**
Request transfer of the app from the owner

Transfer request sent to the owner. To complete, ask the owner to approve the request. This request will be valid for 48 hours.

Figure 7.5 – The app transfer request initiation message

4.  Once received, you need to approve the transfer request within 48 hours. You, as an app owner, will see the following message under the **Manage | Author** option:

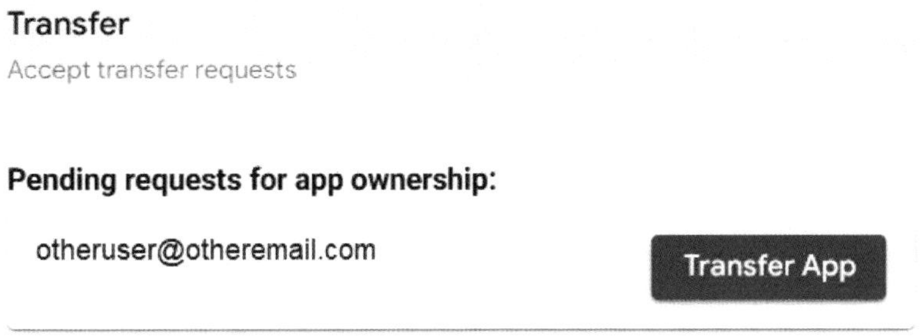

**Transfer**
Accept transfer requests

**Pending requests for app ownership:**

otheruser@otheremail.com                          **Transfer App**

Figure 7.6 – App transfer request approval

5.  When you click on the **Transfer App** button, app ownership is transferred to the user who requested the transfer. The user that requested the transfer sees the transferred app in their **Prototype Apps** or **Deployed Apps** list on the **My Apps** page, depending on the app status.

6.  Before transferring the app ownership to the user requesting the transfer, you need to ensure that the requesting user has edit access to the data source of the app. In the absence of the proper access permission to the data source of the app, the user to whom you are transferring the app ownership will be unable to access the app – the app will be rendered as "not runnable."

7.  Once you transfer the app ownership to the new user, you will no longer have access to that app. If the new app owner wants you to use or coauthor the app, they will have to add you to the list of users in the **Security | Require Sign-in | Manage Users** option.

There are three additional options under the **Author** tab that allow you to copy or delete an app and set certain app editor usage settings of your choice. Let's explore them in detail.

## Setting editor settings, copying, and deleting apps

Let's understand how you can copy or delete an app using the options under the **Author** tab. We will also look at how you can set certain app editor settings.

### Setting editor settings

When you click on the **Editor Settings** option, the app editor presents a settings pane, as shown in the following screenshot. Here, you can select or deselect certain editor settings:

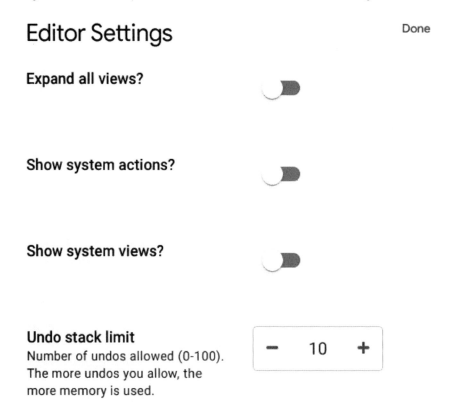

Figure 7.7 – Editor Settings details

When you turn these settings on or off, the resulting editor behavior is as listed in the following table:

| Option | Setting | Resulting editor behavior |
|---|---|---|
| Expand all views? | On | In the UX \| Views option, all the sub-options within a view pane such as View Options, Display, Behavior, and Documentation are displayed by default. |
|  | Off | You need to use the expand or collapse icon ∧/∨ at the top right of each view's pane to see or hide sub-options such as View Options, Display, Behavior, and Documentation of each view pane. |
| Show system actions? | On | All system actions in the app under the Behavior \| Actions option are displayed by default. |
|  | Off | You need to use the Show system actions option under the Behavior \| Actions option to make the system actions visible in the Behavior \| Actions pane. |
| Show system views? | On | All system views are shown by default under the UX \| Views option. |
|  | Off | You need to use the Show system views option under the UX \| Views option to make the system views available under the UX \| Views option. |

Table 7.1 – Editor settings and the resulting behavior

You can set **Editor Settings** as per your liking and those settings will take effect after you perform the next **Save** operation for the editor.

Let's next look at how you can make a copy of an app.

## Copying apps

When you want to make a copy of an app, you can use the **Copy app** option. When you click on the **Copy app** option, the following dialog pane opens:

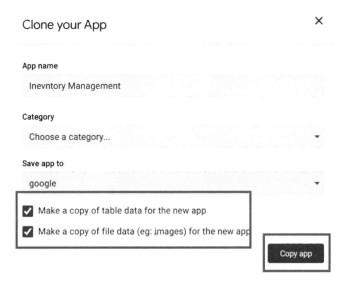

Figure 7.8 – Copying an app

The **App name** field shows the name of the app being copied. While copying an app, you should preferably name the new copy at least somewhat differently by adding a suitable prefix or suffix to the existing app name. The prefix or suffix could be the date of copying or a similar attribute that will identify the new app from the app being copied. You can also select a suitable category for the new copied app from the available options in the **Category** field.

> **Note**
>
> You can choose to make a copy of the app with source table data, images, and other files by ticking those options or you can copy only the app definition without the underlying data, images, and other files.

When you click on the **Copy app** button, the app editor makes a copy of the app. The app is available to you under your account's **My Apps** list.

### Deleting apps

When you want to delete an app, you can use the **Delete App** option. When you click on the option, a dialog pane as shown in the following screenshot opens.

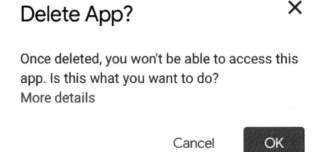

Figure 7.9 – Deleting an app

When you delete the app, you need to be aware that it will not be available anymore in your list of apps and your users will not be able to access it again.

In this section, we have understood how we can use options under the **Manage | Author** tab to analyze app features with respect to the subscription plan. We have also learned how to copy or delete an app. You have also learned about certain app editor settings related to showing or not showing system views and system actions and settings related to expanded or compact view settings panes.

Let's next understand how you can perform various version management activities for an app.

# Performing app version management

Whenever you make changes to an app in the app editor and save those changes, the app editor creates a new version of the app. The app editor also records the details of the changes you have made. The versions list can help you revert to an earlier version. The **Manage | Versions** option shows you the previous app versions as well as having some other sub-options, as shown in the following screenshot:

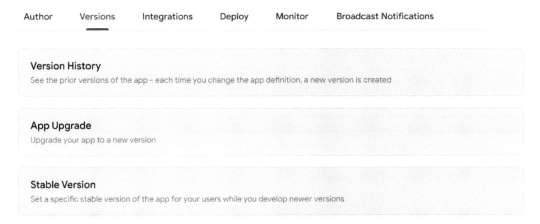

Figure 7.10 – App version management options

As shown in the screenshot, the **Manage | Versions** option allows you to do the following:

- View the previous versions of an app and restore the app to a previous version.
- Upgrade the version of an app to a new version for all users.
- Define a stable version of the app as the version that the users will see until you define a new stable version.

We will understand all these version management options in detail.

## The version history of an app

When you click on the **Version History** option under the **Manage | Versions** tab, it expands to give more details as shown in the following screenshot:

**Version History**

See the prior versions of the app - each time you change the app definition, a new version is created

Editing  Inventory Management    version **1.000015**.

To restore an older version of this app, browse the version history, view the desired version, and restore it.

Get version history

Figure 7.11 – Getting version history

As the preceding screenshot shows, you see the current app version you are editing. If you want to view the previous versions of the app, you can click on the **Get version history** button to see an app's previous versions, as the next screenshot shows:

**Version History**

See the prior versions of the app - each time you change the app definition, a new version is created

Editing 20MAR22 Images in buttons version **1.000018**.

To restore an older version of this app, browse the version history, view the desired version, and restore it.

Get version history

Note: versions saved within the last minute may not show immediately.

| Version | Saved At (UTC) | Changed By | Source | Context | Changes |
|---|---|---|---|---|---|
| 1.000017 View | 2022-03-20T12:51:08.9887409+00:00 | | Saved in app editor | User edit | Expand |
| 1.000016 View | 2022-03-20T11:44:45.7590805+00:00 | | Saved in app editor | User edit | Expand |
| 1.000015 View | 2022-03-20T11:44:31.0461926+00:00 | | Saved in app editor | User edit | Expand |
| 1.000014 View | 2022-03-20T11:43:41.3323072+00:00 | | Saved in app editor | User edit | Expand |
| 1.000013 View | 2022-03-20T11:31:35.924187+00:00 | | Saved in app editor | User edit | Expand |
| 1.000012 View | 2022-03-20T11:22:26.6913894+00:00 | | Saved in app editor | User edit | Expand |
| 1.000011 View | 2022-03-20T11:12:18.5679147+00:00 | | Saved in app editor | User edit | Expand |
| 1.000010 View | 2022-03-20T11:11:24.1653844+00:00 | | Saved in app editor | User edit | Expand |
| 1.000009 View | 2022-03-20T11:10:59.2066585+00:00 | | Saved in app editor | User edit | Expand |
| 1.000008 View | 2022-03-20T11:10:19.602391+00:00 | | Saved in app editor | User edit | Expand |
| 1.000007 View | 2022-03-20T11:09:09.6358743+00:00 | | Saved in app editor | User edit | Expand |
| 1.000006 View | 2022-03-20T11:07:30.7643016+00:00 | | Saved in app editor | User edit | Expand |

Please configure your account settings if you want AppSheet to maintain older versions.

Figure 7.12 – App version history list

You can click on the **View** button of any version to browse that version in the app editor. When you are browsing an earlier version, you get to see the options as shown in the following screenshot:

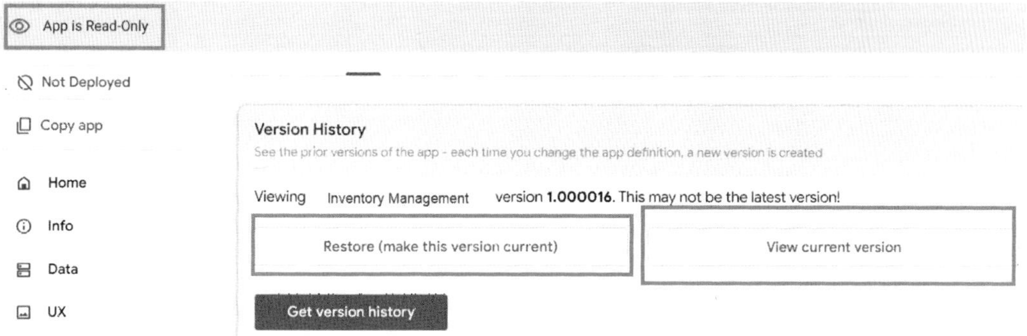

Figure 7.13 – App version restore options

Note the **App is Read-Only** message that the editor shows at the top left of the screenshot. When you are viewing a previous version, you cannot edit its app definition until you restore the version to the current version. You can make a previous version a current version by clicking on the **Restore (make this version current)** option. When you click on this option, the app editor displays a message as shown in the following screenshot:

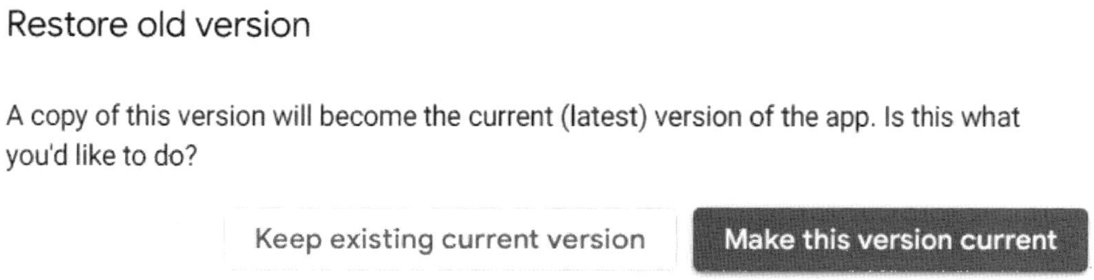

Figure 7.14 – The confirmation message before app version restoration

The message shown in the screenshot draws your attention to the fact that you are about to restore a previous version of the app to the latest version. If you click on the **Make this version current** button, the previous version that you were viewing becomes the current or the latest version.

You can set the number of days for which you want the app editor to recover and show the app version history. You can do so in the **My Account | Enterprise Plan Settings** option:

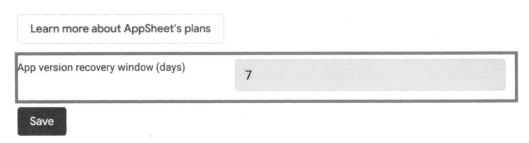

## Enterprise Plan Settings

Use this section for Enterprise account configuration. These options are only available to Enterprise customers.

Learn more about AppSheet's plans

App version recovery window (days)                            7

Save

Figure 7.15 – The app version history recovery window

However, as you can see in the screenshot, you can only set the number of days to retain versions if you have the **Enterprise Plan** subscription. For other subscription plans, you have the default setting of **7** days. This means you can view previous app versions created in the previous **7** days.

Now, we understand how to perform major changes to an app and then roll them out to users with the **App Upgrade** option.

## Upgrading the app version for all users

Sometimes, you want to make major changes to an app, such as adding a new table or changing the structure of existing tables by adding new columns or deleting and moving existing columns. When you are making such major changes to an app, you would not want the app's users to be disturbed by changes being released incrementally until everything is finished. During major app definition change requirements, you can make use of the **App Upgrade** option under the **Manage | Versions** tab. **App Upgrade** allows you to push a major changed version of an app to your app's users.

The **App Upgrade** option works in the following manner. When you want to make major changes to your app, take these steps:

1. First, make a copy of the current version of the app as you learned in the *Copying apps* section of this chapter.

2. Make the major changes you want to make to the copied app. When you are ready with the major changes and have tested the copied app, you need to deploy the copied app using the deployment process described in the *Deploying an app with all features* section of this chapter. If you do not deploy the app before assigning it as a major version with the **App Upgrade** option, the upgrade process will fail with an error such as the one shown in the following screenshot:

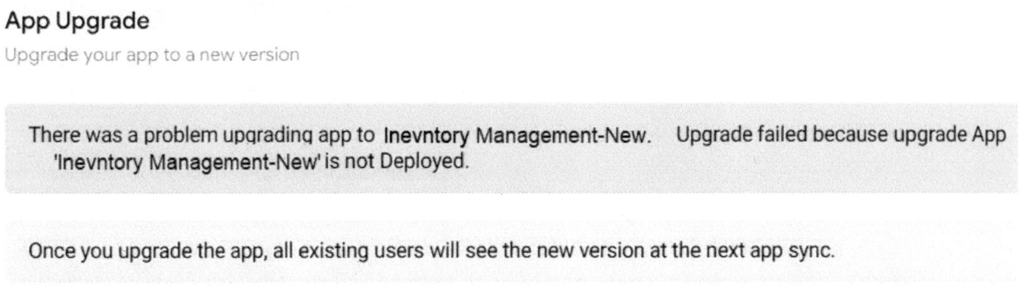

## App Upgrade

Upgrade your app to a new version

There was a problem upgrading app to **Inevntory** Management-New.     Upgrade failed because upgrade App 'Inevntory Management-New' is not Deployed.

Once you upgrade the app, all existing users will see the new version at the next app sync.

Figure 7.16 – App Upgrade failure

As the screenshot shows, the **App Upgrade** process failed because the app version assigned to the upgrade is not deployed.

3. Once you have deployed the copied app after making major changes, you can release this deployed app as the new app version to the app's users through the **App Upgrade** option. The following screenshot shows an example of an app called **Inventory Management-New-123456** being released as the new app version for all users, replacing the existing version:

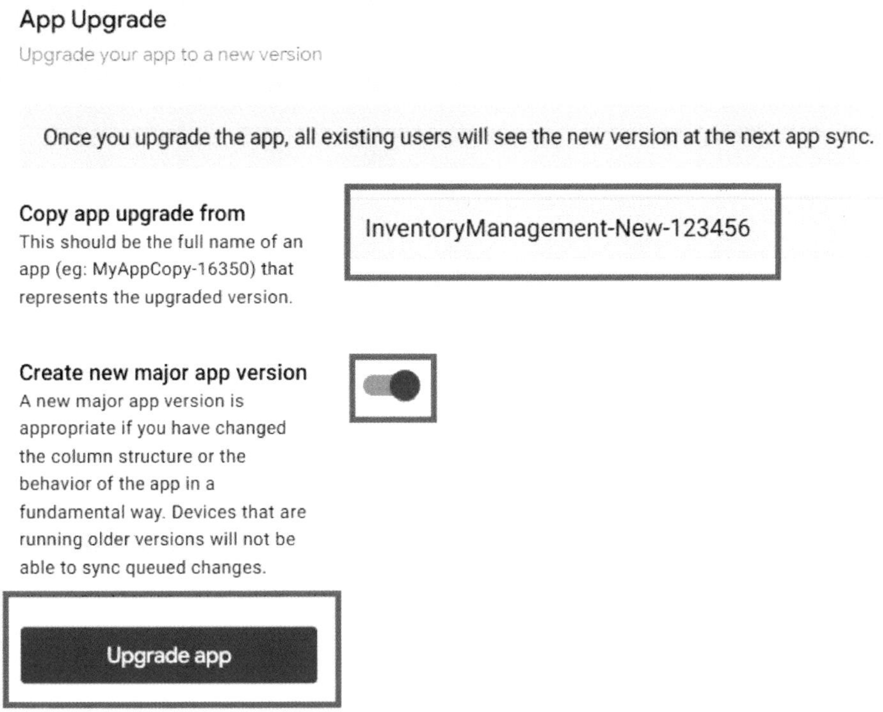

## App Upgrade

Upgrade your app to a new version

Once you upgrade the app, all existing users will see the new version at the next app sync.

**Copy app upgrade from**
This should be the full name of an app (eg: MyAppCopy-16350) that represents the upgraded version.

InventoryManagement-New-123456

**Create new major app version**
A new major app version is appropriate if you have changed the column structure or the behavior of the app in a fundamental way. Devices that are running older versions will not be able to sync queued changes.

Upgrade app

Figure 7.17 – App Upgrade process settings

4.  As the preceding screenshot shows, the modified and deployed **Inventory Management-New-123456** app is being upgraded as the latest app version for the app's users.

5.  You need to insert the name of the app that you have made major changes to and want to release as a new version into the **Copy app upgrade from** setting.

6.  You can get the app name for use in expressions and app editor settings by going to the URL of the app in the app editor. For each app, you get the URL in the app editor with the following format: `https://www.appsheet.com/Template/AppDef?appNam e=InventoryManagement-New-123456&appId=InventoryManagement-New-123456&linkFrom=CopyApp#Home`. In this URL string, the app name is `InventoryManagement-New-123456` and the app ID is also `InventoryManagement-New-123456`.

7.  After inserting the app name into the **Copy app upgrade from** setting, you can turn the **Create new major app version** setting on. Thereafter, when you click on the **Upgrade app** button, the app name that you have entered into the **Copy app upgrade from** option becomes the new app version that all app users will see when they sync the app during their next use.

With this, we have learned how to upgrade app versions. However, we must take certain precautions when performing app upgrades.

### Precautions when performing app upgrades

You need to take the following precautions when performing an app upgrade:

*   As we learned, an app upgrade replaces the earlier version of the app. It is most likely that if users were using the app in offline mode when you performed the app upgrade, they will lose their changes when they are online again. This is because if the app has changed in a major way, the number of columns in the older version and the latest version may not match and changes made by the users when they were offline will fail. As a best practice, you should notify your users about a planned app upgrade beforehand.

*   You should also perform app upgrades when no users are likely to be using the app. As an example, you may have certain apps that the users use during only office hours or the work week. You can perform app upgrades after office hours or during the weekend for such apps.

We will next understand how you can create a stable version of an app for your users till you make major changes to the app.

## Creating a stable version of an app

Whenever you make changes to the app definition, those are typically immediately available to app users. However, if you have an **Enterprise** plan subscription, you can define a stable version of the app. Defining a stable version ensures that until you make changes to the app, the app users will continue to see the stable version. The following screenshot shows how you can define a stable version of an app:

**Stable Version**

Set a specific stable version of the app for your users while you develop newer versions

By default, all your users see the latest version of the app. If you are on an Enterprise plan, you can define a Stable Version instead.

A stable version of this app has not been assigned.

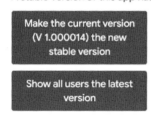

Figure 7.18 – Defining a stable version of an app

You can define any existing version of the app as a stable version using the options under **Stable Version**. You can open any existing version of the app that you want to define as the stable version with the **Version History** option, as discussed earlier in this chapter. As the example in the screenshot shows, you are currently viewing version V1.000014 of the app. The app editor will give you the option of defining version V1.000014 as the stable version. Alternatively, the app editor gives you the option of selecting the latest version of the app that you are working on as the stable version.

As a standard practice, in the majority of scenarios, once you have made all the desired changes to the app, you can define the latest version as the stable version by clicking on the **Show all users the latest version** button.

In this section, we learned how you can perform various app version management activities including restoring a previous version as the current version, defining a stable version, and performing an app version upgrade activity. We will understand how you can deploy the app to your users so that some of the features that are not available in the prototype stage are available to your users next.

## Deploying an app with all features

When you have created and tested an app in the prototype stage to your satisfaction, you can deploy it.

Let us understand the limitations of a prototype app first and why you should consider deploying your app. You can distribute a prototype app to only a maximum of 10 active users. With a prototype app, certain automation features are only available to the app owner. For example, when a **bot** sends an email or SMS, it only delivers it to the app owner in a prototype app.

When you deploy an app, you will need to subscribe to a paid subscription plan depending on the features you are using in the app and the number of active users you have for the app. As you have already learned in this chapter, the **Plan requirements** option under the **Manage | Author** tab allows you to know which subscription plan you will need.

When you go to the **Manage | Deploy** tab, you will see the following options available to you:

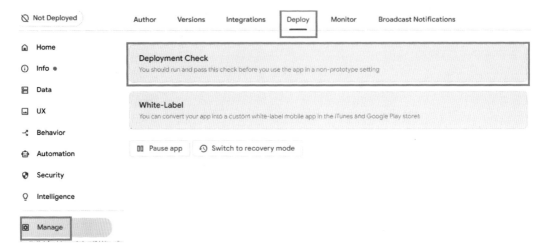

Figure 7.19 – App Deploy options

Let us now understand each option available under the **Manage | Deploy** tab in detail.

## Checking an app's deployment readiness

With the **Deployment Check** option, you can check whether an app is ready for deployment or you need to remove some errors before it can be deployed. When you click on the **Deployment Check** option, you will get the following pane:

Figure 7.20 – The Deployment Check option

When you click on the **Run deployment check** button, the app editor shows you the deployment status of your app, as shown in the following figure:

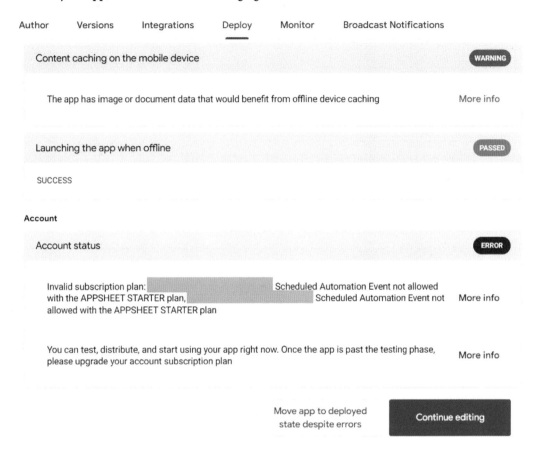

Figure 7.21 – Deployment Check results

The app editor checks the app's deployment status under five different categories – **Definition**, **User Interface**, **Security**, **Performance**, and **Account**. The preceding screenshot shows a small section of the **Deployment Check** results pane.

The app editor displays the results in three different statuses. If we look at the preceding screenshot, there is one **PASSED**, one **WARNING**, and one **ERROR** result:

- **PASSED**: This means the app editor has passed the parameter in the deployment check and you need not take any further action for this parameter.

- **WARNING**: This means the parameter has an issue as indicated in the associated message for the app. The parameters flagged with the **WARNING** status do not prevent you from deploying the app if you want to. However, it is always a good practice to clear as many **WARNING** statuses as possible and move those to the **PASSED** status.

- **ERROR**: These are major errors that you should correct before you can deploy the app.

When the deployment check shows multiple warnings and errors, you can tap the **Continue Editing** button to resume. After you clear all the errors as per the suggested instructions in the deployment check results, you can deploy the app.

We will briefly discuss how you can white label an app and host it on the Apple App Store and the Google Play Store next.

## White labeling an app

The white labeling of an app involves advanced app publishing concepts and procedures for publishing the apps on the Android and iOS app stores. We will only discuss an overview of white labeling an AppSheet app in this book.

With the white labeling option, you can place your app in the Google Play Store and the Apple App Store. You can also use white labeling to remove the AppSheet branding and include your own branding in the app. You can also distribute a white label app on your own.

In the case of non-white label apps, AppSheet app users need to download the AppSheet app from the app stores first. It acts as a host for your developed non-white label AppSheet apps to run on the user's device.

When you publish a white label AppSheet app on the app stores, the app user does not have to download the AppSheet app from the app stores. The user can simply download your white label app on their device.

With white labeling, you can remove most of the AppSheet branding that the user can see in an app. However, at certain places in the app, the AppSheet branding is still visible to the user even after you white label an app. The AppSheet branding is visible in the login and error screens, for example.

You need to be aware that to publish a white label app on the app stores, you will need to undergo the app publishing and approval processes established by those respective app stores.

You will also need an AppSheet core licensing plan with a minimum of 10 licenses to publish a white label app.

Now let us understand how you can pause an app and how you can invoke data recovery mode in an app.

## Additional options under the Deploy tab

There are two additional options under the **Deploy** tab: **Pause app** and **Switch to recovery mode**. Let us understand when you can use these options.

### Pausing an app

At times, you may want to work on the data of your app. In such instances, you would want your users not to use the app. When you click on the **Pause app** option, a dialog pane appears as shown in the following screenshot:

www.appsheet.com says

Use this option to temporarily prevent your users from syncing any data changes. Use this option when you performing data maintenance for a limited time window. Please make sure to Resume the app as soon as possible. Do you want to proceed?

OK          Cancel

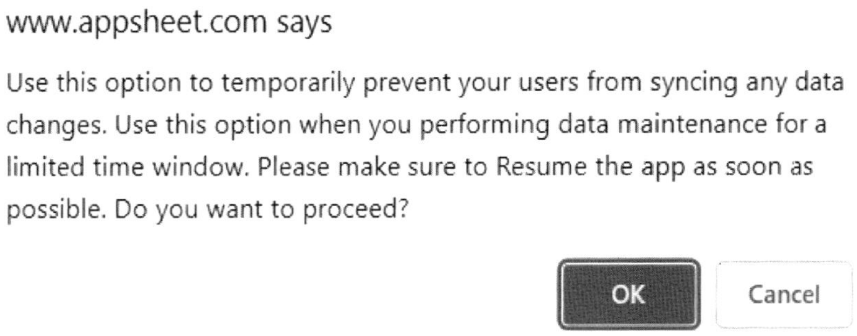

Figure 7.22 – Pausing an app

Once you pause an app, users of your app can no longer make any data changes to the app. When they try to sync the data in a paused app, they will get an error message, as shown in the following screenshot:

# Error

The

**Inventory Management    -   123456**  app did not load successfully. Please contact the app creator.

Unable to fetch app definition. The app creator has paused this app and blocked all data syncs and updates. This is usually done to provide a temporary maintenance window. Please try to sync again la

[0]

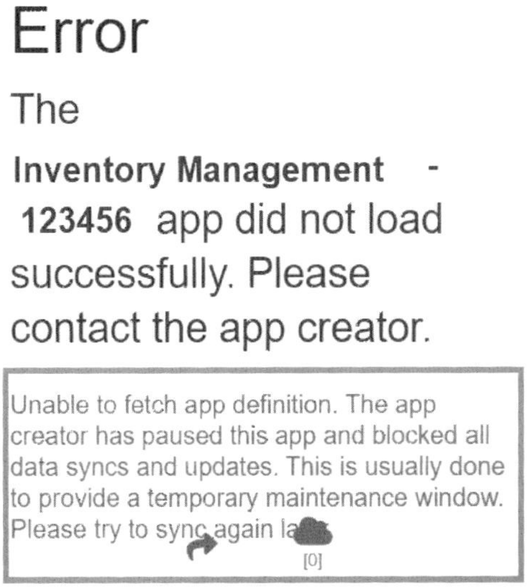

Figure 7.23 – Paused app error message for users

You resume the paused app again by clicking on the **Resume paused app** option. This option shows up in the same place under the **Deploy** option as **Pause app** is shown. When you resume a paused app, your app users can make data changes to the app again.

### Switching to recovery mode

At times, you will find that you have made major changes to an app definition such as adding or deleting columns from the tables in your app. Thereafter, you have upgraded the version of your app. However, it is possible that a few of your app users have not synced the app to get the latest app version on their device and they are still saving their changes to the older version of the app.

In this instance, when the app users try to sync changes made to an older version of the app, the changes will obviously not sync and will not be saved to the data source of the app. This failure to sync is because of a mismatch in the number of columns in the data source and the earlier version of the app. The users will see relevant error messages in the app that let them know their data is not getting saved due to a mismatch in the column structure or a similar reason.

In such cases, the user cannot save the app changes to the app source nor will they be able to use the app anymore until they load the latest app version on their device. When users report such issues to you, you can invoke **recovery mode**. You can invoke either **app recovery mode** or **manual recovery mode**. You can use the recovery mode option as shown in the following screenshot:

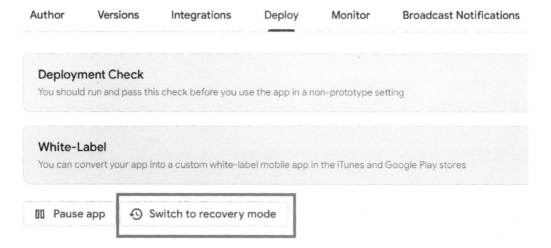

Figure 7.24 – App data recovery mode

Now, let us understand how the app recovery mode works.

## Invoking app recovery mode

When you click on the **Switch to recovery mode** option under the **Manage | Deploy** option, a user who has unsaved changes due to a version mismatch can sync the app. The app automatically creates a recovery folder in the app's root folder and saves the recovery file(s) in this recovery folder. The recovery folder looks as shown in the following screenshot:

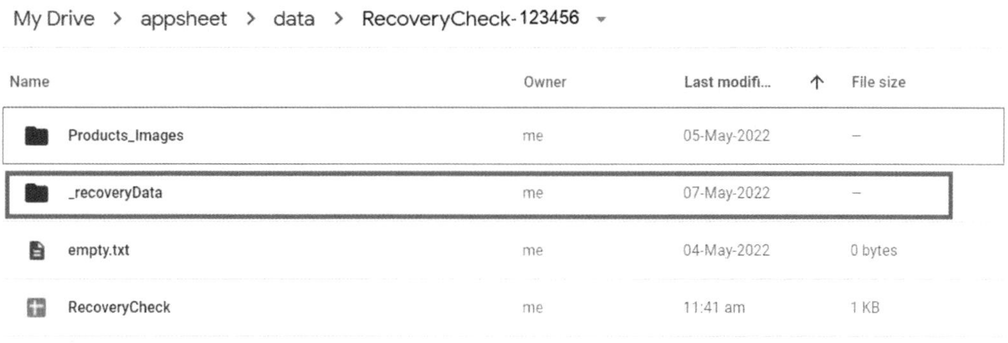

Figure 7.25 – App data recovery folder

The recovery folder named `_recoveryData` contains the recovery file that looks as shown in the following screenshot:

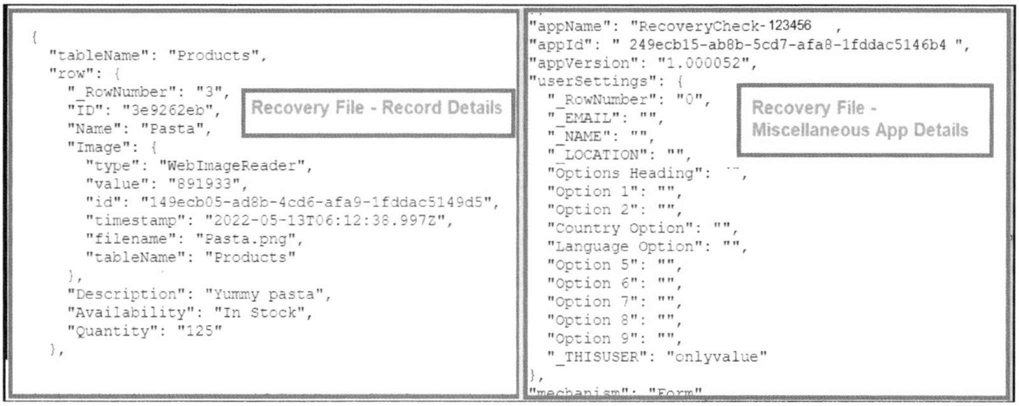

Figure 7.26 – An example of an app data recovery file

As the screenshot shows, the recovery file contains the column value details of the recovered records and various details of the app itself. The recovery file is a file with the `.txt` extension and contains the recovery data in JSON format. You can then manually copy the recovered data to the app's data source in the appropriate tables and columns.

### *Performing manual recovery*

App users can also manually perform recovery steps. When the user realizes they cannot sync the records from their device, they can tap on the app's hamburger menu. They will see the unsaved changes of pending syncs. The following screenshot shows **Sync [3]**, meaning three records are pending to be synced:

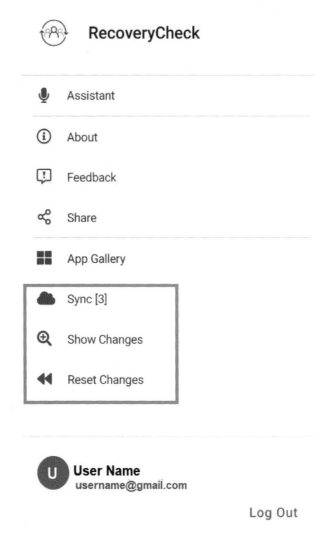

Figure 7.27 – App data recovery (non-synced records)

The user can then tap on the **Show Changes** option. They will see a screen of pending changes as shown in the following screenshot:

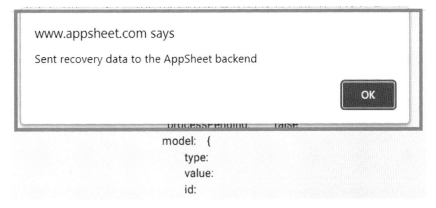

```
              Queued local changes

Action        Params
              {
              tableName:  Products
              row:     {
                   _RowNumber:    2
                   ID:  fc1ccb75
                   Name:   Cake
                   Image:  {
                        _flattenCallbacks:   {
                             }

                        _flattened:   {
                             }

                        _flattenPending:  false
                        _processCallbacks:   {
                             }

                        _processed:
                        _processPending:      false
                        model:  {
                             type:
                             value:
                             id:
                             timestamp:
                             filename:
```

Figure 7.28 – App data recovery (the queued changes screen)

The user will also see a message after a few seconds on the same **Queued local changes** screen, shown in the following screenshot, saying that the queued changes have been saved in the recovery folder. As we learned earlier, the recovery process automatically creates a recovery folder in the app's root folder:

```
www.appsheet.com says

Sent recovery data to the AppSheet backend

                                              OK

              processPending      false
              model:  {
                   type:
                   value:
                   id:
```

Figure 7.29 – App data recovery (the sent recovery data message)

When the user clicks on the **Show Changes** option, the app initiates one more sequence of steps. The app takes the user to the available email provider icons on the user's device and when the user taps on one of those email provider icons, the app copies the recovery data in the body of the email, as the following screenshot shows:

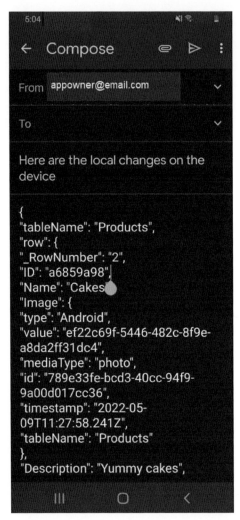

Figure 7.30 – App data recovery (a queued changes email)

The app user can then send the email containing recovery data to themself or the app owner.

Once the queued data is recovered in the recovery folder or sent via email, the user can tap **Reset Changes**. **Reset Changes** will delete those non-synced records from the user's app device. You can then manually copy the recovered data to the app's data source in the appropriate tables and columns. This step completes the data recovery process.

Let us summarize our learning in this section. In this section, you learned how you can move an app from the prototype stage to the deployed stage so that all its features become available to the users, and you can deploy it to more than 10 active users. You learned how you can pause an app when you wish to perform any data maintenance on an app. You also understood how you can perform data recovery in an app.

In the next section, you will understand how you can effectively monitor various app usage activities and analyze an app's sync time performance using the options available under the **Manage | Monitor** tab.

# Monitoring app usage and app sync performance

The options available under the **Manage | Monitor** tab allow you to monitor and manage several app usage parameters:

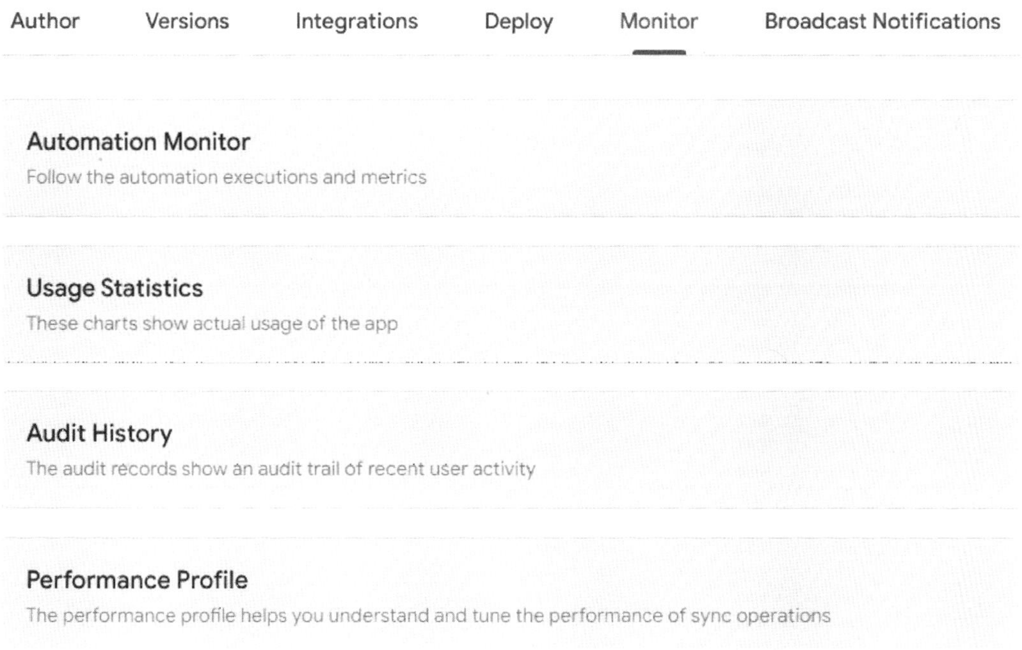

Author        Versions        Integrations        Deploy        Monitor        Broadcast Notifications

**Automation Monitor**

Follow the automation executions and metrics

**Usage Statistics**

These charts show actual usage of the app

**Audit History**

The audit records show an audit trail of recent user activity

**Performance Profile**

The performance profile helps you understand and tune the performance of sync operations

Figure 7.31 – The Manage | Monitor sub-options

As you can see in the preceding screenshot, the **Monitor** option has four sub-options:

- **Automation Monitor:** If you have configured automation in your app, **Automation Monitor** allows you to find out the various steps of the automation a bot is executing and whether there are any errors in the automation. We will not discuss **Automation Monitor** any further in this chapter. You will understand the Automation Monitor in *Chapter 8*.

- **Usage Statistics:** This option lets you know about the app usage pattern of all app users. It also lets you know statistics such as how many users have used the app in a calendar month and how many users have used the app daily in the past month.

- **Audit History:** This option shows a log of the interactions app users have had with the app. **Audit History** shows which user has added, deleted, or edited a record in an app and when a user has invoked an action or automation. It also captures the timestamp in the **Universal Time Coordinated (UTC)** locale of these user activities.

- **Performance Profile:** This shows the app's performance in terms of sync time between the app and the app's data source. You can drill down in this **Performance Profile** log to find out the time taken to sync by various components in the app, such as tables, virtual columns, and some internal activities performed by AppSheet, such as validating your app's subscription plan.

Once you have found out the various usage parameters with the help of the **Monitor** option, you can then take corrective steps to improve the performance wherever it is unsatisfactory.

## Knowing the user's app usage pattern

The **Usage Statistics** option is available under the **Monitor** tab. As the following screenshot shows, you can get the various **Usage Statistics** graphs by clicking on the **Get usage statistics** button:

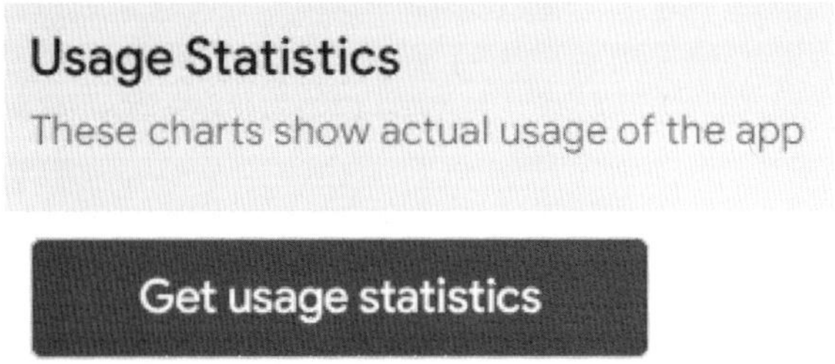

Figure 7.32 – The Usage Statistics option

When you click on the **Get usage statistics** button, you get four different graphs. The first graph under the **Usage Statistics** option shows the total unique users per month for the app in the latest four calendar months, including the current calendar month:

Total unique app users per month

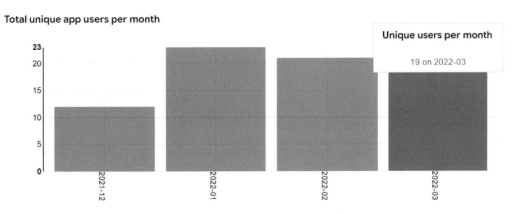

Figure 7.33 – Usage Statistics to view unique users per month

The number of total unique users per month helps you in knowing the monthly usage pattern for your app.

The second graph shows the total unique app users per day in the last 30 days. This graph helps you in knowing the daily app usage pattern:

Total unique app users per day

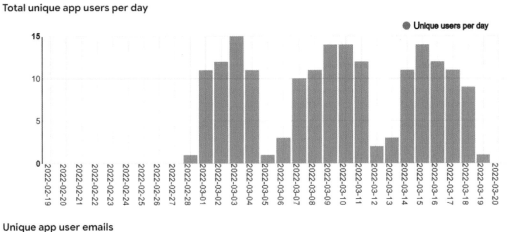

Figure 7.34 – Usage Statistics (unique users per day)

As the screenshot shows, the graph lets you know the aggregated users per day of the app in the last 30 calendar days. With this graph, you can see app usage patterns on a daily basis.

The next or third graph under the **Usage Statistics** option shows **Individual app users per day** in the last 30 calendar days:

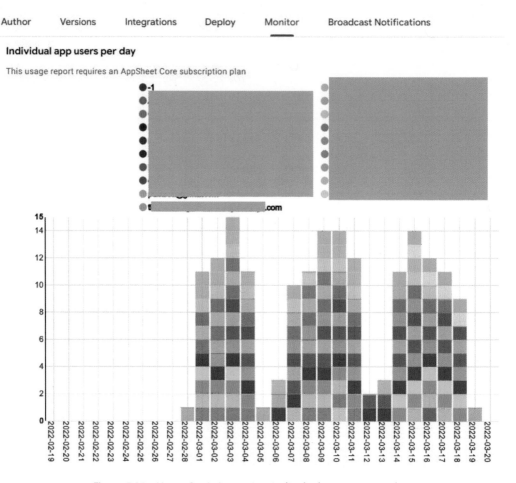

Figure 7.35 – Usage Statistics to view individual app users per day

There are as many different shades of color in the graph as the number of users in that calendar month. Each shade represents one user across the entire graph. This helps you to get an overview of the usage pattern of the app for a user. The graph shows the emails of each user associated with each color shade.

The last or fourth graph under the **Usage Statistics** option shows the per-user drilldown of the app. So, essentially, it shows similar information to the third graph. However, instead of showing all the users in a single graph with a separate color shade for each user as shown in graph three, the fourth graph, titled **Per-user drilldown: app interactions per day**, shows each user's app usage. You need to select the email of the user for whom you wish to know the app usage from a drop-down email list of all app users. This drop-down box is highlighted in the rectangular box in the following screenshot:

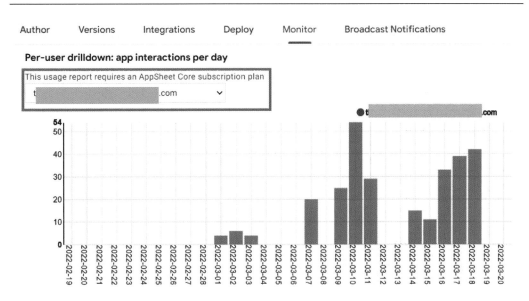

Figure 7.36 – Usage Statistics to view individual app users per day

The graph shows the usage pattern of the selected user on each day in the preceding 30 days. The *Y*-axis represents the number of app interactions by the user on a daily basis. So on March 10, the selected user had the most app interactions, at 54. The users did not use the app on certain days, such as March 4, 5, 6, 8, 12, 13, 19, and 20, 2022, and on none of the days in February 2022.

The third and fourth graphs described in the preceding section are only available under the **AppSheet Core** subscription plan and higher.

Let us next understand how you can monitor user activity for the app at the row level.

## Using Audit History for the row-level user activity

The **Audit History** option takes a deeper dive into user activity. It shows user activity in terms of data change actions such as adding a row, deleting a row, updating a row, performed by a user, and other app data editing activities such as a bot running.

To get the recent audit history of an app, you need to click on the **Audit History** section under the **Manage | Monitor** tab, as shown in the following screenshot:

## Audit History

The audit records show an audit trail of recent user activity

Figure 7.37 – The Audit History option

After clicking on the **Audit History** option, you get a pane as shown in the following screenshot:

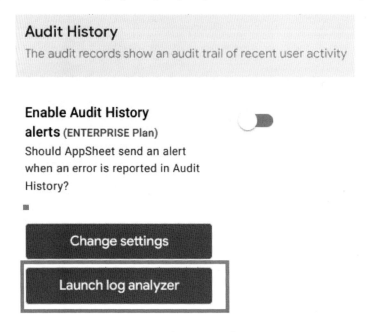

Figure 7.38 – Audit History sub-options

When you click on the **Launch log analyzer** button, you get a long audit history log that has several sections. We will look at these sections in a stepwise manner.

The following screenshot shows the first section of the audit history log that is at the top of the entire log page:

Enterprise Dashboard: Audit Log for 4Actions-Projects-5689905

To use audit log filtering and analytics, please contact us about an Enterprise plan.

| Syncs? ☑ | Adds? ☑ | Updates? ☑ | Deletes? ☑ | Workflows? ☑ | Reports? ☑ | API calls? ☑ | Documents? ☑ |
|---|---|---|---|---|---|---|---|
| Start at (UTC)  3/15/2022 6:33:13 AM | | End at (UTC)  3/22/2022 5:48:07 AM | | Only Display Failures? ☐ | | | |

Your subscription plan allows you to retain logs for 7 days

| TableName | | UserId | | RuleName | | Search | |
|---|---|---|---|---|---|---|---|

For efficiency, the audit log viewer examines at most 1000 records in the specified time range                                    Download 'Search' results

Figure 7.39 – Audit history filtering options

The first section of the audit history log has filter settings to show the audit log records as per your selection. However, the filtering with all the options shown in the screenshot is only available in the **Enterprise** plan subscription.

If your subscription plan is lower than the **Enterprise** plan, you can only do the following:

- See the audit log records for the past 7 days

- Select only the time range in the filter selections

- Get an audit history of a maximum of 1,000 records irrespective of the time range selected

The following screenshot shows the second and third sections of an audit log:

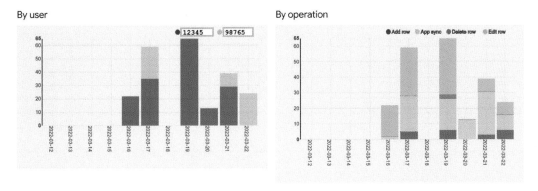

Figure 7.40 – Audit history log graphs

The second section of the audit history log shows two graphs. In the screenshot, the first graph titled **By user** shows that the **12345** user and the **98765** user have performed a certain number of app operations on a daily basis. This graph shows the total number of operations performed by each app user in the app in the last 7 days. The second graph shows the type of app operations performed daily by all the users in the last 7 days. So, the first graph, **By User**, shows that on one specific day, all the users performed 65 row-level operations in the app. This same number of 65 operations on the same day is reflected on the right-hand side graph, **By operation**. So, the total number of operations on each day naturally matches in both graphs, the difference being the left-hand side graph shows row-level operations *by user*, and the right-hand side graph shows operations *by type of operation*.

The second graph, titled **By operation**, shows the number of different operations performed by all the users of the app each day. You can see that on March 19, the app users performed **delete** operations. On March 16, there were no **add** operations and only **edit** operations.

However, the graphs in the preceding screenshot are still a high-level aggregation of app activities by users or operations. If you wish to take an even more detailed look at the result of each of those operations, you can look at the third section of the **Audit History** log, as the following screenshot shows:

| Operation | On | By User | Is Preview | When (UTC) | Duration (sec) | Result | Details | TraceId |
|---|---|---|---|---|---|---|---|---|
| App sync | | | True | 3/22/2022 1:42:58 PM | 0.383 | ✔ Success | 🔍 | Parent |
| App sync – Start | | | True | 3/22/2022 1:42:58 PM | | – | ☰ | Parent |
| Add row | Tasks | | true | 3/22/2022 1:42:56 PM | 0.729 | ✔ Success | 🔍 | Parent |
| Add row – Start | Tasks | | true | 3/22/2022 1:42:56 PM | | – | ☰ | Parent |
| Edit row | Projects | | true | 3/22/2022 1:42:52 PM | 3.137 | ✔ Success | 🔍 | Parent |
| Edit row – Start | Projects | | true | 3/22/2022 1:42:52 PM | | – | ☰ | Parent |
| App sync | | | True | 3/22/2022 1:42:21 PM | 0.281 | ✔ Success | 🔍 | Parent |
| App sync – Start | | | True | 3/22/2022 1:42:21 PM | | – | ☰ | Parent |

Figure 7.41 – Audit History detailed logs

The screenshot shows logs of one *edit*, one *add*, and one *sync* operation. The details of each log record show the following:

- **Operation**: Shows the type of operation.
- **On**: Indicates the table on which the operation took place.
- **By User**: The email and account ID of the user who performed the operation.
- **Is Preview**: Results in **True** if the audit history record is created by using the app in app preview mode or results in **False** if the audit history record is not created by using the app in app preview mode.
- **When (UTC)**: The UTC locale timestamp of when the user performed the operation.
- **Duration (sec)**: The time taken to complete the operation.
- **Result**: The result of the operation: **Success** or **Error**.
- **Details**: The details of the operation. You can click on the binoculars or the list icon to get the results of the operation.
- **TraceId**: The trace ID associated with the audit log records.

Having understood how the audit history log captures operation details, let us look at an example of an erroneous operation captured by the audit history log:

Figure 7.42 – Audit history detailed logs with error log records

The screenshot shows a log record with an error. This means an app operation has an error.

When you click on the binoculars or list icon in any of the audit records, you get a further drilldown of operation details. The following screenshot shows an example of the first part of the details you get when you click on the list icon of an audit record:

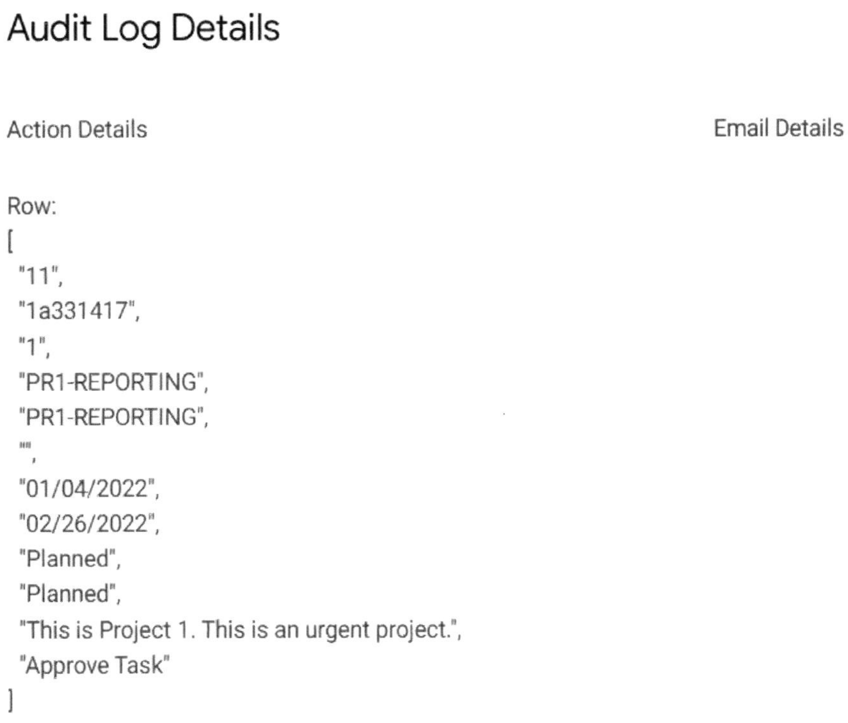

## Audit Log Details

Action Details                                                          Email Details

Row:
[
  "11",
  "1a331417",
  "1",
  "PR1-REPORTING",
  "PR1-REPORTING",
  ""
  ,
  "01/04/2022",
  "02/26/2022",
  "Planned",
  "Planned",
  "This is Project 1. This is an urgent project.",
  "Approve Task"
]

Figure 7.43 – Audit history log details

The preceding screenshot shows the values populated in each column after the user has edited a row. The second part of the details in the following screenshot shows the properties of the edited row.

Properties:
{
  "TableName": "Tasks",
  "tzOffset": "-330",
  "apiLevel": "2",
  "isPreview": "true",
  "checkCache": "true",
  "locale": "en-GB",
  "appTemplateVersion": "1.000080",
  "localVersion": "1.000080",
  "timestamp": "2022-03-22T15:19:54.14Z",
  "requestStartTime": "2022-03-22T15:19:57.506Z",
  "lastSyncTime": "2022-03-22T15:19:16.6403965Z",
  "appStartTime": "2022-03-22T15:19:16.014Z",
  "dataStamp": "2022-03-22T15:19:54.143Z",
  "clientId": "3d61ddac-1667-4342-bd78-eb5b1179d7b4",
  "build": "be67f75bce21332e0568-1647656058661-3fafb797",
  "requestId": "38752091",
  "AppTemplateVersion": "1.000080",
  "RowSize": 128,
  "AppTemplateName": "8d319bed-4f58-411a-a7ac-6642a9226f5f",
  "Operation": "Add row",
  "RecordType": "Start"
}

Figure 7.44 – Audit history log details (properties)

We will now understand the details we get when we click on the binoculars icon. You will see a log record that has captured an error in the app operations:

Properties:
{
  "IfModifiedSinceDate": "2022-03-17T11:31:10.9990667Z",
  "getAllTables": "True",
  "syncsOnConsent": "True",
  "isPreview": "True",
  "apiLevel": "2",
  "supportsJsonDataSets": "True",
  "tzOffset": "-330",
  "locale": "en-GB",
  "tableTimestamps": "0",
  "lastSyncTime": "3/17/2022 11:37:21 AM",
  "appStartTime": "3/17/2022 11:37:20 AM",
  "dataStamp": "3/17/2022 11:37:21 AM",
  "clientId": "52c2e7de-55e1-4913-ad97-07be4105b324",
  "build": "0ec04978f578b6f966d4-1647469093551-60b9af74",
  "hasValidPlan": "False",
  "userConsentedScopes": "data_input,device_identity,device_io,profile,usage",
  "localVersion": "1.000080",
  "version": "1.000080",
  "AppTemplateName": "8d319bed-4f58-411a-a7ac-6642a9226f5f",
  "Operation": "App sync",
  "RecordType": "Stop",
  "Errors": "Error: Data table 'Tasks' is not accessible due to: The service is currently unavailable..",
  "AppTemplateVersion": " ",
  "AppDefinitionChanged": true,
  "Performance": "{\"Version\":1,\"Time\":\"00:00:08.5457039\",\"PerformanceTimingRoot\":{\"Mid\":130,\"Timer\":{\"Time\":\"00:00:08.5457039\",\"ElapsedTime\":\"00:00:00\"},\"Children\":[{\"Mid\":63,\"Timer\":{\"Time\":\"00:00:08.5451431\",\"Ela
  "Result": "Failure"
}

Figure 7.45 – Audit history log details (properties)

As you can see in the screenshot, the last row shows the result as `Failure`. Whenever you see a result is a `Failure` result, you can look for another row in the audit log that starts with `Errors`. In this case, the error says that the data table is not accessible, as the service is unavailable. You can then take corrective actions according to the error message.

When the log record (as well as the log record details) show `Success`, it indicates that the related operation was successful.

You have now learned how monitoring options allow you to fully analyze user activity and row-level operations performed by users. In the next section, we will learn how the **Monitor | Performance Profile** monitoring option will help you to evaluate an app's operation performance in terms of sync time.

## Analyzing an app's sync performance

When an app syncs with its data source, the sync operation reads all the tables and their data from the data source, and virtual columns are recomputed. There are additionally some internal operations required, such as getting the app template and validating the payment plan.

The **Performance Profile** option under the **Manage | Monitor** tab is a powerful option that helps you to identify the slower steps in a sync operation. As in the case of the audit history log, the **Performance Analyzer** dashboard also has multiple sections. We will understand each of those sections now.

The following screenshot shows the first section that shows any recommendation the performance analyzer has for you as an app creator:

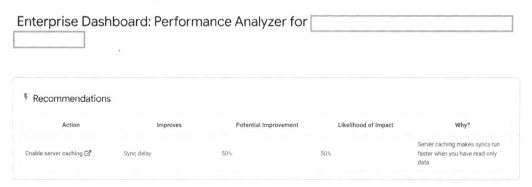

Figure 7.46 – Performance Analyzer Recommendations

As the preceding screenshot shows, the first section of **Performance Analyzer** recommends certain steps to improve the sync performance. In this example, the recommendation from **Performance Analyzer** to the app creator is to enable server caching to improve the sync performance. We learned about **server caching** in *Chapter 5*. You should pay attention to any recommendations and implement those steps when applicable in your app.

The second section of the **Performance Analyzer** log is filter settings, as the following screenshot shows:

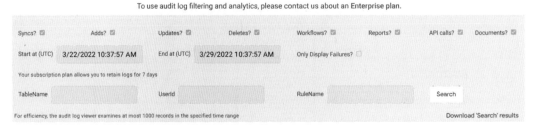

To use audit log filtering and analytics, please contact us about an Enterprise plan.

| Syncs? ☑ | Adds? ☑ | Updates? ☑ | Deletes? ☑ | Workflows? ☑ | Reports? ☑ | API calls? ☑ | Documents? ☑ |
|---|---|---|---|---|---|---|---|
| Start at (UTC) | 3/22/2022 10:37:57 AM | End at (UTC) | 3/29/2022 10:37:57 AM | Only Display Failures? ☐ | | | |

Your subscription plan allows you to retain logs for 7 days

| TableName | | UserId | | RuleName | | Search |

For efficiency, the audit log viewer examines at most 1000 records in the specified time range           Download 'Search' results

Figure 7.47 – Performance Analyzer filtering options

The filter settings and the range of records in days or the number of records available with the **Performance Analyzer** log are the same as those in the **Audit History** log that we learned about earlier, in the *Using Audit History for the row-level user activity* section for the **Audit History** log record details.

The final part of **Performance Analyzer** is the log of each **add, delete, edit, sync, or bot** operation performed by each user. The following screenshot shows how an audit log of each record is captured:

Click on the 🕶 to see performance details for individual operations

| Operation | On | By User | Is Preview | When (UTC) | Duration (sec) | Result | Performance | TraceId |
|---|---|---|---|---|---|---|---|---|
| App sync | | | True | 3/29/2022 3:51:41 AM | 1.304 | ✓ Success | 🕶 | TraceId |
| Add row | Inventory | | true | 3/29/2022 3:51:39 AM | 0.904 | ✓ Success | 🕶 | TraceId |
| App sync | | | True | 3/29/2022 3:51:28 AM | 0.993 | ✓ Success | 🕶 | TraceId |
| Change Bot – **Stock** UpdateRule | | | | 3/29/2022 3:51:25 AM | 0.000 | ✓ Success | 🕶 | TraceId |
| Edit row | Inventory | | true | 3/29/2022 3:51:22 AM | 4.371 | ✓ Success | 🕶 | TraceId |
| App sync | | | True | 3/29/2022 3:50:21 AM | 0.900 | ✓ Success | 🕶 | TraceId |

Figure 7.48 – A Performance Analyzer log for each row-level operation

Each record shows similar details to those we saw earlier for the **Audit History** log record details. There is only one difference in the **Performance Profile** log records. Instead of record details, as in the case of the **Audit History** log, when you click on the binoculars icon, you get the sync performance results of the operation.

When you click on the binoculars icon, you can view the drilled-down results of the sync performance of an operation. You will see many steps listed in the performance details of each log record:

Figure 7.49 – Performance Analyzer logs showing Performance Details

To get the sync time details of each step of the sync performance of an operation, you need to deselect all three options shown at the top right of the image. When you wish to be more selective about the steps that you wish to understand in detail, you can select a combination of the three options that you see in *Figure 7.49*.

When you take a deep dive into the performance detail steps, you will see several steps:

- **InternalAPI_GetAppTemplate**
- **App Template_Clone**
- **ValidatePaymentPlan**
- **Read the tables in parallel**
- **Read a single table**
- **Compute virtual columns**

As an app creator, you can mainly concentrate on the table reading and virtual column steps in a **Performance Analyzer** log to improve the sync performance. Most of the other steps are internal mandatory steps of an app sync operation that you will have no control over.

Let us next understand the relevant steps that you can concentrate on from **Performance Analyzer:**

- **Degree of parallelism:** This indicates the app tables read by the AppSheet server in parallel during a sync operation. The degree of parallelism depends on your subscription plan. The higher the subscription plan, the higher the degree of parallelism. And in turn, the greater the degree of parallelism, the greater the chance of improving the sync time. However, the degree of parallelism is not always helpful. If two tables are being read in parallel and one table takes 30 seconds and the other takes 5 seconds to read, then the total sync time is still 30 seconds or more.

- **Virtual columns:** You should look at the sync time consumed for the computation of virtual columns in each table. Virtual columns with expressions that compute values across multiple rows of a table or compute values across more than one table can significantly increase the sync time. You should try to minimize these virtual columns. Such expressions mostly involve AppSheet functions such as SELECT(), MINROW(), MAXROW(), and LOOKUP().

- **Blanks**: Also remove any blank columns or rows in your data source tables. This will help tables in the app to load faster.

- **Security filters**: You can implement security filters (discussed in *Chapter 6*), to reduce the number of rows downloaded on an app user's device.

- **Server caching**: You can enable server caching mainly for read-only tables in your app. Most of the time, **Performance Analyzer** will give you this recommendation under the **Recommendations** section.

In this section, you learned how you can use the **Monitor** tab to monitor various app usage patterns and an app's sync time performance. Let us now understand how you can broadcast notifications to your app users.

## Sending on-demand messages to app users

At times, you want to convey an important message to all app users. You can write a broadcast message under the **Manage | Broadcast Notifications** option. Only an app user who has *edit definition* rights to the app can construct and send broadcast notification messages. You can construct a broadcast notification message as shown in the following screenshot:

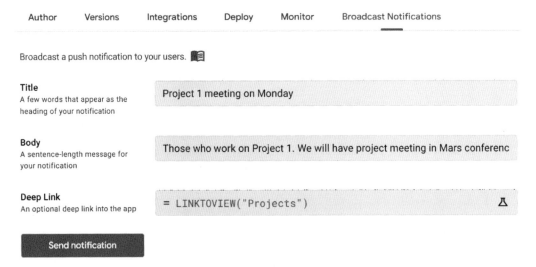

Figure 7.50 – Constructing a broadcast notification message

You need to simply write text in the **Title** and **Body** fields. However, you cannot include any AppSheet expressions the way you can in certain action types in the **To** and **Body** settings. You can also include a deep link expression in the **Deep Link** field to a view in the app in the message. When you write in the three settings and thereafter click on the **Send notification** button, the message is broadcast to all the app users' mobile devices.

The **Broadcast Notifications** settings pane becomes blank immediately after you click on the **Send notification** button. This means you can now type in a new message if you want to.

The following screenshot shows how the notification looks on a mobile device:

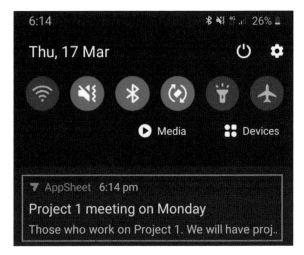

Figure 7.51 – The broadcast notification message on a mobile device

When the user taps on the notification message on their device, it takes them to the view in the app that is configured in the **Deep Link** setting of the **Broadcast Notifications** settings pane. In this current example that we are discussing, when the user taps on the notification message, they are taken to the **Project 1** detail view.

With this explanation of the **Broadcast Notifications** option, we have now gained an understanding of the various options under the **Manage** tab.

## Summary

In this chapter, we learned how you can manage and monitor various app usage activities including app sync performance and certain administrative activities by using the **Manage** tab of the app editor.

We learned how you can deploy an app through the **Manage | Deploy** tab. App deployment is necessary because you can add more than 10 users to the deployed app and all app features such as automation emails going to the intended recipients are enabled in a deployed app. You learned how you or an app user can perform data recovery.

We also learned how we can perform app version management through the **Manage | Versions** tab. Version management is one of the critical tasks that you will need throughout the life cycle of an app, as you make changes to the app to meet the often-changing business needs that any app supports.

Moreover, we learned how we can monitor app usage activities through the **Manage | Monitor** tab. You can monitor usage statistics for a recent time period through the **Monitor | Usage Statistics** option. You can also monitor app usage through the **Audit History** option, at the activity level, such as adding, editing, or deleting a row and bot execution. You can also monitor app sync performance through the **Performance Profile** option. You can use the results of the **Performance Profile** option to improve the app sync performance through several performance improvement measures.

Finally, you learned how you can use the **Manage | Broadcast Notifications** tab to send broadcast messages to your app users and allow them to navigate to a specific view in the app by tapping on the message.

In the next chapter, we will understand how you can use AppSheet automation effectively to create BOTs to  automatically send emails, create new files, and make data changes and also learn to use automation for sending notifications and SMS.

# Part 3 – Advanced Features and External Services

In this part, we will dive into one of AppSheet's key features: automation. Furthermore, we will touch upon some advanced features that will take your apps to the next level and introduce some sample use cases of external services to extend the capabilities of your apps.

This part has the following chapters:

- *Chapter 8, Automating Recurring Data Changes and Scheduling Tasks*
- *Chapter 9, Using Intelligence and Advanced Features*
- *Chapter 10, Extending App Capabilities with Third-Party Services*

# 8
# Automating Recurring Data Changes and Scheduling Tasks

**Automation** is one of the buzzwords used in the context of **Digital Transformation (DX)**. **RoBotic Process Automation (RPA)** is a popular phrase used in the same context as well. AppSheet is no exception; it provides a function to automate the business workflow with a simple setup.

It will help to satisfy the app users' expectations and requirements in various ways by building a functional business application to improve efficiency and productivity. In this chapter, we will review **AppSheet Automation** in depth.

This chapter covers the following:

- What is AppSheet Automation?
- Understanding a bot and its components
- Learning about the Events to trigger your bot
- Deep diving into the **Task** and **Data change** actions
- Conditional workflows using the other Steps

By the end of this chapter, you should be able to create your first Bot, which will automatically send emails, create new files, and make data changes. This kind of Bot is quite frequently used with an AppSheet app to assist you to automate business processes that often require a significant number of man-hours.

To begin this chapter, let's discuss what AppSheet Automation is and how it is useful.

# What is AppSheet Automation?

As of writing this book, AppSheet automates the following processes:

- Sending emails with attachments
- Creating new files with various file types, such as PDF, Excel, CSV, HTML, and so on
- Sending SMSs and notifications
- Running Data change actions
- Calling a webhook
- Running Google Apps Script and capturing the returned values

With most business applications, you need to create files as a part of the functionality you require from the app. For instance, you need to create an invoice with a financial management app and send it to a third party. It could be tedious work to create this file manually, but AppSheet will do so on your behalf, and more importantly, complete jobs of this kind instantly. The app will capture your data and AppSheet Automation will convert the file using your custom templates. File creation and sending mail and notifications are the most frequent and common use cases when it comes to AppSheet Automation, but there are other popular use cases where Automation also invokes Data change actions.

In addition, we can call a **webhook**, which sends a request to a third-party app. This is helpful for integrating your AppSheet app with other apps. Furthermore, as a recent addition in 2022, AppSheet finally connected with Google Apps Script. AppSheet is an add-on service for Google Workspace products, but thanks to the introduction of this new feature, AppSheet can be deeply integrated with Gmail, Google Drive, and other Google products to create new custom functionalities.

We are going to discuss Automation in detail throughout this chapter. Let's briefly review how you are going to develop AppSheet Automation.

In the AppSheet editor, there is an independent main menu called **Automation**. This is the centralized location where we manage AppSheet Automation. The process of automating things involves creating a Bot.

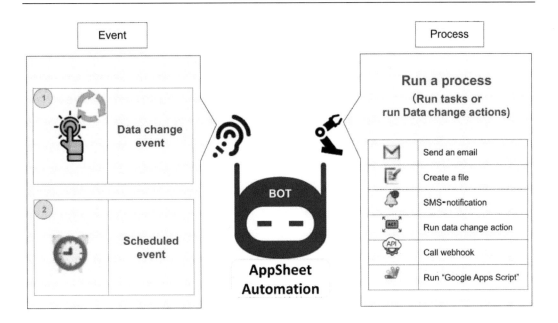

Figure 8.1 – AppSheet Automation infographic

Before we move to a more detailed discussion to understand AppSheet Automation, please refer to the preceding diagram, which provides a visual summary to aid your understanding of the basics of a Bot. AppSheet Automation is managed by a Bot. This Bot is working on a 24/7 basis, watching and listening to your app all the time. Once an Event happens, the Bot will run a Process that you have defined. To understand Bots in detail, firstly, we need to examine the components of a Bot.

## Understanding a Bot and its components

We can create multiple Bots in a single app, but each Bot will manage just a single Process that you want to automate:

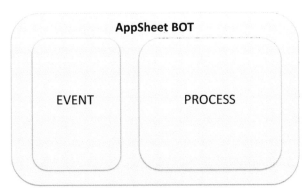

Figure 8.2 – A Bot and its main components

As you can see in the preceding figure, the Bot comprises two main components, which we will review in detail later. The first component is an **Event**. The Event is the component with which we set up when and how the Bot is going to start to work. As its name suggests, we define what sort of **Event** the Bot will handle. The second main component is called a **Process**. Inside the Process, we define what sort of jobs the Bot is going to manage, such as sending mail, creating files, and so on. In other words, the Process is the core part of any Bot you create. To handle a complicated scenario requiring advanced settings, we can build a Bot that can conditionally change its behavior by defining multiple Steps.

A Process comprises one or more Steps. A Step is a sub-component that exists inside a Process:

Figure 8.3 – Anatomy of a Bot with multiple components (Steps) inside the Process

As you can see in the preceding diagram, a Process comprises single or multiple Steps. With simple Bots, there is quite often a Process that contains only a single Step, while it is also possible that the Process comprises multiple Steps for advanced use cases.

In either case, whether the Process contains one or multiple Steps, the Process will execute the Task or Data change action that we defined.

In summary, we can recap the anatomy of a Bot in the simplest terms as follows:

- AppSheet Automation is achieved by building a Bot.
- The Bot is a wrapper for an Event and a Process.
- A Process is a wrapper for single or multiple Steps.

When we look at the settings for a new Bot for the first time, it appears that the settings required are complicated. However, the anatomy of a Bot is actually simple enough to learn. To set up a new Bot, we simply construct each component one by one in sequence.

Once you have named a new Bot, then you need to set up the Event, which defines the "trigger" for when the Bot should run, thus automating the business process. Once the Event is defined, we move to the Process by adding new Step(s). Adding Steps to the Process is as though we are typing the "job description" for the Bot. With the Steps, we define the type of jobs, such as **Task** or **Data change** actions, that we wish the Bot to execute.

Bearing this basic concept for the Bot in mind (how the Bot is built with multiple components), let's have a look more deeply into the key components one by one.

# Event – Data change or Schedule

In the previous sections, we learned about the basic anatomy of an AppSheet Bot, which is built with multiple primary components – an *Event* and a *Process*. As discussed, we need to define the Event to tell the Bot when and how should start its work. Now, let's have a look at the Event component.

## Creating a new Bot

Let's get started with the basic process to create a Bot. Go to **Automation** | **Bots**:

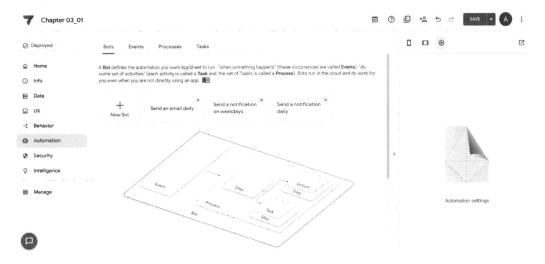

Figure 8.4 – Creating a new Bot

Once you find the **Bots** tab, click on the **+ New Bot** button to create a new Bot. Once the new Bot is created, the next step is to name this Bot. Select a name you believe is appropriate, but we suggest that the name of the Bot should be self-explanatory to tell you what kind of jobs this Bot is going to manage, such as **Sending an email when a new request is in place**:

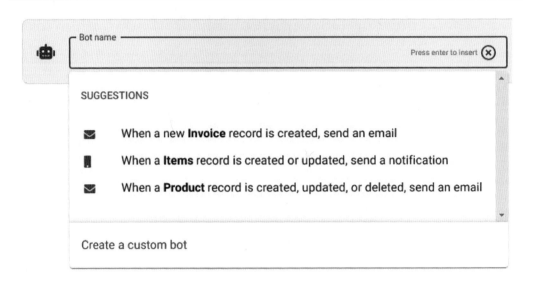

Figure 8.5 – Naming the Bot

Once the name is given to the Bot, please click on the **Create a custom Bot** button at the bottom. This is the first step to adding an Event as a primary component to your Bot:

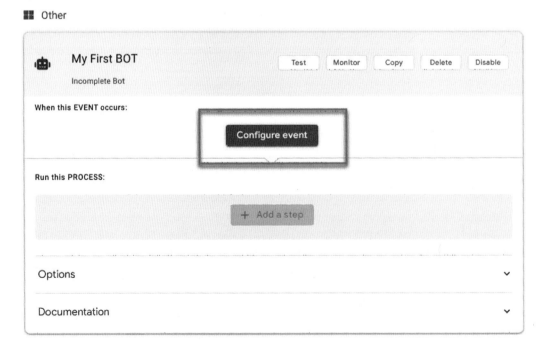

Figure 8.6 – Configuring an Event for the new Bot

After clicking on the **Configure event** button, you will see a new dialog box and can name the Event or proceed to the next step by clicking the **Create a custom event** button at the bottom. The app editor should now change in layout to look like the following screenshot:

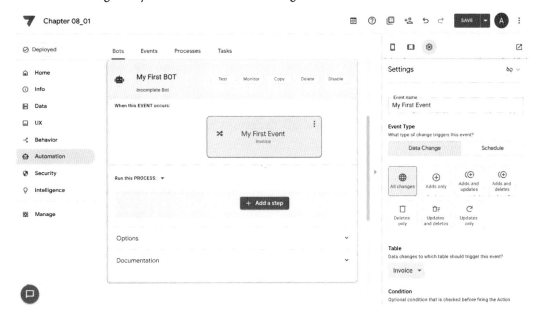

Figure 8.7 – App editor – configure the details for each component

This is a basic layout used to customize a Bot, where the optional settings are wrapped in the pane on the upper right. Usually, a preview is displayed here, but since one of the components in the Bot is selected, this area has turned into a space to configure the Bot. To switch back to the preview, you can toggle the icons at the top. You can find those icons in the following figure. For now, let's make sure the gear-shaped icon is selected by default:

Figure 8.8 – Toggling to preview mode in the Bot settings

Let's continue to work on our Event settings. As previously explained, the Event component is responsible for the trigger to get the Bot to start working. Once an Event happens, such as a Data change or the arrival of a specific date and time, then the Bot will execute the Process. For an Event component, AppSheet provides two different types:

- **Data change event**

  An AppSheet Bot is watching your app on a 24/7 basis. If a certain data change happens, such as a new record being added to a table or the data being updated or deleted, then the Bot listens to these data changes and executes Processes immediately.

  With an IT support ticket management app, for example, you may want to get an email notification once a new support request arrives. In the context of a data change, this is expressed as the addition of a new record to a table where you manage support requests. Hence, in this case, you define the Event with the **Data change** type:

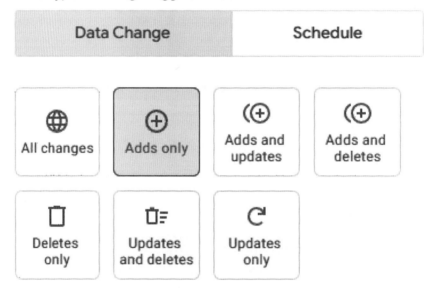

Figure 8.9 – A Data change Event – to be triggered by adding a new record

While the app is being used by a user, naturally, the data of your app will be updated. You capture a particular data change, such as a data change made in a certain column, and use this Event to trigger your Bot. In this sample case, we select **Adds only**, but you must select the appropriate data change type from the list in line with your own needs.

Data changes are always happening in the table of the app. It is an essential step that we direct the name of the table to the Event component that it is associated with. For the **Table** field, please select the name of the table in which a data change happening will trigger the Event. Mistakenly specifying the wrong data table in this field will prevent the Bot from working as expected. Make sure that the name of the table is selected properly.

There is another field – **Condition**. We will discuss this optional setting in a later section in terms of the practical use cases:

### Table

Data changes to which table should trigger this event?

### Condition

Optional condition that is checked before firing the Action

Figure 8.10 – Specifying the name of the table for the Event and condition

**Schedule event**

Schedule is another type of Event where the Bot will start to run when a specific date or time arrives. It is possible that you want to send a notification to app users every week to share some information. The Bot is a server-side operation, meaning the Bot is managed on a 24/7 basis regardless of whether the users are actually using your app or not. The Bot is watching the clock, and once the specified time arrives, the Process will be executed.

As explained, the Event component is an essential one, so you need to set it up based on your requirements whenever you create any Bot. In the following section, let's have a deeper look at Process, which are another major component of any Bot. As previously explained, the Process is the core of the Bot, as it defines the instructions on what your Bot should do (that is, automate) for you.

> **Note**
>
> When you set the Schedule event, please make sure it will not be runnable until you deploy your app. Please refer to *Chapter 7* regarding the app status, either prototype or deployed depending on the specifics, but until your app is deployed, which is subject to a paid license, the Schedule event is not going to work, so you need to pay attention to this.

# How is a Process constructed?

Referring back to the previous section, the Bot is the core of AppSheet Automation, as it defines the jobs you will automate. Roughly speaking, when the condition you set in the Event component is met, the Bot will run. Running the Bot means executing a **Process** – for instance, assuming you made a **Schedule event**, then the Bot will run once the time arrives. Whether you made the Event a **Data change** or **Schedule event**, the Bot is going to execute the **Process** you defined as far as the condition for the Event is satisfied.

Now, let's discuss how to set up a Process in detail.

## Steps for a Task or Data change action

A Bot will do a job for you and most importantly, this process is going to be automated. At the beginning of this chapter, we briefly explained what Automation can do, such as sending emails and creating new files automatically.

To achieve that, we need to set up a **Process** by configuring the Steps involved in that **Process**.

We will explain more options available for the Steps, but let us focus first on Task and Data change actions, as they are the Steps that we must not forget. A Step is a direct child component of a Process. Let us explain how we add a new Step to a Process before we dig into Process further.

## Adding a new step to a Process

Once we have successfully set up the Event, then we need to set up the Process by adding a new Step to it. Click on the **Add a step** button. As you may have done earlier when naming the Bot and Event, you can pass the name of the Step, which should be self-explanatory in terms of what the Step will achieve. Then, click on the **Create a custom step action** to continue.

Now, you should see something similar to the following figure:

Figure 8.11 – New Step configuration

In the center of this tile, there is a dropdown set to **Run a task** by default. We have added the new Step successfully, but we have to configure it further by selecting the **type of Step** from this dropdown:

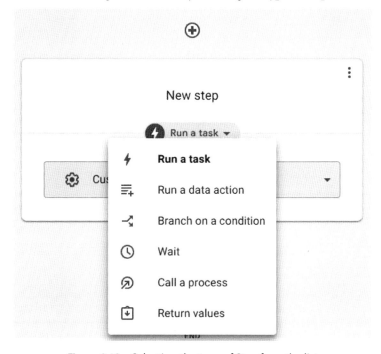

Figure 8.12 – Selecting the type of Step from the list

On clicking this **Run a task** dropdown, you will see the list in the preceding screenshot. There are six available options, but **Run a task** and **Run a data action** are the most important options you need to know. Any Bot you create in the future will have the type of Step specified as we've seen here. In the coming sections, let's focus on those two types of Steps.

## Setting up a task in a Step

A Task is a type of Step where you can manage to automate various business processes such as the following:

- Sending an email
- Sending a notification
- Sending an SMS
- Calling a webhook
- Creating a new file
- Calling a script

At the beginning of this chapter, we first explained the list of the workflows AppSheet Automation can put into action. As you see, the preceding list reiterates what Automation can manage.

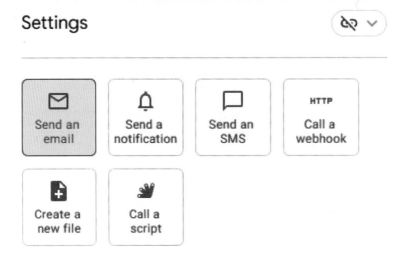

Figure 8.13 – Available types of Task

Once you select a Task for a Step type, then you need to select further the Task type from the list, which you can see in the preceding figure. If you want to automate the sending of an email, you select **Send an email**.

This book is designed for AppSheet beginners: we refrain from explaining all the available Task options in detail due to the page limit of this book. We will explain the detailed setup for the Task of sending an email (along with creating a new file), which is quite commonly and frequently used in AppSheet Automation. We will use practical examples to see how to set it up step by step, but for now, let's review what each Task can achieve.

### Send an email

This is one of the most popular Task types to automate sending emails to one or more recipients. With this Task type, you can send an email to a designated email address. For the email body, you can pull data from inside the app. Furthermore, this Task can be used to generate attachment files, such as PDFs or Excel files. We will dig into more details in a later section. You will learn how to set up this Task by running through a practical example.

### Send a notification

This Task will automate sending notifications to mobile phones. A notification is helpful when you need to call for special attention or share new information among app users, as well as giving a heads-up to users once new important data is saved to the apps by other app users.

*Send an SMS*

This is a similar Task to sending a notification. You can automate sending an SMS to app users.

*Call a webhook*

In a nutshell, a webhook is a service where the app will send messages or information to other apps. The typical use case of this Task is to post a message to chat apps. To learn the basics for this Task, please refer to the *Integrating with Google Workspace products* section in *Chapter 10*, where we will demonstrate the integration of an AppSheet app with Google Chat.

*Create a new file*

This is another popular Task, in addition to sending an email. Through this Task, you can automate the process of generating various types of files. As previously explained, the **Send an email** Task can be used to create email attachment files. This **Create a new file** Task is almost identical in terms of the settings required. The generated files will be saved to one of the default storage services such as Google Drive or OneDrive. If you are using Google account for your AppSheet account, the files will be saved to Google Drive, while it is saved to OneDrive if your AppSheet account is based on Microsoft service.

*Call a script*

This Task was introduced recently in 2022. AppSheet is now in the Google Workspace family and will work closely with other Google Workspace applications, such as Gmail, Drive, and so on. With this Task, we can invoke the Google Apps Script function. Google Apps Script is said to be a low-code solution, but it requires an understanding of JavaScript and coding knowledge, which is out of the scope of this book for an AppSheet beginner, so we will not explain this Task further.

As we have seen by reviewing the available Task types, AppSheet Automation helps to automate common business processes, such as sending an email or creating files. We will deep dive into the **Send an email** Task type in a later section of this chapter so that you are familiar with setting up your first Bot.

In the following section, let us explain another commonly used Step, **Run a data action**. In *Chapter 5*, we went through AppSheet actions in depth. Using a Bot, we can invoke those Actions, but there are some limitations in terms of the type of Actions we are able to run from the Bot.

## Data change actions

We covered the basics for AppSheet actions in *Chapter 5* earlier. AppSheet Actions help to improve the user experience within AppSheet, assisting with navigation from one view to another and helping to change the data for the target columns. With AppSheet Automation, we can invoke Actions by selecting **Run a data action** as the Step type in the **New step** dropdown, as shown in the following screenshot.

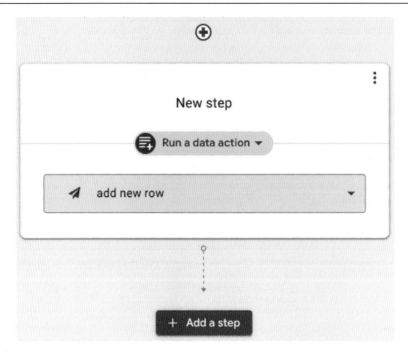

Figure 8.14 – Running a Data change as the Step type

We learned about various types of Actions in *Chapter 5*, and you may remember that there are several Actions that invoke data changes. There are also other Actions, such as exporting data to a CSV file and navigating to another view that are not accompanied by data changes. Please remember that those actions not involving data action can not be invoked in the Step(s).

In the following section, we will run through the basics of setting up a Bot using a practical example. With this exercise, you will learn how to set up a Step for a data change action as well.

## Learning about Bot setup through a practical example

Using what we have learned so far, let's create a new Bot using the sample app. These exercises will guide you through the creation of a Bot that will manage the most frequently used Task (**Send an email**) as well as invoke an Action from the Step.

Sending an email is one of the basic requirements many app creators seek to implement with AppSheet apps. It is often used when you call for actions by other app users, such as giving approvals to the document and applications or you just simply share information by sending mails, and for many other purposes, an automated email is used. When the Bot is run, an email attachment can automatically be created. File creation is another frequently used functionality within Automation. We will cover the Step to create an email attachment file – however, creating an attachment file is almost identical to the **Create a new file** Task type, so once we go through this exercise, you will understand how to set up the Step to create a new file as well.

To follow this example app project, please refer to the sample `Chapter 08_01` folder at `https://www.appsheet.com/templates/sample?appGuidString=7774886c-fcd1-4859-8703-b2263c3c1b10`. For this exercise, let's consider the following requirements:

- The app's purpose is to manage invoices.
- The app creates invoices with line items.
- You wish to create invoices in PDF format, in line with the company template.
- The status of an invoice, such as "Draft" or "Sent," is managed by the `[Status]` column in the invoice table.
- You need to create 2 Task(s) to manage the following:
- Creating an email attachment (an invoice in the form of a PDF).
- Sending an email to a designated recipient with this PDF.
- Once the email is sent out, then the value of the `[Status]` column is changed to "Sent."

This `Chapter 08_01` sample app is based on another sample used in *Chapter 2*, `Chapter 02_01`, at `https://www.appsheet.com/templates/sample?appGuidString=c01096c0-833c-4b88-9ee5-981dbb555b54`. `Chapter 02_01` is a sample app for managing invoices and we call this app the *base app*. This demonstration will start with this base app and we will extend its functionality by adding automation. To follow along with the exercises to come, we recommend you copy the base app to your account (make a sandbox app) and carry on the exercise in this section.

Once your sandbox app is ready, let's start adding some new automation.

Before we dive into the details, let us review in sequence the jobs required to fulfill our app requirements:

- **Preparation**: We need to implement a system to trigger the Bot to run. It is quite common that we place Action which will make a data change in a certain column, and AppSheet Bot will take the data change made by such an Action as a trigger to start jobs. This is preparation work before we start to create a new Bot from a scratch.
- **Creating a new Bot and setting up an event**: We will create a new Bot by configuring an event to run based on data changes made through the Action created during the initial stage of the preparation.
- **Adding the first Step**: Add a new Step (as a child component to the process) in which we will add a task to send an email with an attachment.
- **Adding the second Step**: Add a subsequent Step that will be invoked after the first Step is completed to change a value in the target column of `[Status]`.
- **Testing Bot**: The final test before the app is presented to the users to ensure it works as expected.

## Setting up the column used to trigger the Bot for a data change event

As we can see in the requirements, we want to send an email automatically to the user, but the question is when this automation is going to run. As we learned earlier, automation can either be triggered by a Schedule or Data change event. For this exercise, we would like to create a new data change action to trigger the Bot. Once the user clicks on the Action, this will initiate the data change and in turn, will invoke the Event for Automation to send an email. This is quite a typical implementation with AppSheet Automation for *Event* configurations.

To begin with, we need to add a new **normal column** to the invoice table. Please go to the source spreadsheet and add a new column there. Let's name this column `Trigger`:

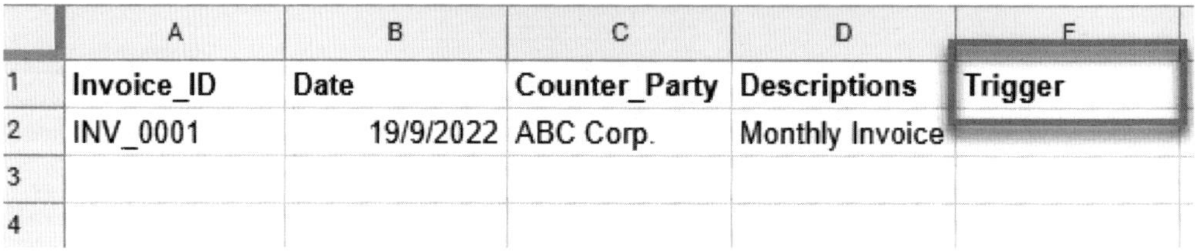

| | A | B | C | D | F |
|---|---|---|---|---|---|
| 1 | Invoice_ID | Date | Counter_Party | Descriptions | Trigger |
| 2 | INV_0001 | 19/9/2022 | ABC Corp. | Monthly Invoice | |
| 3 | | | | | |
| 4 | | | | | |

Figure 8.15 – Adding a Trigger column to the source sheet

Once you have added a new column to the source sheet, go to the **App Editor | Columns** settings and generate the **Invoice** table by clicking on the **Regenerate Structure** button at the top to refresh your table. Once the app editor has refreshed, you will see that the **Trigger** column has been added to this table. Set the data type to **Number** and pass 0 as the initial value. This *normal column* will be used behind the scenes by the system, so we can hide this column by unchecking the **SHOW?** setting:

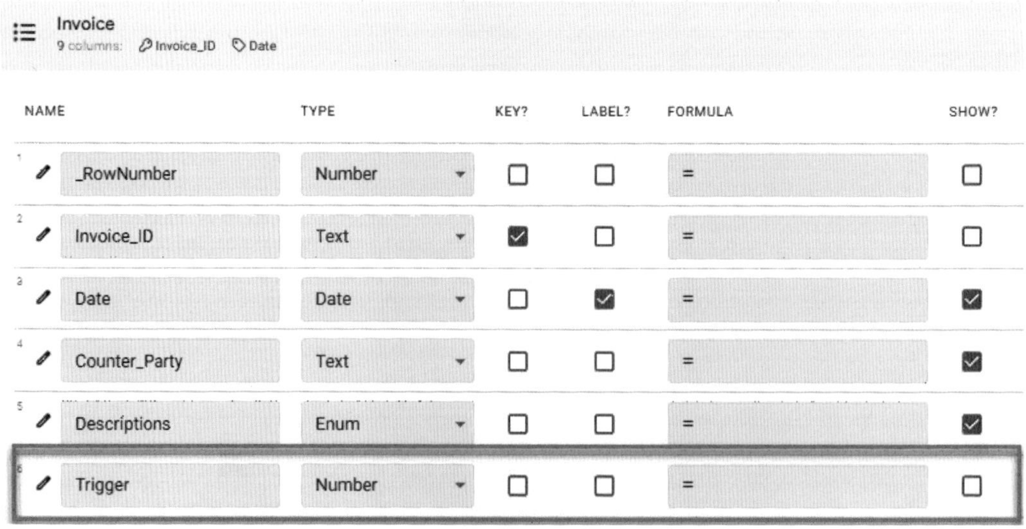

**Invoice**
9 columns:    Invoice_ID    Date

| NAME | TYPE | KEY? | LABEL? | FORMULA | SHOW? |
|---|---|---|---|---|---|
| _RowNumber | Number | ☐ | ☐ | = | ☐ |
| Invoice_ID | Text | ☑ | ☐ | = | ☐ |
| Date | Date | ☐ | ☑ | = | ☑ |
| Counter_Party | Text | ☐ | ☐ | = | ☑ |
| Descriptions | Enum | ☐ | ☐ | = | ☑ |
| Trigger | Number | ☐ | ☐ | = | ☐ |

Figure 8.16 – Detailed settings for the Trigger column

The addition of the column is now complete. The next Step is to create a new action to change the value of this **Trigger** column. So, go to the **Behavior | Actions** tab and click on the **New Action** button. Please see the following screenshot for how you need to configure the data change action:

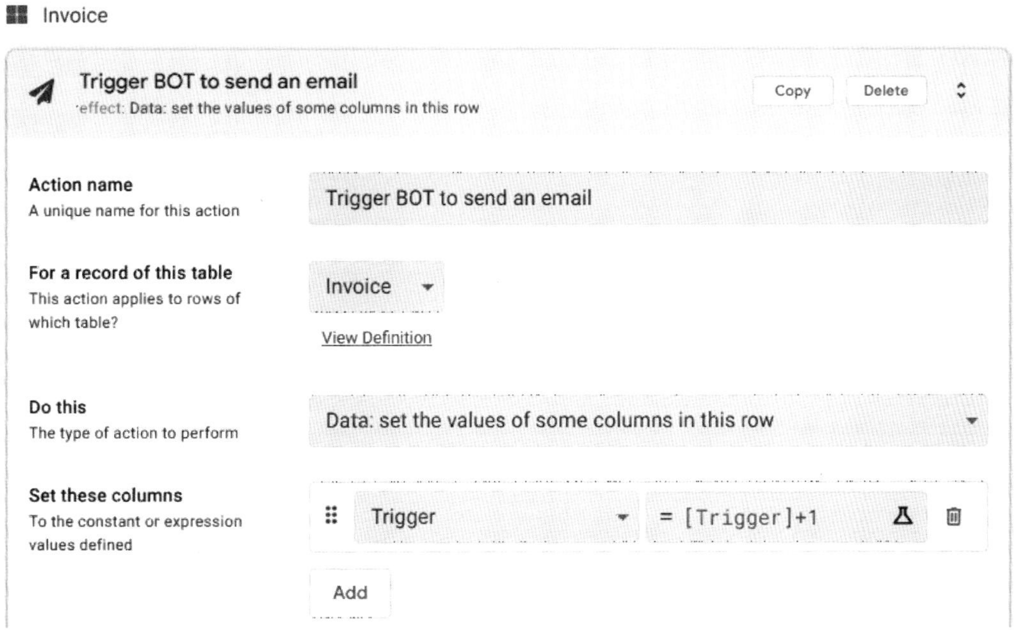

Figure 8.17 – Data change action settings

As you can see, it's of the **Data: set the values of some columns in this row** type, and this Action will increment the value of the **Trigger** column by 1 once the Action is invoked. Remember that you set the initial value of this column to 0.

This Action icon will appear as follows:

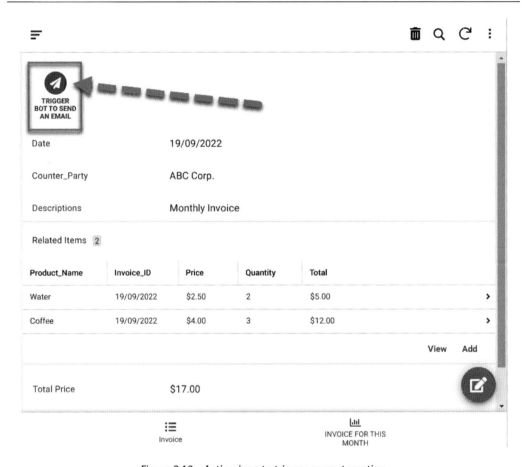

Figure 8.18 – Action icon to trigger our automation

Once the user clicks on this Action icon, it will change the value of the **Trigger** column, meaning the number value will be incremented by one. Then this data change to **Trigger** column made by this Action can be used to trigger the Automation.

The data change action to trigger the Bot is now ready and we will move next to the Automation settings. We will set up an Event to let the Bot listen for data changes made in the **Trigger** column and then start to run the Task to send an email.

## Creating a new Bot by adding a new Event

So far, the preparation work has been done to run automation based on user interaction with the app. We set up an Action to make a data change to the target column for preparation before starting to build a new Bot. Based on that your Action for this data change is ready, let's create a Bot to automate a process to send an email.

To create a new Bot, please visit the **Automation | Bots** tab and click on the **New Bot** action icon. To set this up, please refer to *Figures 8.4, 8.5,* and *8.6* shown earlier in this chapter. The Event you need to specify on this occasion is a **Data change** event. The purpose here is to configure the Event to run the Bot when the **Trigger** column value is changed through the **Data change** action, which we generated earlier:

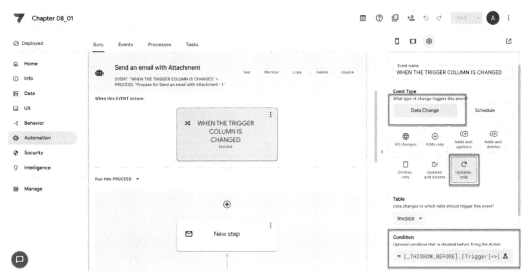

Figure 8.19 – Overall Event settings

We have highlighted with red rectangles the important areas for setting up the Event in the preceding screenshot. First of all, **Event Type** should be **Data change**, and the data change type needs to be set to **Updates only**. With just these two settings, what would happen with the Bot? Well, if you changed the column value in the invoice table, then the Bot would start to run as it would whenever the values in the invoice table are updated, but this is not the behavior that we expect. What we want here is for the Bot to run *only when the Trigger column value is changed.*

To achieve this, we need to configure the **Condition** setting for the Event. What we must do on this occasion is to pass the following expression into it.

Figure 8.20 – Expression to run the Bot conditionally when the Trigger column value is changed

The preceding expression uses the special syntax of [_THISROW_BEFORE] and [_THISROW_ AFTER]. The [_THISROW_BEFORE].[Trigger] expression will return the value before this column value is changed. Similarly, [_THISROW_AFTER].[Trigger] will return the value after the data change is made to the **Trigger** column. Using the < > operator, the overall expression will check whether the [Trigger] column has been changed or not as a result of any **Data change** event happening to the invoice table.

Looking back at the previous settings, we set the **Data change** action to increment the **Trigger** column by 1. Once this Action is invoked, the value for the **Trigger** column is changed. The Bot will listen for data changes made to the **Trigger** column and then start to run.

[_THISROW_BEFORE].[Some Column]<>[_THISROW_AFTER].[Some Column] is quite frequently used syntax when it comes to **Data change** event settings, so please learn it by heart to use it with your apps.

Now we have finished the Event settings, let's move on to the process settings to complete the rest of the work on our Bot.

## Adding a new Step to send an email

As we can see in *Figure 8.19*, we have the + **Add a step** button in the middle of the screen. This is to add a new Step to this particular Bot. For this exercise, the purpose is to send our email. To achieve this, we click on this icon and add a new Step to the Process.

Once you click on the button, your screen should be similar to the following screenshot:

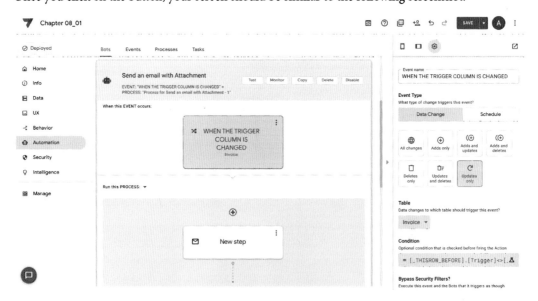

Figure 8.21 – Step settings to send an email

For Task type, **Send an email** should have been selected and highlighted by default. You can leave it as is unless another Task type is selected. Then, under **Email Type**, nothing is selected. To move forward, select **Custom template**. We have another option, **Embedded app view**, which should be selected if you want to send an embedded app view email. Due to the page limit of this book, we are not going to cover the **Embedded app view** email, but if you have an interest, please visit the official AppSheet documentation through the following link: `https://support.google.com/appsheet/answer/11511240?hl=en`.

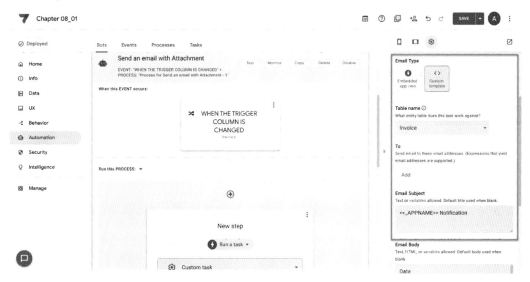

Figure 8.22 – Settings for a Send an email Task

Once you select **Custom template**, the additional settings will become available. Please make sure the invoice table is selected. For the **To** setting, we can direct the email address to which the Bot will send the email. For this exercise, we wish to send an email with an attachment (a PDF file invoice) to the user who initiates the automation. To achieve this, click on the **Add** button and pass the USEREMAIL() expression into **To** setting field.

Let's quickly review the configuration for sending an email attachment.

### Configuring the attachment settings

Go to the **Settings** pane on the right of the app editor and scroll down to the bottom, where you will find the **Attachment settings** section. The available settings can be seen in the following *Figure 8.23*.

The **Attachment settings** section allows us to configure the creation of the file to be attached to the email. To create an email attachment file, a source template is mandatory. This template can be a Google Docs file, an MS Excel or Word document, or another text file.

Let's now review in the following exercise how to use a Google Docs file as the template for your attachment, as it is quite a commonly used template file type with AppSheet. We will also review the available settings for generating the invoice email attachment as a PDF file. For the list of settings, please refer to the next few figures:

- **Attachment Content Type**
- For this exercise, we will create an invoice as a PDF file, so please select **PDF**.

- **Attachment Template**
- Here, we provide the source template file. We will review further settings later in this section.

- We will leave the rest of the settings blank or at their default values for this quick exercise.

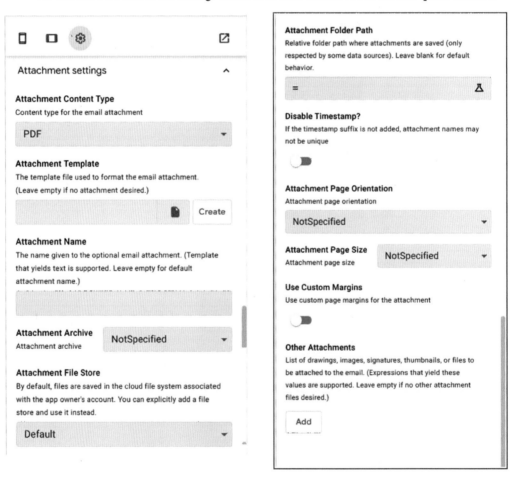

Figure 8.23 – Attachment settings

**Attachment Template** may be the most important option here, as it works as something like a boilerplate for your file. Now, let's create this template file by clicking on the **Create** button. After waiting for a moment, as shown in the following screenshot, you will see the new **View** button and the ID value assigned by Google Drive for the newly created Google Docs template file.

## Attachment Template

The template file used to format the email attachment.

(Leave empty if no attachment desired.)

Figure 8.24 – The new template file is created

Once the **View** button becomes available, please click on it. This will open the template Google Docs file in a new tab of your browser and should look as follows:

# New step Task - 1

## Invoice

Date: <<[Date]>>
Counter_Party: <<[Counter_Party]>>
Descriptions: <<[Descriptions]>>
Trigger: <<[Trigger]>>
Total Price: <<[Total Price]>>

## Items

| Invoice_ID | Product_Name | Price | Quantity | Total |
|---|---|---|---|---|
| <<Start: [Related Items]>><<[Invoice_ID]>> | <<[Product_Name]>> | <<[Price]>> | <<[Quantity]>> | <<[Total]>><<End>> |

Figure 8.25 – Boilerplate for the Automation template

This Google Docs file contains some boilerplate for your template, but you can customize it to meet your requirements. The template uses special syntax to retrieve the relevant values from the invoice table. It is expressed in the format of `<< [Column_Name] >>` and referred to as column name variables or more broadly, template variables. The exact column name is encoded in square brackets. Once the column name variable is used inside the template, it will retrieve the value from the data column at the time when the Bot runs.

In our app, there is a variable called << [Product_Name] >>, which will extract the actual product name from the row where Automation is initiated. The special syntax used in the template is always in the format starting with << and ending with >> operators.

AppSheet Automation templates are quite flexible. We can customize their styles through Google Docs formatting functionality, such as increasing the font size, applying colors, creating tables, and so on.

The template accepts *AppSheet expressions*. We can pass AppSheet expressions as variables to the special syntax, for example <<NOW () >>. This will add a timestamp to the file when the Bot runs:

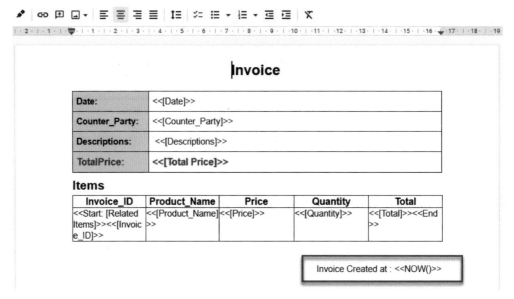

Figure 8.26 – Template with styles and expressions

We just cleaned up the original template file by applying styles that are available in Google Docs. The flexibility in terms of applying the styling is another advantage of Automation, making our AppSheet apps more functional. An AppSheet template is something like a blank canvas, where we can draw freely. We have also seen how, if you have a number of Office templates with fixed styles and layouts, they can be converted into AppSheet templates easily. We also examined how we can retrieve any values required from data tables for use in the template by using template variables. In the case of a file where a complicated calculation is required, the template's capability to accept AppSheet expressions can make many things possible.

Now, let's move back to the app requirements for this exercise. After the email is sent, we want to change the value of the **Status** column to **Sent**. By adding this Action, the app user can easily trace which invoice was sent or not. If your app for this exercise does not have a **Status** column, please create one by following the same Steps we used for adding a **Trigger** column earlier. Make sure the initial value for **Status** is set to **Draft**. Once you are ready, let's move on.

# Running a data change action from a Step

So far, we have added a *Step* to a *Process* to send an email. By adding a new Step under this Step, we can get the Bot do another job after it sends the email. With this sample app, we wish to change data in the Status column by running a data action.

To finish the Process of this Bot, we simply add another new Step.

The required configuration is surprisingly easy:

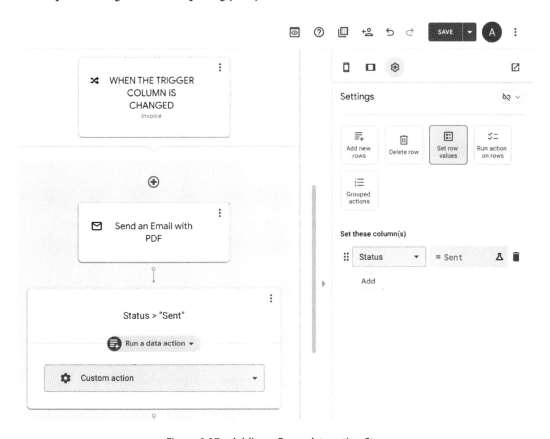

Figure 8.27 – Adding a Run a data action Step

Please add a new Step after **Send an Email with PDF**, and set the Step type to **Run a data action**. On the right-hand pane, select **Set row values** and set the **Status** column to Sent. Please refer to the preceding figure for the overall settings.

With this simple setting, once the **Send an email** Task has been completed, then the Bot will continue to run this **Data change** action.

With this exercise, we have now finished the Bot settings.

We have now built a Bot that is expected to fulfill the requirements we established at the beginning of this exercise. The next step is to test your Bot and see whether it behaves as we expect or not.

## Trying and testing Automation

Testing your Bot is an essential process to make sure it works as expected before you share your app with your users. To carry out testing, please go to your Bot setting tile and check the header area. And then click on the **Test** button:

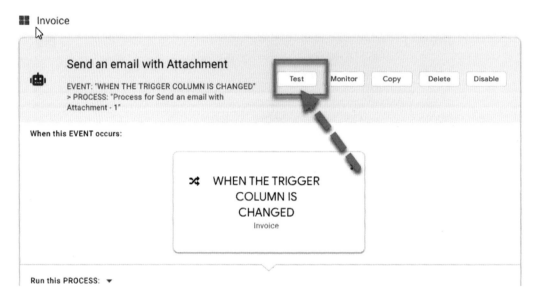

Figure 8.28 – Start testing your Bot

A new tab will open in your browser displaying something like the following figure:

Figure 8.29 – Executing a Bot from a selected record

If we have some records in the invoice table, then they will appear here on this page. With a **Data change** Event action, the Bot is always triggered by data changes made to a particular row. For testing, you can select any row out of the list. In the **Process** column, please click on the **Execute** button to start the test run of your Bot.

Go to your email inbox – if you receive an email with a PDF attachment, this is a sign that the Bot is working perfectly. If it does not, then you need to investigate what's causing the problem. AppSheet provides you with monitoring functionality to find errors and root causes of problems in your Bot:

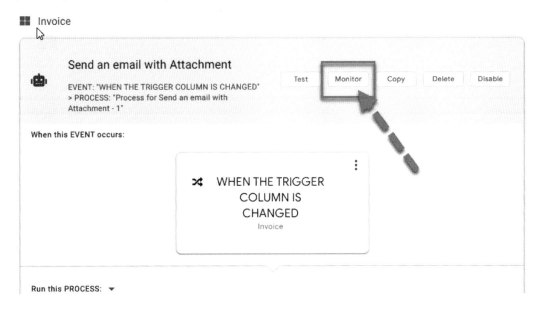

Figure 8.30 – Opening the Monitor app

In the header of the Bot settings tile, you can see the **Monitor** button as shown in the preceding screenshot. When you click on this, the AppSheet Monitor app opens. This app will provide the execution logs for all of the apps you have created. This app is helpful to troubleshoot any issue you may have with a Bot, as we can locate errors in the logs to locate the source of any problem.

## Summary

It is said AppSheet Automation is a particularly tricky function to understand, especially for beginners. We have to admit that this may be true, but we hope our guide helped you to learn the essence of Automation so that you can implement it in your own application having read through this chapter.

To understand Automation better, it is important to understand its anatomy. As we have learned, a Bot is constructed from the two major components of an Event and a Process. The Event settings are rather straightforward to understand, but if we start working with Bots in complex business scenarios, it is possible that you may face some difficulty.

AppSheet Automation can actually do tons of things, including automating extensive business logic and workflows. We could only cover a small part of Automation and just introduce the basics in this chapter. AppSheet's official documentation provides a comprehensive guide for Automation. Please visit the documentation to deepen your knowledge of Automation for continuous study. What we covered in this chapter will help you digest what the official documentation provides: `https://support.google.com/appsheet/answer/11998993?hl=en&ref_topic=11511235`.

With this chapter, we have completed an extensive review of AppSheet's powerful Automation feature, which helps us to automate sophisticated business processes. In the following chapter, we will briefly introduce some advanced AppSheet features driven by **artificial intelligence** (**AI**) to improve the experiences of your app users.

# 9
# Using Intelligence and Advanced Features

AppSheet is not only a data-driven platform for developing feature-rich business applications but is also powered by **artificial intelligence** (**AI**) to give it additional and advanced functionality in terms of data searching, predictions, and data scraping image files. Throughout this chapter, a brief explanation of three different key AppSheet advanced features will be given so that you are familiarized with each feature, driven by the power of machine learning.

Besides the Smart Assistant feature, in order to use the other features, **predictive models** and **optical character recognition** (**OCR**), you need to train your own model as a first step. During this process, you will teach the AI models behind the scenes of AppSheet to get the desired results, such as the result of a prediction based on your own dataset and precise text extraction out of your own images. This training process is an important step in starting to use these unique features.

Throughout this chapter, we will review this training process and then learn how to implement models in your apps. In this chapter, we will cover the following topics:

- Enabling advanced features
- Searching data from an app with Smart Assistant
- Building your own predictive models
- Building an OCR model

Once you enable any of these advanced features, you will be able to implement Google's latest API-based technologies without writing any code. By the end of this chapter, you will understand how to set up each advanced feature, especially the *training model process*, which is fundamental for your own AI models.

# Enabling advanced features

The settings for the advanced features are found in the **Intelligence** pane of AppSheet, as shown in *Figure 9.1*. These advanced features and their functionalities are as follows:

- **Smart Assistant**: Advanced searching function using natural language.
- **Predictive Models**: Once a new data entry is made, you will be able to get the most likely values for your data that you wish to predict.
- **OCR Models (Beta)**: Extracts text that appears in images and saves it as a standardized dataset.

Take a look at *Figure 9.1*, where you can find the three different tabs for each advanced feature in the **Intelligence** pane:

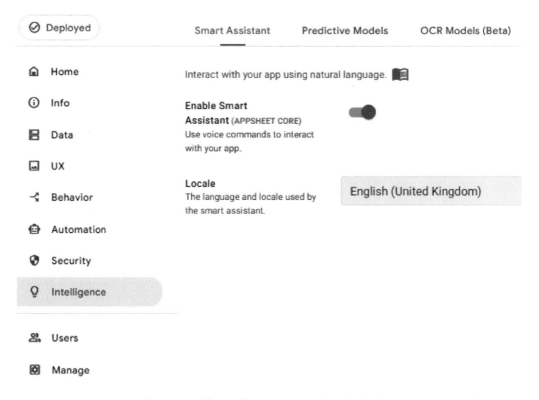

Figure 9.1 – The Intelligence pane and its three tabs

Let's move on to looking at each of these features; we'll learn how to set them up and see what each feature can do for us.

# Searching data from an app with Smart Assistant

In a nutshell, **Smart Assistant** provides app users with advanced searching experiences called **natural language processing**. App users use natural language to search data across the app and tables, returning results matching the searching word(s), just like searching on search engines, such as Google or Yahoo.

This feature is enabled by default once a new app is made. To access this feature, go to the menu and you will see the **Assistant** view, as shown in the following figure. Once the **Assistant** view is open, type some text in natural language into the input field at the top of the view.

On clicking the mic icon, the voice recognition function will be activated. Speak to the app and your app will pick up your words, converting them into text to search:

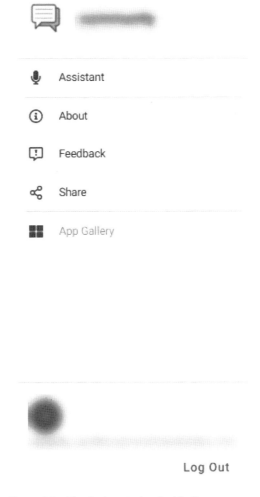

Figure 9.2 – The Assistant view inside the app menu

You can access the menu view via the cloud icon at the top left and then you can find the **Assistant** view to access this feature. Then, you will see the **Smart Assistant** view, which is depicted in *Figure 9.3*:

Figure 9.3 – The Smart Assistant view

Using the Smart Assistant view, you can view data by making requests such as the following:

- *Show me my customers*: To navigate to a table called `Customers`.

- *Go to orders*: To navigate to a table called `Orders`.

- *Show orders with an open status*: A row-level filter can be applied by asking this. This will show the set of rows in the `Orders` table with a status column where the value is `open`.

You can also fire the search action using voice commands, such as the following:

- *Go to John Doe*

- *Send him an email*

These commands will take you to a particular view inside the app and run an appropriate action based on your words. For instance, the first command, *Go to John Doe*, may bring you to a detailed view of this record that contains a `[USER_NAME]` column with a value of `John Doe`. So, this kind of command would be useful to jump to the target view without navigating the nested views inside the app.

Likewise, the second sample command, *Send him an email*, may work to invoke actions with automation. An action may change the value in a certain column. Furthermore, an automation (or bot) may send an email, with the data change event triggered by the preceding data change action.

These two commands could also be combined into a single command, such as *Go to John Doe and send him an email*. This will find a row with `John Doe` in the `[USER_NAME]` column, then invoke the named *Send Email* action on this row.

Smart Assistant is a simple feature to give app users the capability to search data across the app with keywords, similar to the experience of working with a search engine. It is possible users won't notice this feature exists on the app. So, while deploying your app, we recommend you educate your app users about these intelligent features so they can use the app more effectively and have a better experience.

As shown in *Figure 9.1*, enabling Smart Assistant uses a simple toggle with an *on/off* setting option. Now, let's move on to the next advanced feature – predictive models. Unlike Smart Assistant, you need to train AI behind the scenes before using predictive models. Let's dive into the steps you need to follow before you start to use the features of a predictive model.

# Building your own predictive models

Predictive models are an analytical feature only provided for users with AppSheet Enterprise licenses. To enable this feature, you need to purchase the appropriate license. However, without purchasing a license, you can still test this feature—as long as the app is not deployed and remains a prototype for testing purposes.

Predictive models evaluate your data and return the most likely value based on your data when a new row is added to a table. Once a predictive model is built from your existing data, then it will create a model or algorithm.

Typically, it is useful when, for example, you have a data table containing prices with given specifications, such as a product catalog. When a new product is added to the table, the predictive model will estimate the value of the new product behind the scenes using the Google Cloud machine learning algorithm. For other possible use cases, we could collect the feedback from customers or employees through the app and then need to categorize them based on the context of the feedback. Once your feedback is posted, a predictive model helps you to assign it to the appropriate category automatically.

## Creating a new predictive model

To create a new model, go to **Intelligence > Predictive Models**, and then click the **+New Predictive Model** button to proceed, as shown in the following figure:

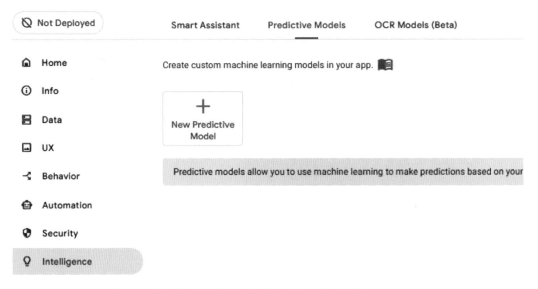

Figures 9.4 – The Predictive Models tab on the Intelligence pane

After you create a new model, you will see a settings screen for your new model. The following figure illustrates the new model configuration for a table that contains data for a mobile phone list with detailed specifications, along with the pricing:

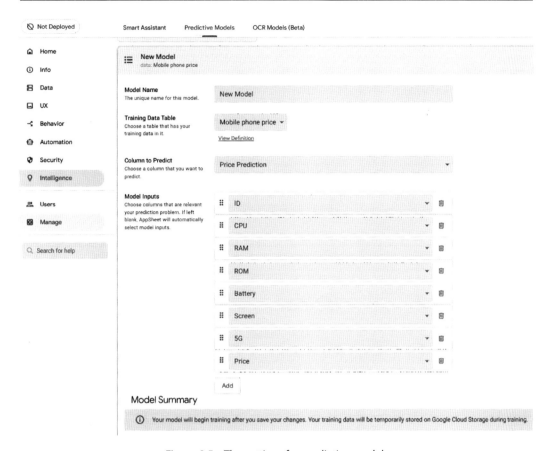

Figure 9.5 – The settings for predictive models

You can see and access this sample dataset through the sample app we prepared for this particular section, called `Chapter 09_01`.

### Steps to enable predictive models

To predict values for a column (i.e. `Price`), you need to create a predictive model following two important steps. First, you train the AI model using an existing dataset. Once the training process is complete, then you are ready to implement the model into your app ready for use.

```
https://www.appsheet.com/templates/Demonstration-for-predictive-
model-feature?appGuidString=e768c099-c021-44e3-9f9d-e21b898ecfc4
```

## Training the model

Once you have created the new predictive model, you need to train the model in order to tune the existing built-in AI algorithm to take all the input columns trained through the existing data and build the prediction patterns. Do the following to train the model:

1.  For **Training Data Table**, pick the data table that works as a source for models. If your dataset is too small (less than 25 rows), the training phase will fail. So, please make sure you have a reasonable amount of data to start training.

2.  Once your data is ready, choose the target column name, and the prediction will yield the result for it.

3.  For **Model Inputs**, choose columns relevant to your prediction model. The selected column and its values will be taken into account for the prediction process. As of the time of writing, AppSheet only supports columns with a data type of Yes/No, Enum, Ref, Price, Decimal, or Number, which can be selected as a *column to predict*. Any other data types not predictable by the models cannot be selected.

Once all the options are set, save the changes in the app editor. The training phase will start once you save the changes and it may take a little while until the whole training process is completed depending on the amount of source data for training. During the training phase, your source data is analyzed as historical data and a new predictive model is created.

## Implementing newly created models into your app

There are two different ways to incorporate newly created prediction models into your app:

*   Adding a virtual column with a *special expression* for your models as an app formula
*   Setting a *special expression* in the initial value for the normal column

At this point, you may ask the question, *What is a special expression?*. Let's explain the concept.

The syntax is PREDICT ("Your Model Name Here"). Place this expression into the initial value for your target or any other column. These expressions can also be used inside the app formula for both physical and virtual columns to get the value as a result of your prediction. Please make sure you change the argument for the expression to your own model name.

For the sample use case here, users will enter the specification of a new mobile phone to add a new record. The predictive model assesses the existing specifications globally and estimates the most likely possible value (that is, the price) of the entered specification.

In the next section, we will look at another AI model – the OCR model – which uses **Google Cloud Vision API**. The beauty of this feature is that it extracts text data inside an image you upload without user intervention. With this particular AI model, you can reduce the number of manual tasks in terms of entering data into apps.

# Building an OCR model

**OCR** is useful for apps – such as a conference management app – where you need to collect the names of attendees or read a product label for inventory management. You may have documents with a fixed style and format, such as names, badges, and labels for stock items on the shelf. Without OCR, the app user needs to manually type into the form view in the AppSheet app to register data. OCR removes the need for this manual process by automatically scanning the document and recognizing the fields and values for each of them.

After taking a photo of the target document and uploading it, OCR extracts the text data from the image file and converts it into a structured set of data automatically. Let's have a look at this powerful feature in detail.

# What are AppSheet OCR models?

AppSheet OCR performs text data scraping out of an image that contains text or handwritten values. With this feature, you can speed up the data entry process. The user takes or uploads an image to the app and the OCR model then extracts the text from the image. It then pushes the data to the target column inside the **form** view.

In a nutshell, OCR is a powerful feature to effectively process structured data without typing text into the input fields, which, in turn, does not require user intervention.

## What types of images are scannable by OCR?

AppSheet's OCR feature can be used when you need to scan multiple documents that all have a fixed layout. The images may contain either printed text or handwriting. For example, a standardized paper of batches of names for a conference or UPS shipping labels could be scannable by AppSheet OCR.

However, please keep in mind that OCR is not capable of scraping text data out of complex formats, such as business cards (which don't always have a unique format), invoices with multiple line items, and forms using checkboxes.

The best way to ensure a high level of performance of the OCR feature is to start with images with a simple fixed format and countable unique text items.

## How do you set and train an OCR model?

To build your OCR model, you will have to first go to **Intelligence** > **OCR Models (Beta)**.

To process a new ORC model, you need to train the model as you do with the AppSheet predictive models feature. To start training, you will need at least four sample images and their values (saved to the backend data source) that you want to be extracted from each image.

The data table must contain an image column, from where text is going to be extracted, and also output columns that save the extracted values. AppSheet will assess the given example images along with the data saved to the source table and come up with a general template to match against new images.

This training phase inspects the text inside the image with the location and then maps it to the target column name where the extracted text values will be saved.

For example, let's assume we are using a simple name card for a conference, as shown in the following figure:

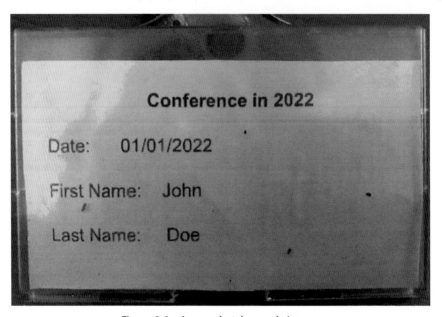

Figure 9.6 – A name batch sample image

The style of the card is fixed (as shown in the preceding figure); the **Date** is placed at the top, followed by the **First Name,** and then the **Last Name**. Based on this, your data table should look as follows:

| ID | Image | Date | First Name | Last Name |
|---|---|---|---|---|
| ABCDE01 | Path to image file | 01/01/2022 | John | Doe |

Table 9.1 – The data table structure

Once your sample images and dataset are ready, click the **+ New OCR Model** button to create a new model. Once the new model is created, you will then see a new settings tile, as illustrated in the following figure:

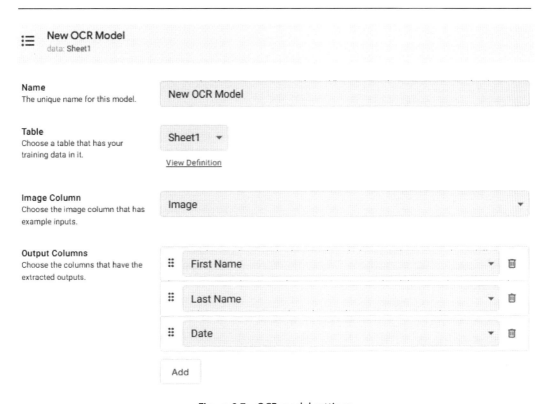

Figure 9.7 – OCR model settings

Once the new model tile is displayed, please follow these steps:

1.  Select your table name for the **Table** option.
2.  For **Image Column**, select the **Image** type column on the selected table. The OCR model will extract the text from the image that you uploaded to this column.
3.  For **Output Columns**, select multiple columns where you want the values to be saved.

Once you save the changes, the first process to create your custom OCR model will run in the background. AppSheet will show the patterns that were found in each example. The extracted text part(s) will be highlighted with background colors on the sample images that are shown at the bottom of the tile. Just check each sample image to ensure that the text you wish to extract from images is properly mapped to the target columns without any errors.

Now that your OCR model has finished training, it's available for use in your app. Once the new image is uploaded to the new form to add a record to the table, your columns will automatically be initialized using the extracted values from the image. Please make sure not to set the initial value for the target columns as it may conflict with the OCR feature.

# Summary

As we discussed in this chapter, AppSheet currently provides advanced AI features driven by Google's machine learning. We hope you got a quick insight into each feature to get started with testing.

Once you do some hands-on testing with them, you may find some functionalities are not returning the results you need. It could be because the machine learning algorithm does not support your complex use cases. For instance, OCR models do not recognize the complicated format of some target images even with fixed styles. It is also possible that you don't get the values expected as a result of running your own predictive models. We have to admit that these advanced features may not accomodate your unique business requirements and the models may not return values with a high level of accuracy due to the limited capabilities of the AI.

It may well be the case that Google's machine learning service becomes more advanced and sophisticated as time goes by. With that, the level of accuracy and reliability of the AppSheet Intelligence services we discussed in this chapter would become more advanced as well. It could result in these advanced features becoming much more capable and even more advanced.

To test these features, we suggest you start with simple use cases for now.

To expand the capabilities of your AppSheet app further, in the next chapter, we will discuss how to enhance your app using third-party services. You will find more flexible, powerful, and practical tricks in the next chapter.

# 10

# Extending App Capabilities with Third-Party Services

There are quite a few open source services available these days. In this chapter, we'll explore a few external services that will add some flavor to your apps, such as a dynamic image with text and a colored background or a dynamic image-based static chart. We will also see how to set up integrations with **Google Workspace** applications such as **Google Chat**.

Throughout this chapter, we will go through a few examples to introduce use cases where we implement third-party services to enhance the functionality of our apps. AppSheet provides a number of different features overall. But the techniques we will learn about in this chapter provide us with additional functions that extend the capabilities of AppSheet. These techniques include improving the visual appearance of your data and connecting to external services.

There are thousands of external services that can communicate with AppSheet. Once you have completed this chapter, we hope you will be able to build your own integrations with your preferred services.

In this chapter, we will cover the following topics:

- Displaying images with dynamic text
- Using QuickChart to generate a dynamic chart as an image
- Integrating with Google Workspace products (connecting to Google Chat)
- Google Apps Script and use cases

We have to admit that the techniques we discuss in this chapter may require a bit of knowledge of coding as well as of APIs in general. To brush up on this knowledge, we suggest that you explore the set of sample apps we have provided. To access those sample apps, please read through the following section on technical requirements.

## Technical requirements

To assist your learning activities through this chapter, we have prepared a few sample apps that you can access from the portfolio site of this book. You can find the set of sample apps that are prepared for this chapter by visiting `https://www.appsheet.com/portfolio/5689905`.

There is a total of eight samples. Each of the sample apps associated with this chapter is named `Chapter 10_N` for your reference.

Let's start with learning more about images and placeholders.

## Displaying images with dynamic text

> *Note*
>
> *Name of the sample app to refer to on the portfolio site: Chapter 10_01*
>
> `https://www.appsheet.com/templates/sample?appGuidString=530fb5cc-`
> `1001-4294-9719-c6e23e8dc865`

In order to increase the visibility of data on your app, you can apply the AppSheet native format rules. They change the color and add icons so a particular section of data stands out.

However, you cannot change the background color using the existing format rules. To highlight some text with color, we can use external services, which will help us generate instant images. These images come with text and background color. But since these are pure images, your text will stand out. For example, a list of line items may have a status such as **Draft** or **Approved** for documentation. With this technique, you can highlight the status of each document, as you can see in the following screenshot:

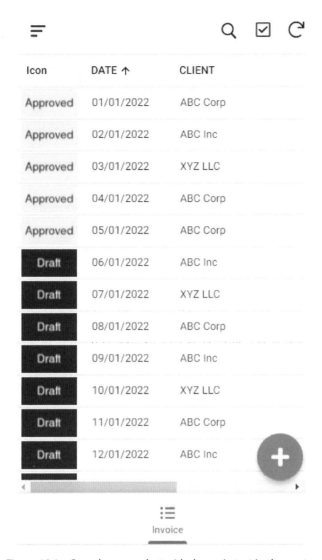

Figure 10.1 – Sample screenshot with dynamic text in the center

This app is designed to generate invoices, and each invoice has a state, either **Draft** or **Approved**, based on the **Status** column on the table. Using the **Status** column value on each row, the service will generate a placeholder with a background color based on the status.

At a glance, app users can easily identify the status of each invoice, whether it is a draft or approved by the line manager, through the label. The data becomes more *recognizable*. Furthermore, if the value in the Status column is changed, the image is automatically regenerated, thanks to AppSheet's virtual column behavior.

## Services to use

You will find various services that provide a URL-based text image generator. Luckily, most of them are open source licensed and free to use. From among the available services, we would like to introduce a service called **placehold.jp**.

To access this service, please visit `http://placehold.jp/en.html`.

In the middle of its landing page, you will find an **Advanced** section, where you can test the service with various optional settings, as can be seen in *Figure 10.2*:

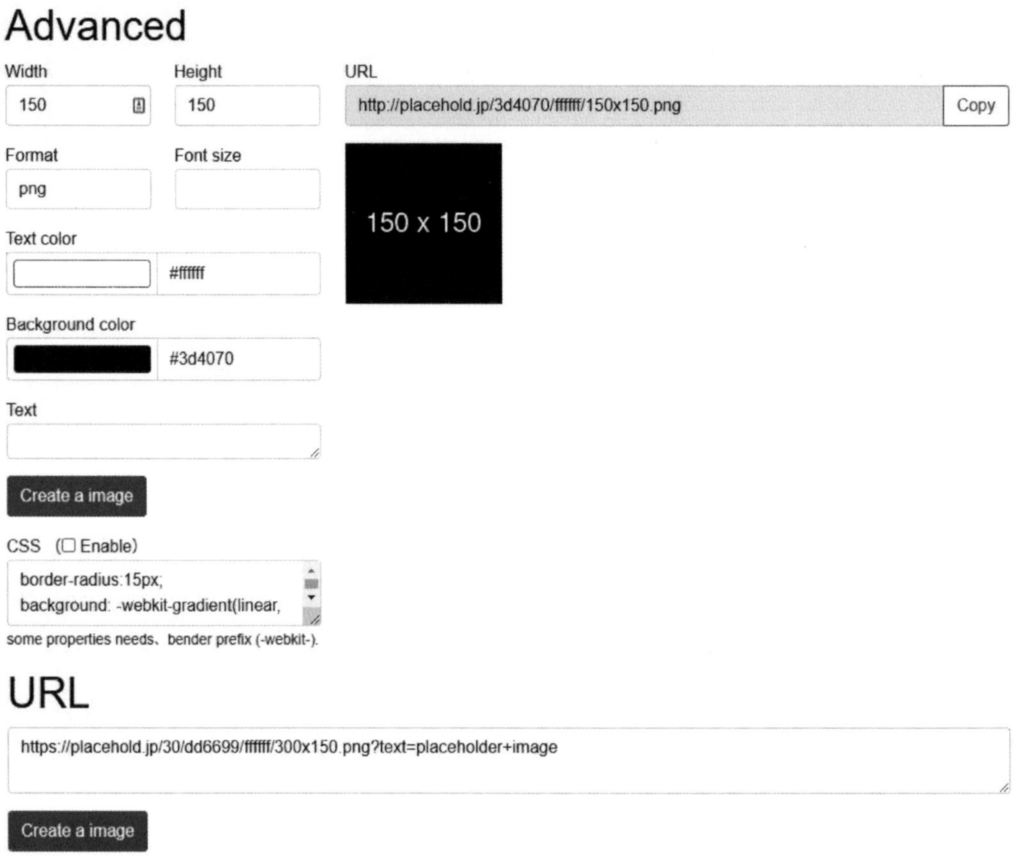

Figure 10.2 – Advanced settings for the custom image with text (from placehold.jp)

Once you have set all the available parameters, such as size, coloring, and dynamic text, you can preview the final version of the image, as shown in the following screenshot. Please make sure to click the **Create a image** button:

Figure 10.3 – URL and image generated/returned by placehold.jp

`placehold.jp` provides a URL-based API endpoint, starting from `http://placehold.jp`. By manipulating the URL further, we can easily control styles, such as background color, text color, and font size. When you pass this URL to the browser, it will yield a rectangle-shaped image with a background color and center-aligned dynamic text.

In the following section, let's review what types of optional controls are available for you to customize the format of the final images.

### A quick guide on using the URL service for a basic text label image

Let's see how we should structure the URL for our own customized placeholder: `https://placehold.jp/60/dd6699/ffffff/300x150.png?text=sample`

The service is based on a URL, which always starts with `http://placehold.jp`, which is called the base URL. By adding a path to this base URL, you are able to control the styles of images, such as the font size and background color:

- **Font size (path):** Immediately after `https://placehold.jp`, the number after the first / (slash) sign is used to control the font size of the text inside the image. The value of this path is always an arbitrary number, such as `20`, `30`, or `40`. This path is omittable.

- **Background color (path):** After the path for controlling the font size, the next path controls the background color of the image. The value required to be passed here is a hex color code (six characters) without the # character at the beginning. Make sure to add / (slash) at the start of the path.

- **Text color (path):** The third path controls the text color. For the background color, only hex color codes are accepted.

- **Image size and image type (path):** After that, add . (dot) followed by the file type, either .png or .jpg. If you wish to render an image as .png, then the full value for this path will be 300x150.png, whereas, in the case of .jpg, it will be 300x150.jpg.

- **Text inside the image (parameter):** To control dynamic text inside the image, we need to add a parameter starting with ?text=. You can pass any arbitrary text to this parameter and it will be displayed as center-aligned text inside the output image. For example, if you want to show the text **Approved**, then the parameter will be ?text=Approved.

An example is shown in the following screenshot:

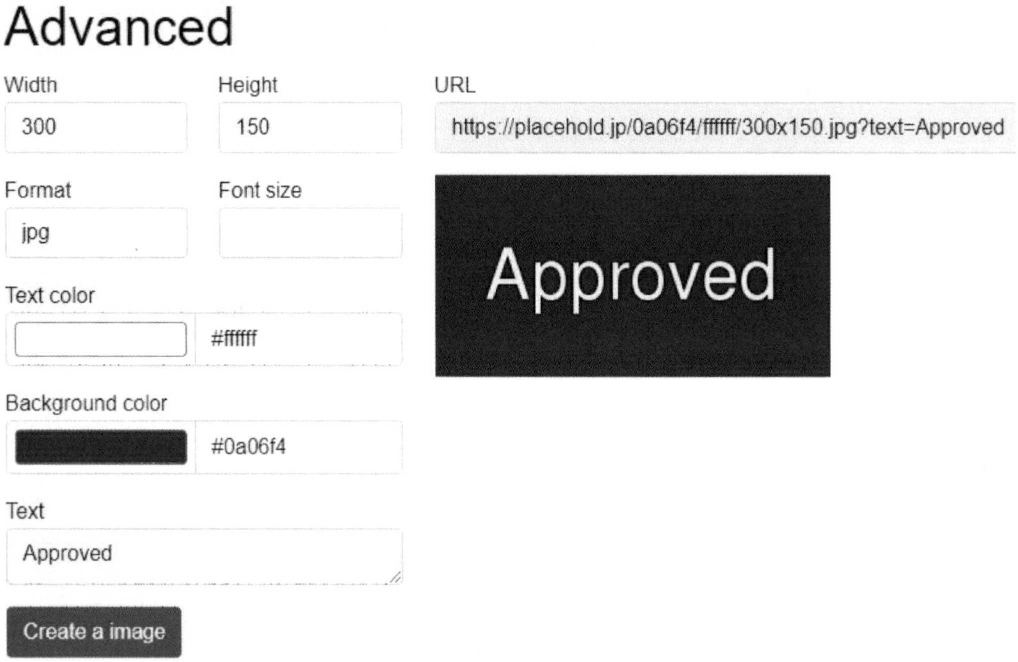

# Advanced

| Width | Height | URL |
|-------|--------|-----|
| 300 | 150 | https://placehold.jp/0a06f4/ffffff/300x150.jpg?text=Approved |

Format: jpg

Font size:

Text color: | #ffffff

Background color: | #0a06f4

Text: Approved

[ Create a image ]

Figure 10.4 – Sample image settings with a rectangle shape and the background color selected

Using the *optional* advanced settings, you can quickly test to see what the final images look like by applying different settings.

Here is the URL to generate the sample label with a blue background shown in the preceding screenshot: https://placehold.jp/0a06f4/ffffff/300x150.jpg?text=Approved.

## *Incorporating an image into an AppSheet app*

Now that we know how to construct a URL that returns the image we want, let's place the image in an AppSheet app. Please have a look at *Figure 10.5* to see how these images appear in your AppSheet apps:

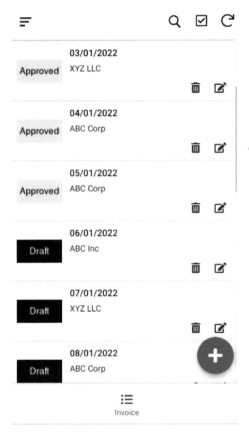

Figure 10.5 – A sample app's deck view with text images

For this sample app, we have a table with the `Status` column that flags the status of each invoice as either **Draft** or **Approved**. By using the values from this **Status** column, the images located on the left side of each line item are added.

Let's review the process to create these text label images, as illustrated in this sample app:

1.  First, create a new virtual column.

2.  Next, add the following app formula:

    ```
    https://placehold.jp/0a06f4/ffffff/300x150.jpg?text="&
    [STATUS]
    ```

3.  Make sure to set the **Virtual Column** data type to the **Image** type.

We are using the & operator to concatenate the string to generate a dynamic URL based on the Status column value. The Status column has different values, either **Draft** or **Approved**. The image created by this virtual column should reflect the value in the **STATUS** column. The text inside the image dynamically changes if you change the value of the **STATUS** column.

## Dynamically changing the label contents

Using the IF and IFS expressions, you can further dynamically change the styles of images based on the column values. For instance, in this sample app, we are switching the style of the images, such as background and text color, depending on the value in the **Status** column.

If the **Status** column value is **Draft**, then we want to present the background in a darker color and white as the text color. Otherwise, the background color should be changed to a lighter color with black text. You can configure this to apply any style you want.

See the following sample expression, which dynamically changes the URL based on the Status column value, using the IF() expression:

```
IF(
[STATUS]="Draft",
"http://placehold.jp/30/3d4070/ffffff/150x
75.png?text=Draft",
"http://placehold.jp/30/eeff99/003366/15
0x75.png?text=Approved"
)
```

This expression will return the images as they appear in *Figure 10.5*.

## Customizing the styles

To change the image styles, you can manually construct a suitable URL, but the website http://placehold.jp provides quick advanced settings to generate the URL for you. You may find it useful and straightforward to use.

For those who know CSS, you can use CSS code to customize the appearance further, such as adding a corner radius and gradient color. In the URL generator, check **CSS Enable** and create an image. You will see a URL with inline CSS being added.

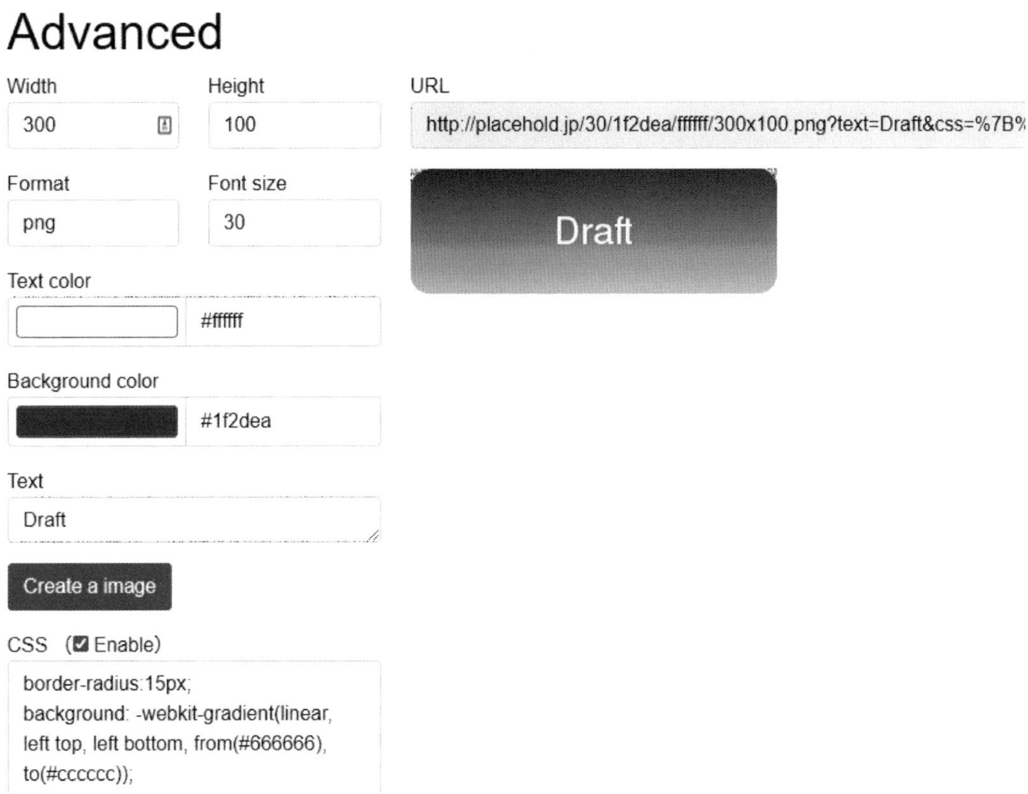

# Advanced

| Width | Height | URL |
|---|---|---|
| 300 | 100 | http://placehold.jp/30/1f2dea/ffffff/300x100.png?text=Draft&css=%7B% |

| Format | Font size |
|---|---|
| png | 30 |

**Text color**

| | #ffffff |
|---|---|

**Background color**

| | #1f2dea |
|---|---|

**Text**

Draft

[ Create a image ]

CSS   (☑ Enable)

```
border-radius:15px;
background: -webkit-gradient(linear,
left top, left bottom, from(#666666),
to(#cccccc));
```

Figure 10.6 – Sample image style applying custom CSS code

For the preceding sample image, CSS code for `border-radius` with `15px` is applied to round the corners of the image.

The technique we have learned in this section to create an image with dynamic text can be used in many ways to make an interface more appealing to your app users; it simply depends on your imagination and creativity. We hope you enjoy this trick and now know how to present your data to facilitate app user navigation over app views.

# Using QuickChart to generate a dynamic chart as an image

AppSheet natively provides a chart-type view where different types of charts are available to present data in a stunning style, such as a bar chart, line chart, or scatter plot.

However, other basic styles, such as a progress bar, radar, and combo chart, are not provided. To present data in these ways, you can use the external open source chart library `QuickChart`.

To find out more about this service, visit the following URL: `https://quickchart.io/`

An AppSheet chart view is generated from a table or slice, meaning the chart will be drawn based on a set of rows and columns. This is good but does not fit the possible use case where the app creator just wants to create a simple chart out of *single row and column values.*

If the data table has columns with numeric values, including percentages, then we are able to draw the chart using values from a single row, to present the progress and occupancy ratio as a chart.

The following screenshot shows a few example chart types from the QuickChart library:

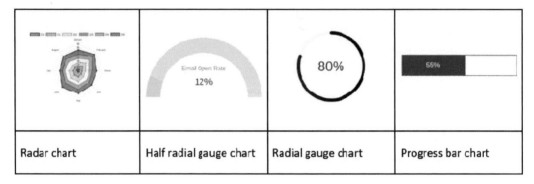

| Radar chart | Half radial gauge chart | Radial gauge chart | Progress bar chart |

Figure 10.7 – Sample chart styles available in QuickChart

There are a number of different types of charts available in QuickChart. The preceding screenshot has been provided as a sample, but other types of charts are also available.

## Building a radial gauge chart

> *Note*
> *Name of the sample app to refer to in the portfolio site: Chapter 10_02* `https://www.appsheet.com/templates/sample?appGuidString= a71fb14c-c0ec-4d4c-9531-25456470f70c`

Let's create a radial gauge chart with the percentage in the middle. We believe this gauge chart is the most commonly and widely used across the AppSheet community.

To use the **QuickChart** service, we pass the URL with various optional parameters, and it returns the image as a result of the HTTP request. In the code block following *Figure 10.8*, you can see the long URL, starting with `https://quickchart.io`, followed by the additional strings. In general, we manipulate such URLs to get the desired dynamic chart as an image.

Let's have a look at a working expression to generate a radial gauge chart in the following screenshot:

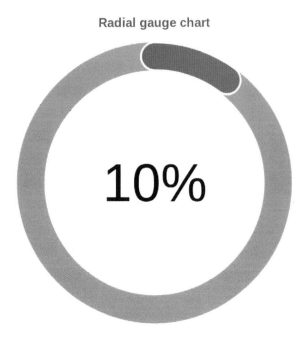

Figure 10.8 – Sample radial gauge chart made by QuickChart

This radial gauge chart is made from the URL highlighted in the following code block. The URL is passed to **Virtual Column** and the data type is set to image:

```
"https://quickchart.io/chart?c={
  type:'radialGauge',
  data:{
   datasets:[{data:["
&
[Ratio]
&
"],backgroundColor:'green'}]
  },
  options: {
  title: {
          display:true,
          text: 'Radial gauge chart'
         },
  centerPercentage: 80,
```

```
    trackColor: 'rgb(255, 165, 0)',
    domain: [0, 100],
    roundedCorners: true,
    centerArea: {
      displayText: true,
      fontFamily: null,
      fontColor: 'rgb(0, 0, 0)',
      fontSize: 50,
      padding: 4,
      backgroundImage: null,
      backgroundColor: 'rgba(129, 236, 236, 0.1)',
      text:"&MID("x'x",2,1)&number([Ratio])&encodeurl("%")
         &MID("x'x",2,1)&"
    }
  }
}"
```

To display QuickChart inside AppSheet, simply create a new virtual column and set the app formula with the QuickChart URL, then set the data type to either image or thumbnail (make sure to surround the URL with double quotes to stringify the URL).

Looks simple, doesn't it? However, there is a bit of a challenge. We want the chart to be dynamic. The chart will present data based on a column value for that particular row, such as Ratio or Percentage, whose data type is set to the Number type.

As you can see in the sample app (*Chapter 10_02*), the full QuickChart URL is constructed using the & operator to concatenate the different portions of the set of strings. The most important parts of the URL and expressions are highlighted.

For the QuickChart URL, one large object (surrounded with curly brackets, { }) is passed after the base endpoint of https://quickchart.io/chart?c=. In other words, to borrow programming terms, it is in the same format as a **JavaScript object**, where the list of the key and value pairs is stored inside a single curly bracket.

This one large object controls all of the image chart. We placed as many chart options as possible in this working expression, so you will see a bunch of key values, which represent the names of the options. You can customize the styles by changing the values for those options. Let's dive into the details of each option one by one.

The following is a list of options to control the styles in a **radial gauge chart**:

| Key & Value pair | Remarks |
|---|---|
| `type:'radialGauge',` | The value to pass to this `type` property is a reserved word. Just pass `radialGauge`. |
| `data:{`<br>`    datasets:[{data:["`<br>`&`<br>`[Ratio]`<br>`&`<br>`"]` | This is an important but tricky part. In order to display data on a chart dynamically, with values taken from columns, we need to pass an AppSheet column expression inside the URL. This makes the image chart dynamically reflect the value of the column on that row. Change the column name to fit your app as necessary. |
| `backgroundColor:'green'` | To set the background color of the lines of the circle. This color is applied to a part of the circle line that represents the measure's percentage. |
| `title: {`<br>`        display:true,`<br>`        text: 'Radial gauge`<br>`            chart'`<br>`    }` | To display the chart title, set the value to `true`, else `false`. The `text` option provides the title to appear over the chart if set to `true`. |
| `centerPercentage: 80` | 80 or 90 yields the best results. |
| `trackColor: 'rgb(255, 165, 0)'` | The color of the radial gauge's track. |
| `domain: [0, 100]` | The domain for the data. The default is `[0, 100]`. |
| `roundedCorners: true` | Determines whether the arc for the gauge should have rounded corners. |
| `centerArea: {`<br>`    displayText: true,`<br>`    fontFamily: null,`<br>`    fontColor: 'rgb(0, 0, 0)',`<br>`    fontSize: 50,`<br>`    padding: 4,`<br>`    backgroundImage: null,`<br>`    backgroundColor: 'rgba(129,`<br>`      236, 236, 0.1)',`<br>`    text:"&MID("x'x",2,1)&number(`<br>`      [Ratio])&encodeurl("%")&MID`<br>`        ("x'x",2,1)&"`<br>`}` | `displayText`: Whether to display the center text value.<br><br>`fontFamily`: The font for the center text.<br><br>`fontColor`: The color of the center text.<br><br>`fontSize`: The size of the center text.<br><br>`padding`: The padding around the center area.<br><br>`backgroundImage`: The image to use for the center.<br><br>`backgroundColor`: The color to use for the center background.<br><br>`text`: The text to display in the center. |
| `text:"&MID("x'x",2,1)&number(`<br>`   [Ratio])&encodeurl("%")&MID`<br>`     ("x'x",2,1)&"` | This is the trickiest part. QuickChart requires you to set the value for this key as follows in order for it to work:<br><br>`text: (val) => val + '%',`<br><br>This causes a problem if we pass the value of `(val) => val + '%'` to the AppSheet virtual column, as it will break up the URL while it is parsed. To avoid this problem, we need to convert this original value to an expression that AppSheet can accept and read to dynamically construct this part of the URL.<br><br>We are using the `MID` expression. As a result of using this expression, the number value in the `Ratio` column is wrapped in single quotation marks; for example, 90 would appear as `'90'`. `%` and must be encoded for the sake of safety. To implement your app, just change the column name listed here so that it matches your column name; otherwise, simply copy this code. |

As previously mentioned, this large object must be in line with the JavaScript object format, so you cannot omit even a single comma to split the key/value pairs. To get your desired chart style, we recommend you simply copy the entire expression we introduced in this section to get started. Just change the column name referenced to fit yours, and double-check to see whether it works.

Once you confirm the chart is displayed, it is time for customization. You can change the value for the color, text, and so on to customize the styles in line with the options listed in the preceding table. If you encounter errors during customization, restore it to the previous expression to debug the issue.

QuickChart provides other useful types of charts that can be used everywhere in your app, such as a progress bar or radar chart. In essence, to build the URL for other charts, the steps you need to take are the same as for the radial chart we built here.

Everything boils down to one large object inside the URL. QuickChart provides QuickChart Maker (visit `https://quickchart.io/chart-maker/`), where you can easily manipulate the other types of charts with the fully compiled URL along with option objects. Just copy the object and place it as a URL parameter to construct a new chart to your taste.

In the next section, we will look at some bonus tips and see some examples of a progress bar chart.

## Bonus tips – a working sample expression for a progress bar chart

In addition to a radial gauge chart, the progress bar chart is the most commonly used among the AppSheet community to display a ratio in a visually appealing way.

> **Note**
> *Name of the sample app to refer to in the portfolio site: Chapter 10_03* `https://www.appsheet.com/templates/sample?appGuidString=bfb484e1-e5d3-48c1-819a-6a21231c9b22`

The following screenshot shows the final version of the progress bar generated at the end. As you can see, this is pretty much a simple single-bar chart, indicating the percentage out of 100. The same chart could be used to express any sort of ratio, coverage, or achievement:

Figure 10.9 – A sample progress bar chart made by QuickChart

The progress bar chart in *Figure 10.9* is generated by passing the following expression into a virtual column. Please make sure that you have a [PERCENTAGE] column in your data table that is referred to inside this expression:

```
///"https://quickchart.io/chart?bkg=white&height=80&c=
type: 'progressBar',
data: {
datasets: [{
data: ["&[PERCENTAGE]&"],
backgroundColor: 'rgba(207, 0, 15, 0.5)',
borderColor: 'rgb(231, 76, 60)',
borderWidth: 5,
datalabels: {
color: 'rgba(0,0,0,0.9)',
font: {
weight: 'bold',
size:40
},
},
}],
},
options: {
responsive: true,

title: {
   align: 'end',
   display: true,
   position: 'right',
   text: 'Progress Bar'

}
}
}"
```

For the backgroundColor key, you can change the dominating proportion of the progress bar's background color on demand. For the sake of clarity, the dominating proportion is the red area in *Figure 10.9*. Other options, such as borderColor and borderWidth, are also customizable.

To make the chart dynamic, we need to pass a column expression for the part right after the `data:` property. In this sample expression, the `[PERCENTAGE]` column expression pushed after `data:` is going to deal with changing the chart dynamically. When the value in the `[PERCENTAGE]` column changes, the expression in the app formula for the virtual column will be recalculated, and the new chart will reflect the latest value.

## Generating a QR code for the image dynamically

*Name of the sample app to refer to in the portfolio site: Chapter 10_04* `https://www.appsheet.com/templates/sample?appGuidString=5fc6efe5-648e-4bf8-96f3-2f9e545e1749`

AppSheet natively provides a barcode and QR code scanning service for when app users are interacting with the app from a mobile phone. Once a column is set to **Scannable** under the column settings, the scanning service on the user's phone opens up to read the code and save the scanned data as text strings. This will accelerate the data entry process for the user. Furthermore, a QR code can be used not only for the data entry process but also for data searching and other useful purposes. Whatever you wish to achieve by having a QR code coupled with your AppSheet apps, the starting point is to generate a QR code inside your app. This short section will guide you on how to generate a QR code using the same service used previously: QuickChart.

QuickChart also provides QR code generators, which means you can create a QR code dynamically out of the datasets on your app. The following base URL will generate the QR code.

After the `?text=` parameter, you can pass any text arbitrarily, which will be converted into a code: `https://quickchart.io/qr?text=AnyTextYouWishToConvertToQR`.

Here, let's assume you wish to convert the `[USER_ID]` columns that store unique values to identify your company's employees. To create a QR code that returns the `User_ID` value after scanning, create a new virtual column on the table where the `[USER_ID]` column resides. Then, pass the following expression for the app formula. Please make sure you set the data type for this virtual column to either `Image` or `Thumbnail`: `https://quickchart.io/qr?text="&ENCODEURL([USER_ID])`.

On your app, it should render a QR code image, something like the one shown in *Figure 10.10*:

Figure 10.10 – A QR code with a basic black-and-white style

The QR code will be displayed inside the AppSheet view as an ordinary image file.

To display a QR code per record column value, you simply create a virtual column and set it as either the `image` or `thumbnail` type, then place the URL strings as an expression. You can further customize the color of the QR code in your preferred style.

Please see the following sample expression, which will generate the QR code shown in *Figure 10.11*:

```
"https://quickchart.io/qr?text="
&ENCODEURL([USER_ID])
&"&dark=f5312a"
&"&light=f9f953"
```

By passing this expression to the app formula in a virtual column with an image type column, this expression will return the following QR code. In this QR code, we set a custom color instead of black with a background color:

Figure 10.11 – QR code with its own color style

We hope you learned a new technique to dynamically create custom images and charts using this useful service. None of the chart types we introduced here in this chapter are provided by AppSheet's native chart views. We just introduced a few sample chart styles to discuss basic tricks to get those dynamic images to work within AppSheet, but you can find other styles of charts as well, thanks to QuickChart's long list of chart styles.

We have placed several sample apps on the portfolio website for this book, where you can learn techniques to instantly implement dynamic charts in your apps by copying the expressions.

In the next section, we will discuss integration with an external service using AppSheet Automation. Using this technique, you will be able to communicate with various external services from AppSheet. To dive deeper, we will consider a typical example to explain how AppSheet communicates with another Google service: Google Chat.

## Integrating with Google Workspace products

*Note*

*Name of the sample app to refer to in the portfolio site: Chapter 10_05* `https://www. appsheet.com/templates/sample?appGuidString=f604304b-69dd-44cc- 9ba8-c206a6844d5f`

Being a Google Workspace product, AppSheet is naturally integrated with various Workspace applications, such as Chat, Gmail, Drive, Sheets, and Docs. In this section, we will introduce a way to integrate your app with Google Chat so that app users can easily post text and other types of messages in target "spaces" inside Chat. To make this happen, AppSheet Automation provides us with a solution.

Please follow this step-by-step guide for integration with Google Chat:

1.  To get the `endpoint` URL from your Google Chat spaces, please go to the Chat space to which you want to submit messages from AppSheet and click **Manage webhooks**, as shown in the following screenshot:

Figure 10.12 – The Manage webhooks menu in Google Chat

2.  You will see a pop-up window asking for the name of incoming webhooks and avatar images. Please put the name you want. The **Avatar URL** field is optional, so you can leave it blank.

## Incoming webhooks
### View Documentation

Name
_____

Avatar URL
_____

Optional; min size 128 x 128px

Save

Figure 10.13 – Naming new incoming webhooks

3.    Then, you will see the link (URL) for the incoming webhook.

## Incoming webhooks
View Documentation

 **appsheet_webhook**
https://chat.googleapis.com/v1/spaces/AAAA4Xdh7Wk/messages?key=AlzaS...        ⋮

Add another

Figure 10.14 – Obtaining the URL for the incoming webhook

Copy this URL to the clipboard.

4.    Go to **AppSheet editor | Automation** and create a new bot.

For more information on AppSheet automation, please refer to *Chapter 8*.

After you have created a new bot by adding an event and a new step, select **Run a task** and create a new task. At the top of the task settings, select **HTTP Call a webhook** for the task type. You can paste the copied URL in the **Url** field.

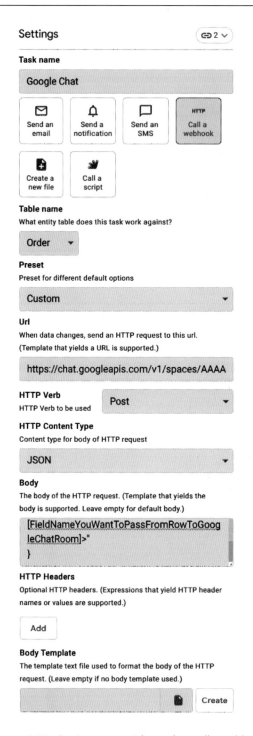

Figure 10.15 – Setting a step with a task to call a webhook

For the basic configuration of this task, refer to the following table:

| Option Name | Value |
| --- | --- |
| Preset | `Custom` |
| Url | Add the one you just copied from Google Chat in the previous step. |
| HTTP Verb | `Post` |
| HTTP Content Type | `JSON` |
| Body | `{`<br><br>`"text":`<br><br>`"<<[FieldNameYo`<br><br>`urWantToPassFro`<br><br>`mRowToGoogleCha`<br><br>`tRoom]>>"`<br><br>`}` |

The **Body** setting is most important. Using the `<<[ColumnName]>>` AppSheet template expression, alter the **JavaScript Object Notation (JSON)** body strings accordingly to fit your app. Just pass the column that contains the text value you wish to send out to Google Chat spaces.

## Adopting a card-style message rather than plain text

According to the Google API documentation, we can do lots more—including sending messages to Google Chat spaces in the style of card views where you can place images and buttons to call for actions, such as to open a URL.

For more details on the Google Chat API, please visit the following site: `https://developers.google.com/hangouts/chat/concepts/cards`.

Using those advanced styling options, it is possible to send text messages that contain a button to call for action. When the receiver clicks the button, you can lead them to a view within the AppSheet app, using AppSheet's opening URL action to move to the target view and page.

Let's assume we are working on an order management app, and we want to submit a text message to a Google Chat space that is shared among team members to give a notification once a new order is placed.

### Sending a card-style message

Rather than sending simple raw text messages to the chat, let's send messages in the card style, using the Google Chat API options. The final message arriving in Google Chat will look like *Figure 10.17*. Constructing this type of card view-style post generally works the same as constructing a simple text message. We simply have to manipulate some JSON body parts, as shown in the following code sample:

```json
{
  "cards": [
    {
      "header": {
        "title": "AppSheet App : Sample App",
        "subtitle": "New Order Data is added to the app",
        "imageUrl": "https://img.icons8.com/external-others-phat-plus/452/external-announcement-email-color-line-others-phat-plus.png"
      },
      "sections": [
        {
          "widgets": [
            {
              "keyValue": {
                "topLabel": "Order ID.",
                "content": "<<[Order ID]>>"
              },
            },
          ]
        },
        {
          "widgets": [
            {
              "keyValue": {
                "topLabel": "Created By",
                "content": "<<[Created By]>>"
              },
            },
          ]
        },
        {
          "widgets": [
            {
              "buttons": [
                {
                  "textButton": {
                    "text": "OPEN ORDER",
                    "onClick": {
                      "openLink": {
                        "url": "https://www.appsheet.com/start/<<_APPID>>?refresh=1&wipe=1<<[Linktorow]>>"
                      }
                    }
                  }
                }
              ]
            }
          ]
        }
      ]
    }
  ]
}
```

Figure 10.16 – JSON body

As you can see in *Figure 10.16*, the JSON body is relatively large. You can access it from our sample app named *Chapter 10_07*. Once you have accessed this sample app, go to the **Automation** pane, and you will find a bot called **Google Chat Card Style**. Then, open the **Card Style Message** task, from where you can copy all of the JSON text into the **Body** field of the webhook step setting and paste it into your apps for testing.

This JSON body yields the following message sent to Google Chat in a card style:

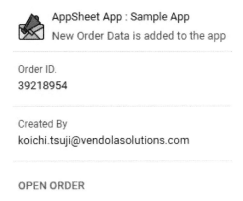

Figure 10.17 – Card-style message to Google Chat

Let's look at the details of this complex JSON body.

In this sample use case, we have the `Order ID.` and `Created By` columns. As the names of the columns suggest, they indicate the unique ID for that particular new order once it is placed, as well as who created the new order by passing the email value.

Those two column values are passed as template expressions to construct the JSON text dynamically using the column values. Change the column names to the ones you wish to send based on your data table.

For the same data table, we have added a virtual column to create a deeplink action that will take the user to the detailed view for this particular order.

We can make a virtual column with the `App` data type and then add the `LINKTOROW()` deeplink expression in order to navigate to the detail view of the order from where the message is sent.

Please review *Figure 10.18* to see what the full expression looks like:

App Formula for column Linktorow (App)

```
LINKTOROW([_THISROW].[Order ID],"Order_Detail")
```

Figure 10.18 – LINKTOROW deeplink expression for a virtual column

In the last part of the JSON object, we placed a `button` widget to present an action button at the bottom of the card to call for action. In *Figure 10.17*, you can see the blue text **OPEN ORDER** at the bottom of the message, which works to invoke the action. You can customize this text as well. Once the user clicks the button, it will open the AppSheet app's detail view for this particular order where the message to Google Chat is sent from.

This will improve the user experience by guiding users to move from Google Chat to the AppSheet app by clicking the **Action** button.

Inside the JSON body, this special expression references the virtual column, which is set to the App type and uses the `linktorow` expression as can be seen in the following URL expression: `https://www.appsheet.com/start/<<_APPID>>?refresh=1&wipe=1<<[Linktorow]>>`.

`<<_APPID>>` is a **template variable** that will dynamically return the app ID you are currently working on. At the end of the URL, we simply add `<<[Linktorow]>>`. This expression will return a link to the detail view for this order once the message is sent out to Google Chat.

So far, we have discussed how to integrate AppSheet with Google Chat, one of the services under Google Workspace, to guide you on how to connect AppSheet with an external service to work together.

Currently, every web-based cloud service—not limited to the ones Google provides—offers an API and/or webhook that enables users to connect to the service from external sources. Google Chat is just one example, but you may find other services you use daily for your own business provide an API/webhook for you.

Integration with an external service through the webhook will expand functionality substantially, but we can also use Google Apps Script. It collaboratively works with AppSheet to add extra features to your app. Let's dive into integration with Google Apps Script.

## Google Apps Script and use cases

AppSheet provides a webhook as a task for automation, where the app creator can send the webhook request to the external services, to invoke any action or post data externally. This is a useful function, but there is no version of a **GET request** available natively inside the AppSheet editor. This is because there is no space to store the response body that we receive as a consequence of such an HTTP request.

Furthermore, the response body (generally in JSON format) varies by API. It is impossible to standardize the method to convert the API response body so that AppSheet can consume it. However, in practical use cases, app creators wish to get the data outside AppSheet and consume it within the app. For this use case, Google Apps Script provides a workaround. These are not purely tips and tricks for AppSheet but are associated more with Google Sheets configuration.

In any case, let's briefly explain how to get data using Google Apps Script and display it within AppSheet apps.

## Displaying the latest currency exchange rate

> *Note*
>
> *Name of the sample app to refer to in the portfolio site: Chapter 10_06* `https://www.appsheet.com/templates/sample?appGuidString=e6e7134c-5965-4e50-9dd6-bc4e6b0509c9`

Let's assume you need to display the latest currency exchange rate in an app. The rates vary from time to time, but various API services provide an endpoint (URL) that returns the currency exchange rates upon request.

To facilitate the explanation, let's use an API service, **ExchangeRate-API** (`https://www.exchangerate-api.com/`).

Before using their services, please check out the terms and conditions of use by visiting `https://www.exchangerate-api.com/terms`.

First of all, let's check the URL (endpoint) for this external service, `https://open.er-api.com/v6/latest/USD`. When you click on this URL, you will see something like the following screenshot in your browser:

Figure 10.19 – Response body in JSON format

This is a *response* in the form of JSON where we can see the latest currency exchange rate against the US dollar.

Using this URL, let's create a quick Google Apps Script. It will extract the currency exchange rate from this response body and save it into Google Sheets.

## Google Apps Script sample code

The following code is to create a custom function called `getRate()`, which will call the HTTP request to `ExchangeRate-API`. Once the exchange rates are called, they are saved in the cell where this function is used inside the spreadsheet cell:

```
function getRate(curr) {

var responseDataGET = UrlFetchApp.fetch("https://open
    .er-api.com/v6/latest/USD").getContentText();

var jsonData = JSON.parse(responseDataGET);

var rate = jsonData['rates'][curr]

console.log(rate)

return rate

}
```

Once the Google Apps Script is ready, we can use the function inside the cell in our spreadsheet. The `getRate()` custom function requires the `curr` argument. For this argument, we need to pass the currency code this service defines, such as GBP, which stands for the British pound sterling. Then, use this `custom` function inside the cell, as shown in the following screenshot:

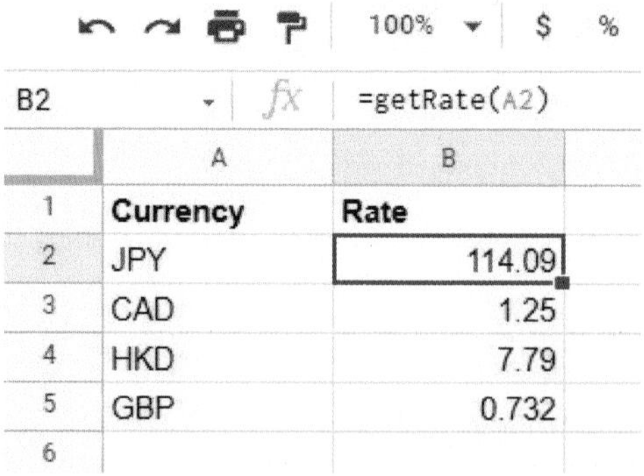

Figure 10.20 – Spreadsheet function made by Google Apps Script

In *Figure 10.20*, we are attempting to extract the currency exchange rates for the **Japanese yen (JPY)**, **Canadian dollar (CAD)**, **Hong Kong dollar (HKD)**, and GBP against the US dollar.

This function anchors the cell beside it to pass the currency code as an argument for this `custom` function. Then, the `custom` function yields the latest exchange rate for each currency against the US dollar.

Once you have the spreadsheet, which is connected to the external service through the `custom` sheet function made by Google Apps Script, you are ready to fetch data from AppSheet.

## Reading data from a spreadsheet

To show the data obtained by Google Apps Script inside the AppSheet app, there is not much required. Simply add this sheet as a table to the AppSheet app. Once the app is synchronized on launch or explicitly synchronized by the app user from the device, the spreadsheet function is re-evaluated and returns the latest currency exchange rate. It is then displayed in the AppSheet app after the synchronization is complete.

Let's recap the steps taken to get the data obtained externally from other services and then display it inside the AppSheet app. The general approach to getting data from external sources and consuming it inside AppSheet is as follows:

1.  Use the API that is provided by the external services outside AppSheet.

2.  Create your own Google Apps Script code to create the spreadsheet `custom` function.

3.  This `custom` function will *return* the data you need. The value the function returns is shown in the cell where the `custom` function is placed.

4.  Once the spreadsheet `custom` function is up and running and getting your required data from the external source into the cells, just connect the sheet from the AppSheet app.

This basic integration between AppSheet and the spreadsheet containing Google Apps Script helps us to display real-time data from third-party services without manually updating the spreadsheet but rather automatically pulling the latest data through the script. In *Figure 10.21*, you can see the exchange rate for each currency displayed through the integration with Google Apps Script:

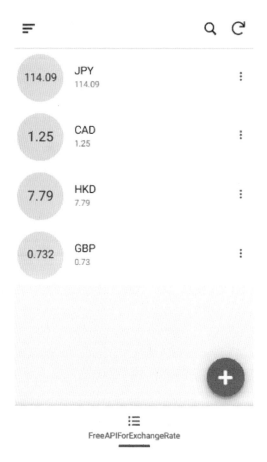

Figure 10.21 – An AppSheet sample view displaying the latest currency exchange rates

Powered by Google Apps Script, AppSheet can connect with various external services to get data from other services and display it inside the AppSheet app. For example, you may have some data in external services you need to pull into your AppSheet app. In that case, integration with Google Apps Script is definitely one of your options.

## Summary

Throughout this chapter, we have introduced several practical techniques you can implement in your apps to improve the style of your app views and also extend the capabilities of your apps.

QuickChart provides better insight into the data you present to app users at a glance and makes your app look more professional with modern styling. Rather than reading the number as text, or the percentage or ratio as a plain number, presenting it in the form of a graphic chart will make it easy to read and visually appealing.

A QR code can be used anywhere, and in any type of app you develop. You may have an inventory management app where you have a collection of products with a `PRODUCT_ID` column. When a new product comes into stock, the app user needs to keep a record by adding new data through the app. Instead of manually typing or selecting the product from a drop-down list, you can present a scanning function where the user scans the QR code attached to the product to instantly capture the `PRODUCT_ID` value. This will make your app efficient as it allows users to enter data quickly into your app.

You should now be able to adopt the techniques we have discussed in this chapter anywhere in the apps that you develop, regardless of the purpose of the app.

The AppSheet portfolio site that we prepared in this book holds several sample apps, so you can copy them to start learning what we discussed in this chapter. Please dive into those sample apps to learn the basics to advance your knowledge and skills to the next stage.

You may encounter difficulties while learning these techniques. The AppSheet community forum (`https://www.googlecloudcommunity.com/gc/AppSheet/ct-p/appsheet`) is a good place to ask for help from those who have advanced skills, such as coding and manipulating URLs to get exactly what you want.

In this chapter, we have made a series of sample apps for you to provide context to the tricks we discussed. These apps will give you a quick insight into how an app is built to implement certain functionalities. In the following chapter, we will talk about *app templates*—a bunch of commonly used app templates that can be used and customized based on the requirement.

You will also learn how to use templates effectively. The chapter will also help you to get an idea of how to use a series of sample apps that we have created for this book, such as how to copy a sample template to make your own app and how to look inside such sample apps. Please make sure to examine the contents by looking inside these template apps, as we believe it is the best way to learn about AppSheet.

# Part 4 – App Templates and Tricks for App Building

In this part, we will explain how you can use app templates when creating a new app or sharing an existing app with other app creators. We will also show you some useful tips and tricks to create advanced functionalities and change app behavior in a user-friendly manner.

This part has the following chapters:

- *Chapter 11, Building More Apps with App Templates*
- *Chapter 12, Tips and Tricks*
- *Chapter 13, Appendix*

# 11

# Building More Apps with App Templates

In the previous chapter, you learned how you can extend an app's capabilities by utilizing third-party services. In this chapter, we will understand how you can use app templates or template apps to build more powerful apps.

In modern IT systems, the concept of templates is very important. Templates help you to build on an already-built foundation. AppSheet apps also use the concept of templates. You can access the various app templates using the following options:

- You can share some of the apps you have created as template apps in your app portfolio for other app creators. You can also create template apps of certain complex functionalities as a self-reference for your own use.

- Many AppSheet app creators have created template apps that demonstrate an AppSheet feature or business functionality. These template apps are available on the app creators' portfolio pages.

- Additionally, the AppSheet website also has a large collection of template apps. You can use these publicly available template apps as building blocks or reference apps to create more complex apps for your own requirements.

We will cover the following topics in this chapter:

- Creating your apps portfolio for other app creators
- Using others' app templates to help with your app development
- Building templates for your self-reference

By the end of this chapter, you will have learned how you can share apps as *public* sample apps on your portfolio page for any AppSheet user to view or copy. You will also learn how you can create teams within your organization and share *team* sample apps with a team. The app templates on a portfolio page mostly demonstrate an AppSheet feature, a business functionality, or a combination of both that other app creators can learn from.

You will understand how you can further build apps by copying the template apps from the AppSheet website or those created by other app creators. You will have also learned how you can build your own template apps repository for your own future reuse and self-reference.

# Creating your apps portfolio for other app creators

You can create teams and public sample apps for use and reference by your team members and other AppSheet app creators. In this section, let's understand how you can define teams and share your apps as team samples or public apps. You will also learn about certain precautions you need to take when you share your apps as public apps.

## Sharing your apps with teams and others

When you are working in teams and want other members of your team to browse or copy an app or change the app definition, you can share the apps as **team sample** apps. You can also share your app as a **public sample** app. Let's understand the procedure for making your apps team sample or public sample apps.

### *Defining your teams*

You need to define your team before you can share your apps as team sample apps. Let's first understand where and how you can define your team:

1. To define teams, you need to have an account with a private domain email, such as yourcompanyname.com, to use the **team sample** option under the **Manage | Author | Team Work** options. You cannot use an account created with a personal email address, such as yourname@gmail.com or yourname@hotmail.com, to define teams.

2. When you log in to your account created with a private domain, you will see the following options on the AppSheet home page at https://www.appsheet.com/home/apps:

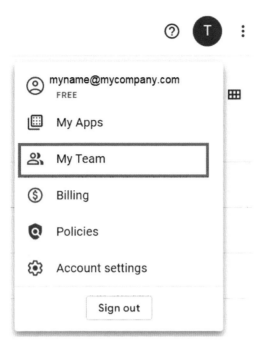

Figure 11.1 – The My Team option on the AppSheet home page

3.    When you click on the **My Team** option, you will see the following page:

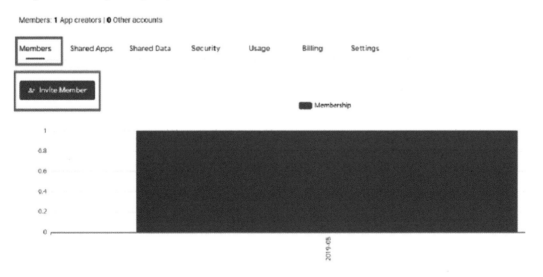

Figure 11.2 – The My Team page and membership chart

4.    You will see the number of members in your team in a chart format. This preceding screenshot shows that the **mycompany.com** account has one team member. You can invite more members by clicking on the **Invite Member** option. When you click on the **Invite Member** button, a form as shown in the following screenshot appears. You can fill in the email addresses of your team members to invite them to join the team and then click on the **Invite** option:

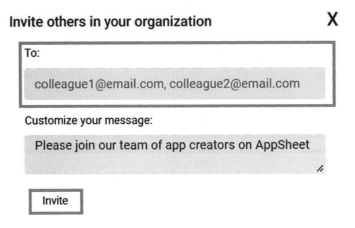

Figure 11.3 – Inviting members to the team

5.    When you scroll down on the **My Team** page, you will see the list of app creators and a list of other account IDs in your team, as shown in the following screenshot:

Figure 11.4 – The team details list

In the preceding screenshot, there are no other app creators and there is only one other account ID, **12345**, that is part of the team.

After having created your team as described in the preceding section, let's now understand how you can share template apps with your team as **team sample** apps.

## *Sharing apps as team samples*

You can share your apps with your team with a procedure, as described in the following steps:

1.  To share the app with your team, you need to first deploy the app using the **Manage | Deploy** options, which we learned about in the *Deploying an app with all features* section of *Chapter 7*.

2.  After you have deployed the app, you can select the **Make this a team sample?** setting under the **Manage | Author | Team Work** options, as shown in the following screenshot:

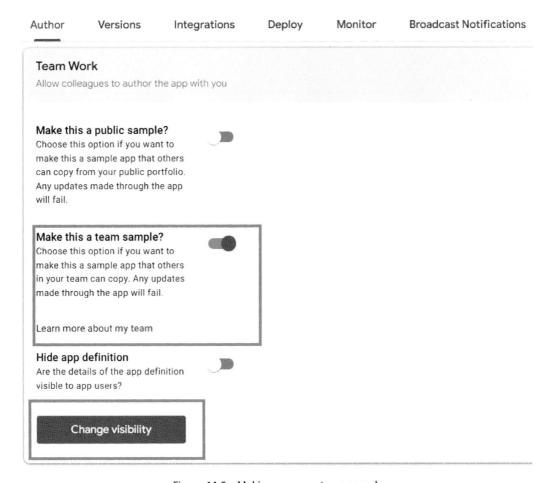

Figure 11.5 – Making an app a team sample

3.  Once you have selected this setting, you can click on the **Change visibility** option to make the app available to other team members under the **Team Samples** option on the **My Team** page:

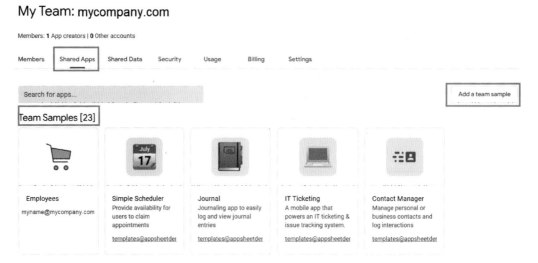

## My Team: mycompany.com

Members: **1** App creators | **0** Other accounts

Members | Shared Apps | Shared Data | Security | Usage | Billing | Settings

Search for apps...

Add a team sample

Team Samples [23]

| Employees | Simple Scheduler | Journal | IT Ticketing | Contact Manager |
|---|---|---|---|---|
| myname@mycompany.com | Provide availability for users to claim appointments | Journaling app to easily log and view journal entries | A mobile app that powers an IT ticketing & issue tracking system. | Manage personal or business contacts and log interactions |
| | templates@appsheetder | templates@appsheetder | templates@appsheetder | templates@appsheetder |

Figure 11.6 – Team sample apps

4. Your team can copy the app as well as the app's data source from there. Once copied, they can make changes to their own copy of the app as per their requirements.

Let's now understand how you can make an app a public sample app.

### Sharing apps as public samples

At times, you may want to share your apps with anyone who has an AppSheet account ID. Generally, you would want to make an app a public sample app when you want to demonstrate a new or different way of achieving a functionality or feature to other AppSheet app creators.

However, you need to be aware that, when you make an app public, anyone with an AppSheet account can browse it. Anyone with an AppSheet account ID can also copy the app definition, depending on the settings that you choose while making the app a public sample.

> **Note**
> You should never create a public sample app with any confidential data. You should also never create a public sample app with a functionality that is very specific or proprietary to your organization that your organization would want to keep confidential.

The process to make one of your apps a public sample is like making a team sample app:

1. To share an app as a public sample app, you need to first deploy it using the **Manage | Deploy** options, which we learned about in the *Deploying an app with all features* section of *Chapter 7*.

2.  Once you have deployed the app, you can select the **Make this a public sample?** setting available under the **Manage | Author | Team Work** options, as shown in the following screenshot:

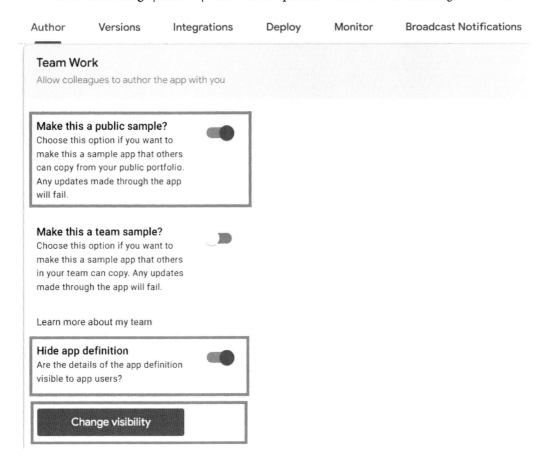

Figure 11.7 – Making an app a public sample

3.  You can also optionally select the **Hide app definition** setting if you do not want the public sample app's definition to be copied by other users. By doing this, other AppSheet app creators can only browse the app but cannot make a copy of the app.

4.  After turning the **Make this a public sample?** setting on and optionally turning the **Hide app definition** setting on, you can click on the **Change visibility** button. These steps make the app a public sample app.

    With the preceding steps, the app made as a public sample app becomes available on your portfolio page for any other AppSheet app creator to browse or copy.

Let's next learn how others can access your portfolio page and how you can add some description to your portfolio page.

### *Adding a description to your portfolio page*

Your public sample apps are available on your portfolio page. Your portfolio page URL follows the pattern of `https://www.appsheet.com/portfolio/Your AppSheet AccountID`. If your AppSheet account ID were `123456`, your portfolio page would be visible at the `https://www.appsheet.com/portfolio/123456` URL.

Since apps configured as public apps will be available on your portfolio page, you need to add a short description to your portfolio page. You can add this description by going to the **My Account | Collab** panes, as shown in the following screenshot:

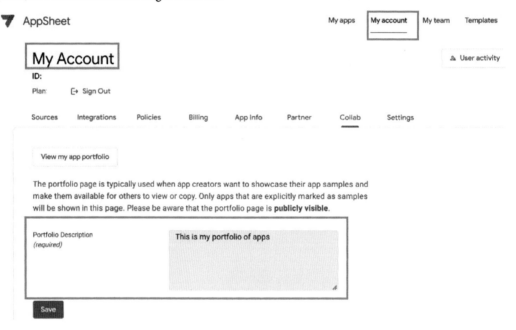

Figure 11.8 – Adding a description to the portfolio page

The preceding screenshot shows the default description that you can modify to add a brief introduction to your portfolio page in the **Portfolio Description** field. You can click the **Save** button after you finish writing the description. You can also see how your portfolio page looks by selecting the **View my app portfolio** option. Your portfolio page is now visible to other app creators, as shown in the following screenshot:

 AppSheet FREE

## This is my portfolio of apps

No apps yet

Shared sample apps will appear here

Figure 11.9 – Portfolio page

Other app creators can copy or browse the apps depending on how you have published them. Other app creators will be able to copy the apps if you disabled the **Hide app definition** option while making the app public.

In this section, you learned how you can define your team, and how you can publish your apps as team sample apps or public sample apps. You also learned how you and others can access your portfolio page and how you can add an introductory description to your portfolio page.

Let's next understand how you can use app templates to build more complex apps as per your requirements.

# Using others' app templates to help with your app development

When you are creating a new app for certain functionality, it always helps to refer to the best practices and innovative, efficient implementations that other app creators have successfully implemented and shared.

You can refer to app templates published on the AppSheet website itself. There are several useful app templates under different categories published on the AppSheet website.

Additionally, you can refer to the app portfolios of other app creators in your team and publicly available portfolios of other app creators.

## Using app templates from the AppSheet website

The **Templates** option is available on the **AppSheet** home page, as shown in the following screenshot:

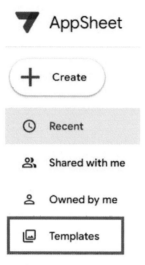

Figure 11.10 – The Templates option on the AppSheet home page

Once you click on the **Templates** option, the **App templates** page appears, as shown in the following screenshot. You can search these apps by using the **Industry**, **Function**, and **Feature** options, as shown in the following screenshot:

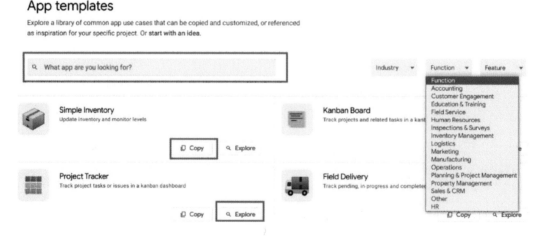

Figure 11.11 – The App templates page

You will find that most of the app templates are listed under the **Function** option.

Alternatively, you can search the template apps by using the search bar, as shown in the preceding screenshot. You can search by functionality keywords, such as `inventory`, `timesheet`, or `orders`. You can also search the apps by app feature keywords, such as `dashboard` or `forms`.

The following table shows the template apps with the most common functionalities and the industries where those functionalities are most used:

| Function | Industries where the function is most used |
|---|---|
| Inventory management<br><br>Field service<br><br>Logistics<br><br>Manufacturing | Automotive, construction, energy, manufacturing, and retail |
| Real estate | Property management |
| Operations<br><br>Inspection and surveys<br><br>Planning and project management<br><br>Human resources<br><br>Sales and CRM<br><br>Attendance/timesheets<br><br>Customer engagement<br><br>Marketing<br><br>Education and training | All industries |

Table 11.1 – Template apps and industries

You can copy the template apps and further modify them as you want. You can click on the **Copy** button to copy an app template, or you can simply browse a template app by tapping on the **Explore** button.

When you click on the **Copy** option, you will get the following form window. You can give a different **App name** to the template app you are copying. You can also optionally select a **Category** option for the app.

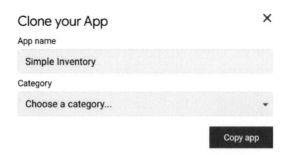

Figure 11.12 – Copying a template app

After learning how to search the template apps by function and industry, let's now learn how you can search the template apps by the AppSheet features.

### Searching template apps by the AppSheet features

At times, you will want to understand how a particular AppSheet feature is implemented. In such cases, you can search the template apps by the AppSheet feature. There are many template apps available for the AppSheet features, such as calendar, chart, dashboard, form, image, map, notification, signature, smart assistant, and automation features. You will often find that the same app appears under the **Industry**, **Function**, or **Feature** categories. This is natural because an app mostly contains several features and more than one functionality.

When you want to copy an app template to modify it, you will find in many instances that a single template app does not exactly match your requirements. In such cases, you can copy the template app that matches them best and build on it further by editing it.

### An alternative way to copy the template apps

Another option to create apps from the templates available on the AppSheet website is to copy those templates using the following steps, as shown in the following screenshot:

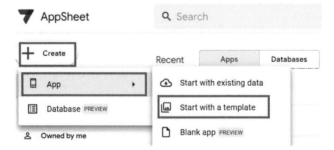

Table 11.2 – An alternative way to copy template apps

1. Go to the **My Apps** page on the **AppSheet** website.

2. Click on the + **Create** option.

3. Another window with **App** and **Database** options will pop up.

4. Click on the **App** option. Another window with three options will pop up. Tap on the **Start with a template** option.

   You will now go to **App templates**.

5. From here on, you can follow the same procedure to copy the template apps we discussed at the beginning of this section.

We have shared a few templates or sample apps as part of this book. You can suitably modify and make use of functionality or AppSheet features implemented in those apps when you build your own apps.

In this section, you learned about the multiple options you have for searching for and then browsing or copying the template apps. You learned that template apps can be useful as building blocks for more complex apps you want to build for your business requirements.

Next, we will discuss how you can build certain template apps just for your own use.

# Building templates for your self-reference

You will find it helpful to have certain template apps readily available for your own reference. These apps are like study notes that you can refer to from time to time. You need not share them as public sample apps. These apps can be simply on your **My Apps** page. Let's discuss a few situations where you will find these template apps useful.

Some of the more complex expressions are mainly date/time expressions and multi-row expressions that have functions such as SELECT(), MAXROW(), and MINROW(). Unlike the metric system, which works on decimals, time and date measurements have very uneven measures, as we discussed in *Chapter 4*.

Additionally, there are somewhat complex AppSheet features such as reference actions, dashboards, charts, URLs for images and files, and so on. It is always useful to have your own template apps ready for complex expressions, features, and business functionalities that you commonly use.

While creating template apps for self-reference, you can use all the available AppSheet features. This is so because AppSheet allows you to create apps with all the AppSheet features available until you deploy the app. Once you have deployed the apps, your subscription plan needs to match the features used in the app. However, you are unlikely to deploy all your template apps, especially those that you create for self-reference. As a result, you can create self-reference template apps with all the available AppSheet features.

Your self-reference template apps will also help you to enhance and test your knowledge of the AppSheet platform. You can mainly create the following templates:

- **Business functionality-based apps**: Sample apps that concentrate on business functionality:

  - Examples of these apps are inventory management, logistics, and operations, project management apps, and property management.

  - You can also create apps with complex calculations such as calculating durations or time differences between two-time values when days overlap. Such calculations will be useful to you when you build timekeeping or attendance apps or any app that has a date/time component.

- **Feature-based apps**: These apps mainly demonstrate AppSheet features and third-party services:

  - You can also create self-reference app templates utilizing the third-party services that we discussed in the previous chapter.

  - You can have self-reference template apps around certain features, such as reference actions, dashboards, calendars, charts, images, barcode or QR code scanning, and files with URLs ready so that you can refer to those functionalities any time you want.

## Summary

In this chapter, we learned how you can create a portfolio page of template apps. We also learned how you can share apps with your teams as team sample apps or with anyone with an AppSheet account as public sample apps.

We also learned about the options that are available for copying template apps created by others. You can copy template apps available on the **App templates** page from the **AppSheet** home page. The second option is to copy the template apps from the **portfolio pages** of the other AppSheet app creators. The third option you have is to refer to the template apps shared with this book.

We also learned that it is a good practice for you to create template apps for your own reference. You learned that you can create template apps for your own ready reference with certain frequently used but somewhat complex functions, including date/time or multi-row functions such as SELECT() and LOOKUP(). You can also build template apps with certain complex features, including reference actions or column types such as images or files referred through a URL.

In the next chapter, we'll learn some practical tips and tricks related to data manipulation, advanced UX, and automation features that will help you to develop apps with custom functionalities.

# 12
# Tips and Tricks

As app creators spend more time in AppSheet, they will naturally find that the learning curve to develop their own functionalities is getting steeper after passing a certain skill and knowledge level. This could happen because the app creators would like to add more advanced functionalities to the apps to implement their own business logic into a single application and in turn, the advanced skills and knowledge are required to add those intelligent functionalities to the app.

Throughout this chapter, you will find the most practical and useful tips and tricks that will help in developing custom functionalities to satisfy the unique needs of your business applications in AppSheet. The tips and tricks that we will introduce in this chapter deal with various aspects of app development, including, but not limited to, data manipulation, advanced UX settings, and using a bot.

We have split the tips and tricks into the following categories:

- Formulas (expressions)
- Actions
- Column settings
- App settings
- Bots and automation
- Views

These tips and tricks are not directly related to each other. We recommend you read through this chapter to get new knowledge bit by bit. We hope this chapter helps you expand your skills to get richer functionalities using these hidden techniques.

# Technical requirements

To assist you in learning the tips and tricks we introduce in this chapter, we have placed several sample apps on the portfolio site of this book. In each section, you will find the name of a sample app. While you read through the tips and tricks, we recommend you take a look at the sample app to see how the tricks are actually implemented.

# Formulas (expressions)

In this section, we introduce some tips and tricks that will help solve common issues that the majority of app creators run into at an early stage when starting to develop an app with AppSheet. Let's dive in.

## Creating a URL to access images and other files

The name of the sample app to refer to on the portfolio site is `Chapter 12_01`:

```
https://www.appsheet.com/templates/sample?appGuidString=a7950813-
c128-4ad2-8bba-9f766034977f
```

Any image files or other files, such as PDF or MS Word files, you save in AppSheet apps will be saved in cloud services such as Google Drive automatically. Typically, there is an image, thumbnail, or file column type and it is easy to access and retrieve the files to show inside the app, as AppSheet automatically creates an action to open the files.

However, app creators quite often need to get the URLs to open the files for various reasons. We need to share those files with someone who does not have access to the app or use those file resources inside other services.

In those cases, we need to have a full absolute path, starting with `https://`, to connect to the files that are saved through the app. Once the files are saved to AppSheet, then the relative path, which is part of the absolute path, is saved as text to the backend data source, but the relative path is not actually linked to the source files.

A simple AppSheet expression will dynamically generate the full path to connect to those files saved on the cloud.

## Setup guide

The workaround is pretty simple. Just create a new virtual column on the table where you have an image or file type column. For the app formula, we pass the following expression, which will return the dynamic full path. Assuming we have an `Image` column in this table, this expression will give you the URL to open the image file. Please make sure you set the column type to `URL` for this case:

| Expression | `CONCATENATE('https://www.appsheet.com/`<br>`template/gettablefileurl?appName=',`<br>`ENCODEURL(CONTEXT(AppName)), '&tableName=',`<br>`ENCODEURL(CONTEXT(Table)), '&fileName=',`<br>`ENCODEURL([Image]))` |
| --- | --- |

To implement this expression in your app, just change the last part of the column name, which is inside the `ENCODEURL()` expression, to match your data. To make this URL open the files properly, please make sure you go to **Security | Options** and turn off the **Require Image and File URL Signing** option, as shown in the following figure:

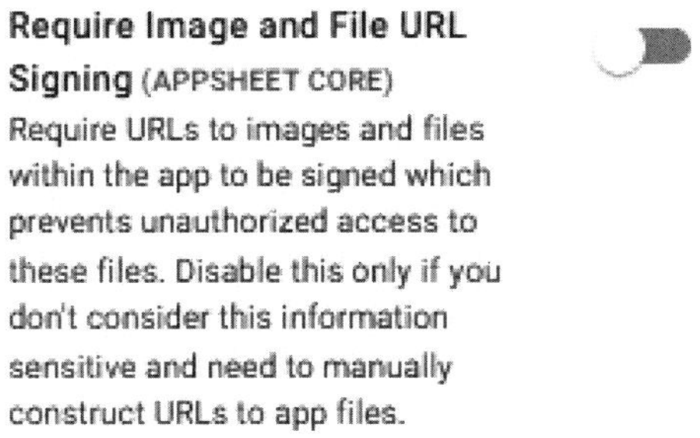

**Require Image and File URL Signing** (APPSHEET CORE)
Require URLs to images and files within the app to be signed which prevents unauthorized access to these files. Disable this only if you don't consider this information sensitive and need to manually construct URLs to app files.

Figure 12.1 – Security option settings

If this option is turned on, then access to saved files is protected, which prohibits the created URL from the expression from accessing a file.

## Bonus tips

It is possible for you or your app users to edit and update the files that a bot generates through cloud storage such as Google Drive – for instance, if a bot generates Excel files and then you edit the data inside the Excel file and save the changes. If you open the file using the URL that this expression returns, you may find that the Excel data is not updated at all. This is because AppSheet is opening your files from the data cached in the server when it was previously accessed, so it is not opening the latest files that are saved in the storage. This is called **file cache**.

In order to avoid this AppSheet behavior and make sure the URL gives access to the latest files, you can modify the expression slightly:

```
CONCATENATE('https://www.appsheet.com/template/
gettablefileurl?appName=', ENCODEURL(CONTEXT(AppName)),
'&tableName=', ENCODEURL(CONTEXT(Table)), '&fileName=',
ENCODEURL([Image]),"&",UNIQUEID())
```

As you can see in the preceding expression, "&",UNIQUEID() is now added as the last argument. By adding this, a unique URL will be generated each time the URL attempts to open the files from the link.

## Calculations between time and duration

The sample app names are as follows:

Chapter 12_02

https://www.appsheet.com/templates/sample?appGuidString=ef15e780-3cd0-400d-b4ff-974b578eb3f5

Chapter 12_03

https://www.appsheet.com/templates/sample?appGuidString=2749141d-1aac-4ae8-90b8-135dcb536f0c

We have to admit that calculations involving time, datetime, and duration values are one of the toughest challenges for most beginners. Let's learn some basics about calculations involving time and duration values that will help you obtain the expected results.

Let's quickly summarize how time and duration values are represented inside AppSheet:

| Time | 00:00:00 | HH:MM:SS; the HH portion is always 2 digits, less than 24 |
| Duration | 001:00:00 | HHH : MM : SS; the HHH portion is always minimum 3 digit. |

Table 12.1 – Time and durations in Appsheet

Let's consider the following example to distinguish the time and duration values:

- 05:00:00: Time type, meaning 5 A.M.

- 005:00:00: Duration type, meaning 5 hours

Now, this is a pretty straightforward example, but what are the data types of these values?

- 24:00:00: Duration type, meaning 24 hours

- 024:00:00: Duration type, meaning 24 hours

Actually, both are recognized as duration types. The first one, 24:00:00, starts with 24 instead of 024, although both choices of syntax express 24 hours. We have to pay special attention to the first two digits of the syntax. If the first two digits are more than 23, AppSheet will recognize it as a duration type. This may sound a bit complicated, but once you get your head around this, you will be able to figure out how to express time and duration values in AppSheet.

Let's move on to discussing the basics for a set of calculations involving time and duration values. In this context, *time* means the value expressed in the form of 00:00:00 or the column value set to the Time type. Similarly, *duration* means a values expressed in the form of 000:00:00 or a column whose type is set to Duration.

The following table illustrates all the possible combinations of time- and duration-related calculations:

| Calculation | Return value type | Example and remarks |
| --- | --- | --- |
| Time + Duration | Time | Timenow() + 001:00:00 (1 hour later from now) |
| Duration + Duration | Duration | "001:00:00"+ "000:01:00" = "001:01:00" |
| Time - Time | Duration | "15:10:00" - "12:00:00" = "003:10:00" |
| Time - Duration | Time | Timenow() - "001:00:00" (1 hour ago from now) |
| Duration - Duration | Duration | "015:10:10" - "012:10:10" = "003:00:00" |
| Duration - Time | Error | This combination does not make any sense |
| Time + Time | Error | This combination does not make any sense |

Table 12.2 – Time- and duration-related combinations

You may have thought that the calculations involving datetime and time values would be easy, but actually, that is not always true. Let us explain. How do you calculate the datetime value for "1.5 days later from now?"

You may suppose the NOW()+1.5 expression will return the result that we need in this case. However, if you test this expression, you will see a result with a datetime value of 2 days from now. The AppSheet will add "2 days" instead of "1 day and 12 hours" to the datetime value that is returned by the NOW() expression, so the result of this expression is not precise. To get the correct result, we need to convert 1.5 days, which is actually a decimal value, into a duration value in AppSheet. There are various equivalent expressions available, but the following sample expressions are one example of converting decimal values which represent days, hours, or minutes into a duration value, which is expressed in a HHH:MM:SS format:

| Convert decimal days into a duration | Convert decimal hours into a duration | Convert decimal minutes into a duration |
|---|---|---|
| ```
concatenate(
floor([Day]*24.0),
":",
floor(([Day]*24.0-
floor([Day]*24.0))*60.00),
":",
floor([Day]*24.0*60*60-
floor([Day]*24.0)*60*60-
floor(([Day]*24.0-
floor([Day]*24.0))*60.00)*60)
)
``` | ```
concatenate(
floor([Hour]),
":",
floor(([Hour]-
floor([Hour]))*60.00),
":",
floor([Hour]*60*60-
floor([Hour])*60*60-
floor(([Hour]-
floor([Hour]))*60.00)*60)
)
``` | ```
concatenate(
floor([Minute]/60.0),
":",
floor(([Minute]/60.0-
floor([Minute]/60.0))*60.00),
":",
floor(([Minute]-floor([Minute]))*60)
)
``` |

Table 12.3 – Sample expression to convert a decimal number into a duration

If you have a decimal value that represents durations such as days, hours, or minutes, then you must remember to convert it into the duration data type expressed in the format of HHH : MM : SS by using the expressions in the preceding table as an example.

## Number division (decimal to be used)

Let's do some quick math. What do you expect that this simple calculation is going to return?

5/2 (5 divided by 2)

Yes, the answer is 2.5. However, when we pass the same mathematic calculation into a virtual column in AppSheet, you may notice the calculation returns 2 as a result instead of 2.5. This is just a simple case, but many will start using AppSheet and face the issue of a calculation not returning the expected result. It is better to know how AppSheet's calculation methodology works before you fall into the trap.

An AppSheet expression always respects the value type. Let's analyze this with the same simple calculation, 5/2.

As you can guess, 5 and 2 are *number types*. The AppSheet expression will return a *number type* as a result if only number type values are used within the calculation. The logic behind it is *number* divided by *number* returns *number*, so this calculation inside AppSheet is returning 2, instead of 2.5, and ignoring the decimal part. The decimal part of the result is rounded down.

If we wish to get 2.5 as a result, we need to change the type of the value inside the calculation. The easiest solution is to change the calculation to *5.0 divided by 2*. Now, you will get a result of 2.5. As you see, we have *5.0* as a decimal value instead of 5. In this way, the calculation has now turned into a *decimal* divided by a *number*, which returns a *decimal* value as the final outcome.

If you have a number-type column and use that column value for the calculation, then the expression would look like *([Number]*1.0)/2*, and return a decimal value.
```

In this section on formulas (expressions), we introduced a few tips and tricks that are worth knowing for new app creators. We hope they will help address the issues you may face during your development work, especially when you initially start to work with AppSheet. In the next section, we wish to address a few tricks related to AppSheet actions.

# Actions

In this section, we will share a few useful tips and tricks for the advanced usage of AppSheet actions. They will help you develop custom features for navigation from one view to another, as well as data manipulations.

## Forcing sync upon navigating to the target view

When you guide your app users to another view by navigating from a certain view, you may need to ensure that the users will access the most recent data at the time they navigate to the next view as much as possible. The most practical solution is to let the app always *sync* upon moving to another view by using a deep link action. For instance, you can set an action to move to another view using the following expression:

```
Linktoview("Next View Name")
```

Once this deep link action is invoked, it moves to the target view without syncing the app. This means the next view the app user is accessing may not really reflect the most recent data, as it is possible that the other app users may have edited data without the current user knowing it. The solution is to make the app sync all the time when the deep link action is activated.

## Setup guide

The solution to this problem is pretty simple. After your deep link expression within the action settings, just add a simple parameter. The expression for **Target** on your custom action looks like this:

```
Linktoview("Next View Name")&"&at="&(NOW() + 1)
```

Please see the following figure to learn how to pass this expression in the action settings:

| Do this<br>The type of action to perform | App: go to another view within this app | ▼ |
|---|---|---|
| Target<br>App link target | = Linktoview("Next View Name")&"&at="&(NOW() + 1) | Ⴥ |

Figure 12.2 – Deep link expression (sample)

After your deep link expression, add the special parameters of `&"&at="&(NOW() + 1)`.

By adding these parameters to the end of the deep link expression, the sync will occur when the user invokes this action and the target view will be displayed after the sync is completed.

## Reference action to update the parent based on the child

The sample app's name is Chapter 12_04: https://www.appsheet.com/templates/ sample?appGuidString=b383fe7f-89e0-4231-8f9b-7339ce2b1b10.

By using the virtual column with de-ref expressions, AppSheet provides us with an easy solution to pull any column value from the parent table into the child table. However, as an app creator, you may need to store and save this value in the child table as a normal column instead of a virtual column.

### Setup guide

In this specific use case, we will employ actions as well as automation to ensure the value in the parent table's column is synced to the normal column of its related child table's row(s). In this sample app, we have the [STATUS] column in the parent table, and we wish to update PARENT_STATUS, which resides in the child table. Based on this assumption, let's get started. The context of this trick is to create a series of actions and wrap them up. Please follow this step-by-step guide:

1.  In the child table, please create an action to change the value in PARENT_STATUS in line with *Figure 12.2* here. The value to pass to the column uses the [PARENT].[STATUS] de-ref expression. Let's name this action UpdateChild:

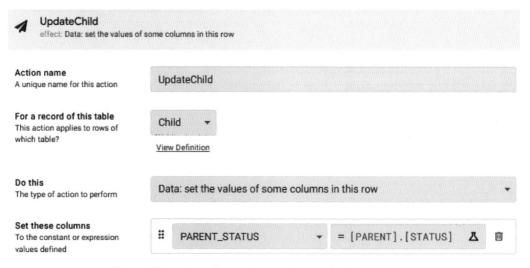

Figure 12.3 – First action to change the value in the child table

2.  In the parent table, create a new action called **execute an action on a set of rows**. The referenced table is selected as a child table and for the referenced rows, the key values of the target records must be specified. In this sample app, we specify a `[Related Childs]` column, which is automatically generated by the system when we set the column in the child table as the `REF` type, and this column holds the key values of the related child records. Hence, it is the easiest way to specify this column for a referenced record, as it retrieves the child records' key values as list-type values. For the referenced action, please select **UpdateChild**, which we just created for the child table in the previous step. Let's name this `Data Change Action`. Please use the following screenshot as a guide for your own actions:

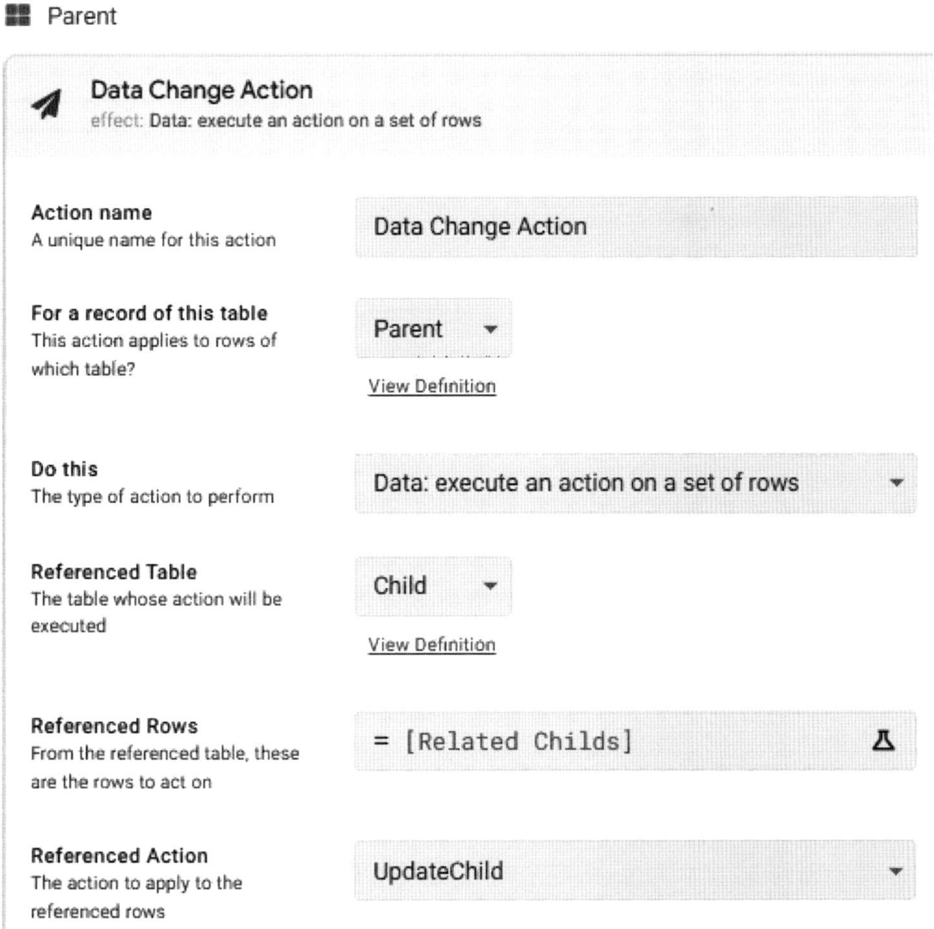

**▦ Parent**

✈ **Data Change Action**
effect: Data: execute an action on a set of rows

**Action name**
A unique name for this action

Data Change Action

**For a record of this table**
This action applies to rows of which table?

Parent ▾

View Definition

**Do this**
The type of action to perform

Data: execute an action on a set of rows ▾

**Referenced Table**
The table whose action will be executed

Child ▾

View Definition

**Referenced Rows**
From the referenced table, these are the rows to act on

= [Related Childs]     ⚠

**Referenced Action**
The action to apply to the referenced rows

UpdateChild ▾

Figure 12.4 – Second action to change the value in the parent table

3.  Go to the **Form** view in the parent table, and then select **Data Change Action** for **Event Actions** under **Behavior**:

Display

**Display name**
The name shown for this view in
the app. Leave this empty to just
use the view name. Or give it a text
value (double-quoted) or a formula

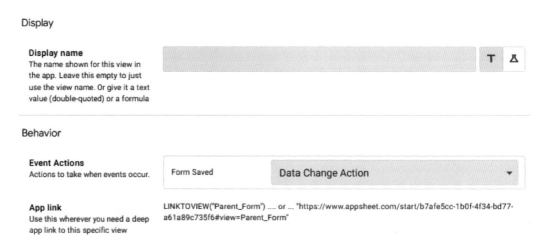

**T**   **𝔸**

Behavior

**Event Actions**
Actions to take when events occur.

Form Saved

Data Change Action

**App link**
Use this wherever you need a deep
app link to this specific view

LINKTOVIEW("Parent_Form") .... or ... "https://www.appsheet.com/start/b7afe5cc-1b0f-4f34-bd77-
a61a89c735f6#view=Parent_Form"

Figure 12.5 – Invoking an action on saving the Form view

Once this is set, **Data Change Action** will run whenever the form for the parent table is saved and update the [PARENT_STATUS] column in the child table.

## Updating child rows based on a data change to the parent row

The sample app's name is Chapter 12_05: https://www.appsheet.com/templates/sample?appGuidString=efd2d852-eeea-451a-a4c5-3830e298aebf.

It is quite a common arrangement where we set the AppSheet expression in the app formula in the *Normal* column to automatically calculate values based on our expression and save the values to a database. Furthermore, it is possible you have this kind of formula in the parent table, and the expression has a dependency on a child table and its rows. In the parent table, you may have the Normal column count the number of related rows in the child table by using a Count([Related Child Tables]) expression. This calculation is only refreshed when this particular row in the parent table is edited or updated. If you add a new row to the child table, then this column does not immediately reflect this data change unless you subsequently update the row in the parent table. How do you get the row in this parent table to automatically refresh the calculation and update the data? A set of simple actions triggered by automation will solve the case.

## Setup guide

To start the discussion here, we assume you have two simple tables that stand as parent and child tables. They are connected by a REF column in the child table. In this child table, you have a number type column and you wish to aggregate the number in the Normal column in the parent table, as well as count the number of related child table rows.

Based on that, the settings of the two tables are going to look like this:

| Parent Table | | | |
|---|---|---|---|
| Column Name | Type | Normal or Virtual | App Formula |
| ID | Text | Normal | UNIQUEID() |
| COUNT_CHILD | Number | Normal | SUM([Related Childs]) |
| SUM_CHILD_NUMBER | Number | Normal | SUM([Related Childs][NUMBER]) |
| CHANGE_COUNTER | Number | Normal | The initial value is set to 0 |
| Related Childs | List | Virtual | REF_ROWS("Child", "Parent") |

Table 12.4 – Column settings for the parent table

Also please find the table settings for the child to the preceding parent table:

| Child Table | | | |
|---|---|---|---|
| Column Name | Type | Normal or Virtual | App Formula |
| ID | Text | Normal | UNIQUEID() |
| PARENT | Ref | Normal | Nil |
| NUMBER | Number | Normal | Nil |

Table 12.5 – Column settings for the child table

## Creating an action

To implement a trick, please create two actions, one for each table:

1. The first action is to change the value in a column in the parent table.

2. For the parent table, create a new action named Counter +1. **Do this** is set to **Data: set the values of some columns in this row.** For **Set these columns, [CHANGE_COUNTER]** is selected, and the [CHANGE_COUNTER] +1 expression is passed:

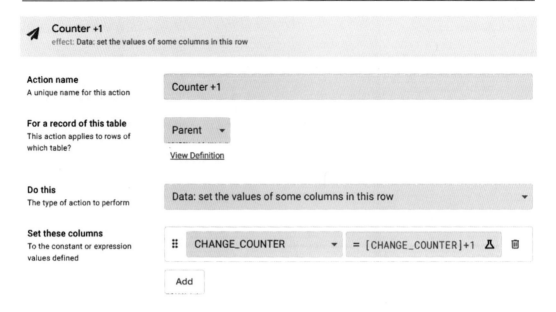

Figure 12.6 – Data Change Action in the parent table

3.  Invoke the action in the parent table from the child table: then, move to the child table to create another action. Name this action ChangeCounterUpOne. **Do this** is set to **Data: execute an action on a set of rows. Referenced Table** is set to **Parent. Referenced Rows** is set to the LIST([PARENT]) expression. Finally, the **Counter +1** action is selected for **Referenced Action**, which was created in the previous step. The expression used here does the trick, but the equivalent expression of SELECT(Parent[ID],[ID]=[_thisrow].[PARENT]) will also do the same:

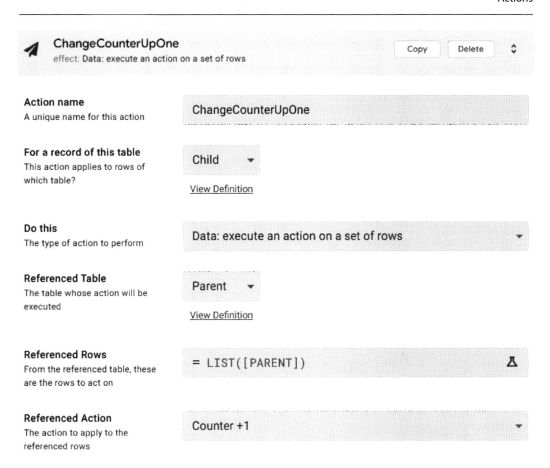

Figure 12.7 – Invoking an action in a parent table from the child table

These actions are only invoked by automation. You can choose to hide an action by selecting **Action Appearance** and setting it to **Do not display** to hide the surface of the app's views.

### Creating new automation

Once the actions are ready, please create a new bot. The event type is set to **Data Change** with the **All changes** option selected. For this event, the child table is selected.

Add a **Run a data action** step to create a new action. From the drop-down list for the actions, select **ChangeCounterUpOne**.

### *How does this trick work?*

We believe the settings for this trick are very straightforward. Once any data changes are made to the child table, such as add, delete, or update, then automation is triggered. Automation is run on the action to increment the number in the column of [CHANGE_COUNTER] by one upon the execution of the automation. Once the [CHANGE_COUNTER] column value is automatically updated, the rest of the columns in the same row of the parent table are also updated, meaning the app formula inside the Normal column is also re-evaluated at the same time as the execution of the automation. We simply update one target column of [CHANGE_COUNTER], but this will trigger the app formula to update the rest of the columns at the same time.

# Column settings

In this section, we would like to introduce a trick that is going to solve one of the most frequently asked questions in the AppSheet community. The question is how to establish a many-to-many relationship between two tables. Let's dive in.

## Establishing many-to-many relationships

The sample app name is Chapter 12_06: https://www.appsheet.com/templates/sample?appGuidString=3fb14df3-062c-46bf-997a-18da2d878be4.

If we set one column to the REF type, then it will construct a *one-to-many* relationship between the two tables. The referenced table in the REF column may have an association with multiple rows. One parent row can have multiple child rows, so it is called a one-to-many relationship. Then, if we wish to establish a relationship between multiple rows on one table with multiple rows on another table, how can we achieve this task? As for real-world examples, we may have an app to manage the order of goods, where the app possibly has a table of products where each record can be related to many records in another table for the orders. Then, the expectation is to see the number of orders when we look at a single product, and similarly, we expect to see the number of related products when we look at a single order. This can be achieved once you explicitly establish many-to-many relationships between products and an order table.

### *Setup guide*

Instead of setting the column to the REF type, select Enumlist with the base type set to REF, and then select the referenced table accordingly. By doing this, this column will pull the key values from the selected rows from the reference tables based on the user's selection. To continue, in the referenced table, add a new virtual column. To make it clear, let's assume table names such as the following:

- Table A with Enumlist with a base type REF column
- Table B, which is referenced by Enumlist in Table A

For the app formula, add the following `Select` expression for a virtual column to `Table B`:

```
Select(Table A[Key Column], IN([_thisrow],[EnumListColumn]))
```

This virtual column is set to the `List` type where `Element type` is set to `REF`. Make sure that `Table A` is selected as the referenced table. This virtual column will create an inline view in `Table B` where a list of related rows from `Table A` is displayed. For both the `Enumlist` column in `Table A` as well as the virtual column in `Table B`, you can use each column for the `De-reference list` expression to retrieve the set of target column values from the referenced table.

You can create a list of the values as an inline view in `Table A`, based on the selection of the values in `EnumList`. The setting is rather simple. Create a virtual column in `Table A` with a `List` type. The element type is set to `REF` and the referenced table is directed to `Table B`. For the app formula, just pass `[Enumlist]` for the same table. Once the values in `Enumlist` are selected and saved, the inline view will be displayed.

# App settings

In this section, we are answering a question that has been asked quite frequently in the community. A problem will come when the app creator is to add a new table with a large number of rows. This can be solved with a simple trick. We will also touch upon useful and practical tips and tricks to deal with files that are saved in a Google Drive folder and how to manipulate those files from an AppSheet app.

## Adding a table with a large number of rows

When you get started with a relatively high amount of rows of a table to create a new app, it is possible you may encounter an error message: *the app has failed to be created due to more than 100,000 rows*. Whenever you create an app from a table with a high number of rows, specifically more than 100,000, you will encounter this problem.

### Setup guide

To solve this issue, please delete some rows from the spreadsheet, leaving only 10 or 100 rows. Add this spreadsheet from the AppSheet editor as a table. Once you have successfully added a new table, go back to your spreadsheet immediately and undo the change to restore the deleted rows. On the app, manually sync the app by clicking on the **Sync** button.

On creating a new table from the sheet, AppSheet returns errors if the number of existing records is more than 100,000. To escape this constraint, just temporarily delete the records so that AppSheet can read this sheet as a table. Once the spreadsheet is successfully connected to AppSheet, then we can simply use the spreadsheet function of `Undo operation` to restore the temporarily deleted data.

## Reading a Google Drive folder as a table

The sample app's name is `Chapter 12_07`: `https://www.appsheet.com/templates/sample?appGuidString=6d753a92-d6c2-407c-a2f3-a29f471f842b`.

One powerful feature of AppSheet is that we can read Google Drive folders and file metadata as tables within an app. To read a Google folder and add it to an app as a table, please refer to the AppSheet documentation (`https://help.appsheet.com/en/articles/5604128-compiling-folder-contents`).

Once a new table is generated out of a folder, you will see the table with a set of columns, as follows:

| Column Name | Values | Example |
| --- | --- | --- |
| `_ID` (Key) | Unique ID provided by Google Drive to identify each unique file | `1kkFBsdsaGtesadsadffadsaU00AfaSpTazwvQ` |
| Path | Relative path, starting from the root position of your folder | `appsheet/data/app_folde/folder_name/fileName.png` |
| File | Filename | `ocument.png` |
| `CreateTime` | Date and time when the file was created | `24/01/2022, 00:14:23 am` |
| `LastModifiedBy` | Email address of who last updated the file | `24/01/2022, 00:14:23 am` |
| `MimeType` | A label used to identify the type of data | `Image/png` |

Table 12.6 – Column details for a table made from a folder

As you can see, this feature will read the target folder and return a set of file metadata. One table row represents a single file. The `_ID`, `Path`, and `File` columns are particularly useful to give you additional capabilities to handle those files in the AppSheet app.

This feature is only available for Google Drive, not for other data sources, such as MS OneDrive or Dropbox.

### *Setup guide*

How can we add a folder as a table?

1. To add a folder as a table to AppSheet, add a new table from the data pane.
2. Click **Documents on Google Drive** and you will see a dialog to pick a target folder in Google Drive.
3. Search for and select the folder you wish to read as a table. Before you click on the **Create table** action button, please make sure the **Collection of Files** button is selected. See *Figure 12.8*, where **Collection of files** is highlighted in blue, meaning this option is selected:

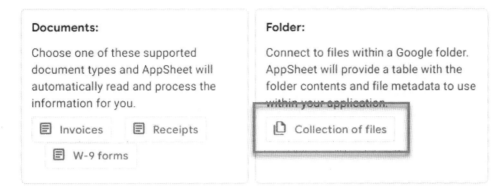

Figure 12.8 – Reading a Google Drive folder as a data table

4.  After selecting one of the folders from your Drive, hit the **Select** button at the bottom. After that, you will see the new table added to the **Data** pane.

5.  Once the folder is added as a table for AppSheet, then we can actually use the data from this table.

By adding a folder as a table, you will see _ID and other useful columns. The [_ID] column represents the unique ID that is provided by Google Drive, and every single file in Drive always has a uniquely indexed ID all the time. Now, we are ready to learn about a set of hidden tricks involving using these file IDs and other column values as a result of connecting to the Google Drive folder.

We will introduce some useful tricks to control files using these _ID values, such as creating download links and manipulating image files. Let's dive in:

*   **Displaying an image and/or downloaded files**: The simplest usage of this table is to display images from either Path or File columns. Set the data type for those columns to either **File** or **Image** depending on the file type (i.e., mime type). For instance, if the file type is either image/jpg or image/png, the actual image will be displayed once you set those column types to the **Image** type. If you set the column to the **File** type, then a system-generated action will enable you to download the file by clicking on the action icon.

- **Creating a URL that reaches out to the files (to display an image or download files):** We quite often see an app creator trying to display an image using a file-sharing link you can get from Google Drive, which looks like this

- `https://drive.google.com/file/d/File_ID/view?usp=sharing.`

- They will find that AppSheet does not show the image properly but rather shows an exclamation mark, which indicates an error. AppSheet is not able to display an image with this URL to share the file with others, even if you made the file publicly available. This is a common problem many app creators face The same applies to us here as well. After we get the file ID through the `[_ID]` column, the expression in the virtual column is supposed to display the image using `https://drive.google.com/file/d/"&[ID]&"/view?usp=sharing`, but it instead ended up with the same error.

- In order to display the image through the full path, which is manually constructed, we suggest alternative expressions such as this, by setting the virtual column data type to **Image**:

```
"https://lh3.googleusercontent.com/d/"&[_ID]
```

With this expression, the source image file saved in the Google Drive folder will be shown correctly. `https://lh3.googleusercontent.com/d/` is a special endpoint, provided by the Google API and other Google image delivery services, which fortunately can be used within AppSheet apps.

If this expression is set to a virtual column with URL  Type, then the AppSheet will create the system action automatically to download the file, using the URL that this expression returns:

```
"https://lh3.googleusercontent.com/d/"&[_ID]&&"=d"
```

For any file type that is an image, Excel sheet, or any other document, if you wish to add functionality that enables the user to download the file, this trick (using an alternative expression) will be useful. When you use this expression for any file type other than images, such as PDF or Excel file, then this URL always downloads a screenshot of the first page of the source file, rather than downloading the file itself. In order to create the download link, please refer to the following screenshot:

---

**Note**

To make this trick work, please make sure you share each file or entire folder by selecting **Anyone with the link.**

---

Figure 12.9 – Publishing the folder

- **Creating a download link and converting the file type**: Using the _ID column value, we can easily create download links inside AppSheet. You just need to click on the URL and then the target file will be downloaded to the user's device. The following expression will generate the download link:

```
"https://drive.google.com/uc?export=download&id="&[_ID]
```

The _ID column can be used to create a dynamic download link as well with this simple expression. The typical use case is to create a virtual column where you place this expression into the app formula. Make sure to set the column type to URL for this virtual column.

Coupled with the Hyperlink() expression, you can manipulate the expression to present the arbitrary text instead of the full URL. An expression of this kind of expression is as follows:

```
Hyperlink("https://drive.google.com/
uc?export=download&id="&[_ID], "Download File")
```

This will generate a UI as shown in the following screenshot. Once the user clicks on the icon or text, the download will begin:

Figure 12.10 – Text with inline action made by the Hyperlink expression

The same expression can be used in the automation template as well. See the following template expression:

```
<<Hyperlink("https://drive.google.com/
uc?export=download&id="&[_ID], "Download File")>>
```

This expression generates a download link for the file that is automatically created. You can implement this trick in your app when you allow the user to download files, including image files.

Next, let's see another trick to download Google app data, such as Google Docs, Sheets, and Slides, in another format by using the _ID value as part of the URL. It will be another simple trick that uses unique URLs.

If the folder includes Google application files, such as Sheets, Docs, or Slides, then we can manipulate the expression further to convert these into other files on download. Similar to other tricks introduced in this section, just create a virtual column and pass the expression based on the original source file with the column type set to URL:

| Original File Type | Converted Into | Expression |
|---|---|---|
| Google Docs | PDF | `https://docs.google.com/document/d/"&[_ID]&"/export?format=pdf` |
| | MS Word | `https://docs.google.com/document/d/"&[_ID]&"/export?format=doc` |
| Google Sheets | MS Excel | `https://docs.google.com/spreadsheets/d/"&[_ID]&"/export?format=xlsx` |
| | PDF | `https://docs.google.com/spreadsheets/d/"&[_ID]&"/export?format=pdf` |
| | CSV | `https://docs.google.com/spreadsheets/d/"&[_ID]&"/export?format=csv` |
| Google Slides | PDF | `https://docs.google.com/presentation/d/"&[_ID]&"/export/pdf` |
| | MS PowerPoint | `https://docs.google.com/presentation/d/"&[_ID]&"/export/pptx` |

Table 12.7 – List of expressions to convert file types

- For PDF, Excel, Docs, or Word documents, by using a special URL, we actually show a preview image of those files. By adding the folder as a table to AppSheet, we can see the name of the file, but it is not enough to see which contents are in there by seeing the filename alone. Using this special URL trick, you can get the image for the first page of the target file and render the image to your app.

First of all, let's see the special expression that carries out this trick:

```
"https://lh3.googleusercontent.com/d/"&[_ID]
```

When this expression is used in a virtual column with _ID for any file type, including but not limited to an image, Excel, Google Sheets, Google Docs, Word, or PDF file, and VC is set as the image type, it works like a preview for the file. The most useful use case of this trick is to display the preview image for a PDF file. For PDF files, we are currently unable to embed previews for PDFs due to the lack of embedding file functionalities with AppSheet. However, with this URL, we can present the first page of the PDF as a fixed and static image to present.

> **Note**
> To make this trick work, please make sure you use the **Anyone with the link** setting for each file or folder to be shared.

- **Cropping, resizing, flipping, and rotating images:** Currently, AppSheet does not provide a capability for those operations to manipulate the image files. Using the same endpoint of `https://lh3.googleusercontent.com/d/` and adding some hidden parameters to the end of this endpoint, we can freely manipulate the image files. Let us explain what hidden parameters are going to be.

Figure 12.11 – Sample image file (original)

Using the image in *Figure 12.11* as a sample, please find the list of URLs that could be used in the expression to manipulate the image in different ways in the following table:

| For cropping images | | | |
|---|---|---|---|
| **Cropping** | **Params** | **Sample** | **Sample Expression** |
| Crop to a square shape | c | | `https://lh3.googleusercontent.com/d/"&[_ID]&"=c` |
| Crop to a circle shape | cc | | `https://lh3.googleusercontent.com/d/"&[_ID]&"=cc` |
| Smart cropping from the midpoint of the image. | P | | `https://lh3.googleusercontent.com/d/"&[_ID]&"=p` |
| **For resizing images** | | | |
| **Resizing** | **Params** | **Sample** | **Sample Expression** |
| Maximum width, maintaining original aspect ratio. | w# | | `https://lh3.googleusercontent.com/d/"&[_ID]&"=w300` |
| Maximum height, maintaining original aspect ratio. | h# | | `https://lh3.googleusercontent.com/d/"&[_ID]&"=h600` |
| Force the scaling, ignoring the original aspect ratio. Requires both w and h to be explicitly set. | s | | `https://lh3.googleusercontent.com/d/"&[_ID]&"=w300-h600-s` |
| **Rotating images** | | | |
| **Editing** | **Params** | **Sample** | **Sample Expression** |
| Flip horizontally | fh | | `https://lh3.googleusercontent.com/d/"&[_ID]&"=fh` |
| Flip vertically | fv | | `https://lh3.googleusercontent.com/d/"&[_ID]&"=fv` |
| Rotate by # degrees (must be one of the following: 90, 180, 270) | r# | | `https://lh3.googleusercontent.com/d/"&[_ID]&"=r90` |

Table 12.8 – List of expressions to manipulate image files

As you can see in the preceding tables, the parameter being passed to the end of the URL will change the behaviors and show different results for the output image. We hope you enjoy these hidden tricks, which are not in the official AppSheet documentation.

Until now, we have mostly talked about manipulating image files using this trick. For the next set of tips and tricks, we will provide you with an easy solution to display other media-type files as well:

- **Playing a video or audio file**: If you want to display a playable video file that has been saved and the file ID obtained from the table, you can still do so in an embedded style.

- The first step is to set the column type to `show` and the category to `Video`. Then, for the content file, just pass the following expression. Again, the files or the folder that contains those files must be *published* (anyone with a link can access the file); otherwise, AppSheet cannot access those files:

```
"https://drive.google.com/uc?id="&[_ID]
```

The overall column setting is going to look like the following figure:

Figure 12.12 – Show type column settings

Audio files, such as MP3s, are rendered as an audio player UI:

Figure 12.13 – Audio player sample

You save lots of these media files to your Google Drive folder, but I hope you will now see how easy it is to display these files inside AppSheet.

It is always possible that you have a folder that contains different types of files. Some of them might be image files, while others are application files, such as MS Excel and Word files. There is a mixture of various file types. We have discussed a number of tips and tricks, but you will notice that each tip was connected to a specific file type. After reading the files from the folder, you can easily track the file type by relying on the `MimeType` column.

- Using the listed URL-based tricks with AppSheet's conditional expressions, an AppSheet conditional expression of `IFS()` or `SWITCH()` could help dynamically generate some of the URLs that were introduced in this section. In this case, the `MimeType` column identifies the type of file, which act as a key to change the URL conditionally. Those are typical mime types you rely on to identify each file type.

- Just for your guidance, the following table illustrates the combination of mine types and the actual file types:

| File Category | Mime Type | File Type |
| --- | --- | --- |
| Image | `image/png` | PNG file |
| | `image/jpeg` | JPEG file |
| | `image/gif` | GIF file |
| Video | `video/mp4` | MP4 file |
| Audio | `audio/mpeg` | MP3 file |
| PDF | `application/pdf` | PDF file |
| CSV | `Text/csv` | CSV file |
| Application Files | `application/vnd.google-apps.spreadsheet` | Google Sheets |
| | `application/vnd.google-apps.document` | Google Docs |
| | `application/vnd.google-apps.presentation` | Google Slide |
| | `application/vnd.openxmlformats-officedocument.spreadsheetml.sheet` | MS Excel file |
| | `application/vnd.openxmlformats-officedocument.wordprocessingml.document` | MS Word file |

Table 12.9 – List of mime types for different file types

For our sample app, `Chapter 12_07`, we created one virtual column in a table called `Sample_Files`. This is a sample use case where we anchor the `MimeType` column and get the value dynamically to identify the file type in a human-readable way. For this table, there is a virtual column that constructs the download link for the file. As a working use case, we control the visibility of this column by using a conditional expression and hiding this column if the file type is a Google application, as it can't be downloaded.

# Bots and automation

In this section, let us introduce some of the two tips and tricks that can solve the most frequently asked questions by using AppSheet Automation as a solution.

## Creating sequential numbers by using a bot

The sample app's name is `Chapter 12_08`: `https://www.appsheet.com/templates/sample?appGuidString=17237b1f-5f16-4b31-8b2a-269aafeb0274`.

We observed a number of the same questions in the community asking how to get sequential numbers. They could be used, for instance, as document IDs, job IDs, or for other different purposes. An AppSheet app should be usable by multiple users at any time. When app users are accessing the same app at the same time, they are working on the same app, which is copied to the devices the app users are using. This makes the task of creating sequential numbers difficult, as concurrent app users could generate the exact same number. Before diving deeper, let's get started with the usual implementation of this type of feature, and then confirm the source of the problem that makes this task difficult. Then we'll look at the solution, which is sure to generate unique sequential numbers without fail.

## Setup guide

When we add a new row to a table, AppSheet's native behavior is to append a new row to the table, meaning the new row is added at the very bottom of the spreadsheet. In other words, a new row will always have the maximum number of `_rowNumber` values at the point in time that the row is added. In the meantime, `_rowNumber` is equal to the number you will see on the spreadsheet on the left-hand side, starting from 1 from the top. Hence, the newly added row always has the max number of `_rowNumber` columns theoretically. We can utilize this `_rowNumber` column value to create sequential numbers. For this section, let's avoid relying on this `_rowNumber` column value and use another column to discuss the tricks needed.

To start the setup, please add a normal column, called `Sequential_Number`, which is set to the `Number` type. To sequentially add a new, unique number when the new row is added, you may think of using the following expression to generate the initial value for this field:

```
Max(Select(SequentialNumber[Sequential_Number],[_
Thisrow]<>[ID]))+1
```

Yes, you are on the right track, but the problem is this simple expression potentially generates a duplicated number if there are other users who are using the app concurrently. A simple test would verify what would happen if you had another concurrent user doing the same operation – that is, adding a new row to this table. You will see that you get a certain number for this column. Likewise, the row that is created concurrently by another user would get the exact same number, so the number is duplicated. This is because the devices of simultaneous users and your device are going to return the exact same number when the new row is added at almost the same time. This is the root cause of the problem that is making it difficult to manage to get sequential numbers.

Now, the point of the problem is hopefully clear to you. Let's discuss how to set up your app to ensure you always get sequential but unique numbers.

To achieve this, we create a new bot. For the event component with the bot, you set **Event** to **Data Change** and trigger **Adding new row** to this table. The event setting should be simple. The bot simply adds a new row to this table.

Then, for the **Process** and **Step** components, you create a task to run an action.

The settings for the action in **Step** are as follows:

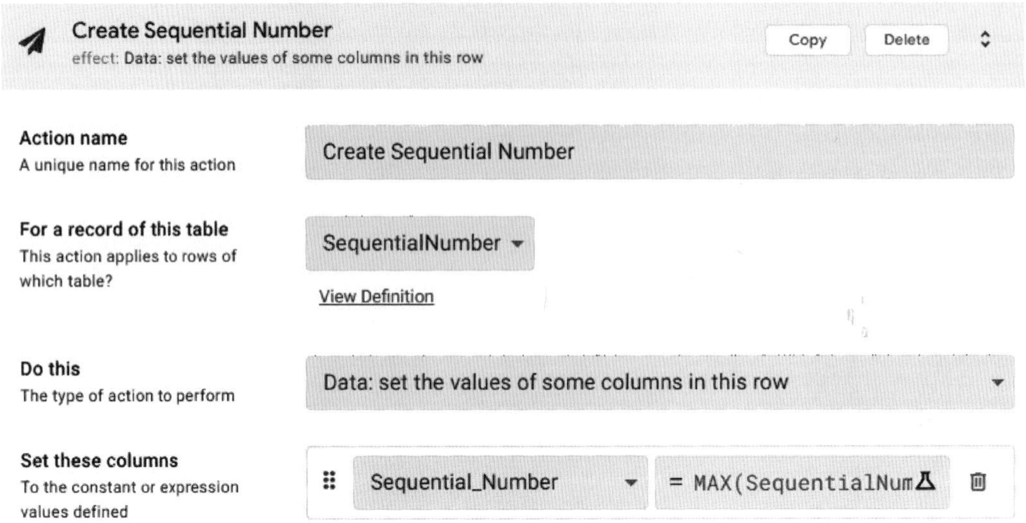

Figure 12.14 – Data Change Action

For **Set these columns,** just pass the same expression we set for the initial value:

```
MAX(Select(SequentialNumber[Sequential_Number],[ID]<>[_
Thisrow]))+1
```

Once the new row is added, then the bot is going to run in order to push the value (number) being returned by the expression you pass to the task. A bot is a server-side process and each unique request for a data change given by app users will be handled one by one, on a first come, first served basis. For instance, when you add a new row, a request to the AppSheet server is given to start the task – in this case, to run the action to change the data value in the target column with the expression. When the task is run, the expression evaluates the entire table and the values of its rows at the point in time at which the bot is run. Therefore, there is no crossover with other operations – that is, a data change request that may be made at almost the same time by another app user. If another user adds a new row, but the request to change data arrives after your request, then the request will be placed in the queue. The request will not be processed until your request is dealt with.

All of the data change requests given to the bot are handled one by one, and the expression defined inside the **Data Change** action in each bot is evaluated whenever the bot is running.

In this way, we are able to ensure the MAX(Select(SequentialNumber[Sequential_Number],[ID]<>[_Thisrow]))+1 (SequentialNumber[Sequential_Number])+1 expression returns the correct value. More precisely, it will add an incrementing number to the target field, which is what we wish to achieve.

## Bonus tips

Once we manage to get the sequential numbers, thanks to AppSheet Automation, we are able to use this sequential number for other purposes. As initially discussed, you may need to get a document ID or job ID using a sequential number as a part to construct those ID values, such as `INV1_20200101`, `INV2_20200101`. This unique ID will be incremented by 1 once the new unique ID is generated.

The easiest solution is to set the virtual column and assign the expression as follows:

```
"INV"&[Sequential_Number]&"-"&Text([Date], "YYYYMMDD")
```

Of course, this expression is just an example; your final expression will vary depending on how you wish to "style" the unique ID, where the sequential number resides.

> **Note**
> For the table where you create the sequential number to which you are applying this trick, we strongly suggest that you have a normal `ID` column as a key, using `UniqueID()` with the initial value expression.

## Creating a dynamic URL to open files created by a bot

The sample app's name is `Chapter 12_09`: `https://www.appsheet.com/templates/sample?appGuidString=0f1925b0-c6a5-4870-bc29-8bdca0476132`.

One of the more frequent use cases of automation could be sending an email with an attachment file, or creating new files. In either case, the files, such as PDF or Excel documents, Automation-generated, can be saved to a cloud file storage service, such as Google Drive. In this case, it is possible that you may have a question: how do we reach those files from the AppSheet apps? How do we generate the links to reach the files?

The solution is rather simple: just make a virtual column to generate the URL dynamically.

## Setup guide

To start our discussions, firstly, let's recap the automation functionalities to generate files. There are two tasks, namely the following:

- **Send an email**: This task will generate the file that will be attached to the automated email when it is sent out and the same file is archived in the cloud service

- **Create a new file**: This task is simply to create files, such as PDF or Excel files, and then they are saved to the cloud as well

The next question you may have is where the files would be saved. By default, both tasks will create a folder directly inside the default app folder. If you are not sure what the default app folder is, you can find it in **Info** > **Properties** > **Default app folder**:

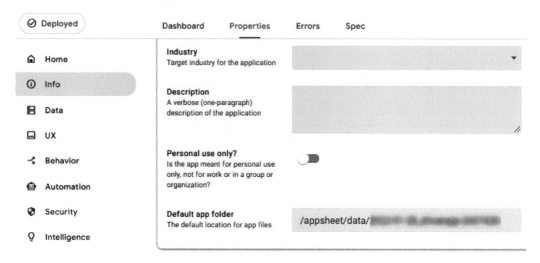

Figure 12.15 – Default app folder

To make this clear, let's assume we are currently working on an app with an app ID of MyFirstApp-1234567. Then, your default app folder path is going to be appsheet/data/MyFirstApp-1234567 by default. The files will be saved in a subfolder of this default app folder. See the following table. You can see the folder location where the generated files by the respective task will be saved:

| Task Name | The location of the folder the generated files are saved |
| --- | --- |
| Send an email task | A folder named Attachments, directly under the default app folder<br><br>Example: appsheet/data/MyFirstApp-1234567/Files |
| Create a new file task | A folder named Files, directly under the default app folder<br><br>Example: appsheet/data/MyFirstApp-1234567/Attachments |

Table 12.10 – Default folder path where the files are automatically saved by Automation

Let's further assume that you create PDF files with those tasks. You have the option to explicitly name the files when Automation generates those new files. To continue the discussion, let's simply use the key value of the source row from which the file is going to be created. Let's assume the ID column is set as the key for this table. Based on this assumption, the settings are going to look like this.

For the **Send an email** task, please check the following points in order to proceed:

- The attachment template is properly generated
- For the attachment name, pass the ID column, using a template expression
- For the attachment archive, select **AttachAndArchive**
- Enable **Disable timestamp**

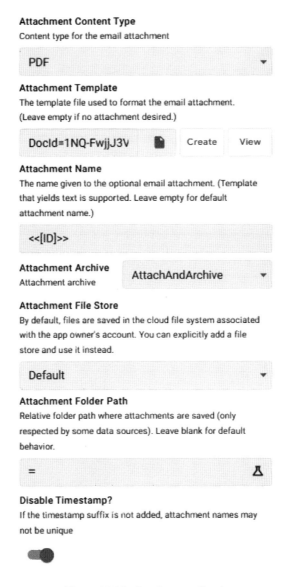

Figure 12.16 – Send an email task

With these email task settings, the PDF will be generated and sent as an attachment to the recipients. At the same time, the same PDF file will be saved to the default folder of `appsheet/data/ MyFirstApp-1234567/Attachments`. The PDF filename is always the key value of the row from where this automation is invoked.

In *Figure 12.17*, you will find the settings for a task to create a PDF file. You will find the settings are almost identical to the settings for the **Send an email task**. For this **Create a new file** task, ensure the following points are met:

- A template is properly generated
- For **File Name Prefix**, pass the column expression to name the file with the row's key value

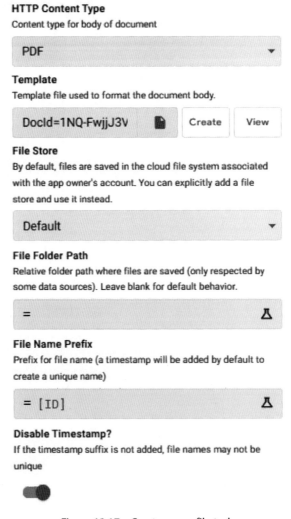

Figure 12.17 – Create a new file task

Now, we have finished with the basic setup for Automation. It's now time to test your bot on your app on your own. Please read *Chapter 8* to conduct testing with a bot. Hopefully, your bot has successfully generated the folders and files as expected.

To reach those files from your app, please create a virtual column in the same table as where your bot resides. Then, set the column type to URL and pass the following expressions:

| Task Name | Expression |
| --- | --- |
| Send an email task | `https://www.appsheet.com/template/getappfileurl?ap-pName="&context("AppName")&"&ilename=Attach-ments"&"/"&[ID]&".pdf` |
| Create a new file task | `https://www.appsheet.com/template/getappfileurl?appN-ame="&context("AppName")&"&ilename=Files"&"/"&[ID]&".pdf` |

Table 12.11 – Expressions to reach the saved files

Once you have saved the changes in the app editor, you will find URLs in the detail view with clickable actions to open the files.

Before you test this, please make sure that the following optional setting in the **Security** pane is turned off (**Security | Options**):

**Require Image and File URL Signing** (APPSHEET CORE)
Require URLs to images and files within the app to be signed which prevents unauthorized access to these files. Disable this only if you don't consider this information sensitive and need to manually construct URLs to app files.

Figure 12.18 – Image file security setting

If this option is enabled, then you will not be able to open the file with those URLs, as the file is protected for security reasons. Please make sure to turn off this option to make this trick work.

### Bonus tips

If the bot runs on the same row, and files with the same name are repeatedly created with the same bot, then the latest run will overwrite the previous file. This may cause a problem when you open the files from the URL, due to AppSheet's file cache system. Once the file is opened through the URL, the file data is cached. The subsequent operation to open the file through the same URL is reading file data from the cache rather than the raw file itself. This causes a problem, as the app user may not see the most recent file and could access the previously opened file. To solve this possible issue, you alter the expression by adding `&"&"&UNIQUEID()` to the end:

```
"https://www.appsheet.com/template/
getappfileurl?appName="&context("AppName")&
"&ilename=Attachments"&"/"&[ID]&".pdf"&"&"&UNIQUEID()
```

# Views

In this section, we wish to introduce a trick that is useful for controlling the **View type** option of **Inline View**. By default, you may see **Inline View** as **deck**, **table**, or **gallery**, but you can explicitly control those types. For example, you can change the **Inline View** type to either a **chart** or **map** type if you want.

## Creating a chart or map view

The sample app's name is `Chapter 12_10`: `https://www.appsheet.com/templates/ sample?appGuidString=e29e2aba-9fe8-4a19-a339-f60851285815`.

We are pretty sure you will have a question: "What are an inline chart and an inline map?" Okay, these are probably not official terms used in the AppSheet community, but we named them this way to help you out. Let's dive deeper into this.

See the sample detail view in the following figure. This view is for the parent table's row and we will normally see **Inline View** at the bottom, which comes from the **List** type view (the virtual column, which is automatically generated when we set a column to the REF type in the child table). By default, this sort of **Inline View** is typically set to a **deck**, **card**, or **table** view, always depending on the data in the child table.

If you go further down, you will see a **map** view, which we are calling an "inline map" view in this particular instance. Then, go further down, and at the bottom, there is a **chart** view, which we call an "inline chart" view.

These views originate from a set of child rows associated with the parent rows. When it comes to both the map and chart views, if they are independent views rather than in the **Inline** style, then they should contain all of the rows those views originated from. However, as you can see, this trick makes it possible to display the data on both a chart and a map that are associated with the parent row.

Overall, this unique technique is going to give you control over the style of an inline view and make your own detail view look nicer, then present data in different ways to appeal to your app users.

> **Note**
>
> Currently, it is not possible to set **Inline View** to **calendar** style.

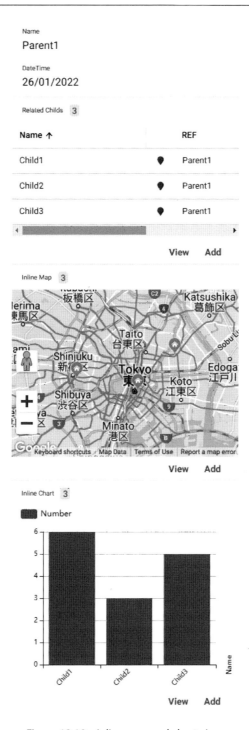

Figure 12.19 – Inline map and chart view

## *Setup guide*

Let's now see how to set this up. How can we create these inline views, in either **chart** or **map** style? Actually, it is not really difficult and you may find it quite simple once you get to know the tricks behind it:

1.  **Creating slices**

    The first step is to create two slices from the child table. Let's name them:

    I.    `Slice for Inline Chart`
    II.   `Slice for Inline Map`

2.  **Creating a view out of slices**

    Out of `Slice for Inline Chart`, please create a new view and set it as a **chart** view. Similarly, create another new view out of `Slice for Inline Map` and then set it to **Map** view.

    Most importantly, please make sure you set **Position** to the **ref** position. Otherwise, this trick will not work.

3.  **Creating a virtual column set to the List type with REF as the element type**

    In the parent table, create two virtual columns.

The first virtual column is for **Inline View** with a **chart** view type. Let's name this column `Inline Chart` and pass the following expression:

```
REF_ROWS("Slice for Inline Chart", "REF")
```

In the same way, create another virtual column named `Inline Map`, and pass the following expression:

```
REF_ROWS("Slice for Inline Map", "REF")
```

Then, please make sure you set the column type to **List** and the element type to **Ref**. For **Referenced table name**, make sure each virtual column is targeting the slice name that is the same as the slice name of your expression:

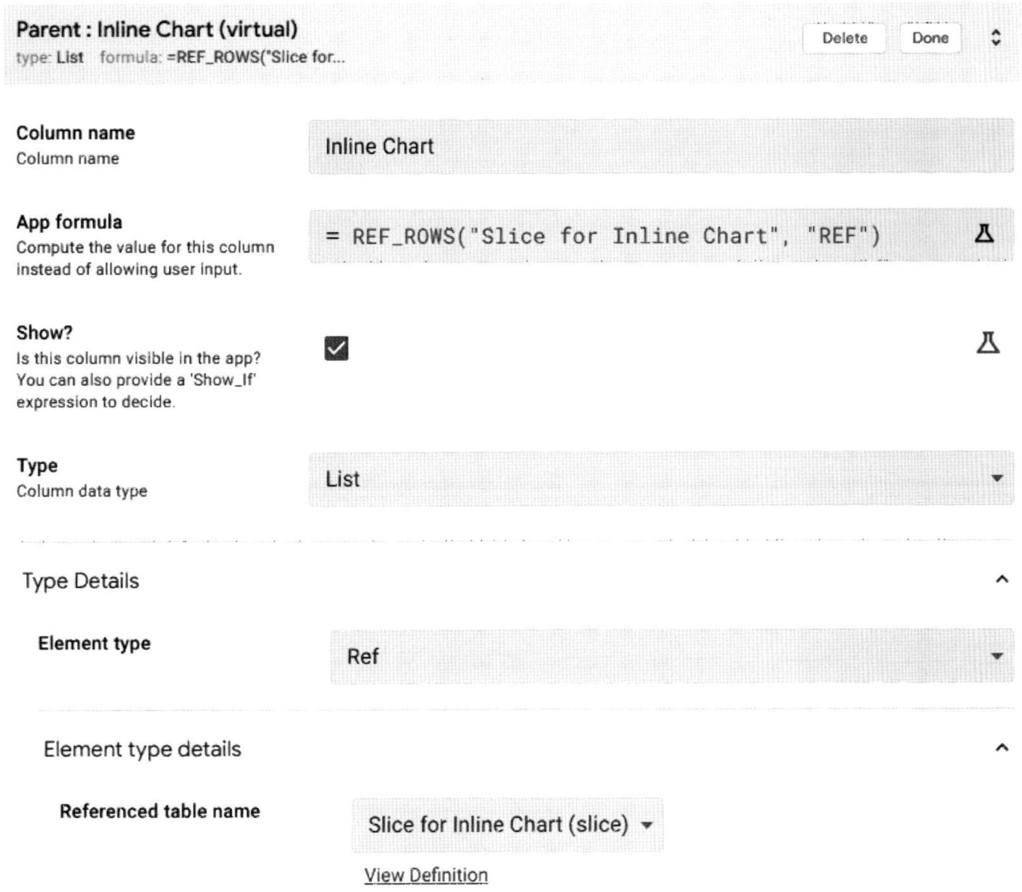

**Parent : Inline Chart (virtual)**
type: List    formula: =REF_ROWS("Slice for...    `Delete`   `Done`   ↕

**Column name**
Column name

Inline Chart

**App formula**
Compute the value for this column
instead of allowing user input.

`= REF_ROWS("Slice for Inline Chart", "REF")`   ⚗

**Show?**
Is this column visible in the app?
You can also provide a 'Show_If'
expression to decide.

☑   ⚗

**Type**
Column data type

List   ▼

Type Details   ⌃

   **Element type**

   Ref   ▼

  Element type details   ⌃

    **Referenced table name**

    Slice for Inline Chart (slice)   ▼

    View Definition

Figure 12.20 – Virtual column to show inline chart view (sample)

Please pay attention to the app formula, where the REF_Rows () expression is referring to the slice name and **Referenced table name** is also directing the slice for the chart view.

**Parent : Inline Map (virtual)**
type: List   formula: =REF_ROWS("Slice for...                    [ Delete ]   [ Done ]   ⇕

**Column name**
Column name

> Inline Map

**App formula**
Compute the value for this column
instead of allowing user input.

> = REF_ROWS("Slice for Inline Map", "REF")                         ⚗

**Show?**
Is this column visible in the app?
You can also provide a 'Show_If'
expression to decide.

> ☑                                                                 ⚗

**Type**
Column data type

> List                                                              ▼

**Type Details**                                                     ⌃

**Element type**

> Ref                                                               ▼

**Element type details**                                             ⌃

**Referenced table name**

> Slice for Inline Map (slice)   ▼
>
> View Definition

Figure 12.21 – Virtual column to show inline map view (sample)

Please make sure the app formula with the REF_ROWS() expression has two arguments. The first one is to address the slice name we created only for the map view, while the second argument is required to direct the REF column in the child table.

Now, you should see both the inline map and chart views when you access the detail view for the parent table. To understand this trick better, we need to learn why and how it works.

AppSheet automatically picks the default view style for any **Inline View** when it is systematically created, so we do not actually have much control over this behavior. However, there is a fixed rule with AppSheet that **Inline View** is the default view for the respective table and slice. To make a long story short, each table and slice always has default views and any **Inline View** is presented based on this default view type. How the default view is determined by AppSheet is a complicated story, so we will avoid elaborating in depth here in this book, but for this trick, we are using this AppSheet default behavior to control the style of **Inline View** at will.

The view we created in the second step of *Creating a view out of slices* from the newly created slice from the first step is actually the default view for this slice. The key point when making this view the default view for a slice was that we set the location to the **ref** position. By doing so, this view was recognized as the default view for that particular slice. Your virtual columns refer to this slice, so AppSheet naturally picks up the manually generated default view and sets it as the given **Inline View** at the end.

## Summary

In this chapter, we introduced unique tricks that are useful for adding new functionalities to your applications. We were limited due to the space available in this book in terms of the number of tricks we could present. AppSheet provides an uncountable number of tips and tricks to extend its functionalities.

# 13
# Appendix

You have almost read through the whole book, and we hope you now have good knowledge of how to build an app using the various AppSheet features. Using the knowledge you have acquired throughout this book, it is time for you to start to build your own application with AppSheet suitable for your own business requirements. However, you may notice that you need more advanced knowledge and techniques to fulfill your own requirements while developing your apps. Once new advanced functionalities are required within your app, it is natural that you will be required to apply more advanced settings to implement the app's behaviors and functionalities.

This book is designed for absolute beginners who are starting their journey with AppSheet. We have only mentioned the really basic things, which are the minimum things to know. The number of things AppSheet can do is extensive, and AppSheet can do what you believe is impossible. We hope you have got off to a good start with AppSheet, but we have to say that you have just opened the door to the AppSheet world.

## Joining the AppSheet community to be a citizen developer

To be confident and competent in AppSheet to develop apps as you want, further and continuous study in AppSheet is inevitable. Please keep working on AppSheet to learn more.

You are possibly aware that there is an AppSheet community that has been up and running for years. As your next step, we encourage you to sign up with the community at `https://www.googlecloudcommunity.com/gc/AppSheet/ct-p/appsheet`.

The AppSheet community has been driving the growth of AppSheet and it always stays active. An uncountable number of problems have been solved, thanks to the contributions of the community members. The community is where you can ask questions to solve any issue you might have. In addition, the community platform is one of the AppSheet resources where you can apply a search to find out how to solve your issues. Skilled app creators share new ideas, tips, and tricks to apply advanced functionalities to your apps.

## AppSheet is growing endlessly

AppSheet is growing every day. New functionalities and features, as well as the enhancement of the existing functions, are added to the platform all the time. The knowledge we have today about AppSheet would become out of date if we stopped continuing to learn.

Looking back at 2021 and 2022, we witnessed a series of new changes that enhanced the AppSheet capabilities and let app creators do more. For instance, there is now powerful integration with a series of Google Workspace products. AppSheet is a pure no-code platform, but it now controls another Google solution, Google Apps Script, which is a low-code service. Yes, it requires knowledge of coding, but, indeed, AppSheet has now made something possible that was previously believed impossible, in just a few years.

As of writing this book in late 2022, a number of new features, such as the new desktop UX and the new data connection to AppSheet's database, are in play. They are expected to be released as new official features in the near future.

We expect the introduction of new features to continue in the future, which means learning about AppSheet is never-ending. There are always things to learn.

## Summary

To end this book, we wish to emphasize on the most important thing in Appsheet.

*"Enjoy learning and building apps with AppSheet!"*

We hope you embark on the journey with us to become an active AppSheet citizen developer. Thank you for reading!

# Index

## A

**actions 139, 140**
  settings pane, configuring 143-147
**actions types 141**
  system-generated actions 141-143
**actions types, usage**
  app actions 141
  data actions 141
  external actions 141
  grouped actions 141
**app**
  copying 195, 196
  creating, from data 11-13
  deleting 196
  deploying, with all features 203
  deployment readiness, checking 204, 206
  Deploy tab, options 207
  editor settings, setting 194, 195
  features, analyzing 190
  Plan requirements tab 190, 192
  stable version, creating 202, 203
  usage, monitoring 213, 214
  usage pattern 214-216
  version history 197-200
  version, upgrading for users 200-202
  white labeling 206

**app actions for navigation**
  conditional navigation 149
  CSV export or import actions 150
  deep link expressions 148
  unconditional navigation 148
  using 147
**app creators**
  used, for creating apps portfolio 304
**app ownership**
  transferring 190-193
**App settings**
  Google Drive folder, reading
    as table 332-340
  table with large number of rows, adding 331
**AppSheet 49**
  access control 172
**AppSheet actions**
  sync, forcing upon navigation
    to target view 323, 324
**AppSheet app**
  building 4
  ideas, converting 5
  image, incorporating 277, 278
  offline settings 166
  prerequisites 5
  sync settings 166

**AppSheet Automation 232, 233**

**AppSheet community 355**

  growth 356

  reference link 355

**AppSheet editor**

  basics 13-17

**AppSheet expression**

  used, for calculation between time
     and duration 320-322

  using, for number division 322

**AppSheet OCR models 267**

  setting 267-269

  training 267-269

  types of images, scanning by 267

**AppSheet, view 51**

  adding 51

  for this data 53

  position 53

  view name, assigning 52

  view type 53

**apps internal terminology**

  managing, through Localize tab 85

**apps portfolio**

  creating, for app creators 304

  description, adding to portfolio
     page 310, 311

  sharing, as public samples 308, 309

  sharing, as team samples 307

  sharing, with teams 304

  teams, defining 304-306

**app templates**

  building, for self-reference 315

  business functionality-based apps 316

  copying 314

  feature-based apps 316

  searching, by AppSheet features 314

  using, for development 311

  using, from AppSheet website 312-314

**app upgrades**

  performing, precautions 202

**app users**

  adding, as co-author 175

  adding, as normal users 173, 174

  adding, to AppSheet 173

  app role, defining 175-178

  editing permissions, defining 173

**app version management**

  performing 197

**arithmetic calculations**

  performing, with math functions
     and expressions 112

**artificial intelligence (AI) 259**

**Audit History option**

  sync performance, analyzing 223-226

  using, for row-level user activity 217-223

**Automation 231**

**automation functionalities**

  email, sending 343

  new file, creating 343

**auto re-open 63**

**auto save 62**

# B

**backdrop layout 72**

**bot**

  used, for creating sequential
     numbers 340-342

**Bot 233**

  automation, testing 256, 257

  column, setting up to trigger data
     change event 246-248

  components 233, 234

  creation, by adding new Event 248-250

  data change action, running 255

  email attachment setting,

configuration 251-254

email, sending 250, 251

setup, learning through practical
example 244, 245

used, for creating sequential
numbers 340-342

**bulk actions 153**

# C

**calendar view 64**

**card-style message**

adopting 291

sending 292-294

**card view 71**

**chart view 78**

**child rows, based on data change**

action, creating 327-329

automation, creating 329

updating 326, 327

**child table 32**

**column-level functions**

versus row-level functions 127-129

**column order 60, 62**

**column settings**

analyzing 17

**column type configuration 19**

column group settings 22-30

data types, defining 19, 20

keys 21

labels 22

**conditional functions and expressions**

decision making 97

IF() function 98

SWITCH() function 99, 100

**conditional navigation 149**

example 149, 150

**CONTEXT() function 133, 134**

**CSV export or import actions 150**

CSV file, importing to add or update
view records 151, 152

view records, exporting to CSV file 151

**CSV files**

working with 147

# D

**dashboard view 76**

interactive mode 76, 77

tabs in mobile view 76

view entries 76

**data**

app, creating from 11-13

preparation, in right format 10, 11

searching, from app with Smart
Assistant 261-263

**data change actions**

bulk actions, using in multiple rows 153

configuring 152

INPUT() function, using 152, 153

in summary views 154, 155

reference actions 157-160

row, adding to table with current
row values 156, 157

setting, for columns in row 152

**data control**

additional security measures for
safety, implementing 185, 187

security filter per table, creating 183, 185

sending, to security options 183

sending, to user device 183

**date and time functions and expressions**

date calculations, performing 116

datetime value components, extracting 117

duration calculations, in decimal
value results 122-124

duration calculations, performing 116-119
  parameters 116
  time calculations, performing 116
  week-based calculation functions 119-122
date calculations
  performing, with date and time
    functions and expressions 116
deck view 65
deck view, options 66
  data locations 67
  group aggregate 66
  group by 66
  image shape 68
  nested table column 67, 68
  show action and actions 68
  sort by 66
deep link expressions 147, 148
Deploy tab, options
  app recovery mode, invoking 209
  manual recovery, performing 210-212
  Pause App option 207, 208
  recovery mode, switching to 208
dereference expression (de-ref) 37
dereference list 38-41
detail view 55
  column order 60
  display mode 60
  header column 57, 58
  image style 60
  main image 56, 57
  max nested rows 61
  quick edit columns 58, 59
  slideshow mode 61
  sort by 59
  use card layout 55
Digital Transformation (DX) 3, 231
display mode 60

display name 63
display pane 79
  settings 79
drop-down lists
  choice, constructing ways 41-44
  creating, to assist data entry 41
duration calculations
  performing, with date and time
    functions and expressions 116
  versus time calculations 320-322
dynamic chart as image
  generating, with QuickChart 279, 280
dynamic text
  label contents, modifying 278
  services 274, 275
  styles, customizing 278, 279
  URL service, using for text label image 275
  used, for displaying images 272, 273
dynamic URL
  creating, to open files created by bot 343-347

E

enumlist-type real column 104
enumlist-type virtual column 104
EOWEEK() function 121
event actions 165, 166
Event component 234
  Bot, creating 235, 237
  data change or schedule actions 235
Event component, types
  data change event 238, 239
  schedule event 239
ExchangeRate-API
  reference link 295
expressions 88
external actions 161

**external actions for external communications**
email  161, 162
file opening  162-164
message  161, 162
phone call  161, 162
using  161
website navigation  162-164

**F**

**file cache  319**
**finish view  63**
**foreign key  32**
**format rule  82**
creating  82, 83
options  83
**form style  62**
**form view  61**
auto re-open  63
auto save  62
column order  62
display name  63
finish view  63
form style  62
max. nested rows  62
page style  61, 62
save/cancel position  62
**functions  88**

**G**

**gallery view  70, 71**
**GET request  294**
**Google Apps Script  294**
currency exchange rate, displaying  295
data, reading from spreadsheet  297, 298

sample code  296
use cases  294
**Google Chat  271**
**Google Cloud Vision API  266**
**Google Workspace  271**
**Google Workspace products**
card-style message, adopting  291
integrating with  288-291
**grouped action**
used, for executing multiple actions  164, 165

**H**

**header and footer**
options  84
**header column  57, 58**

**I**

**image**
displaying, with dynamic text  272, 273
incorporating, into AppSheet app  277, 278
**image style  60**
**Intelligence pane**
advanced features, enabling  260

**J**

**JavaScript object  282**
**JavaScript Object Notation (JSON)  291**

**L**

**large layout  73**
**list functions and expressions  106**
COUNT() function  111
enumlist-type real column  104
enumlist-type virtual column  104

INDEX() function  109
INTERSECT() function  112
MAX() function  109
MIN() function  109
SELECT() function  107
SORT() function  107
TOP() function  109
UNIQUE() function  111
used, for manipulating multiple
    values  104-106
list layout  71, 72
list-type view  63
    backdrop layout  72
    calendar view  64
    card view  71
    deck view  65
    gallery view  70, 71
    large layout  73
    list layout  71, 72
    map column  74
    map type  75
    map view  74
    minimum cluster size  75
    photo layout  72
    secondary data column  74
    secondary data table  74
    table view  68
Localize tab
    used, for managing apps internal
        terminology  85

**M**

main image  56, 57
many-to-many relationships
    establishing  330
map column  74
map type  75

map view  74
math functions and expressions
    AVERAGE() function  115
    MOD() function  114
    RANDBETWEEN() function  115
    SUM() function  114
    used, for performing arithmetic
        calculations  112
max nested rows  61
minimum cluster size  75
miscellaneous functions  130
    CONTEXT() functions, using  134
    CONTEXT() function, using  133
    TEXT() function, using  134, 135
    using, in app user  130-133
multiple functions
    using, in single expressions  136, 137
multiple values
    manipulating, with list functions
        and expressions  104-106

**N**

natural language processing  261
Near Field Communication (NFC)  30
normal columns
    versus virtual columns  22

**O**

OCR model
    building  267
offline settings, AppSheet app
    usage  167, 168
onboarding view  63
    finish view  63
    image  63
    second short blurb  63

short blurb 63

title 63

**on-demand messages**

sending, to app users 226, 227

**optical character recognition (OCR) 259**

# P

**page style 61, 62**

**parent table 32**

**photo layout 72**

**placehold.jp service 274**

reference link 274

**predictive models 259**

building 263, 264

creating 264, 265

enabling 265, 266

**Process component 234**

constructing 240

data change actions 243, 244

setting up 240, 241

Task or Data change action 240

**Process component, task**

email, sending 242

file, creating 243

notification, sending 242

script, calling 243

setting up 241, 242

SMS, sending 243

webhook, calling 243

# Q

**QR code for image dynamically**

generating 286, 287

**QuickChart**

QR code for image dynamically,
generating 286, 287

radial gauge chart, building 280-284

sample expression, working for
progress bar chart 284-286

URL 280

using, to generate dynamic chart
as image 279, 280

**QuickChart Maker**

reference link 284

**quick edit columns 58, 59**

# R

**radial gauge chart**

building 280-284

options 283, 284

**record-level operations**

performing, with table functions
and expressions 124

**reference action 157, 324**

example 160

using, to update parent based
on child 324-326

**referenced table 32**

**REF type columns 30-34**

**reverse reference 33**

**RoBotic Process Automation (RPA) 231**

**row-level functions**

evaluating 127

versus column-level functions 127-129

# S

**sample expression**

working, for progress bar chart 284-286

**save/cancel position 62**

**secondary data column 74**

**secondary data table 74**

sequential numbers
creating, by using bot 341, 342
single expressions
multiple functions, using 136, 137
single-sheet-type view 55
detail view 55
form view 61
onboarding view 63
slice
creating, from table 44, 46
slideshow mode 61
Smart Assistant
used, for searching data from app 261-263
sort by 59
source table 32
sync settings, AppSheet app
app to cloud 167
cloud to data source 169
system-generated views 51

**T**

table
used, for creating slice 44, 46
table functions and expressions
column-level functions, versus
row-level functions 127
ORDERBY() function 125, 126
used, for performing record-
level operations 124
table settings
analyzing 17
checking 17-19
table view 68
column order 69
column width 69
enable quick edit 69, 70
tabular format 10

template variable 294
text
manipulating, with text functions
and expressions 101
TEXT() function 134, 135
text functions and expressions
CONCATENATE() function 101
FIND() function 103, 104
SUBSTITUTE() function 103
used, for manipulating text 101
text label image
background color (path) 275
font size (path) 275
image size and image type (path) 276
text color (path) 276
text inside image (parameter) 276
URL service, using 275, 276
theme colors and icons
app logo 84
branding 83
launch image 84
primary color 83
theme 83
time calculations
performing, with date and time
functions and expressions 116
versus duration calculations 320-322
type-casting 91
examples 91

**U**

unconditional navigation 148
example 148
Universal Time Coordinated (UTC) 214
URL
creating, to access images and files 318, 319
service, using for text label image 275, 276

**use card layout  55**

**useremail() expression**

using  180, 181

**User Experience (UX)  49**

pane, reviewing  50, 51

**user permission levels**

controlling, with expressions  178

expression, passing to table
  permission control  181-183

useremail() expression, using  180, 181

userrole() expression, using  178-180

**userrole() expression**

using  178-180

# V

**view events  80**

**view events, actions**

action settings, for form views  81

behavior settings, in deck views  81

behavior settings, in gallery views  80

behavior settings, in table views  80

controlling  80

**Views  348**

chart or map view, creating  348

setup guide  350-353

**view type  54, 76**

chart view  78

dashboard view  76

display pane  79

list-type view  63

single-sheet-type view  55

**virtual table  46**

# W

**webhook  232**

# Y

**Yes/No functions and expressions**

AND() function  93

CONTAINS() function  95

decision making  92, 97

IN() function  95

ISBLANK() function  96

ISNOTBLANK() function  96

NOT() function  93

OR() function  93

`Packt.com`

Subscribe to our online digital library for full access to over 7,000 books and videos, as well as industry leading tools to help you plan your personal development and advance your career. For more information, please visit our website.

## Why subscribe?

- Spend less time learning and more time coding with practical eBooks and Videos from over 4,000 industry professionals

- Improve your learning with Skill Plans built especially for you

- Get a free eBook or video every month

- Fully searchable for easy access to vital information

- Copy and paste, print, and bookmark content

Did you know that Packt offers eBook versions of every book published, with PDF and ePub files available? You can upgrade to the eBook version at `packt.com` and as a print book customer, you are entitled to a discount on the eBook copy. Get in touch with us at `customercare@packtpub.com` for more details.

At `www.packt.com`, you can also read a collection of free technical articles, sign up for a range of free newsletters, and receive exclusive discounts and offers on Packt books and eBooks.

# Other Books You May Enjoy

If you enjoyed this book, you may be interested in these other books by Packt:

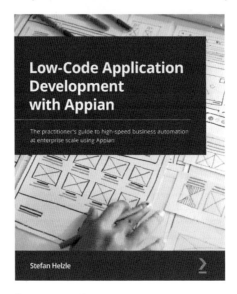

**Low-Code Application Development with Appian**

Stefan Helzle

ISBN: 9781800205628

- Use Appian Quick Apps to solve the most urgent business challenges
- Leverage Appian's low-code functionalities to enable faster digital innovation in your organization
- Model business data, Appian records, and processes
- Perform UX discovery and UI building in Appian
- Connect to other systems with Appian Integrations and Web APIs
- Work with Appian expressions, data querying, and constants

**Microsoft Power Apps Cookbook - Second Edition**

Eickhel Mendoza

ISBN: 9781803238029

- Learn to integrate and test canvas apps
- Design model-driven solutions using various features of Microsoft Dataverse
- Automate business processes such as triggered events, status change notifications, and approval systems with Power Automate
- Implement RPA technologies with Power Automate
- Extend your platform using maps and mixed reality
- Implement AI Builder's intelligent capabilities in your solutions
- Extend your business applications' capabilities using Power Apps Component Framework
- Create website experiences for users beyond the organization with Microsoft Power Pages

## Packt is searching for authors like you

If you're interested in becoming an author for Packt, please visit `authors.packtpub.com` and apply today. We have worked with thousands of developers and tech professionals, just like you, to help them share their insight with the global tech community. You can make a general application, apply for a specific hot topic that we are recruiting an author for, or submit your own idea.

## Share Your Thoughts

Now you've finished *Democratizing Application Development with AppSheet*, we'd love to hear your thoughts! Scan the QR code below to go straight to the Amazon review page for this book and share your feedback or leave a review on the site that you purchased it from.

`https://packt.link/r/1803241179`

Your review is important to us and the tech community and will help us make sure we're delivering excellent quality content.

# Download a free PDF copy of this book

Thanks for purchasing this book!

Do you like to read on the go but are unable to carry your print books everywhere?

Is your eBook purchase not compatible with the device of your choice?

Don't worry, now with every Packt book you get a DRM-free PDF version of that book at no cost.

Read anywhere, any place, on any device. Search, copy, and paste code from your favorite technical books directly into your application.

The perks don't stop there, you can get exclusive access to discounts, newsletters, and great free content in your inbox daily

Follow these simple steps to get the benefits:

1.  Scan the QR code or visit the link below

https://packt.link/free-ebook/9781803241173

2.  Submit your proof of purchase
3.  That's it! We'll send your free PDF and other benefits to your email directly

Printed in Great Britain
by Amazon